ESSENTIALS FOR design

ADOBE® INDESIGN® CS

level one

Robin B. McAllister

Prentice Hall
Upper Saddle River, New Jersey 07458

Library of Congress Cataloging-in-Publication Data
McAllister, Robin B.
Adobe InDesign CS, level one/[Robin B. McAllister]
p.cm. — (Essentials for design)
Includes index.
ISBN 0-13-146643-7 (alk. paper)
1. Adobe InDesign. 2. Desktop publishing I. Title. II. Series

Z253.532.A34M43 2004
686.2'2544536—dc22 2004045396

Publisher and Vice President: Natalie E. Anderson
Executive Editor: Jodi McPherson
Acquisitions Editor: Melissa Sabella
Editorial Assistant: Alana Meyers
Senior Media Project Manager: Cathleen Profitko
Senior Marketing Manager: Emily Knight
Marketing Assistant: Nicole Beaudry
Senior Managing Editor: Gail Steier de Acevedo
Project Manager, Production: Vanessa Nuttry
Manufacturing Buyer: Vanessa Nuttry
Interior Design: Thistle Hill Publishing Services, LLC
Cover Design: Blair Brown
Cover Printer: Coral Graphics
Printer/Binder: Von Hoffman Press

Credits and acknowledgments borrowed from other sources and reproduced, with permission, in this textbook appear on the appropriate page within the text.

10 9 8 7 6 5 4 3

ISBN 0-13-146643-7

ABOUT THE SERIES EDITOR

Ellenn Behoriam is president and founder of Against The Clock, Inc. (ATC), one of the nation's leading content providers. Ellenn and her staff have successfully produced many of the graphic arts industry's most popular and well-received books and related series. These works include the *Electronic Cookbook*, *Workflow Reengineering*, *Teams and the Graphic Arts*, *Adobe Photoshop Creative Techniques*, *Adobe Illustrator Creative Techniques*, and *QuarkXPress 6: Creating Digital Documents*, the foundation for the QuarkXPress Trainer certification programs. The Against The Clock Series, published in concert with Prentice Hall/Pearson Education, includes more than 26 titles that focus on applications for the graphic and computer arts industries.

Against The Clock also worked with Pearson to develop the *Companion for the Digital Artist* series. These titles focus on specific and fundamental creative concepts, including design, Web site development, photography, typography, color theory, and copywriting. The concise and compact works provide core concepts and skills that supplement any application-specific education, regardless of which textbooks are being used to teach program skills.

Under Ellenn's leadership and direction, ATC is currently developing more than 20 titles for the new *Essentials for Design* series. Her staff and long-established network of professional educators, printers, prepress experts, workflow engineers, and business leaders add significantly to ATC's ability to provide current, meaningful, and effective books, online tutorials, and business-to-business performance and workflow-enhancement programs.

ABOUT THE AUTHOR

Robin McAllister has been speaking and writing about creating effective pages since before desktop publishing was invented, and has been involved in the printing and publishing industry since the late 1960s. In the process of teaching others, he has written various "how to" guides and training manuals for general distribution and to solve company-specific issues. Rob is the author of a series of eight books for Delmar Publishers on a variety of desktop-publishing topics.

Rob is a team leader within America Online's Computing Community. He is also a technical editor for *Electronic Publishing* and has been writing and editing for Against The Clock for over five years.

ACKNOWLEDGMENTS

We would like to thank the professional writers, artists, editors, and educators who have worked long and hard on the *Essentials for Design* series.

Special thanks to Deborah Zerillo, Editorial Assistant, for her help in keeping us all together.

And thanks to the dedicated teaching professionals: Sharon Neville of L & N Design; Janet C. Frick of Training Resources LLC; Jill Mudge of Souhegan High School; and Sherri Brown of Trident Technical College. Your insightful comments and expertise have certainly contributed to the success of the *Essentials for Design* series.

Thank you to Laurel Nelson-Cucchiara, copy editor and final link in the chain of production, for her help in making sure that we all said what we meant to say.

And to Melissa Sabella, Jodi McPherson, and Vanessa Nuttry, we appreciate your patience as we begin this new venture together.

CONTENTS AT A GLANCE

TABLE OF CONTENTS

HOW TO USE THIS BOOK

Essentials courseware from Prentice Hall is anchored in the practical and professional needs of all types of students. The *Essentials* series presents a learning-by-doing approach that encourages you to grasp application-related concepts as you expand your skills through hands-on tutorials. As such, it consists of modular lessons that are built around a series of numbered step-by-step procedures that are clear, concise, and easy to review.

Essentials books are divided into projects. A project covers one area (or a few closely related areas) of application functionality. Each project consists of several lessons that are related to that topic. Each lesson presents a specific task or closely related set of tasks in a manageable chunk that is easy to assimilate and retain.

Each element in the *Essentials* book is designed to maximize your learning experience. A list of the *Essentials* project elements, and a description of how each element can help you, begins on the next page. To find out more about the rationale behind each book element and how to use each to your maximum benefit, take the following walk-through.

WALK-THROUGH

Project Objectives. Starting with an objective gives you short-term, attainable goals. Each project begins with a list of objectives that closely match the titles of the step-by-step tutorials. ▶

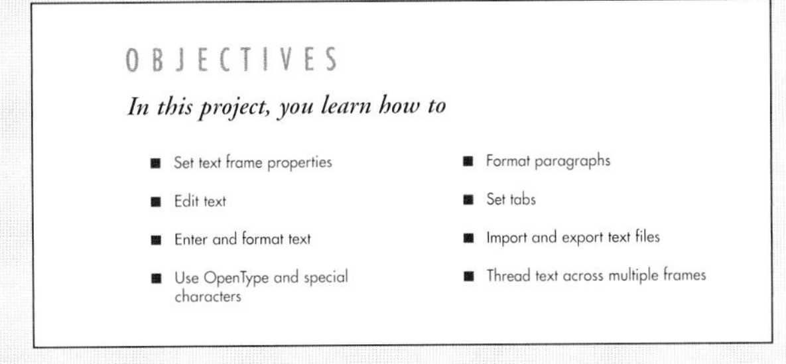
OBJECTIVES

In this project, you learn how to

- Set text frame properties
- Edit text
- Enter and format text
- Use OpenType and special characters
- Format paragraphs
- Set tabs
- Import and export text files
- Thread text across multiple frames

◀ **Why Would I Do This?** Introductory material at the beginning of each project provides an overview of why these tasks and procedures are important.

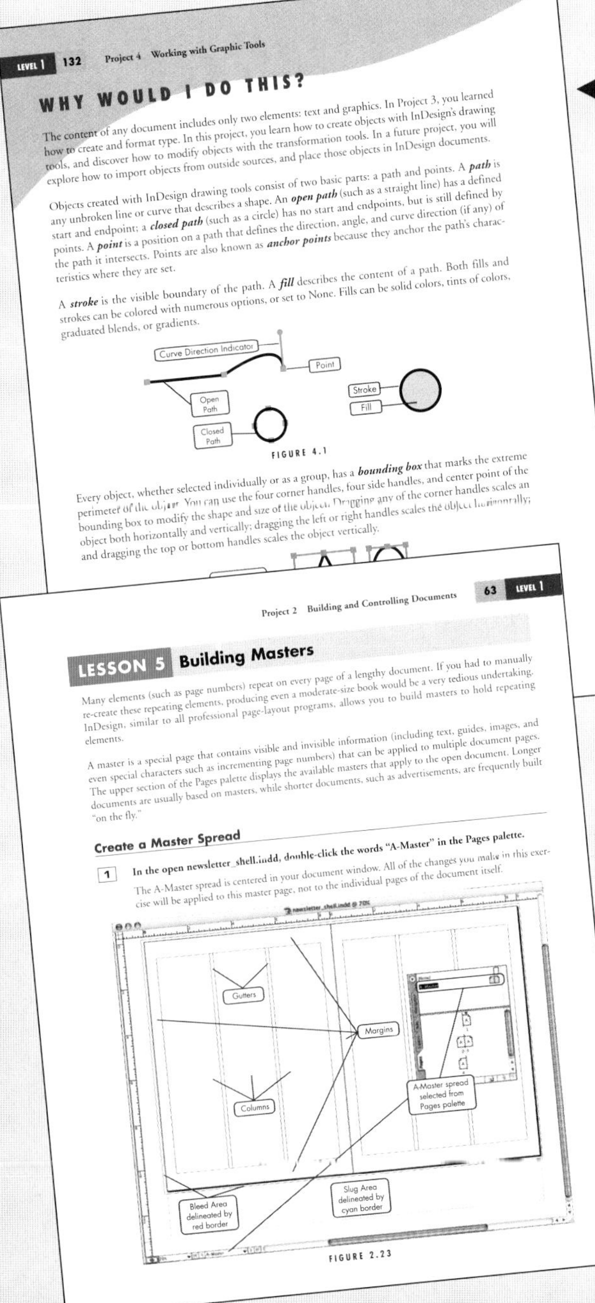
LEVEL 1 132 Project 4 Working with Graphic Tools

WHY WOULD I DO THIS?

The content of any document includes only two elements: text and graphics. In Project 3, you learned how to create and format type. In this project, you learn how to create objects with InDesign's drawing tools, and discover how to modify objects with the transformation tools. In a future project, you will explore how to import objects from outside sources, and place those objects in InDesign documents.

Objects created with InDesign drawing tools consist of two basic parts: a path and points. A *path* is any unbroken line or curve that describes a shape. An *open path* (such as a straight line) has a defined start and endpoint; a *closed path* (such as a circle) has no start and endpoints, but is still defined by points. A *point* is a position on a path that defines the direction, angle, and curve direction (if any) of the path it intersects. Points are also known as *anchor points* because they anchor the path's characteristics where they are set.

A *stroke* is the visible boundary of the path. A *fill* describes the content of a path. Both fills and strokes can be colored with numerous options, or set to None. Fills can be solid colors, tints of colors, graduated blends, or gradients.

FIGURE 4.1

Every object, whether selected individually or as a group, has a *bounding box* that marks the extreme perimeter of the object. You can use the four corner handles, four side handles, and center point of the bounding box to modify the shape and size of the object. Dragging any of the corner handles scales an object both horizontally and vertically; dragging the left or right handles scales the object horizontally; and dragging the top or bottom handles scales the object vertically.

Project 2 Building and Controlling Documents 63 LEVEL 1

LESSON 5 Building Masters

Many elements (such as page numbers) repeat on every page of a lengthy document. If you had to manually re-create these repeating elements, producing even a moderate-size book would be a very tedious undertaking. InDesign, similar to all professional page-layout programs, allows you to build masters to hold repeating elements.

A master is a special page that contains visible and invisible information (including text, guides, images, and even special characters such as incrementing page numbers) that can be applied to multiple document pages. The upper section of the Pages palette displays the available masters that apply to the open document. Longer documents are usually based on masters, while shorter documents, such as advertisements, are frequently built "on the fly."

Create a Master Spread

1 In the open newsletter_shell.indd, double-click the words "A-Master" in the Pages palette.

The A-Master spread is centered in your document window. All of the changes you make in this exercise will be applied to this master page, not to the individual pages of the document itself.

FIGURE 2.23

Visual Summary. A series of illustrations introduces the new tools, dialog boxes, and windows you will explore in each project. ▼

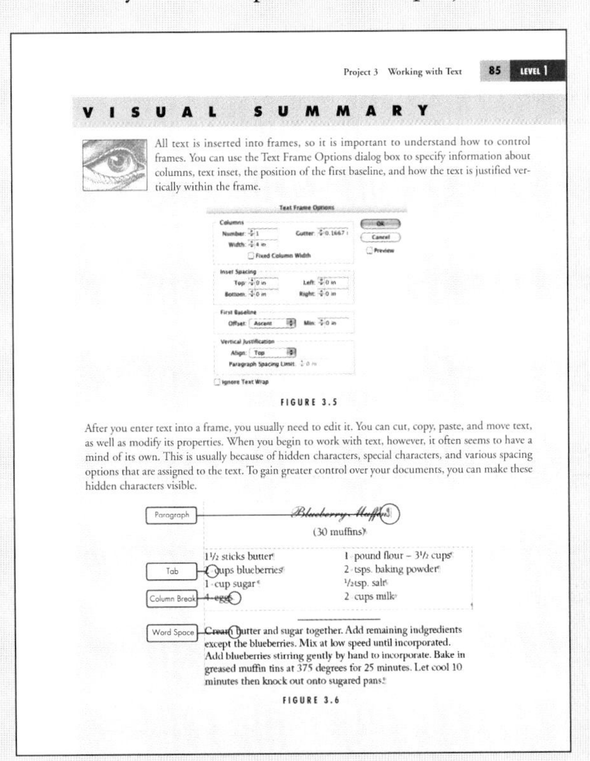
Project 3 Working with Text 85 LEVEL 1

VISUAL SUMMARY

All text is inserted into frames, so it is important to understand how to control frames. You can use the Text Frame Options dialog box to specify information about columns, text inset, the position of the first baseline, and how the text is justified vertically within the frame.

FIGURE 3.5

After you enter text into a frame, you usually need to edit it. You can cut, copy, paste, and move text, as well as modify its properties. When you begin to work with text, however, it often seems to have a mind of its own. This is usually because of hidden characters, special characters, and various spacing options that are assigned to the text. To gain greater control over your documents, you can make these hidden characters visible.

FIGURE 3.6

◀ **Step-by-Step Tutorials.** Hands-on tutorials let you learn by doing and include numbered, bold, step-by-step instructions.

If You Have Problems. These short troubleshooting notes help you anticipate or solve common problems quickly and effectively.

To Extend Your Knowledge...

INSERTING BREAK CHARACTERS

You can insert a variety of break characters. You can access the Insert Break Character menu from the Type menu or by Control/right-clicking.

Type of Break	Keyboard Shortcut	Action
Column Break	Numeric Keypad Enter	Move text to the next column, or to the next linked text frame
Frame Break	Shift-Numeric Keypad Enter	Move text to the next linked text frame
Page Break	Command/Control-Numeric Keypad Enter	Move text to the next page.
Odd Page Break	None (available from menu only)	Force text to the next odd-numbered (right-hand) page
Even Page Break	None (available from menu only)	Force text to the next even-numbered (left-hand) page
Forced Line Break (Soft Return)	Shift-Return/Enter	Force a line break without starting a new paragraph
Paragraph Return	Return/Enter	Start a new paragraph

To Extend Your Knowledge. These features provide extra tips, alternative ways to complete a process, and special hints about using the software.

CAREERS IN DESIGN

THE GRAPHIC ARTS MARKETPLACE

The graphic arts industry, by its very nature, extends into many other industries. The term "graphic designer" has become something of a catch-all term that can include designers (who are responsible for the appearance of print or Web documents), illustrators (who "draw" images on the computer or on another medium), page-layout specialists (who assemble text and images for print production), or Web-publishing specialists (who assemble text and images for Web presentation).

When you enter the field of graphic design, you will likely work in a position that can offer you the greatest amount of experience. You might work for a Fortune 500 company, a real estate agency, a school or hospital, advertising agency, or a printer. In the course of your responsibilities, you may produce a letterhead package on Monday, assemble a brochure on Tuesday, and work on an annual report for the rest of the week.

As you gain experience, you will discover which areas of graphic design you enjoy, and in which you excel; you will likely build upon those areas. Some of the areas in which you may eventually specialize are listed below:

- Advertising design (brochures, magazine and newspaper ads, direct mail)
- Publication design (books, magazines, catalogs, annual reports, directories)
- Specialty design (menus, posters, postcards)
- Package design (labels, boxes, bags, wrappers, display packaging, merchandising display)
- Illustration (information graphics, editorial illustration, technical illustration)
- Corporate identity design (logos, stationery, business cards, signage)

Careers in Design. These features offer advice, tips, and resources that will help you on your path to a successful career.

End-of-Project Exercises. Extensive end-of-project exercises emphasize hands-on skill development. You'll find two levels of reinforcement: Skill Drill and Challenge.

Project 5 Working with Images 219 LEVEL 1

SKILL DRILL

Skill Drills reinforce project skills. Each skill reinforced is the same, or nearly the same, as a skill presented in the lessons. Detailed instructions are provided in a step-by-step format. You should complete these exercises in order.

1. Create a Catalog Cover

Your client, Premier Products, produces catalogs for corporate employee programs. The winter catalog appropriately features gifts for the holidays, in addition to a number of items people might want to purchase for themselves. In the following Skill Drills, you compose the cover and inside front cover for this year's catalog. We placed a couple of initial items to help you get started.

1. Open premier_catalog.indd from your Project_05 folder. Be sure you are on Page 1.

   Some text is in place, but you will create frames and import images. Notice that the text frame in the upper right is irregularly shaped. It was created with the Pen tool.

2. Create a new rectangular frame that fills the entire page, including bleed area.
3. Fill the frame with the graduated tint swatch labeled Light Gradient. Set it as a Linear gradient at a –35° Angle in the Gradient palette.
4. Use the Selection tool to select the frame containing the gradient. Place holiday_cover.tif.
5. With the frame still selected, Choose Object>Arrange>Send to Back to send the frame to the back.

   You could also use the keyboard shortcut Command/Control-Shift-[.

6. Center the image in the frame. Choose Object>Fitting>Center Content.

   It sits too high in the frame, but it's centered horizontally.

7. Use the Direct Selection tool to select the image. Set the Y position to 2.75 in, with one of the upper proxy-reference handles selected.
8. Save the document to your WIP_05 folder. Leave it open for the next Skill Drill.

2. Convey the Main Offer

1. In the upper right-hand corner, create a new frame at X: 5.5 in, Y: –0.125 in (the top of the bleed area). Extend the frame to the right-hand bleed area, with a Height of 2.6 in.
2. With the frame active, place the palmy_beach.tif photo.
3. Send the frame to the back. Choose Object>Arrange>Bring Forward, or press Command/Control-] to bring it forward one level.
4. Click the image with the Direct Selection tool and change its X and Y percentages to 75%. Drag the image around until the two people are visible in the frame.
5. With the Direct Selection tool active, click the lower-left anchor point of the frame, and drag it up and to the right until the image disappears from below and to the left of the arrow.

LEVEL 1 126 Project 3 Working with Text

CHALLENGE

Challenge exercises expand on, or are somewhat related to, skills presented in the lessons. Each exercise provides a brief introduction, followed by instructions presented in a numbered-step format that are not as detailed as those in the Skill Drill exercises. You should perform these exercises in order.

1. Place Text into the Ad Shell

Many design projects are simple one-page layouts that appear in a magazine or newspaper. The ad in this exercise uses images already placed on the page, as you might find when you work from comps created with placeholder text. The exercise focuses on text placement and formatting, using InDesign's built-in tools to complete the ad.

The ad in this project has some initial copy already typed in, but it's not formatted. The two required images are already placed exactly where the ad manager specified, and their position cannot be changed without approval. The ad designer set up some guidelines for specifying the position of text elements.

1. Open cheese_ad.indd.

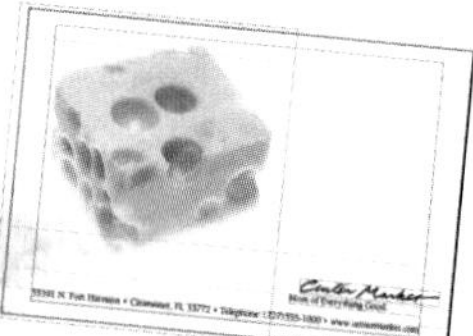

FIGURE 3.69

2. Place cheese_ad_text.txt.

   This is a plain text file, so it requires no import options; but make sure the Use Typographer's Quotes box is checked.

3. Position the file at the second horizontal guideline, 3.75 inches from the top edge of the page and the left margin.

   The text frame fills the width between the margin guides, and the red plus sign indicates overset text. The text wraps around the Center Market logo because the designer already applied a text wrap to the logo.

Save the file as "cheese_ad.indd" in your WIP_03 folder.

Portfolio Builder. At the end of every project, these exercises require creative solutions to problems that reinforce the topic of the project. ▶

LEVEL 1 184 Project 4 Working with Graphic Tools

PORTFOLIO BUILDER

Spam Stopper Logo

Info Management developed a new product called Spam Stopper that reduces the amount of spam that filters in through your e-mail. Spam Stopper gives you almost complete control over what is filtered out, and it can "learn" what you consider spam. To keep costs down, the product is only available over the Internet as a downloadable file.

Your assignment is to use type elements and InDesign's graphics to create a catchy logo. You should create at least three unique ideas for presentation to the company's management. Some ideas you may wish to consider include:

- Use of the international "No" symbol
- Incorporating a stop sign (8-sided polygon)
- Replacing letters with graphic symbols

Let your imagination run. Remember, there is no "right" solution.

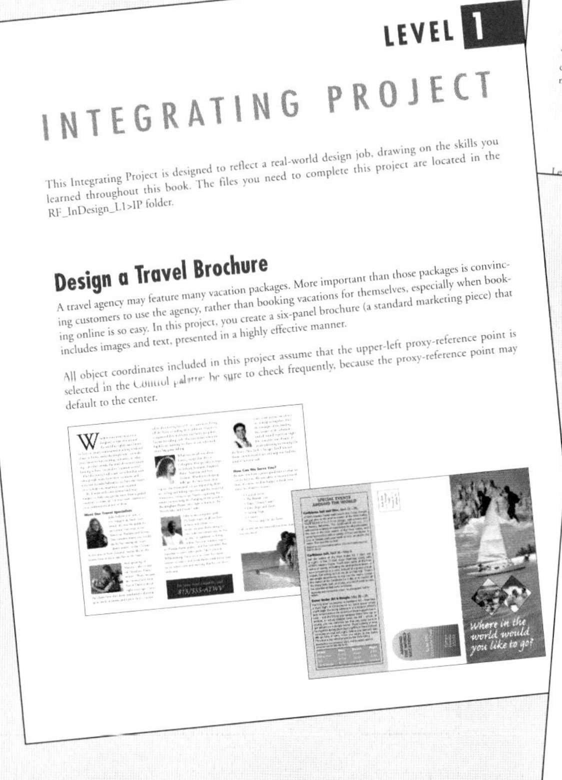

LEVEL 1

INTEGRATING PROJECT

This Integrating Project is designed to reflect a real-world design job, drawing on the skills you learned throughout this book. The files you need to complete this project are located in the RF_InDesign_L1>IP folder.

Design a Travel Brochure

A travel agency may feature many vacation packages. More important than those packages is convincing customers to use the agency, rather than booking vacations for themselves, especially when booking online is so easy. In this project, you create a six-panel brochure (a standard marketing piece) that includes images and text, presented in a highly effective manner.

All object coordinates included in this project assume that the upper-left proxy-reference point is selected in the Control palette; be sure to check frequently, because the proxy-reference point may default to the center.

Where in the world would you like to go?

◀ **Integrating Projects.** Integrating projects are designed to reflect real-world graphic-design jobs, drawing on the skills you have learned throughout this book.

Task Guides. These charts, found at the end of each book, list alternative ways to complete common procedures and provide a handy reference tool. ▶

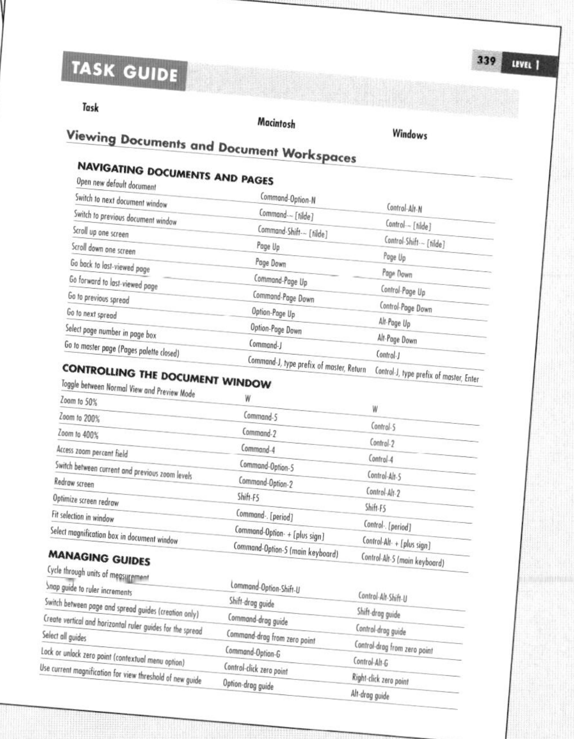

TASK GUIDE 339 LEVEL 1

Task	Macintosh	Windows
Viewing Documents and Document Workspaces		
NAVIGATING DOCUMENTS AND PAGES		
Open new default document	Command-Option-N	Control-Alt-N
Switch to next document window	Command-~ [tilde]	Control-~ [tilde]
Switch to previous document window	Command-Shift-~ [tilde]	Control-Shift-~ [tilde]
Scroll up one screen	Page Up	Page Up
Scroll down one screen	Page Down	Page Down
Go back to last-viewed page	Command-Page Up	Control-Page Up
Go forward to last-viewed page	Command-Page Down	Control-Page Down
Go to previous spread	Option-Page Up	Alt-Page Up
Go to next spread	Option-Page Down	Alt-Page Down
Select page number in page box	Command-J	Control-J
Go to master page (Pages palette closed)	Command-J, type prefix of master, Return	Control-J, type prefix of master, Enter
CONTROLLING THE DOCUMENT WINDOW		
Toggle between Normal View and Preview Mode	W	W
Zoom to 50%	Command-5	Control-5
Zoom to 200%	Command-2	Control-2
Zoom to 400%	Command-4	Control-4
Access zoom percent field	Command-Option-5	Control-Alt-5
Switch between current and previous zoom levels	Command-Option-2	Control-Alt-2
Redraw screen	Shift-F5	Shift-F5
Optimize screen redraw	Command-. [period]	Control-. [period]
Fit selection in window	Command-Option- + [plus sign]	Control-Alt- + [plus sign]
Select magnification box in document window	Command-Option-5 (main keyboard)	Control-Alt-5 (main keyboard)
MANAGING GUIDES		
Cycle through units of measurement	Command-Option-Shift-U	Control-Alt-Shift-U
Snap guide to ruler increments	Shift-drag guide	Shift-drag guide
Switch between page and spread guides (creation only)	Command-drag guide	Control-drag guide
Create vertical and horizontal ruler guides for the spread	Command-drag from zero point	Control-drag from zero point
Select all guides	Command-Option-G	Control-Alt-G
Lock or unlock zero point (contextual menu option)	Control-click zero point	Right-click zero point
Use current magnification for view threshold of new guide	Option-drag guide	Alt-drag guide

STUDENT INFORMATION AND RESOURCES

Companion Web Site (www.prenhall.com/essentials). This text-specific Web site provides students with additional information and exercises to reinforce their learning. Features include: additional end-of-project reinforcement material, online Study Guide, easy access to *all* resource files, and much, much more!

Before completing the projects within this text, you need to download the Resource Files from the Prentice Hall Companion Web site. Check with your instructor for the best way to gain access to these files or simply follow these instructions:

1. From an open Web browser, go to http://www.prenhall.com/essentials.

2. Select your textbook or series to access the Companion Web site. We suggest you bookmark this page, as it has links to additional Prentice Hall resources that you may use in class.

3. Click the Student Resources link. All files in the Student Resources area are provided as .sea files for Macintosh users and .exe files for those using the Windows operating system. These files do not require any additional software to open.

4. Click the Start Here link for the platform you are using (Macintosh or Windows).

5. Once you have downloaded the proper file, double-click that file to begin the self-extraction process. You will be prompted to select a folder location specific for your book; you may extract the file to your hard drive or to a removable disk/drive.

   The Start Here file contains three folders:

   - **Fonts.**
   - **RF_InDesign_L1.** You can place this folder on your hard drive, or on a removable disk/drive.
   - **Work_In_Progress.** You can place this folder on your hard drive, or on a removable disk/drive.

6. Locate the project files you need from the list of available resources and click the active link to download. There is a separate file for each project in this book (e.g., Project_01, Project_02, etc.).

7. Once you have downloaded the proper file, double-click that file to begin the self-extraction process. You will be prompted to select a folder location specific to your book; you should extract the project-specific folders into the RF_InDesign_L1 folder that was extracted from the Start Here file.

Resource CD. If you are using a Resource CD, all the fonts and files you need are provided on the CD. Resource files are organized in project-specific folders (e.g., Project_01, Project_02, etc.), which are contained in the RF_InDesign_L1 folder. You can either work directly from the CD, or copy the files onto your hard drive before beginning the exercises.

Before you begin working on the projects or lessons in this book, you should copy the Work_In_Progress folder from the Resource CD onto your hard drive or a removable disk/drive.

Fonts. You must install the ATC fonts to ensure that your exercises and projects will work as described in the book. Specific instructions for installing fonts are provided in the documentation that came with your computer.

If you have an older version (pre-2004) of the ATC fonts installed, replace them with the fonts in this folder.

Resource Files. Resource files are organized in project-specific folders, and are named to facilitate cross-platform compatibility. Words are separated by an underscore, and all file names include a lowercase three-letter extension. For example, if you are directed to open the file "graphics.eps" in Project 2, the file can be found in the RF_InDesign_L1> Project_02 folder. We repeat these directions frequently in the early projects.

The Work In Progress Folder. This folder contains individual folders for each project in the book (e.g., WIP_01, WIP_02, etc.). When an exercise directs you to save a file, you should save it to the appropriate folder for the project in which you are working.

The exercises in this book frequently build upon work that you have already completed. At the end of each exercise, you will be directed to save your work and either close the file or continue to the next exercise. If you are directed to continue but your time is limited, you can stop at a logical point, save the file, and later return to the point at which you stopped. In this case, you will need to open the file from the appropriate WIP folder and continue working on the same file.

Typeface Conventions. Computer programming code appears in a monospace font that `looks like this`. In many cases, you only need to change or enter specific pieces of code; in these instances, the code you need to type or change appears in a second color and `looks like this`.

INSTRUCTOR'S RESOURCES

Instructor's Resource Center. This CD-ROM includes the entire Instructor's Manual for each application in Microsoft Word format. Student data files and completed solutions files are also on this CD-ROM. The Instructor's Manual contains a reference guide of these files for the instructor's convenience. PowerPoint slides with more information about each project are also available for classroom use.

Companion Web site (www.prenhall.com/essentials). Instructors will find all of the resources available on the Instructor's Resource CD-ROM available for download from the Companion Web site.

TestGen Software. TestGen is a test generator program that lets you view and easily edit test bank questions, transfer them to tests, and print the tests in a variety of formats suitable to your teaching situation. The program also offers many options for organizing and displaying test banks and tests. A built-in random number and text generator makes it ideal for creating multiple versions of tests. Powerful search and sort functions let you easily locate questions and arrange them in the order you prefer.

QuizMaster, also included in this package, enables students to take tests created with TestGen on a local area network. The QuizMaster utility built into TestGen lets instructors view student records and print a variety of reports. Building tests is easy with TestGen, and exams can be easily uploaded into WebCT, Blackboard, and CourseCompass.

Prentice Hall has formed close alliances with each of the leading online platform providers: WebCT, Blackboard, and our own Pearson CourseCompass.

OneKey. OneKey lets you in to the best teaching and learning resources all in one place. OneKey for *Essentials for Design* is all your students need for out-of-class work conveniently organized by chapter to reinforce and apply what they've learned in class and from the text. OneKey is all you need to plan and administer your course. All your instructor resources are in one place to maximize your effectiveness and minimize your time and effort. OneKey for convenience, simplicity, and success.

WebCT and Blackboard. Each of these custom-built distance-learning courses features exercises, sample quizzes, and tests in a course management system that provides class administration tools as well as the ability to customize this material at the instructor's discretion.

CourseCompass. CourseCompass is a dynamic, interactive online course management tool powered by Blackboard. It lets professors create their own courses in 15 minutes or less with preloaded quality content that can include quizzes, tests, lecture materials, and interactive exercises.

Performance-Based Training and Assessment: Train & Assess IT. Prentice Hall offers performance-based training and assessment in one product — Train & Assess IT.

The Training component offers computer-based instruction that a student can use to preview, learn, and review graphic design application skills. Delivered via Web or CD-ROM, Train IT offers interactive multimedia, and computer-based training to augment classroom learning. Built-in prescriptive testing suggests a study path based not only on student test results but also on the specific textbook chosen for the course.

The Assessment component offers computer-based testing that shares the same user interface as Train IT and is used to evaluate a student's knowledge about specific topics in software including Photoshop, InDesign, Illustrator, Flash, and Dreamweaver. It does this in a task-oriented, performance-based environment to demonstrate students' proficiency and comprehension of the topics. More extensive than the testing in Train IT, Assess IT offers more administrative features for the instructor and additional questions for the student. Assess IT also enables professors to test students out of a course, place students in appropriate courses, and evaluate skill sets.

INTRODUCTION

Introduced in 2000, Adobe InDesign is a robust, design-oriented publishing package. As its name indicates, this page-layout program provides the tools you need to design and create effective pages. It allows you to integrate text and graphics — prepared in the program itself or imported from other sources — and produce files that may be printed to a local or networked printer, taken to a commercial printer or other graphic arts service provider, or published to the World Wide Web.

Since its initial release, InDesign has offered designers the tools they need to exercise precise control over every element on the document page. In addition, InDesign's automated features allow designers to speed up the production process. The latest release of the product, InDesign CS (version 3), offers an expanded user interface that provides additional tools and utilities to improve the digital workflow. InDesign CS includes numerous features that allow designers to handle text and manage documents with greater efficiency than ever before.

This book is designed to introduce you to the tools and features of InDesign, as well as teach you how to produce professional-looking documents quickly and easily. After you learn the basics, you discover shortcuts and alternate methods to produce the same results — but with far less repetitive action. Becoming an expert is hard work, but it should also be fun and fulfilling.

We encourage you to look at the big picture — what you're actually creating — and make design and production decisions based on that reality, rather than establishing a blanket rule for production. The skills you learn can be applied to virtually any document, from a business card to a 208-page catalog.

As you progress through this book, pay attention not only to the details — the step-by-step tasks associated with lessons within the projects — but also to the principles behind them. Most hands-on exercises and Skill Drills demand absolute attention to detail; but many of the Challenges and Portfolio Builders provide opportunities to express your personal creativity. In addition, we encourage you to go beyond the projects and experiment on your own, rather than limit yourself solely to the ideas presented in this book.

The lessons in this book focus on design and print-production techniques. You should realize, however, that just because a program allows you to perform a certain function, it does not necessarily mean it is the best way to attain your goal; we include cautions about these types of situations. As you work through this book, we hope you gain the skills and confidence to use type and images to create effective layouts that look good in print.

LEVEL 1

PROJECT 1

Taking a Tour of Adobe InDesign CS

OBJECTIVES

In this project, you learn how to

- Create thumbnails, comprehensive sketches, and mechanical proofs
- Navigate within and between pages of a document
- Efficiently manage palettes to optimize screen space
- Use rulers, guides, and other measuring devices
- Create a basic letterhead using drawing and type tools
- Import graphics and text into a document
- Print a document
- Use the built-in and online help systems

WHY WOULD I DO THIS?

InDesign CS is a powerful page-layout program from Adobe Systems. As you become acquainted with the design and production of electronic documents, you will discover that moving from design to production to finished document is a step-by-step process. InDesign helps you complete the publishing process effectively, whether you are producing stationery packages, advertisements, forms, or complex magazine layouts. InDesign also allows you to think beyond print documents; you can create rich PDF documents and repurpose your print documents for the Web.

When you first open InDesign, you may find the array of palettes and tools somewhat intimidating. As part of Adobe's Creative Suite, InDesign is closely integrated with the newest versions of Photoshop, Illustrator, GoLive, InCopy, and Acrobat. A standard Adobe interface facilitates the process of learning each of these programs, since they share a number of commands and features. As you progress through this book, you'll find that there is usually more than one way to accomplish almost every task, and you'll discover which method is best suited to your personal workflow.

With InDesign, you can type and style text, use drawing tools to create rectangles and ellipses, and print your document, just as you can in word-processing programs. You can also import text from word processors and bring in a variety of graphic file types. InDesign gives you far more control over the placement and appearance of text than most word processors; but InDesign isn't a word processor, so some of the more advanced word-processing functions, such as the ability to check grammar, are not available.

Beyond these basic functions, InDesign allows you to draw complex illustrations — although we recommend that you use a dedicated drawing program such as Adobe Illustrator, Macromedia FreeHand, or CorelDRAW to create such images. You can add interactivity to PDF documents and include rich content, such as sound and Macromedia Flash movies. You can also manage color and create features specific to long documents, such as tables of contents and indexes.

In this project, you learn about the design-to-production process, progressing from a hand-drawn thumbnail to a comprehensive sketch to a final electronic mechanical. A ***mechanical*** is a document that is ready to be ***output*** (printed) to film for production on a printing press. You learn to find your way around the document window and to manage InDesign's palettes. You also learn to use rulers, guides, and measuring devices as you create a document. You not only learn to type text into your document and to use the basic drawing tools, you also import text and graphics that have been created in another program, and then print the document. Finally, you learn how to access Adobe's extensive help functions.

VISUAL SUMMARY

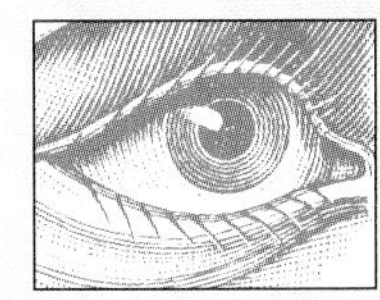

A document within InDesign can be of almost any size — with horizontal or vertical dimensions as small as 0.1667 inches or as large as 216 inches (18 feet). It can range from a business card or a bookmark to a magazine, novel, or textbook. Regardless of size, each page is built in the same workspace, using the same suite of tools.

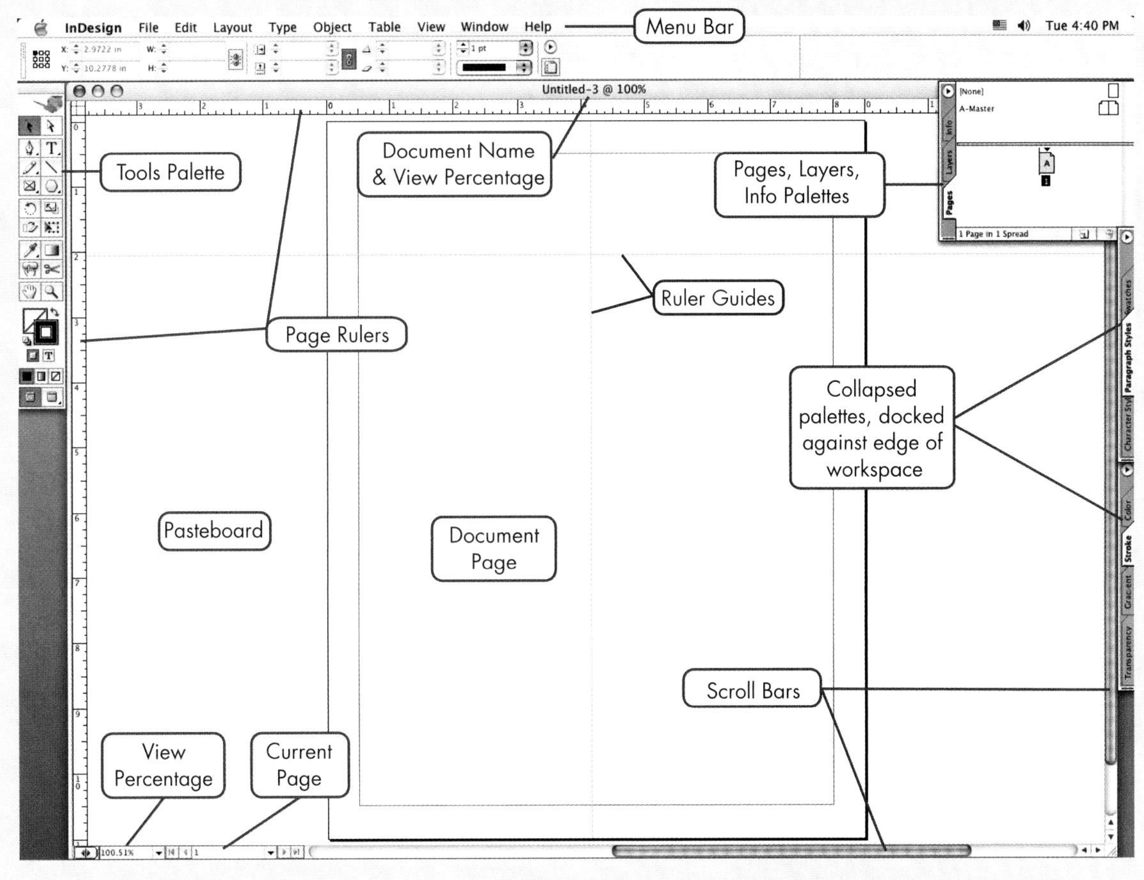

FIGURE 1.1

As you learn your way around InDesign, you open a multi-page document and navigate through its pages using the Pages palette, View percentage menu, and the Hand and Zoom tools. ***Palettes*** are extremely powerful devices for producing documents. They organize various tools that you can use to affect type, graphics, color, and document layout, among other functions. InDesign offers 35 different palettes; you must learn to manage these palettes if they are to be truly useful. Palettes can be grouped, collapsed, or docked. They can also ***float*** in the workspace (floating palettes can be placed anywhere in your workspace). Some palettes, such as the Tools palette, can be reshaped to a single vertical or horizontal bar.

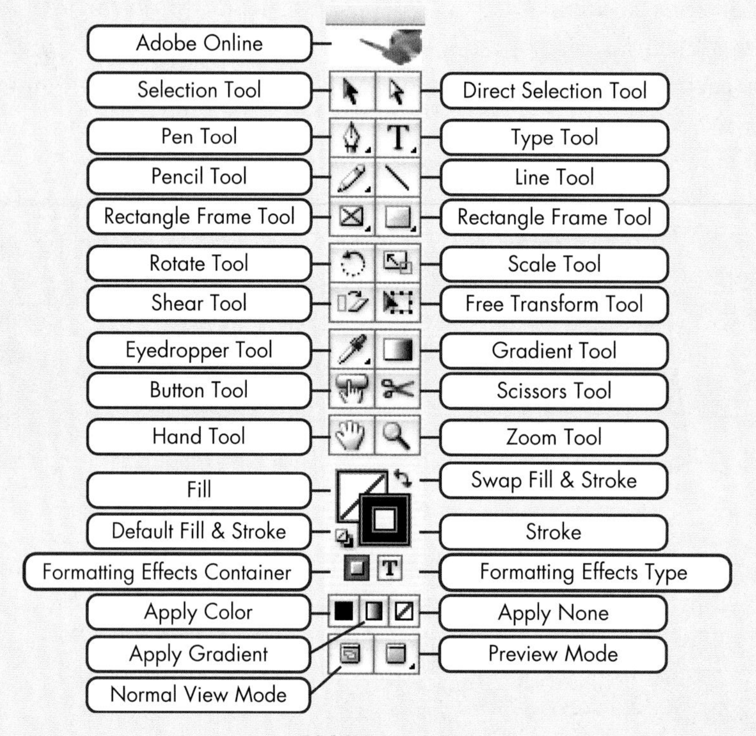

FIGURE 1.2

Rulers and guides complement the workspace, so you can quickly make gross adjustments to your documents. The Info palette and Navigator palette, together with the Control palette, allow you to place elements at precise locations on a page. This is extremely important when laying out pages, such as advertisements, where space is at a premium and even the slightest misalignment could stand out as a grave error.

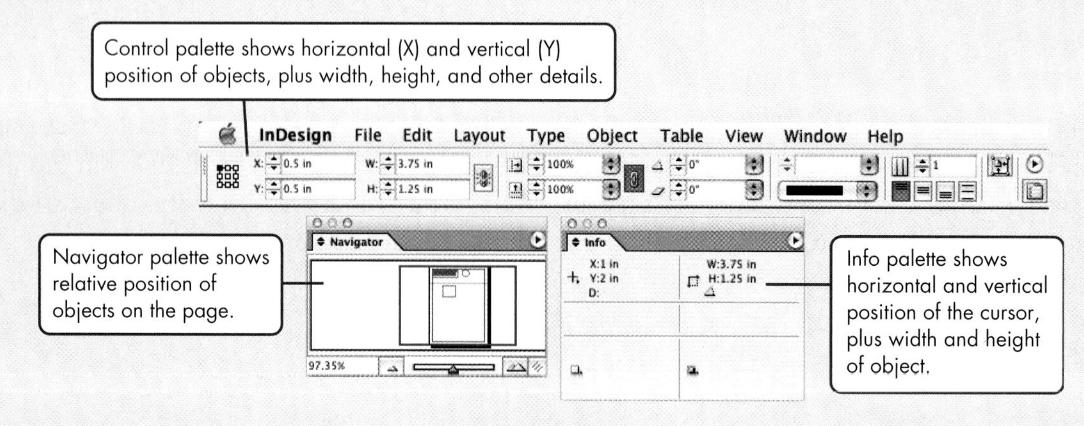

FIGURE 1.3

LESSON 1 Working Through the Design-to-Production Process

Producing a document is a multi-step process. Even the most experienced designers don't often sit down at the computer and begin typing and drawing without first doing some preliminary planning. Instead, they typically begin by hand-sketching their ideas for the document that they will later create on the computer. This sketch, called a ***thumbnail***, may be actual size, to scale, or simply a visual reminder of the elements they want to include — many an award-winning ad started as notes on a napkin or placemat. After the sketch is completed, the designer creates a ***comp***, or comprehensive sketch, which is the artwork used to present an accurate layout to the client.

In the following two exercises, you create both a thumbnail and a comp of an ad that is slated to run in a local business magazine. Later in this project, you turn your design into a finished ad.

Create a Thumbnail

1. **On a blank sheet of paper, use a pencil or pen to draw a rectangle approximately 4.5 inches wide and 7 inches high.**

   The rectangle represents the area and frame of the ad you will produce.

2. **Draw a horizontal line approximately 3 inches from the top of the rectangle. Draw an "X" through the resulting rectangle at the top of the ad.**

   A frame filled with an "X" is the universal indicator that a picture will be inserted later.

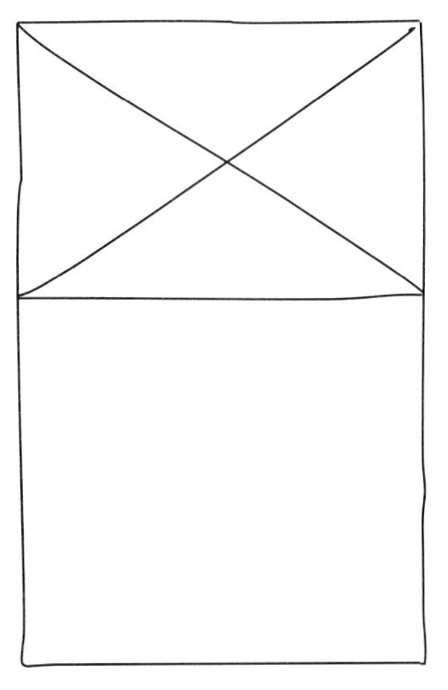

FIGURE 1.4

3. **Directly below the picture box, draw a box approximately 0.75 inches high. Print "Two line headline goes here" on two lines within this box.**

4 **Below the headline, in two columns, draw several horizontal lines.**

These lines indicate where body type will be inserted.

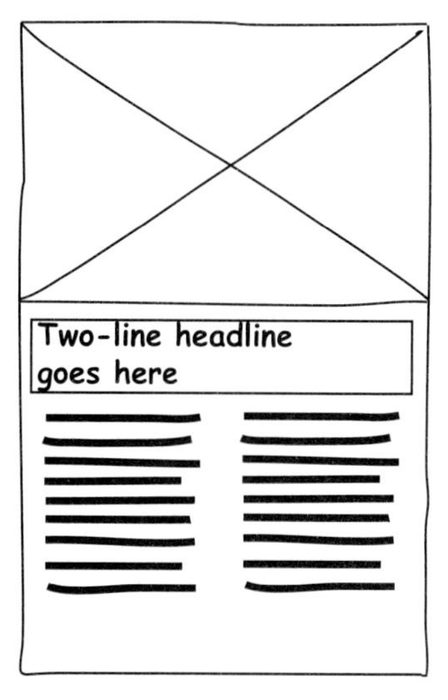

FIGURE 1.5

5 **At the bottom of the sketch, add another small picture box with a line under it.**

The picture box indicates the company logo, and the line under it represents the address information.

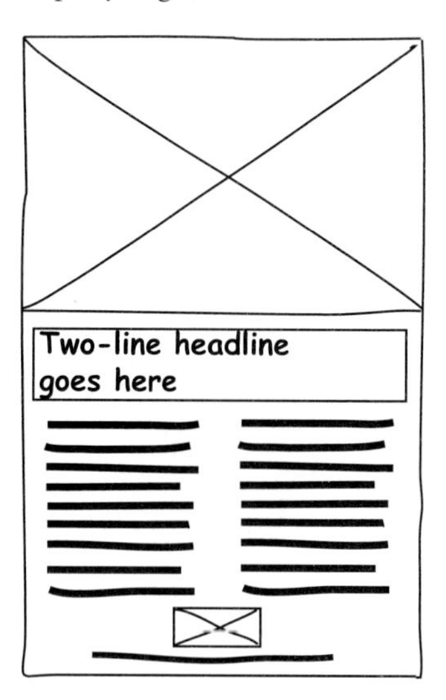

FIGURE 1.6

Refer to your thumbnail sketch as you create your comp in the next exercise.

Convert the Thumbnail to a Comp

1 **Double-click the InDesign application icon from your desktop (Macintosh), or choose it from the Start>Programs menu (Windows).**

The InDesign application launches.

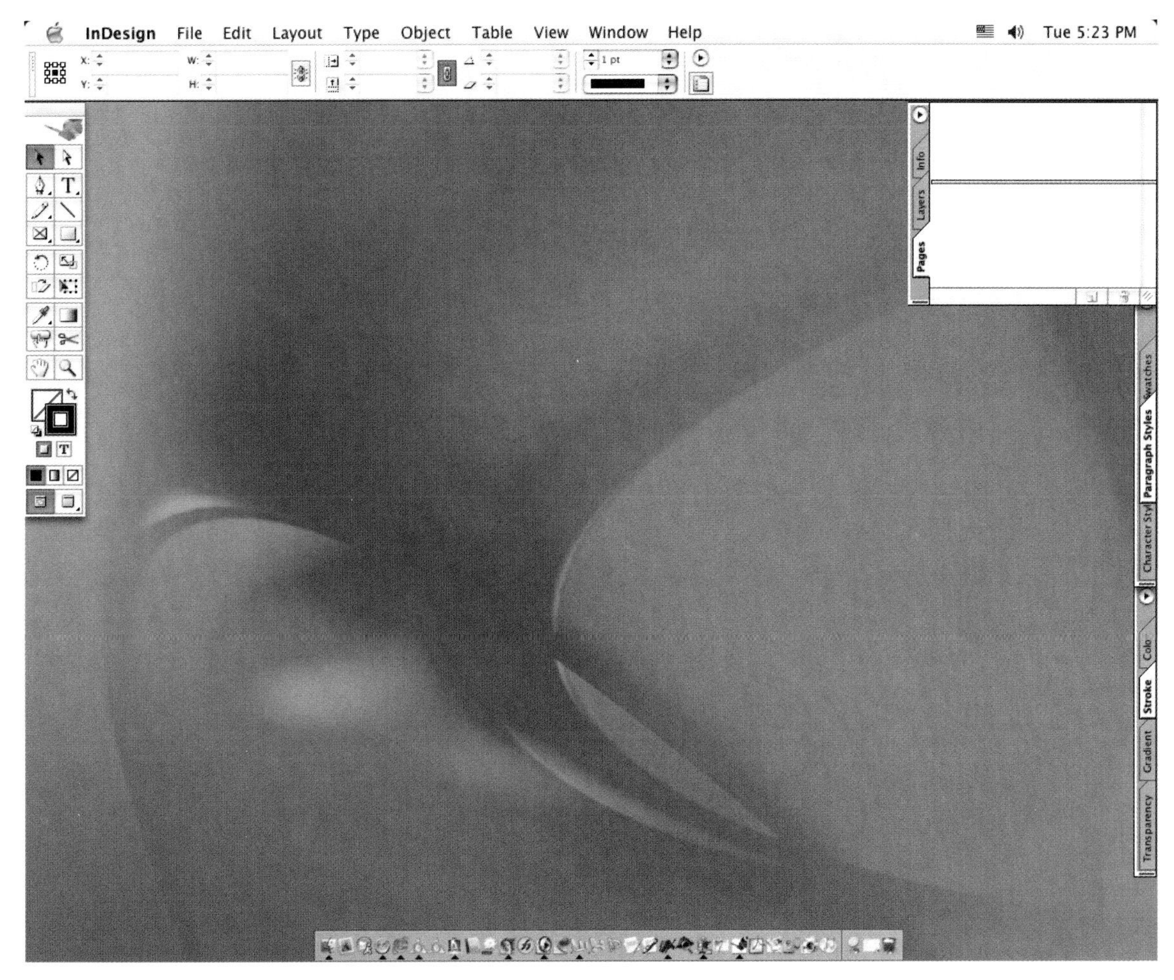

FIGURE 1.7

2 **Choose File>Open.**

The Open a File dialog box appears. You can also access this dialog box by pressing Command/Control-O, the universal command for opening files from Adobe applications.

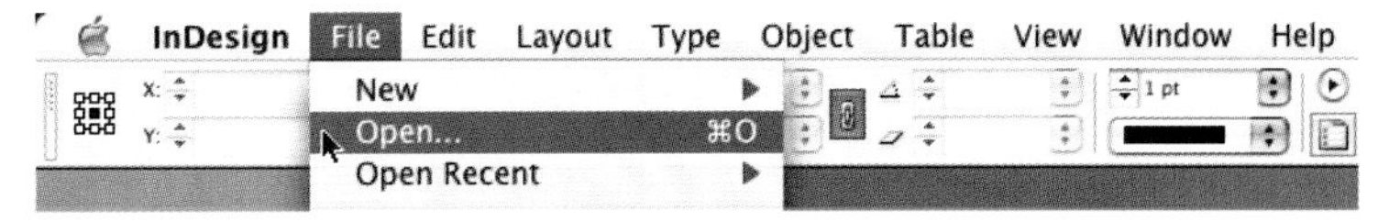

FIGURE 1.8

3 **In the From field, navigate to the RF_InDesign_L1>Project_01 folder. Highlight the file soupcomp.indd in the list that appears. Click the Open button.**

Unless otherwise instructed, you can find all files used throughout this book in the project-specific folder within the RF_InDesign_L1 folder. For this project, look in the Project_01 folder.

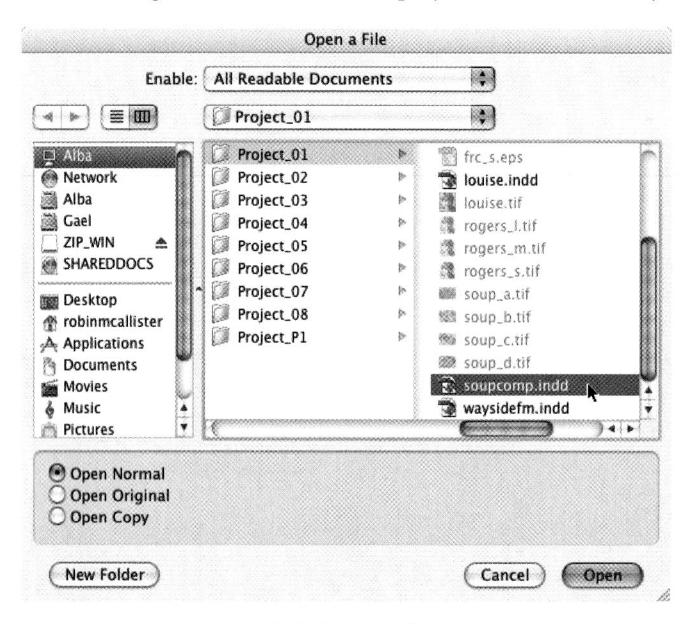

FIGURE 1.9

4 **Choose the Rectangle tool in the Tools palette.**

The Rectangle tool is activated. You can use this tool to draw a frame on the document page. Notice that the cursor changes to crosshairs.

5 **Click the Rectangle tool at the intersection of the upper and left blue guides. Drag down and to the right to create a rectangle that fills the area between the blue guides.**

Although the blue guides nearly obscure the frame, you can tell it's there because of the eight handles of the ***bounding box***, an imaginary box that marks the perimeter of all frames, regardless of their shape. The guides are locked so you do not accidentally move them.

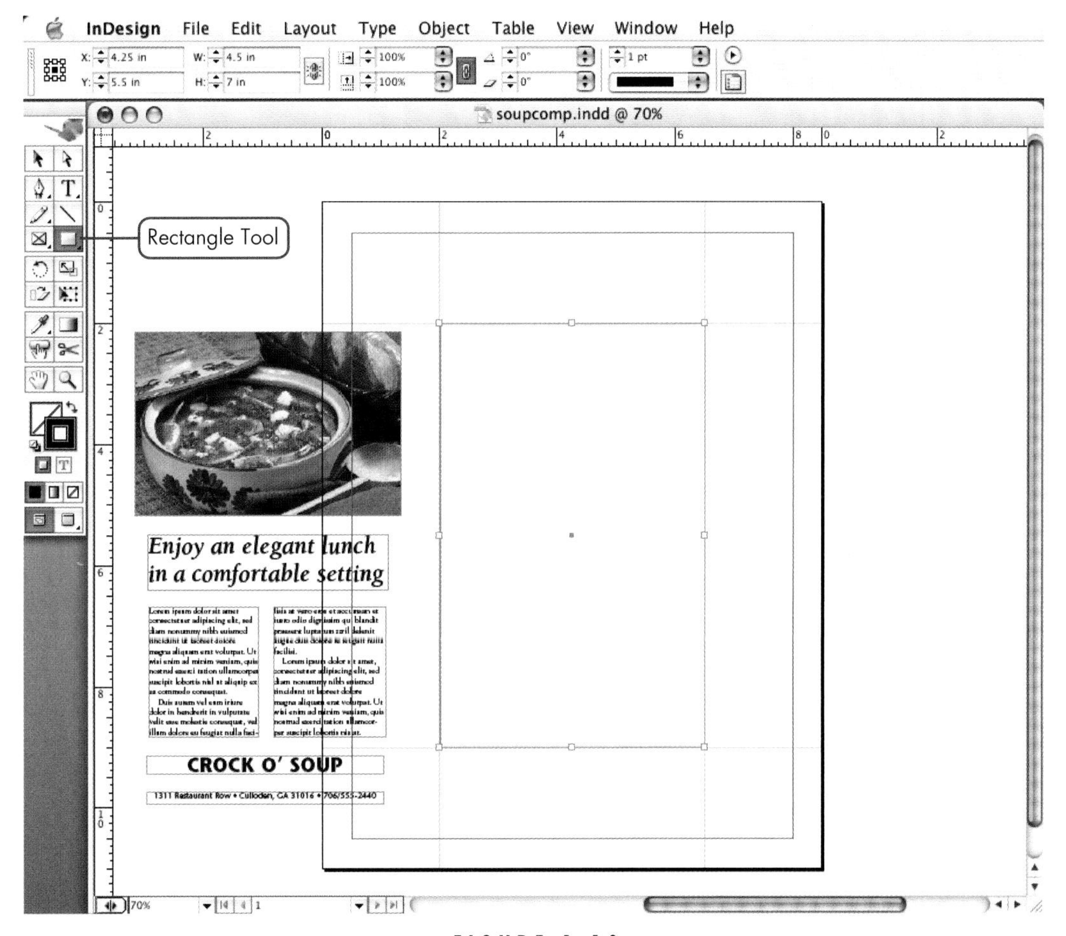

FIGURE 1.10

6 **Choose the Selection tool in the Tools palette.**

The cursor changes to a pointer arrow.

7 **One at a time, click each of the elements at the left of the screen, and drag them into place to approximate your thumbnail sketch.**

These are not necessarily the final images or headlines, and the text is ***Greeked*** (dummy text is used to fill the area to approximate the ad's final appearance).

Enjoy an elegant lunch
in a comfortable setting
CROCK O' SOUP
1311 Restaurant Row • Culloden, GA 31016 • 706/555-2440

FIGURE 1.11

8 **Choose File>Save As.**

The Save As dialog box appears.

9 **Navigate to your Work_In_Progress>WIP_01 folder.**

Save all the files that you work through in the exercises in the project-specific folder in your Work_In_Progress folder. For this project, use the WIP_01 folder.

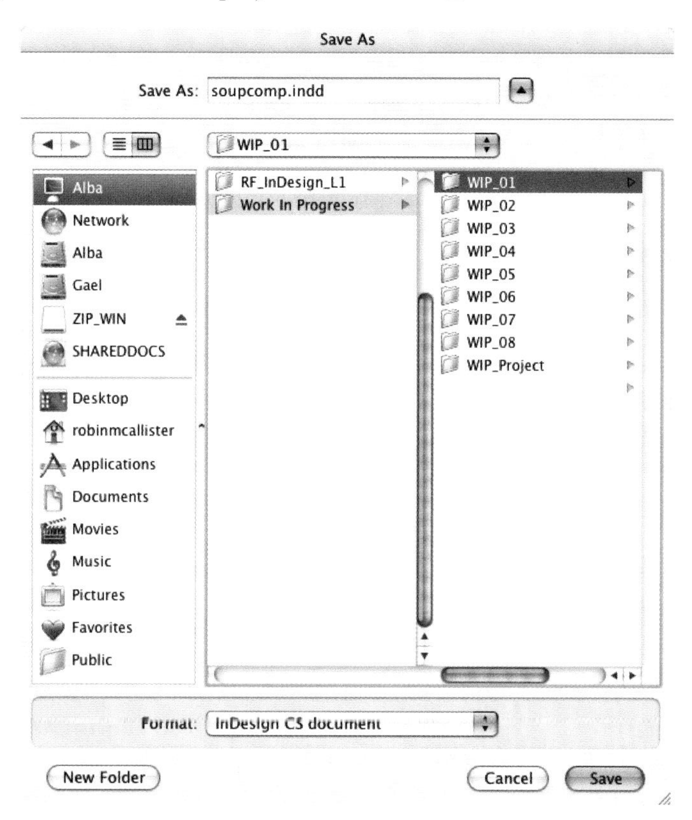

FIGURE 1.12

10 **Click the Save button to save the document.**

The file name remains unchanged (soupcomp.indd), but you're putting it in a new location.

11 **Choose File>Close to close the window.**

You can also close a window by pressing Command/Control-W, or by clicking the Close button on the document window.

To Extend Your Knowledge...

CONVERTING THUMBNAILS TO COMPS

While a thumbnail conveys the bare bones of a document — whether it is an ad, a magazine article, or a book design — the comp brings a feeling of reality to the design. Type is tangible (even if it is Greeked gibberish), the customer's logo is in place, and there are "real" graphics that convey the look and feel of the final piece. Comps (you usually submit at least three) may be accompanied by several versions of text. During the comp stage, the design becomes tangible, even to the graphically impaired.

LESSON 2 Navigating an InDesign Document

InDesign offers a number of options for navigating through a document. As you gain familiarity with the program, you will undoubtedly develop your own preferences for moving around a single page, or moving from one page to another within a lengthy document.

When you work on documents, you should use the largest monitor available. A large monitor allows you to have multiple windows open at the same time, as well as makes it possible to view more of a page or spread (at a readable size) than a smaller monitor. Even the largest monitor, however, will not accommodate viewing a large poster in a workable view percentage, or a letter-sized document set in small type.

The ability to navigate the page and know your exact location will be very helpful when you are creating documents under a deadline — as will the ability to quickly navigate from page to page using keyboard shortcuts, or using the Pages palette. In the following exercise, you become familiar with InDesign's Pages palette and navigation tools by opening and navigating a four-page document.

Navigate an InDesign Document

1 **Choose File>Open. Choose louise.indd from the RF_InDesign_L1>Project_01 folder.**

Remember, you can also access the Open a File dialog box by pressing Command/Control-O. The document opens to the first page. You can tell which page you are viewing by looking at the number at the bottom of the page.

FIGURE 1.13

2 **In the Pages palette (in the palette bay in the upper-right corner of your screen), progressively double-click each page in the document. When you have finished your tour, go back to Page 1.**

If you don't see all four pages in the palette, drag the bottom-right corner of the palette to expand it, or use the scroll bar on the right-hand side. ***Scroll bars*** help you move rapidly (horizontally or vertically) in a document page or other list (such as this list of pages) in an open window.

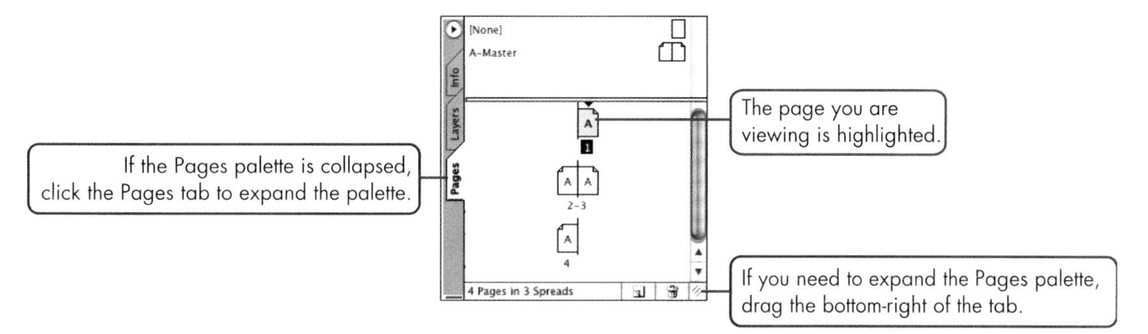

FIGURE 1.14

3 **Click the arrow that is next to the View Percentage field at the lower left of the document window. Choose 200% from the pop-up menu that appears.**

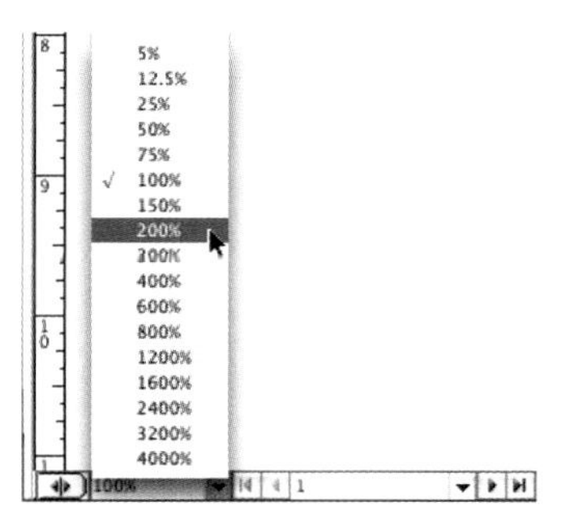

FIGURE 1.15

4 **Choose Window>Navigator.**

The Navigator palette opens. The Navigator shows the current view percentage and a thumbnail of the page, called a ***proxy image***. The proxy is particularly useful when you are viewing a page at a large percentage and want to move to another area of the page. You can also change the view percentage from the Navigator palette.

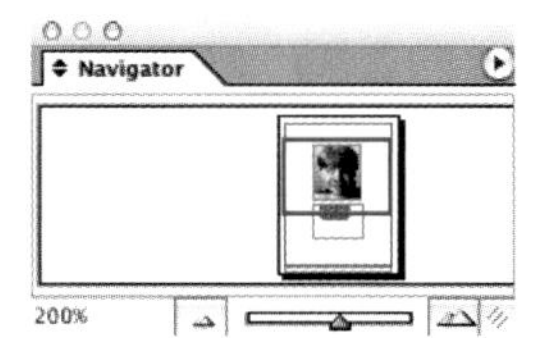

FIGURE 1.16

5 **Click-hold the red box and drag it around.**

6 **Use the slider in the Navigator palette to change the View Percentage.**

The portion of the image displayed in the actual document window changes to reflect the position of the red box relative to the proxy image.

7 **In the document window, click in the Current Page field to the right of the View Percentage field. Enter the number "3". Press Return/Enter to go to this page.**

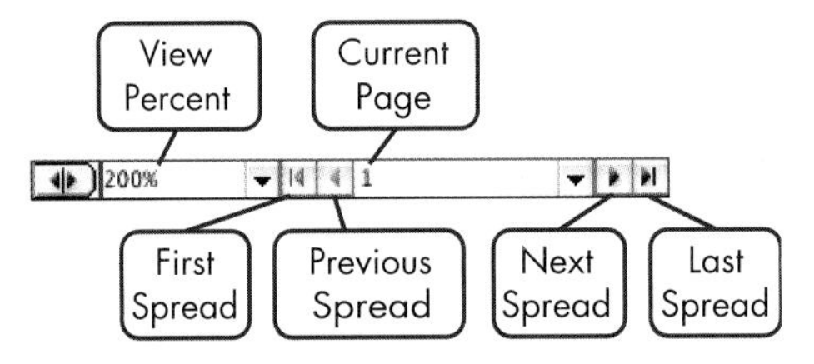

FIGURE 1.17

The Navigator palette confirms that you are on Page 3. Pages 2 and 3 adjoin one another; collectively, they are referred to as a ***spread***. You can also go to a specific page by pressing Command/Control-J, then typing the page number into the Current Page box.

8 **From the main menu, choose View>Fit Spread in Window.**

Both pages of the active spread fit into the open window. The Current Page box indicates that you are on Page 2, even though Page 3 is also visible.

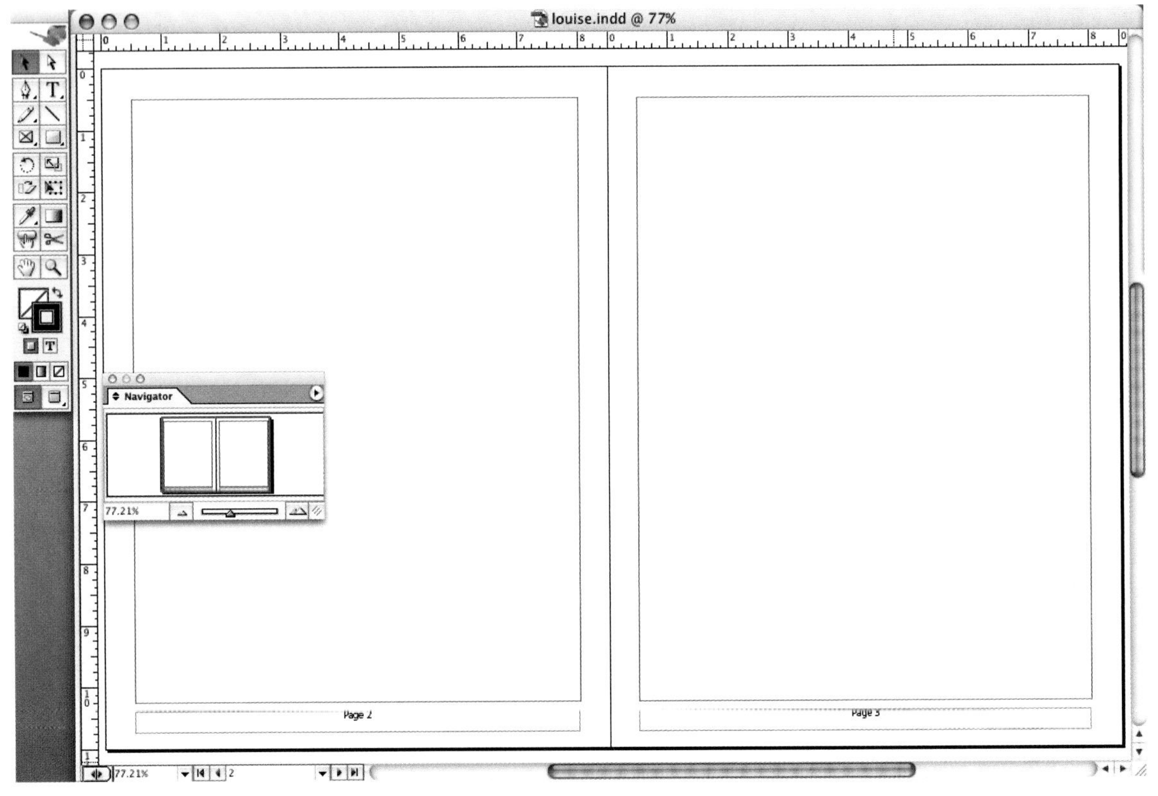

FIGURE 1.18

9 **At the bottom of the document window, click the Next Spread button (to the immediate right of the Current Page field).**

Page 4 is now centered in the window.

10 **Click the First Spread button (at the far left of the Current Page field).**

Page 1 appears once again.

11 **Choose the Hand tool in the Tools palette.**

Using the Hand tool is a fast and easy way to move pages so you can access different areas.

12 **Click anywhere on the page and hold down the mouse button. Drag the page around the open window.**

The page movement is mirrored by the proxy image in the Navigator palette.

13 **Save the document (File>Save As), leaving the file name louise.indd. Leave the file open for the next exercise.**

As instructed earlier, save all files to your WIP_[Project Number] folder, unless otherwise instructed.

You can also save the document by pressing Shift-Command/Control-S.

Explore the Control Palette

1 **In the open document, choose View>Fit Page in Window.**

Page 1 is fit to the window. You could also press Command/Control-0 to fit the page to the window.

2 **If the Control palette is not visible, choose Window>Control.**

The Control palette can be docked at the top or bottom of your screen, or it can float. It defaults to docking at the top, which is where it appears throughout this book.

3 **Choose the Selection tool. Click the tool anywhere on the photo in the middle of the page. Note the information in the Control palette.**

The Control palette is ***context-sensitive*** — its content changes to reflect the active tool. The Control palette not only gives you information about text, image frames, and content, it allows you to manage them, too.

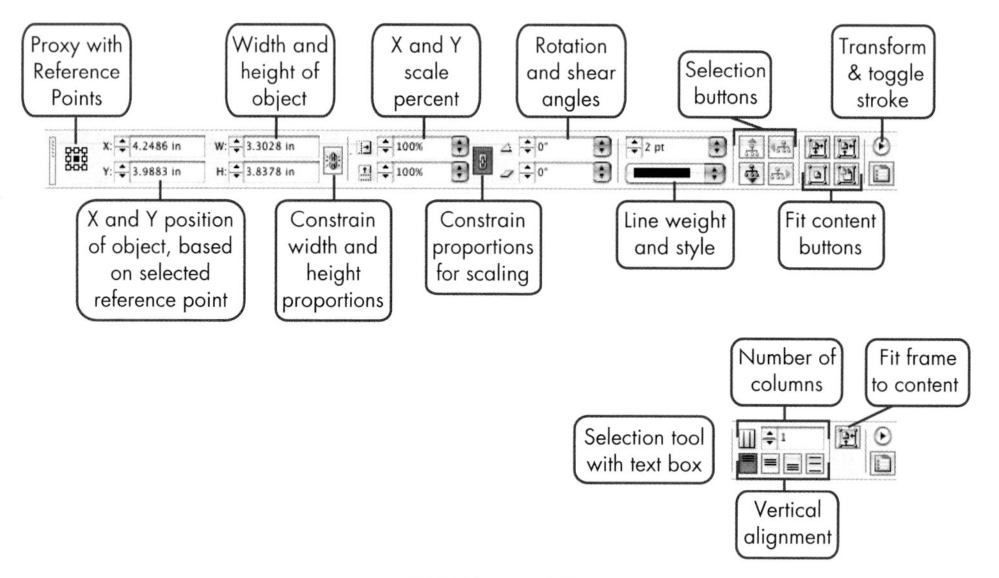

FIGURE 1.19

4 **With the Selection tool still active, click in the text block and note the difference in the information in the Control palette.**

5 **Activate the Type tool. Click the Character Formatting Controls icon in the Control palette, if it is not already highlighted. Click the word "Louise".**

You can perform virtually every character-related function from the Character Control palette that appears.

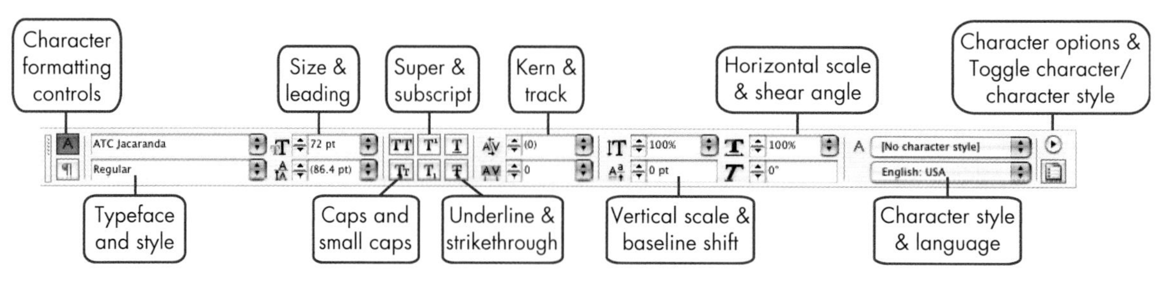

FIGURE 1.20

6 **Click the Paragraph Formatting Controls icon in the Control palette.**

The Paragraph Control palette displays virtually every function related to the formatting of entire paragraphs.

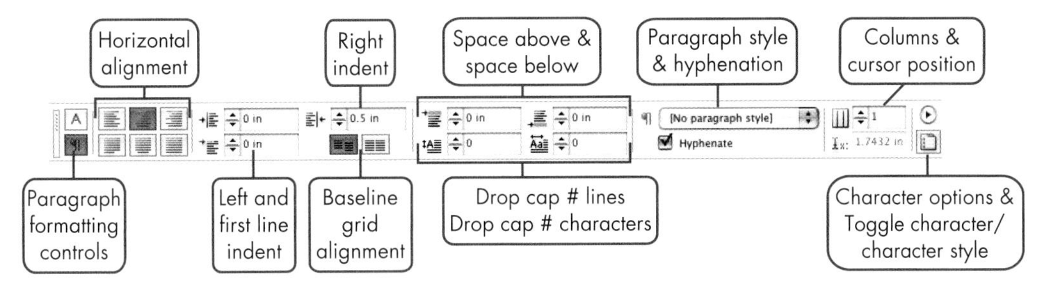

FIGURE 1.21

7 **Save the document (File>Save) and leave it open for the next lesson.**

To Extend Your Knowledge...

WORKING WITH CONTEXT-SENSITIVE PALETTES

The Control palette is context-sensitive, so it provides a consistent interface for working with your creative tools, and is always in the same place. In addition, it takes up a minimal amount of real estate on your screen that could quickly become crowded with palettes, were it not for InDesign's workspace organization.

You will probably virtually ignore the dedicated Transform, Character, Paragraph, and Stroke palettes. When you are referred to these palettes in projects within this book, feel free to use the Control palette instead — when it provides the same information in a similar format. As we stated earlier, you will develop your own personal working style as you become more familiar with InDesign.

LESSON 3 Managing Your Working Area

In this lesson, you learn how to manage the InDesign palettes to maximize your on-screen real estate. It's important to conserve as much screen space as possible, because you will often zoom in on your pages to tweak details — or to read the type, if you are using small point sizes. When your palettes aren't managed properly, you waste both space and time.

Palettes can be ***docked*** (grouped together) in collections called ***palette bays***. The entire collection can then be compressed and tucked neatly out of the way against the edge of the screen (Macintosh) or InDesign window (Windows). In some cases, especially with palettes that you access only briefly, you might choose to allow palettes to float.

The context-sensitive Control palette, which you used in the previous lesson, is particularly feature-rich. It takes up a small amount of space, so you will probably choose to leave it open most of the time. You will likely keep the rest of the palettes compressed as much as possible to maximize your working space.

Manage Your Working Area

1 **Continue in the open document.**

2 **Click the tab of the Navigator palette and drag it into the palette bay that contains the Pages, Layers, and Info palettes.**

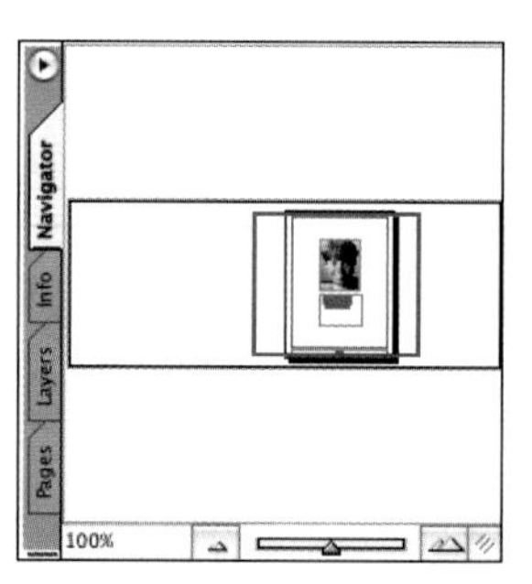

FIGURE 1.22

3 **Click the tab of the Pages palette to bring it into view.**

Clicking the tab of any palette brings it to the front of a group and makes it the active palette.

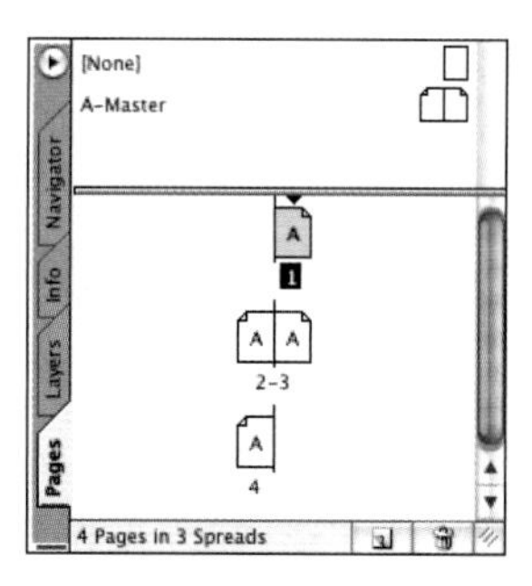

FIGURE 1.23

4 **Click the tab of the Pages palette, and then release the mouse.**

The entire palette bay is collapsed and "stuck" against the edge of your screen.

FIGURE 1.24

5 **Click the tab of the Navigator palette to expand it to full size and make it the active palette.**

6 **Hold down the mouse button and drag the tab of the Navigator palette away from the group.**

The Navigator palette becomes a floating palette again.

7 **Click the Navigator palette's Close button.**

You can also deselect the Navigator palette in the Window menu to close it.

8 **Close the document without saving.**

To Extend Your Knowledge...

CUSTOM WORKSPACES CAN BE SAVED

You may want to save groups of palettes as palette bays for specific types of work. InDesign allows you to save sets of palettes as named ***workspaces***. Even the position of the palettes is retained — so you always know where the palettes are located. To save a custom workspace, choose Window>Workspace>Save Workspace, enter a workspace name, and click Save.

LESSON 4 Creating Simple Documents

Now that you have been introduced to some of InDesign's tools, you will use the Type and Line tools, in conjunction with rulers and guides, to create a simple letterhead. ***Rulers*** are used as aids to visual measurement and to apply guides to the page; ***guides*** are used to align objects to the page. As you progress through the book, you will be introduced to additional tools.

New Document Dialog Box

In the New Document dialog box, you can define the size of a document, the number of pages, whether to use facing pages, and whether a text frame should appear on each page. You can also establish the document's orientation as either ***portrait*** (vertical) or ***landscape*** (horizontal). You can define the number of columns, the space between each column (called the ***gutter***), and all four margin widths. The options that appear when you click the More Options button allow you to specify ***bleed*** (the area beyond the page that is required if ink is to print to the edge of the page) and ***slug*** (information that prints on the sheet, but is not included within the specified page size, or ***trim size***).

Although InDesign has many advanced tools that offer expanded control over the document being produced, you will frequently use the basic tools introduced in this lesson, and produce documents similar to the letterhead in the following exercise. As you continue in this book and the advanced book on InDesign (Level 2), you will discover that a firm understanding of the basic tools allows you to quickly expand your skill set.

Use the Tools

1 **Choose File>New to create a new document.**

The New Document dialog box appears. You can also press Command/Control-N to access the New Document dialog box.

2 **Click the Facing Pages button to uncheck it. Click OK.**

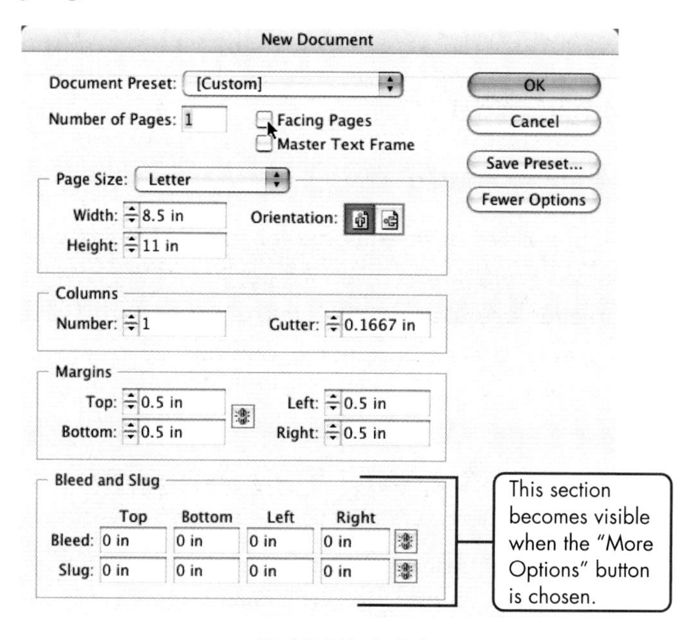

FIGURE 1.25

3 **Choose InDesign>Preferences>Units & Increments (Macintosh) or Edit>Preferences>Units & Increments (Windows).**

4 **In the Ruler Units section, set the Origin to Page, and set the Horizontal and Vertical to Inches. Click OK.**

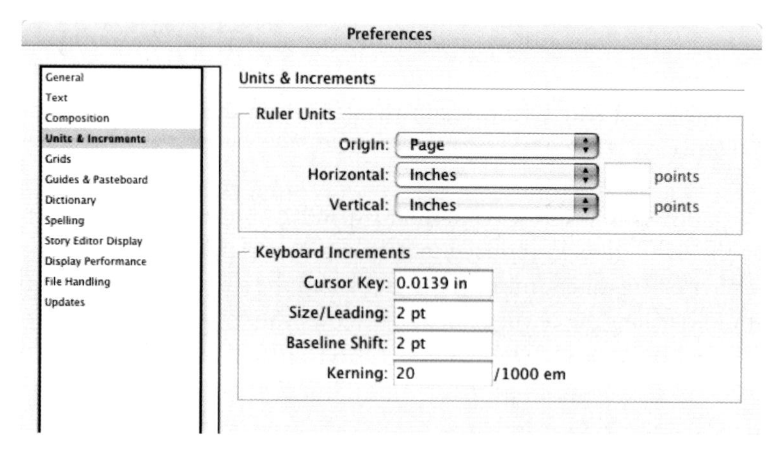

FIGURE 1.26

5 **Click in the horizontal ruler at the top of the page and drag a guide down to the 1.5-inch mark.**

Look at the Y coordinate in the Control palette to check the guide's position. With a guide selected, you can type the position into the Control palette.

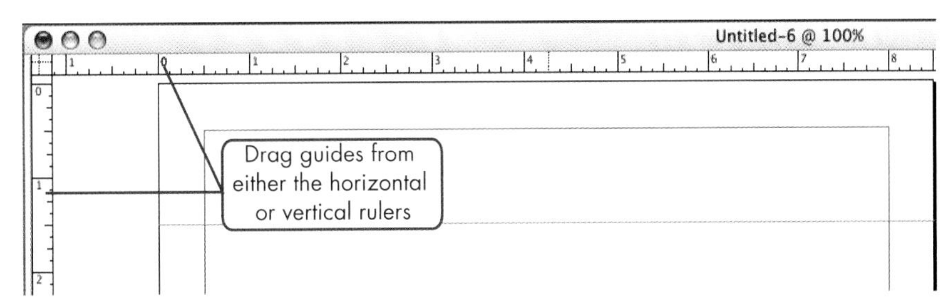

FIGURE 1.27

If you have problems...

If you can't set the guide at exactly the correct position by dragging with the mouse, you can adjust the guide manually by switching to the Selection tool, clicking the guide, and typing "1.5" in the Y field of the Control palette.

6 **From the vertical ruler at the left of the page, drag guides to the 2.5-inch and 6-inch marks.**

7 **Choose the Type tool in the Tools palette. Drag a frame from the upper-left margin to where the guide intersects the right margin at 1.5 inches.**

This frame delineates the text area. In InDesign, all text and images are placed in ***frames***, which are simply containers. The text cursor is automatically positioned at the top left of the frame. You will soon learn how to center text within the frame.

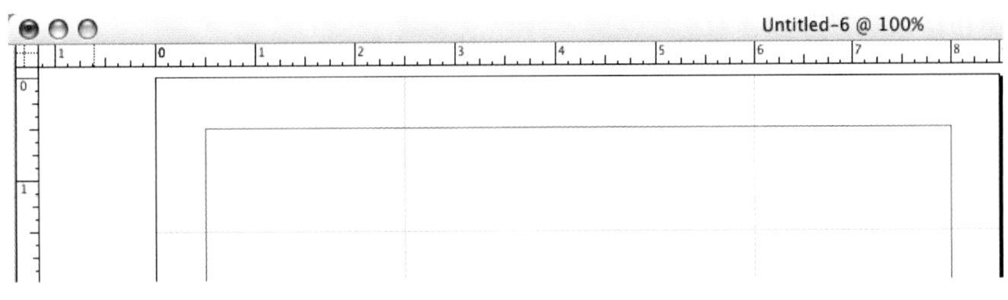

FIGURE 1.28

8 **Type your name, and then press Return/Enter. On the next line, type your address [space], press Option/Alt-8 [space], type your city, [space], type your state [2 spaces], type your Zip code, and then press Shift-Return/Enter. On the third line, type your telephone number.**

These three lines of text are aligned left and set in your computer's default typeface. Pressing the Return/Enter key enters a ***paragraph return***, which is sometimes called a ***hard return***. A paragraph return creates a new paragraph. Holding the Shift key while you press Return/Enter enters a ***line feed***, or ***soft return***, which keeps the two lines together in the same paragraph. Option/Alt-8 accesses the bullet character in both the Macintosh and Windows versions of InDesign.

9 **Place the cursor in front of your name. Drag to highlight your name. In the Character Control palette, set the Font as ATC Laurel and Bold as the Style. Set the Size at 30 pt. Apply the default Leading (36 pt).**

Highlighting text selects it for formatting. Text elements are discussed in detail in Project 3.

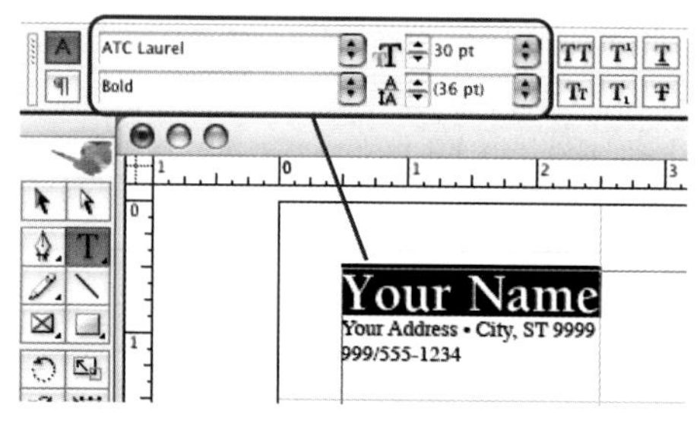

FIGURE 1.29

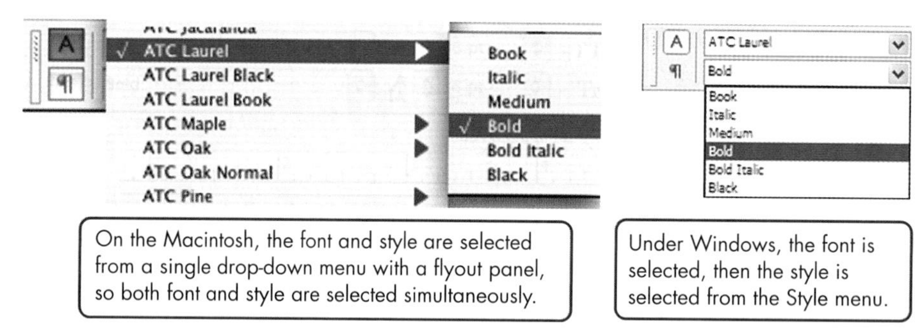

FIGURE 1.30

10 **Select the address and phone number lines. Set the Font as ATC Oak Normal. Set the Size to 14 pt and the Leading to 18 pt.**

11 **Highlight all of the text. In the Paragraph Control palette, click the Align Center button to center the text horizontally in the frame.**

The keystroke shortcut for centering text is to select the text and press Shift-Command/Control-C.

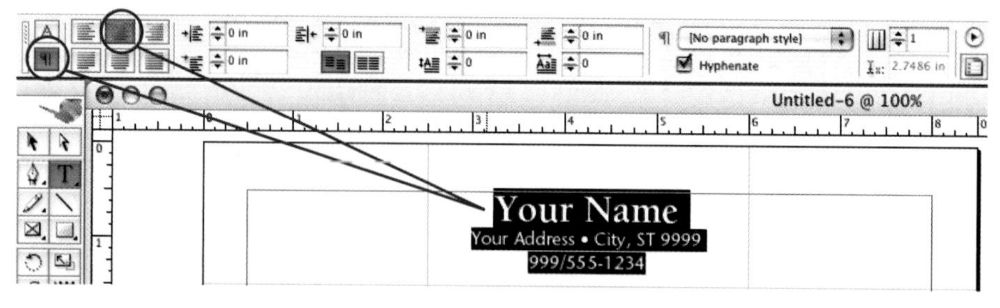

FIGURE 1.31

12 **Choose the Line tool in the Tools palette. Hold down the Shift key, click the left guide at the 1.5-inch mark, and drag to the right guide.**

This draws a straight line between the two vertical guides. Holding the Shift key constrains the line to 45-degree increments. Check the Control palette to ensure that it reads X: 2.5 in, Y: 1.5 in, L: 3.5 in.

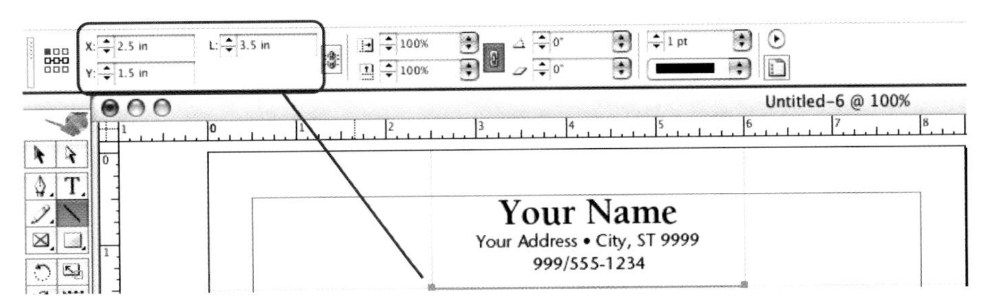

FIGURE 1.32

13 **Choose the Selection tool in the Tools palette. Click anywhere on the page to deselect the line.**

14 **Click the Preview Mode icon to preview the page (see Figure 1.33).**

You can also preview a page by pressing the "W" key.

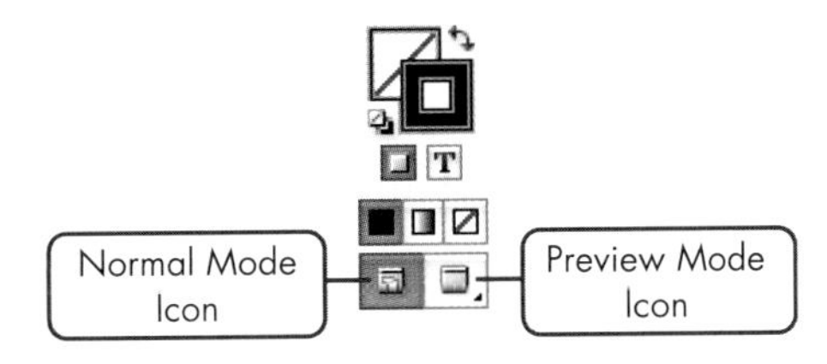

FIGURE 1.33

15 **Save the file to your Work in Progress>WIP_01 folder with the name "letterhead.indd".**

16 **Close the document.**

To Extend Your Knowledge...

MANAGING THE FALL OF TYPE

When you work with a document's design — particularly when you need to fit text to a specific area to achieve a graphically appealing look — you will often force lines to break using soft returns and other devices. Hard returns execute paragraph parameters, such as indents, rules (lines) above or below, and additional line spacing, while soft returns simply move the following text to the next line.

LESSON 5 Importing Graphics and Text

Not everything that finds its way to a page begins in InDesign. When you want to include text and graphics that were created in an application other than InDesign, they must be placed into your InDesign document. When text and graphics are ***placed*** (instead of copied) into a file, they can take advantage of InDesign's powerful filters that can read characteristics applied to the imported document from the original program.

Large blocks of text often originate in word-processing programs — in many cases, such text is already formatted so it can flow into your document without the need to assign character or paragraph styles. If text files are copied instead of imported, they may lose all of their formatting. Although artwork can be drawn in InDesign, it usually originates in a program dedicated to creating vector graphics (such as Adobe Illustrator) or a program that manipulates raster graphics (such as Adobe Photoshop).

In the following exercise, you finish the design-to-production process you began in Lesson 1. You open a document that has some placeholder frames, and then you accurately position the frames and fill them with text and images. The resulting mechanical should closely resemble the comp you created in Lesson 2.

Reposition Frames

1 **Open crockad.indd from the RF_InDesign_L1>Project_01 folder.**

To the left of the page are four blank frames (the two columns that will hold text are grouped together) and two frames filled with text. If you do not see the frames, choose View>Show Frame Edges.

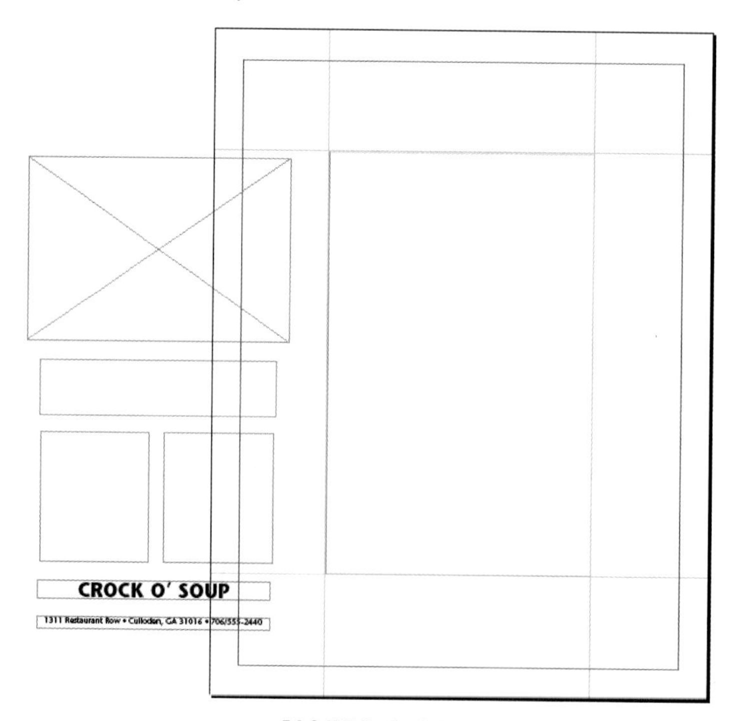

FIGURE 1.34

2 **Use the Selection tool to click the top frame (the one with the "X"). Use the Control palette to position the frame at X: 2 in, Y: 2 in. Be sure the proxy-reference point is set to the upper left.**

There are nine proxy-reference points that correspond the eight handles of an object's bounding box and its center point. The X and Y positions refer to the positions of the proxy-reference point selected. Positioning objects and performing actions such as rotations are based on the proxy-reference point.

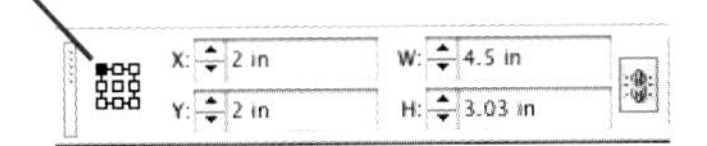

FIGURE 1.35

3 **Click the frame that will hold the headline. Position it at X: 2.25 in, Y: 5.15 in.**

4 **Click the two linked text boxes. Position them at X: 2.25 in, Y: 6.15 in.**

5 **Click the Crock O' Soup frame. Position it at X: 2.25 in, Y: 8.375 in.**

6 **Click the address frame. Position it at X: 2.25 in, Y: 8.7 in.**

All of the frames are in their correct locations. You are ready to import the text and image.

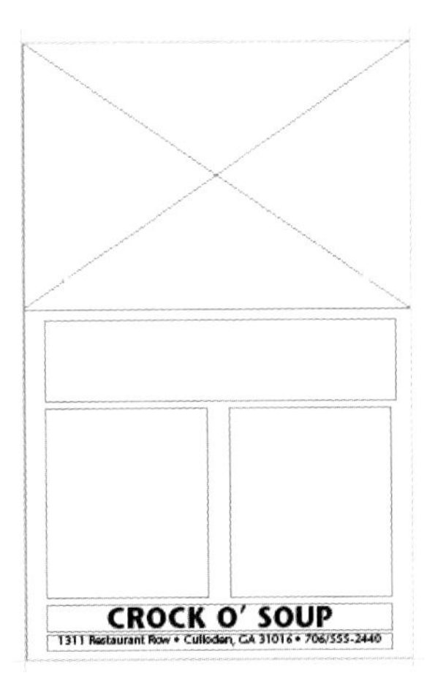

FIGURE 1.36

7 **Save the ad as "crockosoup.indd" in your Work_In_Progress>WIP_01 folder. Leave the file open for the next exercise.**

Import Graphics and Text

1 **Continue in the open document.**

2 **Use the Selection tool to click the graphic frame. Choose File>Place.**

The Place dialog box appears. The keystroke shortcut to place either graphics or text is Command/Control-D.

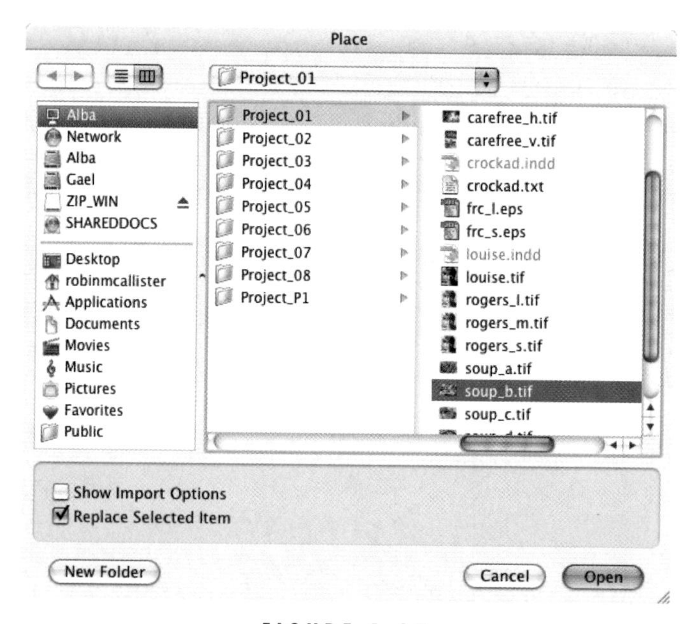

FIGURE 1.37

3 **Navigate to the RF_InDesign_L1>Project_01 folder. Choose one of the soup_.tif images. Click the Open button.**

Comps often incorporate images that merely represent the final image. You can decide which image you like best for this exercise.

FIGURE 1.38

4 **Choose the Type tool in the Tools palette. Type (with no quotation marks) "Enjoy an elegant lunch in a comfortable setting" in the headline frame below the image.**

5 **Use the Type tool to select all of the headline text. Set the Font as ATC Laurel Bold Italic, 30-pt Size, with 33-pt Leading. In the Control palette, set the Tracking for the headline at –5.**

Tracking adjusts the spacing of a group of letters so they are closer together or farther apart. ***Kerning*** adjusts the spacing between character pairs. In this case, you are tracking the text so it fits in the allotted space. You can select all type in a text frame by manually highlighting all the text, choosing Edit>Select All, or pressing Command/Control-A.

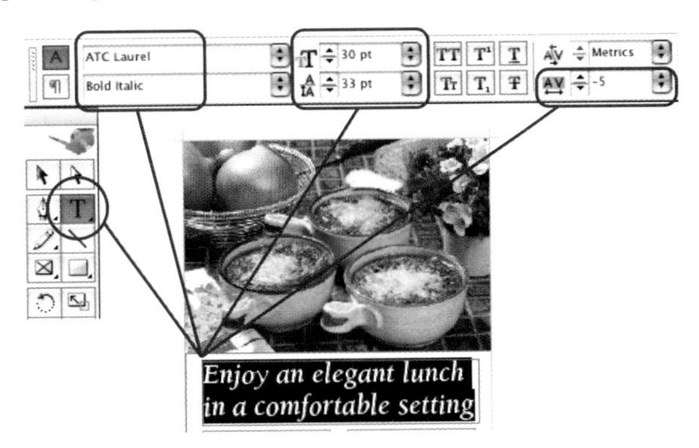

FIGURE 1.39

6 **Click the Type tool in the left column of the linked pair of frames. Choose File>Place and place crockad.txt.**

Remember, you can access the Place dialog box by pressing Command/Control-D. The text has been pre-formatted, so it fits the space available in these frames.

To Extend Your Knowledge...

QUICK AND EASY NAVIGATION TIPS

To change page views quickly and easily, use the keyboard shortcuts.

- Command/Control-1 brings the page to 100%
- Command/Control-2 is 200%
- Command/Control-4 is 400%
- Command/Control-5 is 50%

To fit the page in the open window, press Command/Control-0. To fit the spread in the window, press Command-Option-0 (Macintosh) or Control-Alt-0 (Windows).

Using the Navigator palette is one of the fastest and easiest ways of getting around a page or spread when the entire page doesn't fit on your screen.

7 **Use the Selection tool to click the border surrounding the ad. Choose Object>Arrange> Bring to Front.**

The Bring to Front command places the border in front of the text and image, forming a frame around the entire ad. The border was behind all the elements you added to the ad. If it were not brought to the front, the image at the top would cut off that portion of the border.

8 **Deselect the border. Click the Preview Mode button to preview your ad.**

Remember, you can press the "W" key to preview your page. Check your ad to be sure everything is in place.

FIGURE 1.40

9 **Save the ad and leave it open for the next exercise.**

LESSON 6 Printing a File

There are a number of reasons why you might want to print a document. Whether you need to distribute a file for client approval or proofread it off-screen, InDesign includes many print options.

When you print a document to your desktop printer, there is a limited number of available options. If you print documents to film or direct to plate, however, there are many criteria to take into consideration. In this exercise, you learn the most basic steps involved in printing a document. You explore the advanced printing options in Project 8.

Print Your Ad

1 **In the open document, choose File>Print.**

The Print dialog box (which is quite extensive) appears. Another way to access the Print dialog box is to press Command/Control-P.

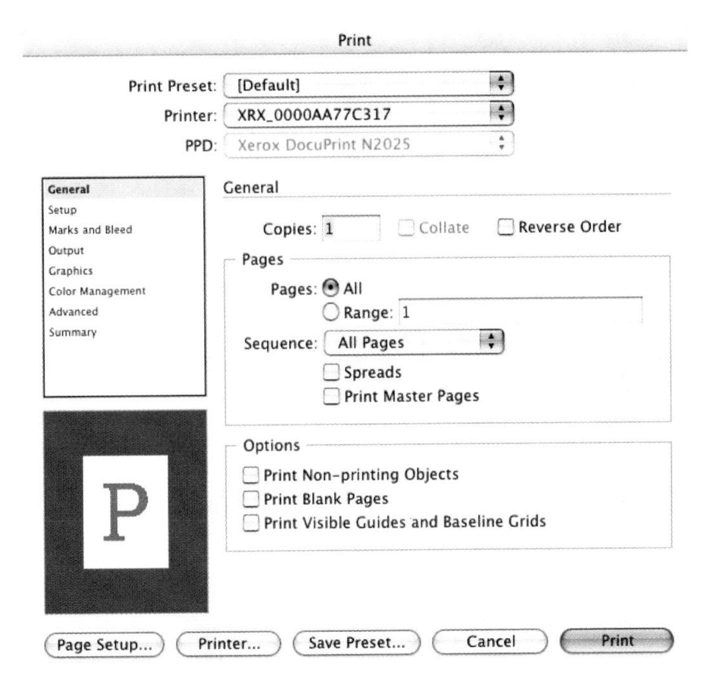

FIGURE 1.41

2 **Accept the default settings and click the Print button.**

This sends the document to your default printer, exactly as if it were a word-processing document. It should produce a printed document that is acceptable for proofreading or distributing within an office environment.

If you have problems...

We assume that your computer is set up with a default printer. If the file doesn't print, chances are that you have not selected a default printer. Check to see if a printer has been selected and if it is turned on.

3 **Close the file without saving.**

If you receive the message, "Save changes to the Adobe InDesign document "crockosoup.indd" before closing," click the Don't Save button.

To Extend Your Knowledge...

PRINTING WITH EFFICIENCY

When setting up files for printing, a printing service provider may have several different "printers" in use. They may use an ink jet printer for inexpensive color proofing, a black-and-white laser printer, and several high-end output devices — they may even print direct to plate. To make managing printing to multiple devices easy, InDesign allows you to save any printing setup as a ***preset***. This feature saves substantial time and eliminates errors that can occur if the wrong device is selected.

LESSON 7 Getting Help

If you want additional information about using InDesign, one of the best places to go is the source. The InDesign application comes with an extensive Help database, which is installed on your computer when you load the software. The Adobe Systems Web site is another valuable asset. If you have Internet access, you can refer to the most up-to-date information available.

Help features available online include an overview of InDesign, answers to frequently asked questions (FAQs) and in-depth product information. There are also customer stories, reviews of the product, and a listing of events and seminars where you can go to learn more about InDesign. Announcements and listings of third-party plug-ins are also featured.

Use the Help Features

1 **Choose the Help menu.**

From the Help menu, you can access either the help files that reside on your computer or online support from the Adobe Web site.

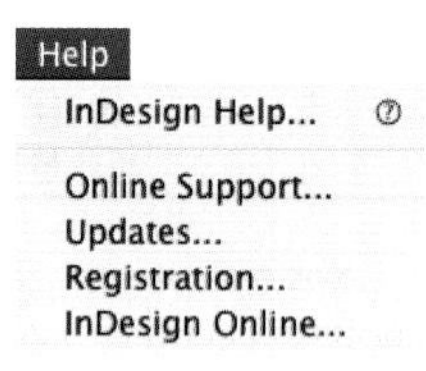

FIGURE 1.42

2 **Choose InDesign Help.**

Your default browser opens, and you see a list of help topics that reside on your computer. These files are installed on your computer, so they cannot be updated.

3 **Return to InDesign. Choose Help>Online Support.**

Your browser takes you to the InDesign page at the Adobe Web site. From here, you see a list of the top support issues. You can also type a question of your own. This site should contain up-to-date information. Another way to access the InDesign home page on the Adobe Web site is to click the InDesign Online icon in the Tools palette.

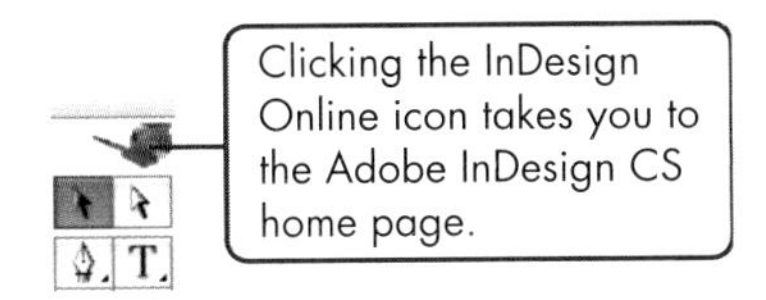

Clicking the InDesign Online icon takes you to the Adobe InDesign CS home page.

FIGURE 1.43

CAREERS IN DESIGN

THE GRAPHIC ARTS MARKETPLACE

The graphic arts industry, by its very nature, extends into many other industries. The term "graphic designer" has become something of a catch-all term that can include designers (who are responsible for the appearance of print or Web documents), illustrators (who "draw" images on the computer or on another medium), page-layout specialists (who assemble text and images for print production), or Web-publishing specialists (who assemble text and images for Web presentation).

When you enter the field of graphic design, you will likely work in a position that can offer you the greatest amount of experience. You might work for a Fortune 500 company, a real estate agency, a school or hospital, advertising agency, or a printer. In the course of your responsibilities, you may produce a letterhead package on Monday, assemble a brochure on Tuesday, and work on an annual report for the rest of the week.

As you gain experience, you will discover which areas of graphic design you enjoy, and in which you excel; you will likely build upon those areas. Some of the areas in which you may eventually specialize are listed below:

- Advertising design (brochures, magazine and newspaper ads, direct mail)
- Publication design (books, magazines, catalogs, annual reports, directories)
- Specialty design (menus, posters, postcards)
- Package design (labels, boxes, bags, wrappers, display packaging, merchandising display)
- Illustration (information graphics, editorial illustration, technical illustration)
- Corporate identity design (logos, stationery, business cards, signage)

SUMMARY

In this project, you learned that publishing is a process, not a discrete action. You took an ad from its inception, through the comp stage (when it would be presented to a client), and on to completion. You even printed a proof. You also learned to navigate within and between the pages of a document.

You learned that the InDesign palettes are very valuable tools, and that it's important to make them as accessible as possible without wasting a great deal of valuable screen space. You learned how to manage palettes and enhance their value during production. You also learned how to define specific workspaces that allow you to be more productive as you develop personal work habits and experience a variety of workflows.

You learned to use some basic tools, including the Selection, Rectangle, Hand, Line, and Type tools. The Type tool may be the most important tool you will use in InDesign. (In future projects, you will learn how to exert precise control over your text.) You also learned the importance of InDesign's ability to import text and graphics from other programs.

KEY TERMS

Bleed
Bounding box
Comp
Context-sensitive
Control palette
Dock
Floating palette
Frame
Greeked text
Guide
Gutter
Hand tool
Hard return
Help files
Import
Kerning
Landscape orientation
Line feed
Mechanical
Navigator palette
Palette
Paragraph return
Portrait orientation
Preset
Proxy image
Ruler
Scroll bar
Slug
Soft return
Spread
Thumbnail
Tracking
Trim size
View Percentage box
Workspace

CHECKING CONCEPTS AND TERMS

SCREEN ID

Identify the indicated areas from the list below:

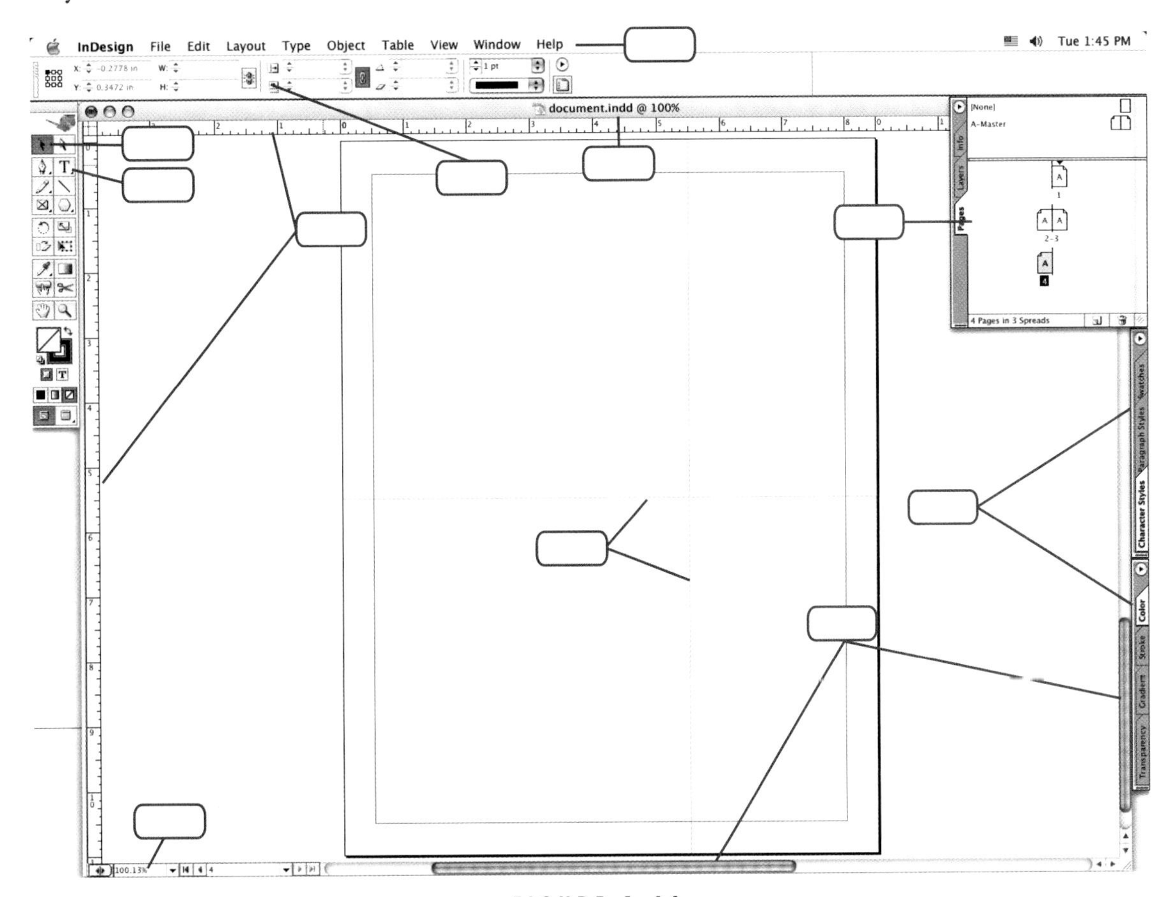

FIGURE 1.44

a. Collapsed palette bays
b. Control palette
c. Document name
d. Expanded palette group
e. Ruler guides
f. Menu bar
g. Rulers
h. Scroll bars
i. Selection tool
j. Type tool
k. View Percentage

MULTIPLE CHOICE

Circle the letter of the correct answer for each of the following.

1. What functions can you perform using InDesign?
   a. Type and style text.
   b. Draw complex illustrations.
   c. Add rich content to documents.
   d. All of the above.
2. What is a mechanical?
   a. Any document that "moves," such as a Flash movie.
   b. A document that is ready to be output to print production.
   c. A function that you perform automatically.
   d. The process of using InDesign's tools.
3. What is a bounding box?
   a. An imaginary box that marks the perimeter of all frames.
   b. An animated box that jumps across a page.
   c. Any rectangle.
   d. An object's proxy image, viewed in the Navigator palette.
4. The Hand tool is used to __________.
   a. move objects around on the page
   b. select and move individual points in an image
   c. navigate from page to page
   d. move a page around in a window
5. The Navigator palette allows you to ________.
   a. know where you are on the page, relatively, when zoomed into an object
   b. know the X,Y coordinates of an object
   c. navigate between pages
   d. manage the appearance of text and graphics
6. What is a docked palette?
   a. A palette that is grouped with other palettes.
   b. A palette that has all features visible.
   c. A palette you placed against another palette.
   d. A palette that is combined with other palettes in a palette bay.
7. Which is not true of text?
   a. It may be imported from another program.
   b. Its size and style can be managed from the Control palette.
   c. It may be typed directly on the page, without a frame.
   d. It may be aligned in the Control palette or with keyboard commands.
8. Which of the following is true of a mechanical?
   a. Images may be imported, but text must be typed in InDesign.
   b. Accuracy is very important.
   c. There can be no deviation from what is presented in the comp.
   d. It must be produced in black and white.
9. Which of the following is not true of the Control palette?
   a. It changes appearance depending upon what tool is being used.
   b. You can use it to accurately place objects on the page.
   c. You can change the size of type and images.
   d. You can colorize black-and-white photos.
10. How can you get the most up-to-date help and support available for InDesign?
    a. Ask a friend who uses InDesign.
    b. Choose InDesign Help from the Help menu.
    c. Take an advanced course in InDesign.
    d. Choose Online Support from the InDesign Help menu.

DISCUSSION QUESTIONS

1. In this project, you learned that the process beginning with design and ending with production is not entirely computer-based. You were encouraged to begin the process with a sketch, progress to a comprehensive computer-based rough design, and then to complete your mechanical. Why is this process more desirable than simply sitting down at the computer and beginning to design? Are there any disadvantages to working this way?

2. When you produced a comp, and then a mechanical, you used two different methods of placing frames on the page: dragging to a guide, and positioning on an X,Y coordinate. In what circumstances would it be better to use one method instead of the other?

3. InDesign's palettes are unique, in that different palettes function in different ways. What are the advantages and disadvantages of context-sensitive palettes? Discuss the relative values of floating palettes over docked palettes, and free-standing palettes over palette groups.

SKILL DRILL

Skill Drills reinforce project skills. Each skill reinforced is the same, or nearly the same, as a skill presented in the lessons. Detailed instructions are provided in a step-by-step format. You can work through one or more exercises in any order, although Drills 2 and 3 must be done in succession.

1. Navigate a Multi-Page Document

You created the front matter portion (pages that appear before the main content) of a cookbook being published by a nationally famous inn. Before you assemble the pages and send them out for printing, you want to check them for accuracy.

1. Open the document waysidefm.indd.
2. Expand the Pages palette so you can see the page icons for all six pages in the document.
3. Click the Next Page button in the lower left of the open window.

   You now see Page 2 — verses from Longfellow's "Tales of a Wayside Inn."
4. Choose Window>Navigator to open the Navigator palette.
5. Choose View>Fit Spread to Window to fit the spread to the window.

   The proxy in the Navigator palette shows that the entire spread is visible. You could also use the keyboard shortcut Command-Option-0 (Macintosh) or Control-Alt-0 (Windows) to fit the spread to the window.

6. Choose the Zoom tool in the Tools palette. Click twice on the title, "Tales of a Wayside Inn."

   The title is centered on the screen, and the Navigator shows its position relative to the spread. The view percentage depends on the size of your monitor.

7. In the Pages palette, double-click the left page in Spread ii-iii. When the spread appears in the window, double-click again.

   This reduces the spread so Page ii fits and is centered in the window.

8. Use the Hand tool to drag the spread so the entire spread is visible in the window.

9. Save the document in your WIP_01 folder and close it.

2. Create a Concert Flyer

A coffee shop that promotes folk concerts hired you to produce custom flyers and tickets for an upcoming event. You will use the same information for both promotional pieces.

1. Create a new letter-size document without facing pages, and with 0.5-in margins. Save it as "rogers_flyer.indd" in your WIP_01 folder.

2. Drag a vertical guide to the center of the page (4.25 in on the horizontal ruler).

3. Choose File>Place and place the file frc_l.eps. Choose the upper-center proxy-reference point (at the left of the Control palette) and position the placed file at X: 4.25 in, Y: 0.5 in.

4. Place the main image (rogers_l.tif) with the upper center positioned at X: 4.25 in, Y: 2.5 in. Be sure to deselect the frame created for the previous image you placed, or you will replace it with this image. Simply click to place this image — do not click and drag.

5. Choose the Type tool in the Tools palette. Click the left margin at the 8-in mark. Drag diagonally to the intersection of the right and bottom margins.

6. Use the Character Control palette to apply the following: Set "Louise Rogers" in 60-pt ATC Jacaranda; set "In Concert" in 36-pt ATC Oak Normal; set "1201 Flatrock Bridge Road • Rye, NY 10580 • (914) 555-FOLK" in 18-pt ATC Oak Normal. Allow the Leading to default. Press the Return/Enter key after the first two lines of type.

7. With the cursor still in the last line, enter "0.5 in" in the Space Before Paragraph field in the Paragraph Control palette.

8. Choose Edit>Select All to select all the type in this text frame. Click the Align Center icon in the Paragraph Control palette.

9. Be sure nothing is selected. Click Preview Mode in the Tools palette (or press the "W" key) to view your document in Preview mode. Save the document and leave it open for the next Skill Drill.

FIGURE 1.45

3. Print Your Flyer

Now that you have created the poster, it's time to print it. If you have a color PostScript printer, it will appear similar to the preview. If you do not have a PostScript printer, the first image you inserted (Flatrock Café Presents) may appear jagged.

1. With rogers_flyer.indd open, access the Print dialog box (File>Print).
2. If you have more than one printer installed on your computer, select the printer that will be best for this document. Bear in mind that this is a color image, and that the size is "letter," so a larger-format printer is not necessary.
3. Click Print. You are presented with a warning.
4. Click OK and allow the document to print. If it does not print, your printer is not compatible with PostScript files.
5. Close the document without saving.

4. Create a Concert Ticket

The second part of the promo package is the concert ticket. You will create the ticket — a custom-size document — to complement the poster you made.

1. Create a new document with a Width of 4 in, Height of 2 in, Landscape orientation, and 0.125-in margins on all sides. Save the file as "rogers_ticket.indd" in your WIP_01 folder.
2. Click the View Percentage field in the lower left of the open window. Highlight the number that is there, and type "200". Press Return/Enter.

   The document window zooms to 200%.
3. Choose File>Place and place rogers_s.tif at the upper-left margin (X: 0.125, Y: 0.125).
4. Click the Type tool at the intersection of the upper margin and the 1.75-in point, horizontally. Drag a 1.5-in text box to the right margin (X: 1.75 in, Y: 0.125 in, W: 2.125 in, H: 1.5 in).
5. Use the Character Control palette to apply the following: Set "Louise Rogers" in 30-pt ATC Jacaranda; set "Live In Concert" in 14-pt ATC Pine Bold Italic; set "September 17, 2004 • 8:00 PM" in 10-pt ATC Oak Normal; set "ADMIT 1 – $10.00" in 10-pt ATC Oak Normal. Allow the Leading to default. Press the Return/Enter key after each line.
6. Center all type. From the Paragraph Control palette, add a 0.25-in Space Before the last two lines.
7. Choose the Rectangle Frame tool in the Tools palette. Drag a frame with the following parameters: X: 1.75 in, Y: 1.585 in, W: 2.125 in, H: 0.2014 in.
8. Place the small Flatrock Café logo (frc_s.eps) in this frame. Choose Object>Fitting>Center Content.
9. Use either the Frame tool or the Type tool to drag a frame from X: 1.75 in, Y: 1.8 in to the right margin and slightly below the bottom margin. Set the Font to 5.5-pt ATC Oak Normal. Type the following in the frame: "1201 Flatrock Bridge Road • Rye, NY 10580 • (914) 555-FOLK".
10. Click the Align Center button in the Paragraph Control palette.
11. Switch to the Selection tool. Click Preview Mode in the Tools palette (or press the "W" key) to preview your ticket. Save the document and close it.

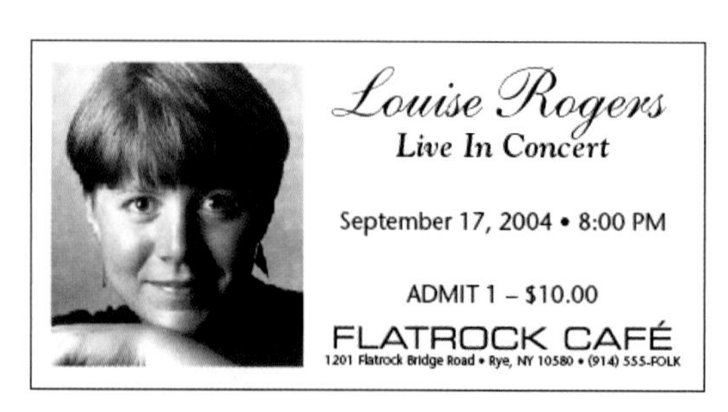

FIGURE 1.46

CHALLENGE

Challenge exercises expand on, or are somewhat related to, skills presented in the lessons. Each exercise provides a brief introduction, followed by instructions presented in a numbered-step format that are not as detailed as those in the Skill Drill exercises. You should do the exercises in the order presented.

1. Designing a Travel Ad

You work for a travel agency that specializes in resort escapes. A Florida escape — Bali Hai Beach Resort — is to be featured in the November issue of AAA's Northeast and Midwest regional magazines. The specifications for both magazines are the same, and the ad will be a full page (8.25 × 10.5 in), so you will not need to use a border. When you design your ad, be sure to leave enough room for your margins (at least one-half inch).

While this exercise calls for designing only one ad, it would be more practical to develop at least two designs. This is an opportunity to use your creative energies. Your first task is to create a hand-sketched thumbnail.

1. Sketch your page dimensions, 8.25 × 10.5 in.
2. Choose one of the two photos that your client provided. One is in a horizontal format (7.25 × 4.85 in) and the other in a vertical format (4.125 × 6 in). Draw a box with an "X" to indicate that it is a picture box.
3. Add the headline. The creative director specified it as, "Relax... without a care in the world." The headline was built into the vertical photo, but not the horizontal photo.
4. Add some lines to indicate the position of the text. There are eight or nine lines, depending on the size of the text box and the number of columns you choose to use.

   Based on the concept of centering the text under the photo, two columns of text look better with the horizontal photo, while one column of text looks better with the vertical photo.
5. Add the Bali Hai Beach Resort logo. It is a circle of approximately 1.5-in diameter.
6. Add the street and Web addresses on a single line:
   6900 Gulf Boulevard, Siesta Key, FL 34242 • 941-555-6900 • www.balihairesort.com.
7. Keep the file open for the next exercise.

2. Executing the Travel Ad

Your client approved your rough sketch, so it's time to build the ad. You created your own sketch, so your ad may look different from others' — and different from the samples shown below. The process of building the ads, however, should be very similar.

1. Create a new document with no facing pages to the dimensions you designed your ad (8.25 × 10.5 in). Make sure the rulers are visible.
2. Place the photograph you are going to use (carefree_h.tif or carefree_v.tif) and position it at X: 4.125 in, Y: 0.5 in, using the top-center reference point in the proxy.

3. If you are using the horizontal photo, create a text frame the width of the text area and about 1-in deep. Type the headline on two lines. Select a Font, Size, and Leading. We chose a Font of 36-pt ATC Laurel Bold, 38-pt Leading, and Tracking of –30. If you wish to add color to the headline, click the tab of the collapsed Swatches palette, then release it. With the text highlighted, click a color that you like.

   If you are using the vertical photo, skip to Step 4; the headline is built into the vertical photo.

4. Create a text frame, approximately 4.25 in × 1.75 in, centered below the photo. You can adjust the frame to fit the text after the text is flowed into it. To define two-column text, place the cursor in the frame and choose Object>Text Frame Options. You can adjust the number and width of columns, as well as the width of the gutter between them, in the Text Frame Options dialog box that appears.

5. Place the text in balihai.txt. It was pre-formatted.

6. Place the logo (balihai.ai) at the bottom center of the page.

   It is an Illustrator document in its native format.

7. Create a text box that flows across the bottom of the logo. Type the address text here and apply a Font, Size, and Style. We chose 12-pt ATC Oak Normal.

8. Switch to the Selection tool and preview your completed ad.

FIGURE 1.47

9. Save the document in your WIP_01 folder as "balihai.indd".

10. Print the document, and then close the file.

PORTFOLIO BUILDER

Create a Comprehensive Design

As you know, graphic design is a process. A designer doesn't simply sit down at her computer and immediately begin combining text and images. An experienced designer usually begins the process by creating a rough sketch of the document by hand. Then she creates a rough sketch of the document by hand. Then they will create a comprehensive design (comp) on the computer, rendering the design with reasonably accuracy. Only when the client has approved the comp does production begin in earnest.

You were hired by a magazine publisher who is going to launch a new quarterly publication, *RV Adventure.* The sales staff needs samples of the magazine well in advance of the actual launch. The editorial staff will provide initial content, and another team is working on the internal layout. It is your responsibility to design "knock 'em dead" covers to get this project launched.

The dimensions of the magazine are 8.25 × 10.5 inches. The name of the magazine, a tag line (to be determined), and listing of main articles will comprise the text for the cover.

Search stock image Web sites such as www.photospin.com for appropriate artwork or photographs. You may work with the low-resolution versions of any imagery you wish to use.

PROJECT 2

LEVEL 1

Building and Controlling Documents

OBJECTIVES

In this project, you learn how to

- Work with InDesign's preferences and default settings
- Open, close, and save documents
- Open, close, and save templates
- Explore the anatomy of an InDesign page
- Create new document spreads
- Build master pages
- Apply masters to document pages

WHY WOULD I DO THIS?

One of the keys to efficiently creating effective pages and multi-page documents is understanding how InDesign manages a document file and its many parts. This project helps you understand preferences and default settings, and guides you through the basics of document structure and management.

In Project 1, you created, opened, closed, and saved documents, and used standard and custom page sizes. The standard sizes used in the United States are Letter, Legal, Tabloid, Letter-Half, and Legal-Half. The international paper sizes A4, A3, A5, and B5, as well as Compact Disk, are also included as standard sizes. The skills you learn in this project provide you with additional control over pages and groups of pages. Although InDesign's multitude of controls can seem overwhelming at first, they are designed to help you produce documents faster and more efficiently than you could with a less powerful publishing vehicle.

When you define preferences, InDesign can accommodate your preferred workflow. You can save groups of preference settings as named presets. Preferences that are set when no document is open are ***universal preferences*** — they are applied to every document that you create with InDesign. If you set preferences when a specific document is open, however, those preferences (called ***document preferences***) apply to that document only.

You will discover that there are many parts to a page and a spread. A spread in InDesign can be either a single page or multiple pages that abut one another horizontally. Each element contributes to the overall look and feel of the document. Some elements of the page are meant to be viewed by the reader; others are used only as references during the final printing process.

Masters (also called ***master pages***) act as the building blocks for document pages. Masters speed production and improve precision by containing recurring page elements (such as page numbers and borders). Elements that occur on a master automatically appear on every page to which that master is applied. Masters are also flexible; while working on an individual document page, you can quickly and easily modify any item that appears on a master.

In this project, you learn to adjust many of InDesign's preferences, and to define the default settings that you use throughout the exercises in this book. You experiment with other preferences and see how they affect a document. Some preferences, such as those that relate to text, are discussed in greater depth in later projects. When you combine what you learn in this project with what you learned in Project 1, you will have the necessary foundation to begin building documents of your own.

VISUAL SUMMARY

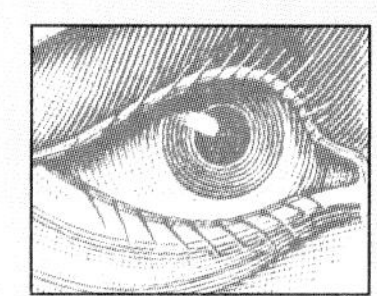

The Preferences menu, located under either the InDesign menu (Macintosh) or the Edit menu (Windows), contains 12 different panes for fine-tuning the way InDesign works for you. As you scan the preferences in Figure 2.2 below, it may strike you that a large proportion is closely related to text and text handling. Although a picture may be worth a thousand words, when it comes to printed documents, text is still of paramount importance.

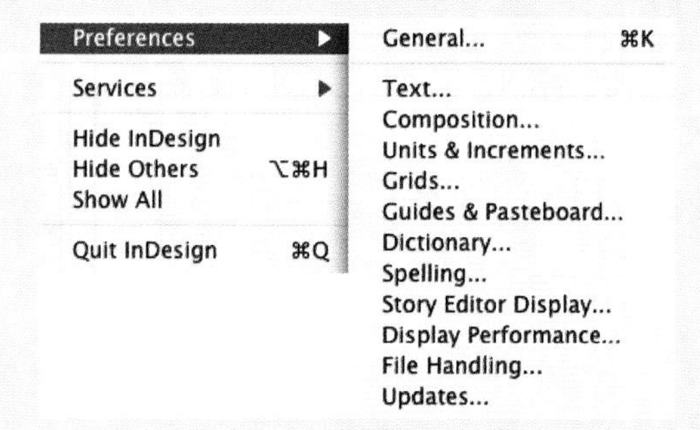

FIGURE 2.1

When most people think of a "page," they visualize a blank sheet of paper. A ***page***, as defined by InDesign, includes areas that extend beyond the physical boundaries of the sheet of paper. An InDesign page contains many invaluable aids for the design and production processes, even though they are invisible on the final printed document. Some of these aids, such as margins and columns, are probably familiar to you; others may be new.

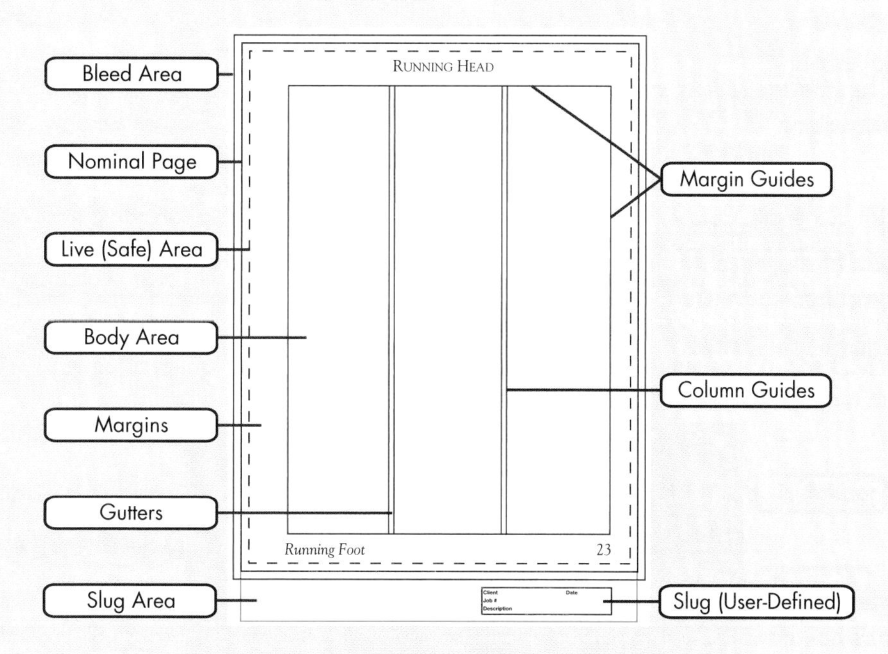

FIGURE 2.2

In Project 1, you navigated through a document using the page icons in the lower half of the Pages palette. The top half of the Pages palette displays all of the master pages created for a particular document. Elements placed on masters repeat — but may be altered — on all document pages to which the master is applied.

A document can have more than one master. For example, you could create one master that defines the elements of a chapter-opening page, another that defines standard document pages, and a third that defines a section-opening page. Each page icon in the lower half of the Pages palette reflects the letter of the master that was applied to that page.

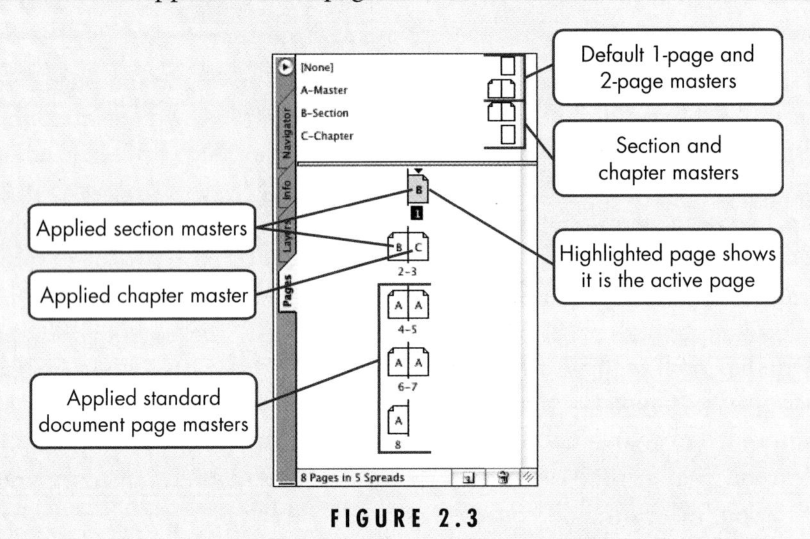

FIGURE 2.3

LESSON 1 Working with Preferences and Defaults

As you know, the Preferences panes are accessed from the InDesign menu (Macintosh) or the Edit menu (Windows). While you may wish to reset some preferences on a document-by-document basis, you will most likely retain most preferences without resetting them. Preferences, for the most part, reflect the way you want to work, and how you prefer to view documents, or they may reflect the way your company prefers you to work, to encourage consistency among documents.

General Preferences

The General Preferences pane contains options that don't fit neatly into the other preferences panes, or those that might readily be overlooked. Once the General Preferences are set, you rarely alter them, since they are the most basic preferences in your InDesign workflow.

The Page Numbering options allow you to choose how the pages in your document are numbered. When Section Numbering is used, the actual page numbers are displayed beneath the icons in the Pages palette. For example, if the first page of a 12-page document is defined as Page 11, the icons are numbered 11–22. When Absolute Numbering is selected, the icons are numbered beginning with 1. Icons for a 12-page document are numbered 1–12.

In the General section, you can choose how tool tips and the Tools palette display. ***Tool tips*** are the hints and labels that display when the cursor hovers over a tool icon. There is virtually no difference between Fast and Normal (which refer to the time it takes for the tip to appear). You can turn off tool tips by selecting None. After you become well acquainted with InDesign, None will likely be your preference. While you learn to use the application, however, the tool tips will be useful. The next menu affects only the appearance of the Tools palette. It can remain at its default appearance (double column), or set to appear as either a single column (vertical) or a single row (horizontal).

Rarely will you need to change the Overprint (Black) Swatch at 100% setting found in the Print Options section. Type and objects that are 100% black print correctly on top of any color.

In the Font Downloading and Embedding section, the option to subset fonts with large glyph counts is the most practical choice. A ***glyph***, for all intents and purposes, is a single character. A ***font subset*** includes only the specific characters used within the document, which is downloaded to the printer upon final output. This is a practical way to save significant amounts of time during the printing process.

The Clipboard options apply when files are copied into InDesign instead of placed through the File menu. You achieve the best results when you place files, which is the method used throughout this book.

Some InDesign functions may display a warning dialog with a "Don't ask again" option. Clicking the Reset All Warnings button resets the "Don't ask again" status to Off.

Text Preferences

While most text preferences are addressed in Project 3, those that affect the entire document and your workflow are addressed here. With the exception of the Character settings, most Text preferences are left at their defaults to ensure a consistent interface.

Character settings depend on the characteristics of individual fonts, so they should be addressed on a document-by-document basis, instead of being defined universally.

The Type Options settings should all be turned on. Take a moment to review the Type Options, as follows:

- ***Use Typographer's Quotes*** automatically converts prime (') and double prime (") marks into an apostrophe (’) and open (“) or close (”) quotes.
- ***Automatically Use Correct Optical Size*** affects only Multiple Master fonts. Choosing this option enhances the readability of Multiple Master fonts in small sizes.
- If the ***Triple-Click to Select a Line*** option is turned off, three clicks selects an entire paragraph. If you activate this option, three clicks selects only a single line of text, four clicks selects an entire paragraph, and five clicks selects all text in the frame.
- ***Adjust Text Attributes when Scaling*** applies only to the display in the Character Control palette and the Character palette. The actual attributes are always adjusted when scaling.

- ***Apply Leading to Entire Paragraphs*** allows you to place your cursor in the paragraph and apply ***leading*** (the space between lines; "leading" rhymes with "wedding") simultaneously to all lines in the paragraph. If this option is not selected, you must manually highlight every line that should receive the leading attribute.
- If you were creating dynamic documents that will be updated on a regular basis, you would check the ***Create Links When Placing Text and Spreadsheet Files*** option. This is a good idea for spreadsheets, which take up a specified amount of space; it is not a good choice for text, however, which could reflow incorrectly, resulting in additional work to fix the problem.
- The ***Input Method*** options are used primarily with Asian text.

Units & Increments Preferences

These preferences affect how the horizontal ruler is displayed, as well as the horizontal and vertical units of measurement (which can be different). It also affects the increments that are used when you modify elements with keyboard shortcuts.

The Origin of the rule may be defined as Spread, Page, or Spine. When defined as Spread, the width of the entire spread is used and the origin is in the upper-left corner of the spread. When defined as Page, each page has its own origin (zero point) in the upper-left corner. When defined as Spine, the measurement begins in the upper-left corner; but if there are multiple pages that originate from the binding spine, which is the case in a fold-out, the measurement continues across the width of the pages on that side of the binding spine.

In the Keyboard Increments section, you can define the amount of increase or decrease made with various keyboard shortcuts. By default, selecting an object and pressing the cursor key moves the element 0.0139 inch (one point). Keyboard shortcuts for modifying size, leading, and baseline shift default to 2 points, and the kerning and tracking values are measured in 20/1000 em (an ***em*** is a variable value, based on point size; an em in 10-point type is 10 points wide).

Grids

Grids allow you to visually or automatically align type and elements within a document. The grid makes it easy to align objects by "magnetically" attracting (snap-to) and locking items to the gridline.

Notice that the default Baseline Grid settings and Document Grid settings have different increments (subdivisions). The Baseline Grid is set to increment every 1/6 inch, and the Document Grid is set to increment every 1/8 inch. The Baseline Grid is intended to assist in placing type, which is based on the points and picas measurement system; the increment of the Baseline Grid normally depends on the leading defined for the document, so it's not practical to define universally.

File Handling

InDesign's File Handling preferences give you control over the manner in which the file itself, rather than its components, is saved and managed. This is particularly important in the event of a system or program crash, and when you are working on a large project in collaboration with others.

The Document Recover Data options allow you to choose where InDesign will place recovered files in the event of a system crash.

The Save Document Preview Image option shows a small view (thumbnail) of the first page of the document when you click the file to open it; this option is a rarely used.

Version Cue, available with the entire Adobe Creative Suite, keeps track of the most recent versions of the document you are working on, maintains file security, and assists in organizing your projects, whether you are working alone or in collaboration with others.

Display Performance

These preferences control how images and other page components are displayed on your screen. When working with large images, you generally need to choose between high-quality image representation and performance. High-quality-image displays require more processing power from your computer.

There are three options in the Default View menu: Optimized performance substitutes a gray box for any images in your file; Typical performance shows standard screen images; High-Quality performance shows the best quality (but slowest-painting) images.

The quality levels can be adjusted with the Adjust View Settings sliders, but the default values are usually fine.

In the exercises in this lesson, you learn to set universal preferences, which are applied to every document you create with the InDesign application. In addition, you experiment with defining document preferences, which are associated with only one specific file. You also learn to override universal preferences from within an individual document.

Define Some Universal Preferences

1. **Launch InDesign, if it is not already open. Do not create a new document. If a document is open, close it without saving.**

2. **Choose InDesign>Preferences (Macintosh) or Edit>Preferences (Windows) to open the Preferences dialog box.**

   The keyboard shortcut to access the Preferences dialog box is Command/Control-K. As you saw in the introduction to this lesson, you can control the way InDesign handles many functions by editing the settings in the 12 panes of the Preferences dialog box.

3 **Click the General category in the function pane of the Preferences dialog box.**

The General Preferences dialog box opens.

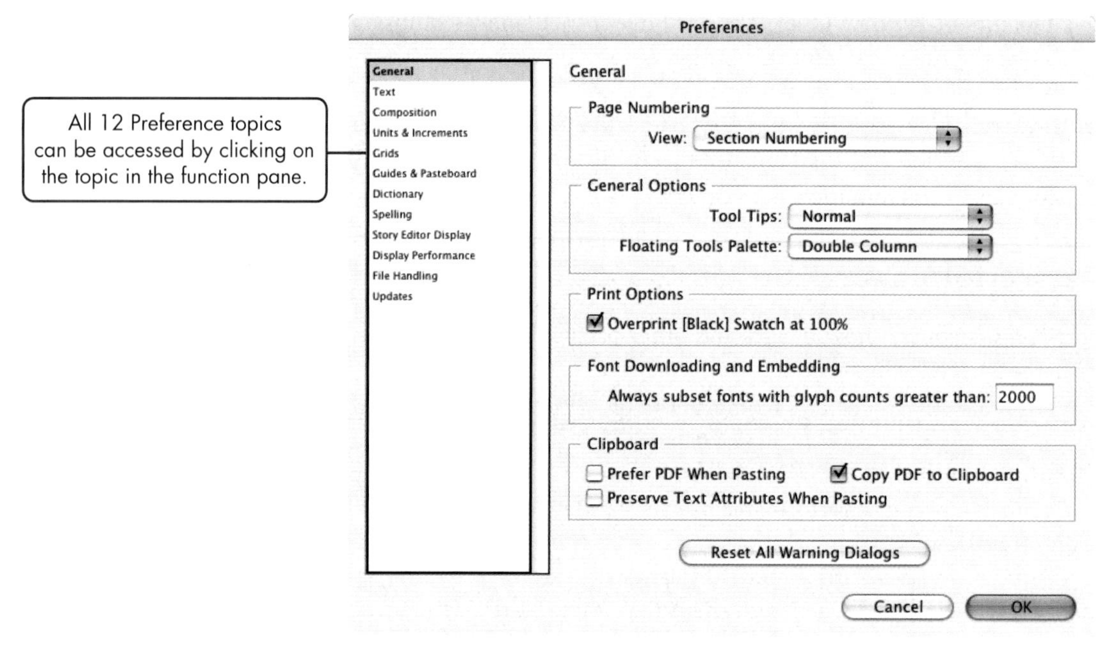

FIGURE 2.4

4 **Leave all of the General preferences at their default settings.**

5 **Click Text in the function pane of the Preferences dialog box.**

The Text Preferences dialog box opens.

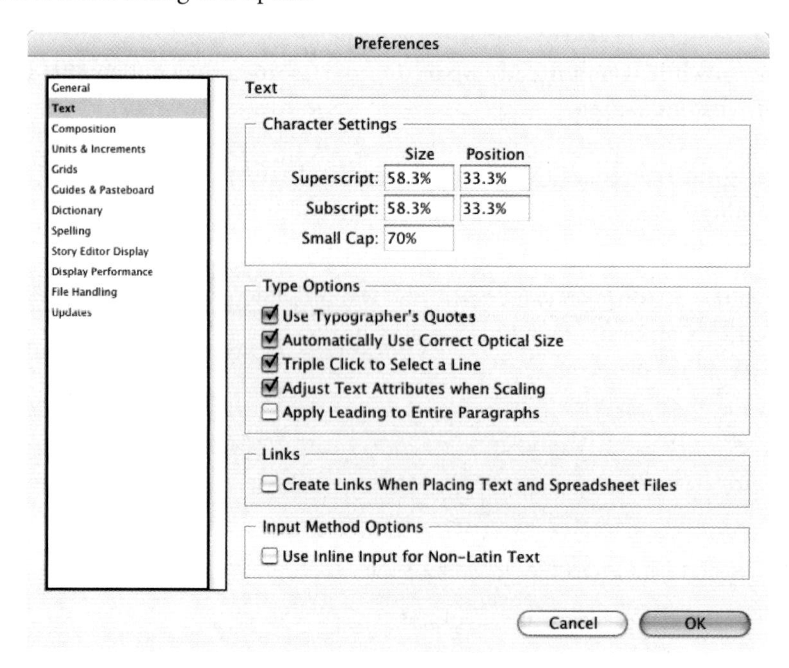

FIGURE 2.5

6 **Click Apply Leading to Entire Paragraphs. Leave the rest of the Text preferences as they are.**

The feature is activated, allowing you to simply click the cursor in the paragraph and type in or select the appropriate line spacing.

7 **Click Units & Increments in the function pane of the Preferences dialog box.**

The Units & Increments dialog box opens.

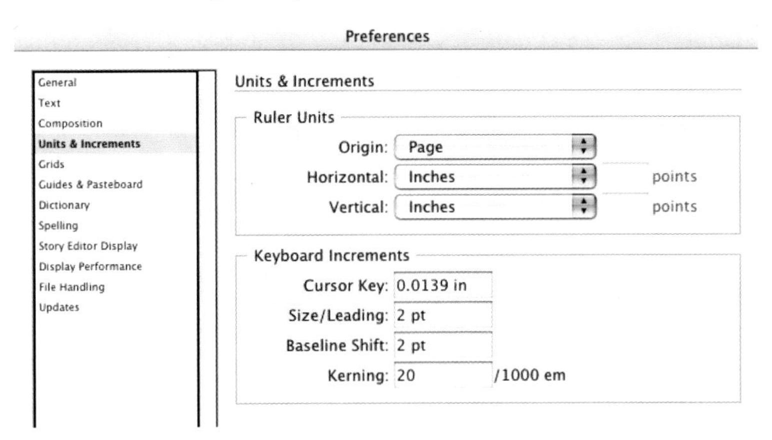

FIGURE 2.6

8 **Change the Origin to Page and the Horizontal and Vertical values to Inches. Leave the Keyboard Increments at their default settings.**

9 **Click Grids in the function pane of the Preferences dialog box.**

The Grids Preferences dialog box opens.

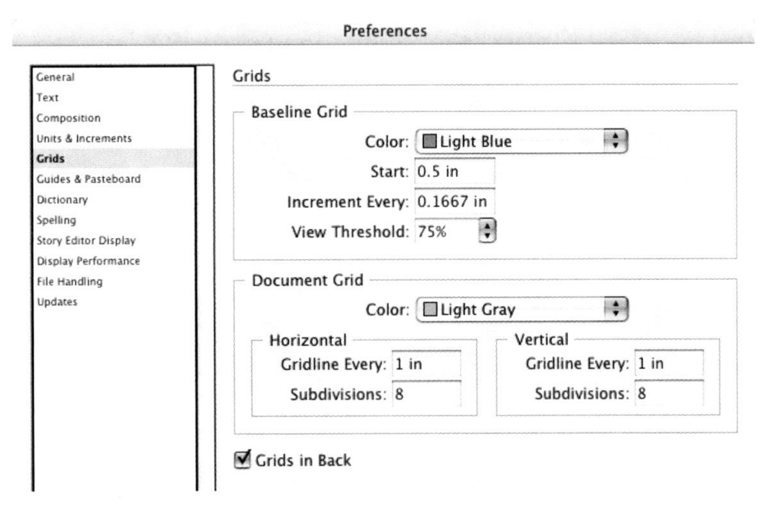

FIGURE 2.7

10 **Leave all of the Grids preferences at their default settings.**

11 **Click File Handling in the function pane of the Preferences dialog box.**

The File Handling dialog box appears.

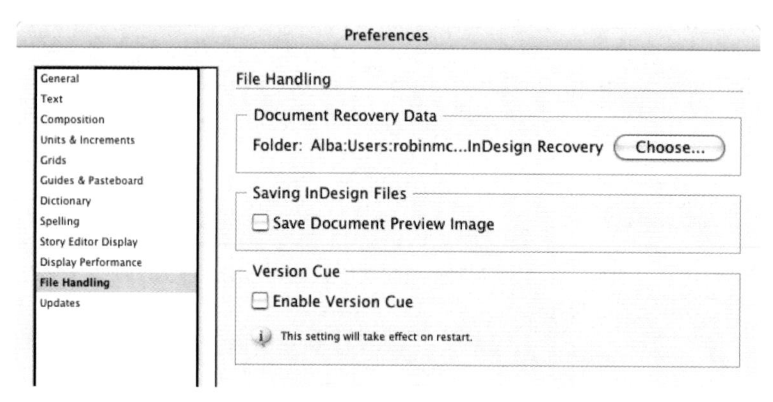

FIGURE 2.8

12 **Leave all of the File Handling preferences at their default settings.**

13 **Click Display Performance in the function pane of the Preferences dialog box.**

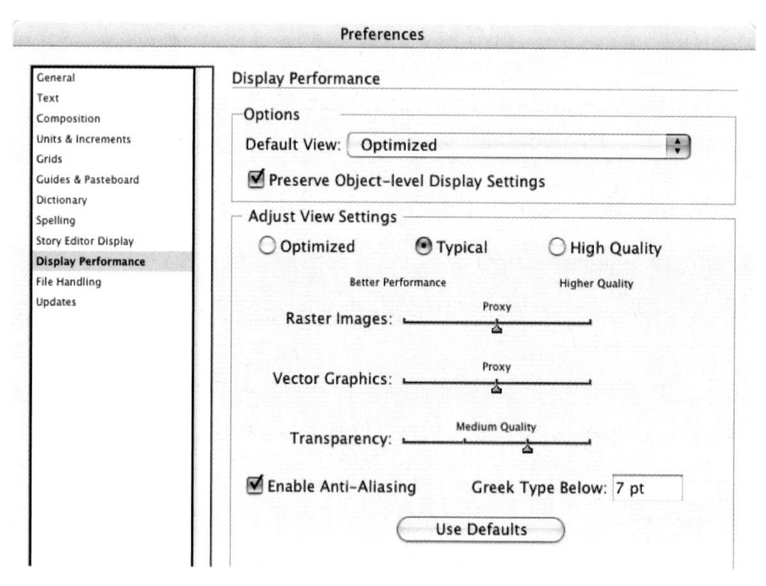

FIGURE 2.9

14 **Choose Optimized from the Default View menu. Check the Preserve Object-level Display Settings box.**

Selecting the Optimized view means that all the images in your document appear as grey boxes by default. You can override this setting to make certain images visible (View>Display Performance or Object>Display Performance), but the Preserve Object-level Display Settings option must be activated for these overrides to be retained; otherwise, all images default to the Optimized preference.

15 **Click OK to save your changes as universal preferences and close the Preferences dialog box.**

Define Some Document-Specific Preferences

Even though you can define any preferences as either universal or document preferences, you can only see their effects when they are applied to a specific document. In this exercise, you set some document-specific preferences and learn how to override universal preference settings.

1 **Open salad.indd from your Project_02 folder.**

This file is one of the chapters from the Wayside Inn cookbook. The image on the first page is grayed-out, transparency is turned off, and the type is lower quality.

2 **Click the lower-right corner of the image to select it. Choose Object>Display Performance>Typical Display.**

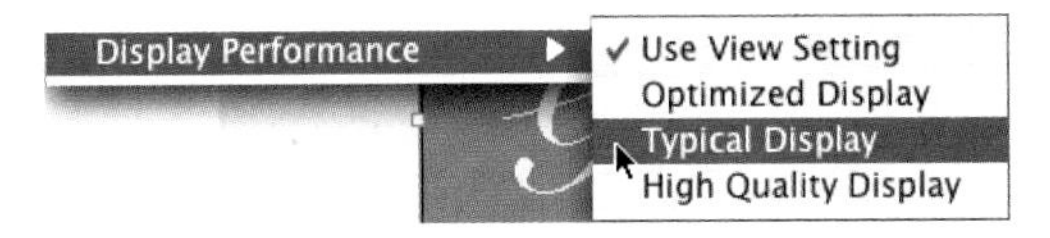

FIGURE 2.10

You clicked the Preserve Object-level Display Settings button in the Display Performance dialog box, so this particular image becomes visible. The other elements on the page remain rough.

3 **Choose View>Display Performance>Typical Display. Be sure the Allow Object-Level Display Settings option is checked.**

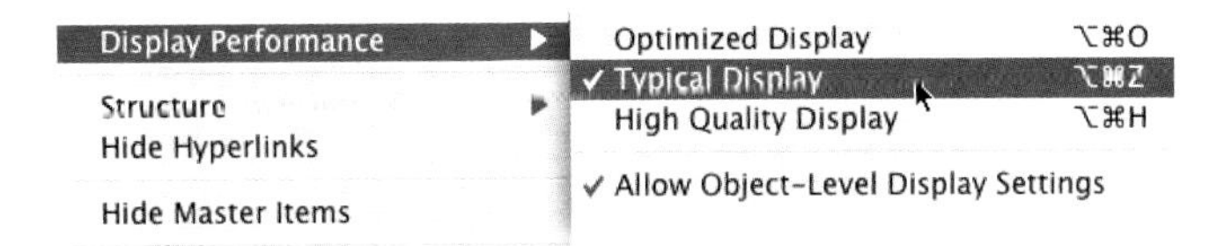

FIGURE 2.11

Using the menu to set the display performance from within a document overrides the universally defined preference. The other features in the document, including type and drop shadows, now appear at a higher quality. If you wish, you can return to Object>Display Performance and click High Quality Display to see how the higher-quality display looks.

4 **Make sure the Pages palette is open; if not, click the Pages tab to open it.**

5 **Choose InDesign>Preferences (Macintosh) or Edit>Preferences (Windows) to open the Preferences dialog box. From the General Preferences pane, click Absolute Numbering. Click OK.**

The Pages palette switches from displaying the document's actual page numbers to displaying their absolute positions in the document. The checkerboard pattern on Page 33 indicates that there is transparency on the page.

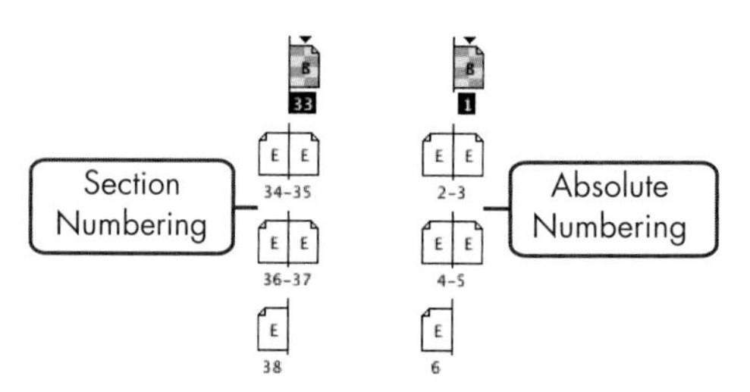

FIGURE 2.12

6 **Double-click the numbers of Pages 2 and 3 to center the spread on the screen.**

The page ruler extends from 0 to 12 inches, crossing the entire spread.

7 **Return to the General Preferences dialog box. Reset the Page Numbering View to Section Numbering.**

8 **In the Units & Increments pane of the Preferences dialog box, set the Ruler Units Origin to the Page option. Click OK.**

Each page is now measured from 0 (at the left of the page) to 6 inches (at the right of the page).

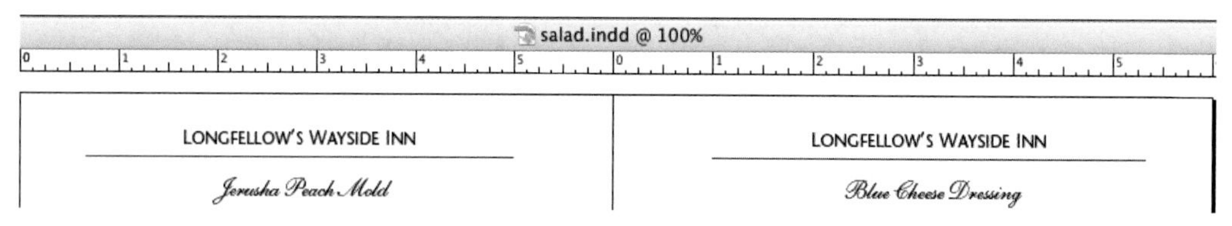

FIGURE 2.13

9 **Close the document without saving.**

10 **With no document open, return to the Display Performances Preferences dialog box and set the Default View to Typical, with the Preserve Object-level Display Settings box checked. Click OK.**

To Extend Your Knowledge...

A NOTE ABOUT INDESIGN'S SPREADS

In common graphic arts terminology, a spread is two or more pages that face or abut each other in a publication. InDesign considers all pages, even stand-alone pages, to be part of a spread. You should be aware of this potentially confusing terminology.

LESSON 2 Opening, Closing, and Saving Documents and Templates

In Project 1, you learned the basics of opening, closing, and saving documents. In this project, you explore some options that allow you to produce and manage documents more effectively.

Opening a File

In the Open a File dialog box, you can choose to show All Readable Documents or All Documents. Windows users can also choose to show only files in InDesign, InDesign Interchange, PageMaker (6.5–7.0), or QuarkXPress (3.3–4.1x) format. All of these formats are included in the Macintosh All Readable Documents file list.

Three selections are available in the lower left of the Open a File dialog box. You can specify whether a file should be opened as Normal, Original, or Copy. The Open Normal option opens document files and opens a copy of template files; this is the most commonly used option. The Open Original option allows you to open the original file, even if it's a template (which is useful if you want to change the template). The Open Copy option allows you to open a copy of a document file instead of the original file, which could be useful if you plan to keep multiple versions of a document.

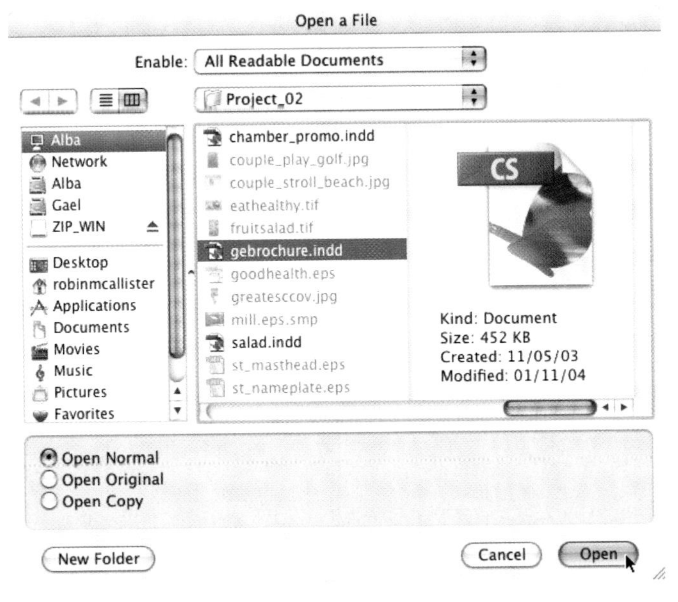

FIGURE 2.14

Open, Close, and Save Documents and Templates

1 **Choose File>Open. Choose gebrochure.indd from the list in your RF_InDesign_L1>Project_02 folder. Click Open.**

The brochure opens. You can also press Command/Control-O to open a file. This keyboard shortcut assumes the Open Normal option.

2 **Choose File>Save As. Choose InDesign CS template in the Format (Macintosh) or Save as type (Windows) menu.**

The name of the document changes to gebrochure.indt. A ***template*** is a document format; templates are used as the basis for creating subsequent documents.

FIGURE 2.15

3 **Close the file.**

4 **Open the template you saved in Step 2.**

An Untitled document opens. To prevent you from accidentally overwriting the template file, you cannot simply save the document (even though the Save option is available in the menu). You must assign a name to the file. Even if you accidentally assign the same name as the template, the file will have a different extension — ".indd" (document) instead of ".indt" (template).

5 **Close the document without saving.**

6 **Choose File>Open Recent.**

A list of recently opened documents appears. This feature can be particularly helpful when you want quick access to a file that you recently worked on, and you don't have time to search through a long list of readable documents to find it.

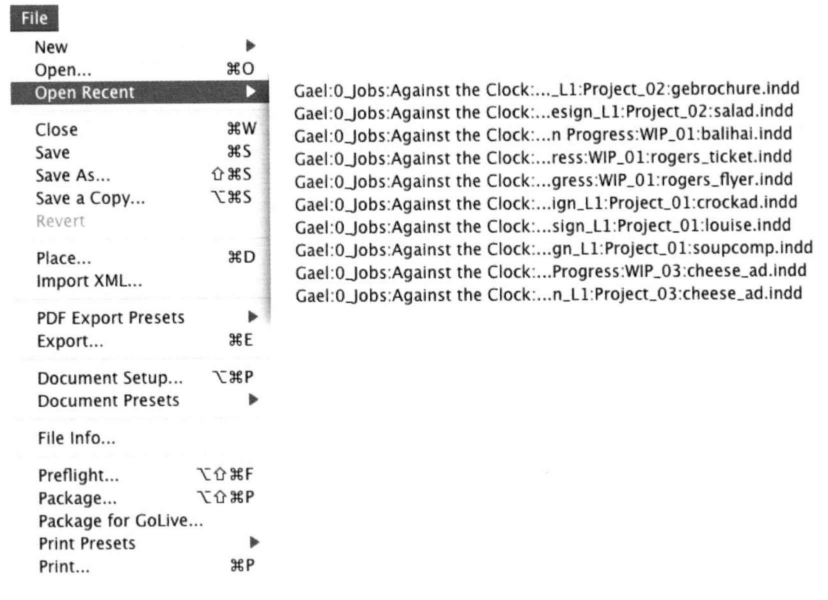

FIGURE 2.16

7 **Highlight one of the document (.indd) files in the list.**

8 **Choose Save a Copy, and save the copy in your WIP_02 folder.**

By default, InDesign keeps the original file name and adds the word "copy" prior to the file extension. You can edit the file name, if you prefer (for manual version control and management).

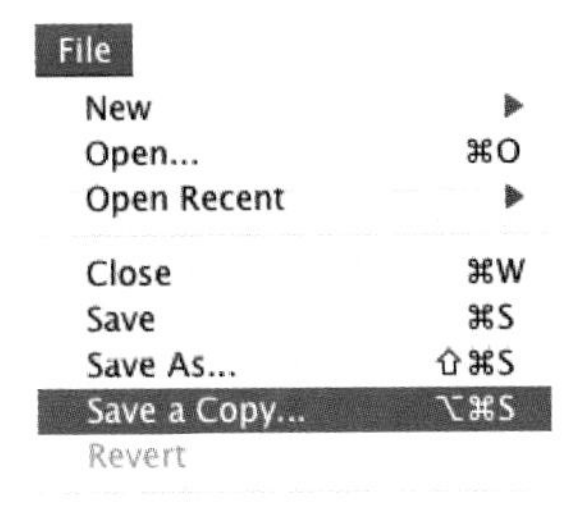

FIGURE 2.17

9 **Choose File>Open. In the Open a File dialog box, click the Open Original button. Re-open the gebrochure.indt template you saved in Step 2.**

The actual template file, instead of an Untitled document, opens. This option is useful if you need to make changes to a template.

10 **Close the file without saving.**

To Extend Your Knowledge...

USE TEMPLATES AND SAVE OPTIONS TO MANAGE DOCUMENTS

When you save a document as a template, you can use the template as the basis for other documents. You will have already positioned your running heads and feet, all the paragraph and character styles (discussed in Project 6), and the page layout/s that will be included in the document. This not only saves time, it also ensures consistency from document to document.

If you get into the habit of saving a document as a copy or using the Save As option, you will automatically have control over each version of the document. As hard as it is to believe, sometimes clients will order changes, and then ask you to "put it back the way it was." If you retain multiple versions of the project, you can comply with this sort of request quickly and easily.

LESSON 3 Exploring Page Anatomy

As you discovered in the Visual Summary, a page is more than simply a blank sheet of paper upon which you position words and images. A typical page includes a number of standard elements that enhance the readability of documents and guide readers from one element to another.

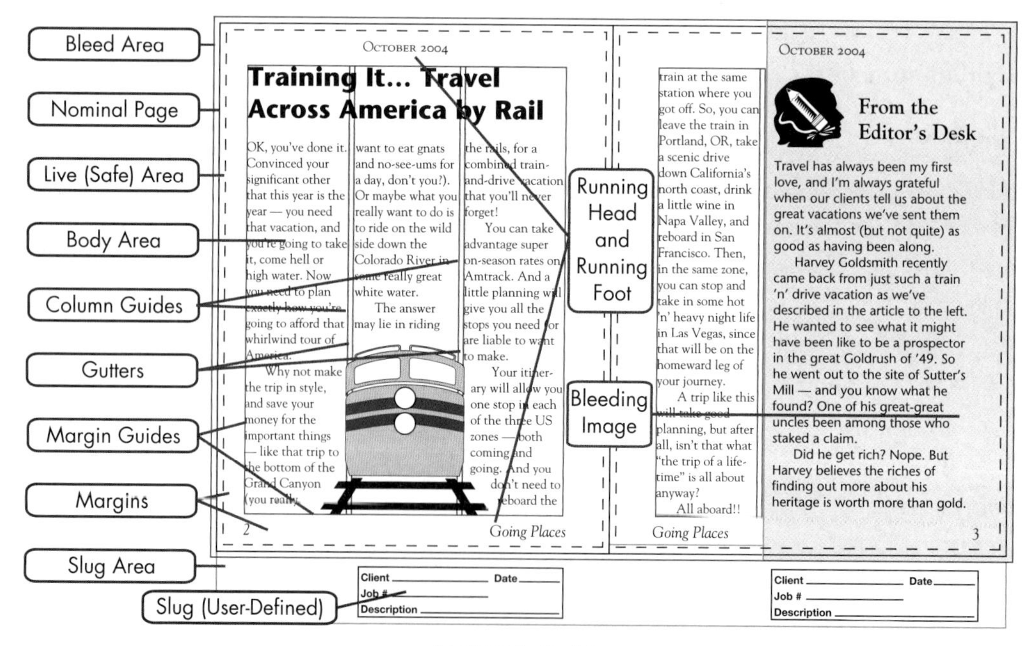

FIGURE 2.18

Explore a Document

In this exercise, you open a document and identify the elements of a two-page spread.

1 **Open chamber_promo.indd from the Project_02 folder.**

The file opens to the Page 2–3 spread.

2 **If it is not already visible, open the Pages palette (click the Pages tab if it is compressed in the palette bay, or choose Window>Pages).**

The Pages palette shows that this document is divided into three sections. If the file didn't open to the Page 2–3 spread, you can double-click the numbers "2, 3" below the page icons in the Pages palette to open the correct spread.

The pages beginning each section have an arrow above them. The two sections for the covers of the booklet (using the C-Master) are numbered 1–2 (front cover) and 3–4 (back cover). The pages in the section of the main booklet content (using the A-Master) are numbered 1–8.

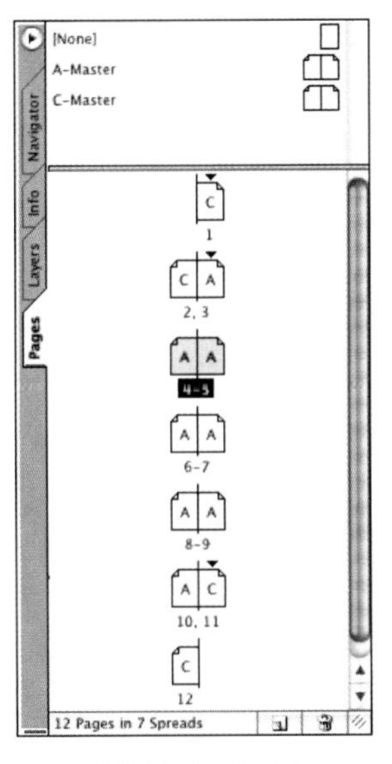

FIGURE 2.19

3 **If guides and frames are not already visible, choose View>Show Guides and View> Show Frame Edges.**

Viewing the frames helps you identify page geometry. Viewing guides allows you to see the bleed and slug areas. You can press Command/Control-H to show or hide frame edges and Command/ Control-; (semi-colon) to show or hide guides.

4 **Identify the following elements on Pages 2–3: Bleed area, Body area, Columns, Gutters, Live area, Margins, Running feet (also called footers), and Slug area.**

Running feet and running heads automatically appear on every page to which the master is applied.

5 **Save the file using the same file name. Close the document.**

To Extend Your Knowledge...

PHYSICAL CHARACTERISTICS ARE IMPORTANT

When designing documents, keep in mind the characteristics of the physical product. You should consider the thickness of a document, how it will be bound, and any special sizing requirements. For example, if you want your document to be filed for convenient reference, it should fit into a file drawer without being folded.

LESSON 4 Creating New Documents

In Project 1, you created basic new documents without paying much attention to the details of the process. In this lesson, you use the New Document dialog box to set the page options for a four-page document. You create multiple columns and specify the space between columns. You also pay attention to the page margins, as well as the bleed area around the page that allows you to print off the edge of the page.

Create a New Spread

1 **Choose File>New>Document to create a new document.**

The New Document option is automatically assumed if you use the keyboard shortcut Command/Control-N instead of the menu selection. You will learn about creating books and libraries, the other two options in the File>New menu, in *Essentials for Design: InDesign Level 2*.

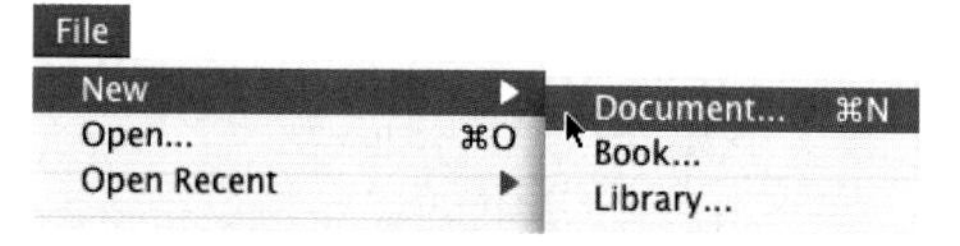

FIGURE 2.20

2 **If the More Options button is visible, click it to reveal the Bleed and Slug fields at the bottom of the New Document dialog box.**

For many documents, bleeds and slugs are unimportant. For that reason, these specifications are usually in a hidden menu. In this exercise, however, you are going to create a document with all of its "anatomical parts," including bleeds and slugs.

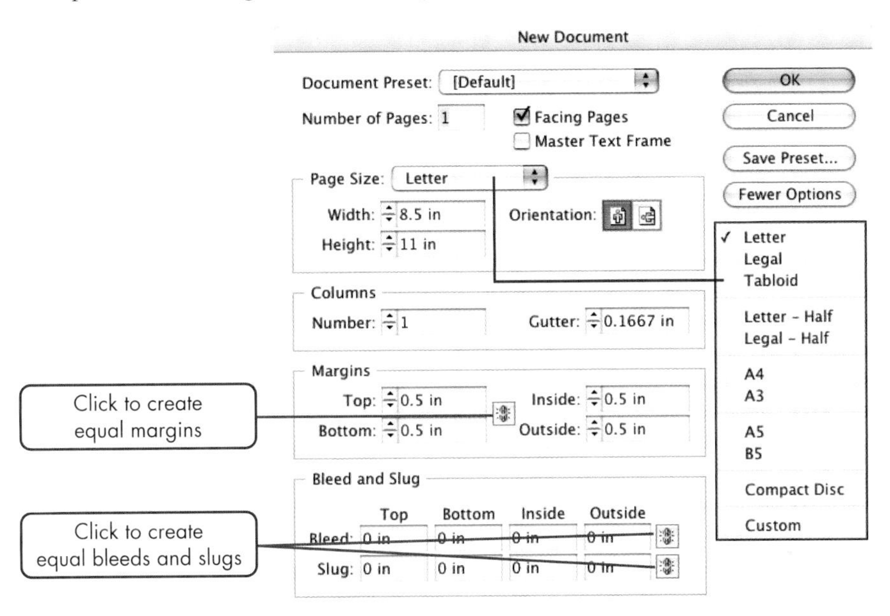

FIGURE 2.21

3 **Change the Number of Pages to "4". Leave the Facing Pages box checked. Click the Master Text Frame box.**

These are the settings for creating the basic format of a four-page newsletter.

4 **Change the Columns Number to "3" and leave the Gutter set to 0.1667 in (the default).**

Three columns result in lines of text that are easy to read, and allow you to add variety to the document. The default gutter width is 1/6 inch, which is the width of a ***pica*** in printing terms.

5 **Change the Top and Bottom Margins to "0.75 in". Leave the Inside and Outside Margins at the default 0.5 in.**

Top and bottom margins allow room for running heads and feet (headers and footers) on each page. Headers and footers require margins slightly larger than the half-inch side (inside and outside) margins.

6 **Click the Top Bleed field and enter "0.125 in". Click the Linking button to create equal-sized bleeds. Set the Bottom Slug field to "2 in".**

A bleed of 0.125 inch is adequate for most projects; however, you should check with your printer to see what bleed he prefers. The large bottom slug allows room for client information.

7 Click OK. As a last check, choose Preferences>Units & Increments and ensure that the Ruler Units Origin menu is set to Page.

8 Save the document as "newsletter_shell.indd" in your WIP_02 folder. Leave the document open for the next exercise.

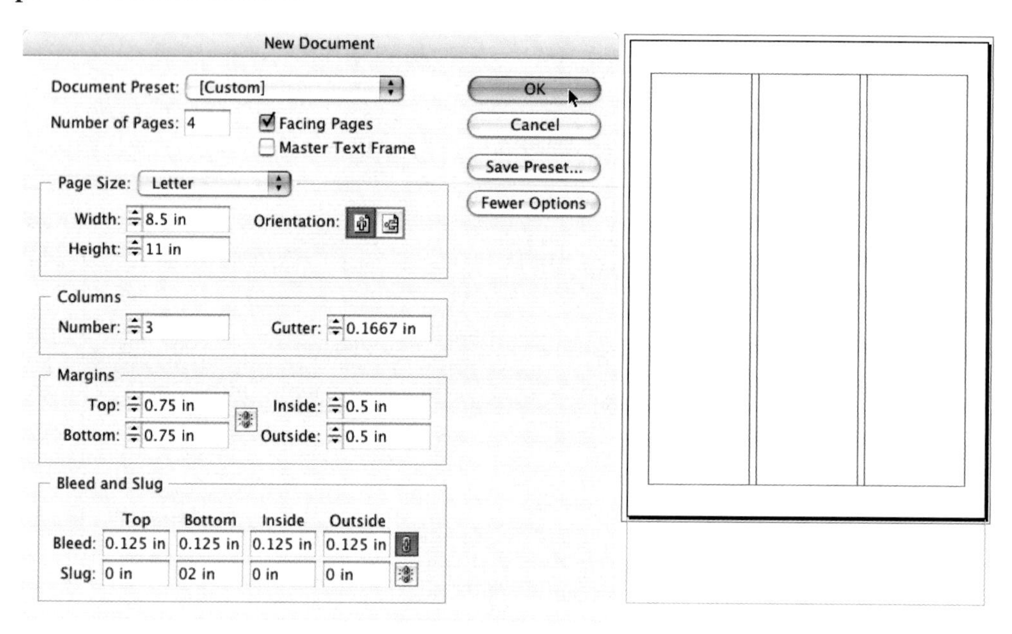

FIGURE 2.22

To Extend Your Knowledge...

BLEEDS AND SLUGS

Printers use sheets of paper that are larger than the finished documents. After the ink is printed, the large sheets are then cut to the finished size. To prevent a thin white border from appearing at the edge of the trimmed page, images need to bleed (extend) beyond the dimensions of the finished page so a little excess can be trimmed off.

A slug allows you to add information to the oversized press sheet, such as customer name, job number, and other information about the project. This can be stored with the job for future reference.

LESSON 5 Building Masters

Many elements (such as page numbers) repeat on every page of a lengthy document. If you had to manually re-create these repeating elements, producing even a moderate-size book would be a very tedious undertaking. InDesign, similar to all professional page-layout programs, allows you to build masters to hold repeating elements.

A master is a special page that contains visible and invisible information (including text, guides, images, and even special characters such as incrementing page numbers) that can be applied to multiple document pages. The upper section of the Pages palette displays the available masters that apply to the open document. Longer documents are usually based on masters, while shorter documents, such as advertisements, are frequently built "on the fly."

Create a Master Spread

1 **In the open newsletter_shell.indd, double-click the words "A-Master" in the Pages palette.**

The A-Master spread is centered in your document window. All of the changes you make in this exercise will be applied to this master page, not to the individual pages of the document itself.

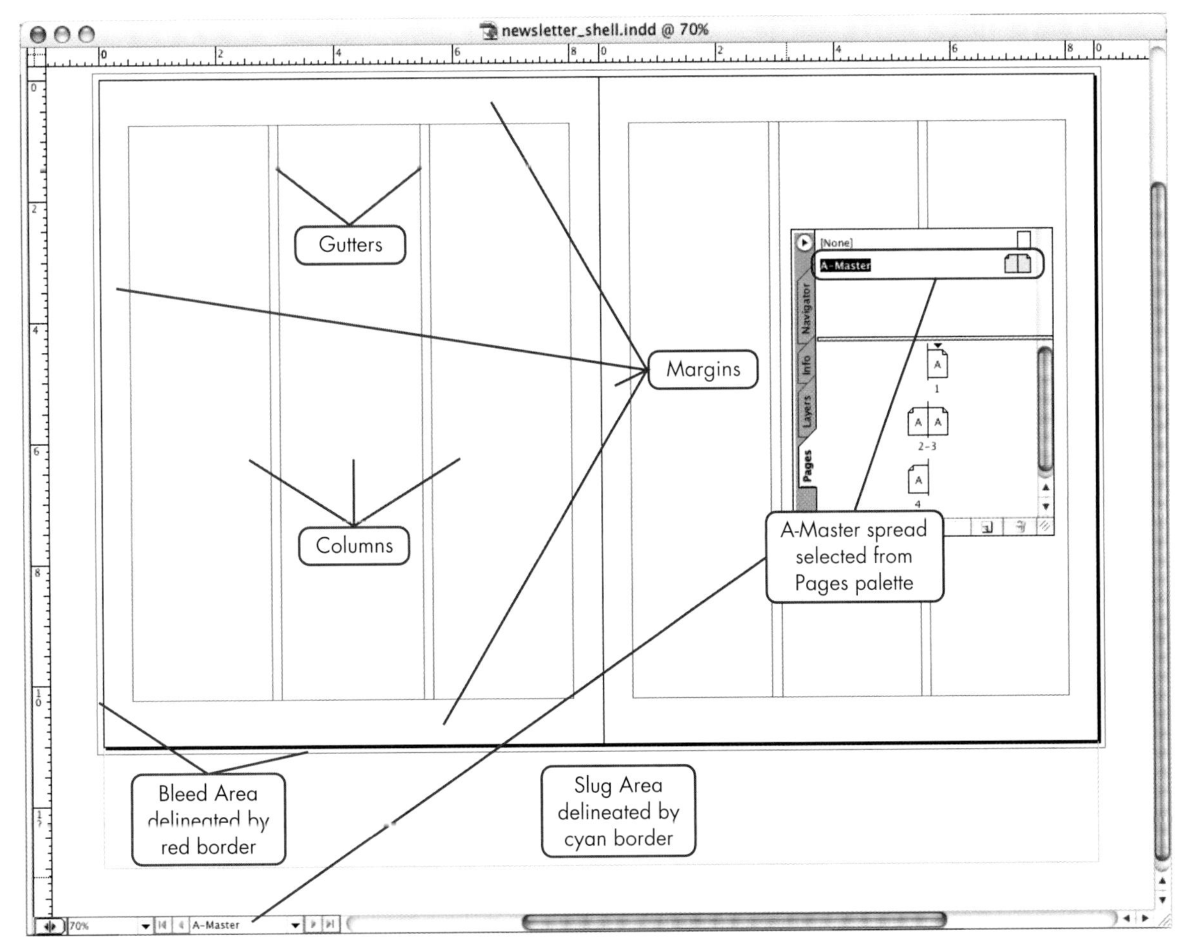

FIGURE 2.23

2 **Choose the Type tool in the Tools palette. Drag the tool cursor to create a text frame below the three-column box on the left master.**

The resulting text frame appears outlined in blue. It doesn't matter where you start the text frame, nor what size you make it, because you will use the Control palette to precisely size and position it.

3 **If the text frame does not appear, choose View>Show Frame Edges.**

4 **Choose the Selection tool in the Tools palette. Click the upper-left proxy-reference point in the Control palette. Enter the following dimensions for the text frame you just created:**

X: 0.5 in **W: 7.5 in**
Y: 10.375 in **H: 0.25 in**

The page proxy allows you to select one of nine distinct reference points for an object. You can use the proxy-reference point to accurately position the object on the page and specify its dimensions.

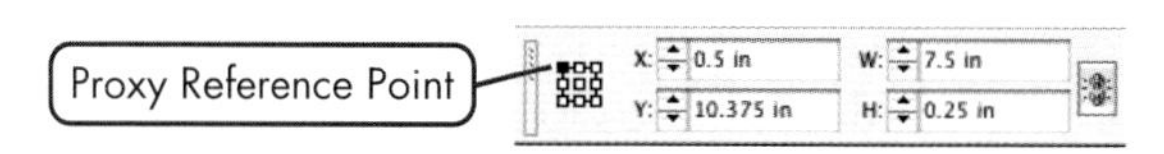

FIGURE 2.24

5 **Press Return/Enter to apply these settings and close the Control palette.**

The text frame is not resized and repositioned until you press Return/Enter.

6 **Create another text frame on the right master with the same position and dimensions:**

X: 0.5 in **W: 7.5 in**
Y: 10.375 in **H: 0.25 in**

7 **Choose the Type tool in the Tools palette. Click the frame you created on the left master. Type the word "Page", and then press the Spacebar.**

8 **Choose Type>Insert Special Character>Auto Page Number.**

An "A" appears in the text frame after the word "Page." The "A" is a marker for InDesign's automatic page-numbering system. You could also insert the page number by pressing Command-Option-Shift-N (Macintosh) or Control-Alt-Shift-N (Windows). Another way to access the Special Character menu is to Control-click (Macintosh) or right-click (Windows).

9 **In the Control palette, click the Paragraph icon. Click the Align Center icon.**

The text you just entered is centered in the text frame.

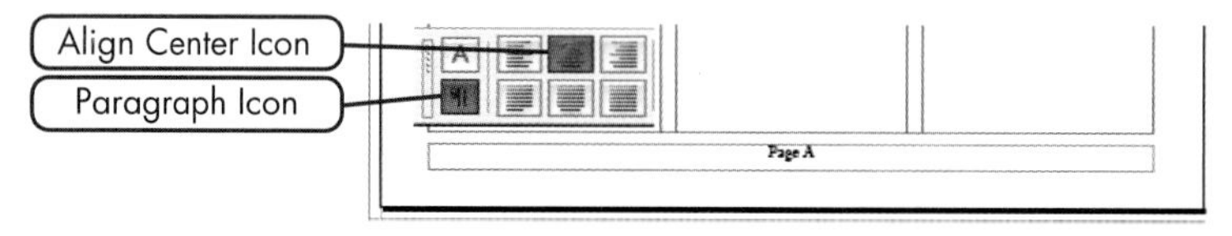

FIGURE 2.25

10 **Repeat Steps 7–9 on the right master.**

11 **In a similar fashion, create headers for both the left and right masters, positioned as follows:**

X: 0.5 in	**W: 7.5 in**
Y: 0.5 in	**H: 0.25 in**

12 **Center the words "Sundae Times" in the header text frames.**

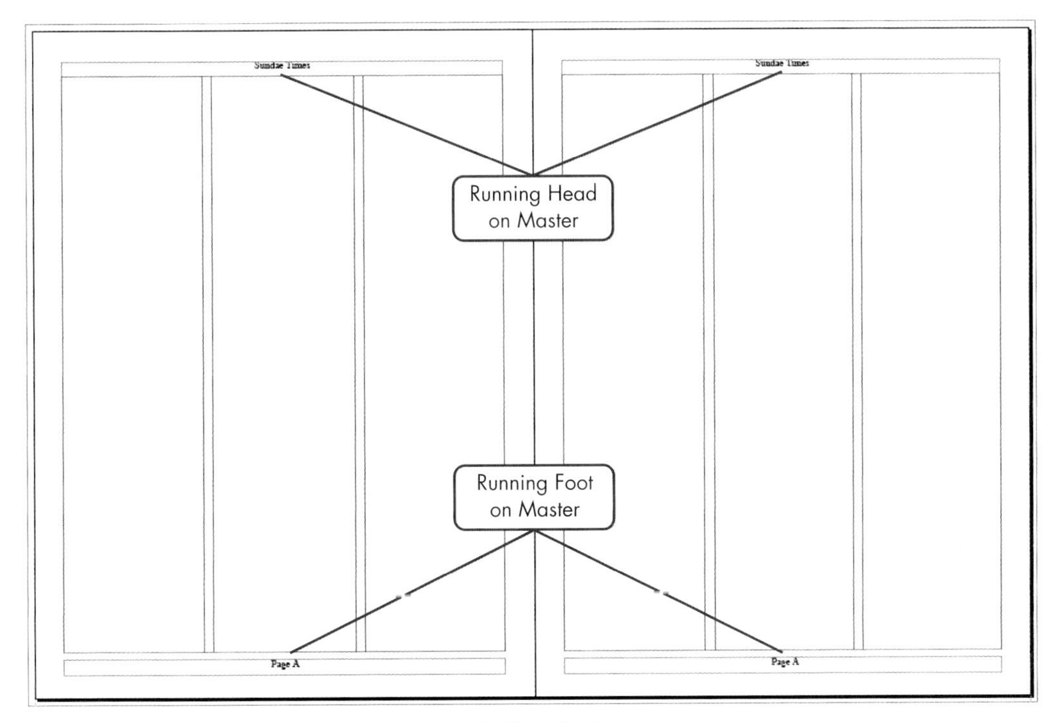

FIGURE 2.26

13 **Double-click Page 1 in the Pages palette.**

The items placed on the A-Master appear on Page 1. The "Page A" that resulted from inserting the automatic page number is now "Page 1." If you click the other pages in the document, you can confirm that they are numbered consecutively.

14 **Save the document as "newsletter_master.indd". Leave it open for the next exercise.**

Add Multiple Masters

1 **Continue in the open newsletter_master.indd.**

2 **From the Pages palette Options menu, choose New Master.**

The New Master dialog box appears.

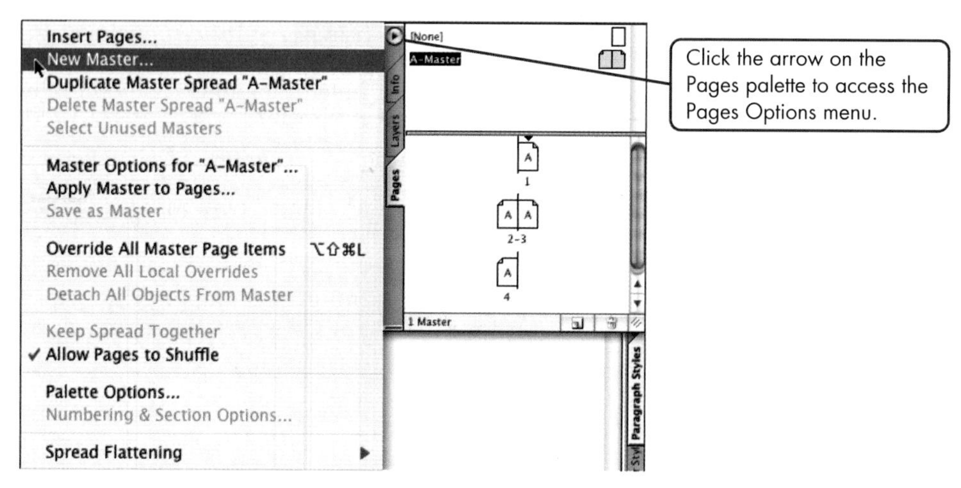

FIGURE 2.27

3 **Name the new master "Nameplate", and base it on A-Master. Leave the Number of Pages at 2. Click OK.**

InDesign automatically assigns the new master the prefix of "B." Once you click OK, the new B-Master spread appears. This will be the master for Page 1 of the newsletter. You need to remove the page number and add the nameplate.

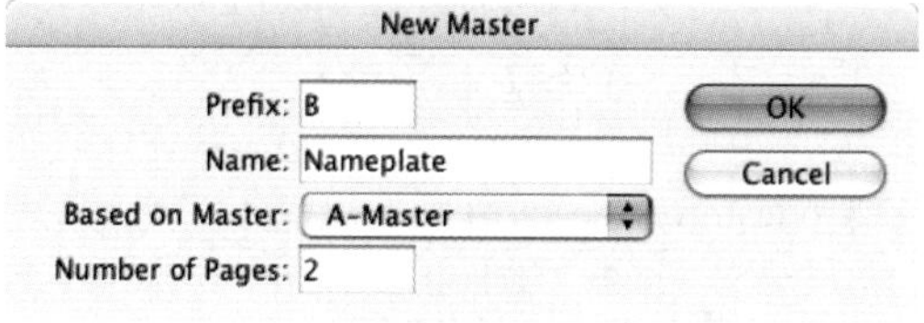

New Master
Prefix: B
Name: Nameplate
Based on Master: A-Master
Number of Pages: 2
OK
Cancel

FIGURE 2.28

4 **Choose the Selection tool in the Tools palette. Press Command/Control-Shift and click the text frame on the right-hand B-Nameplate master that contains the page-number placeholder.**

To change the content of a text frame on a master that's made from another master, you have to press Command/Control-Shift and click once. This prevents inadvertent changes. After you Command/Control-Shift-click a frame once, you don't need to do it again.

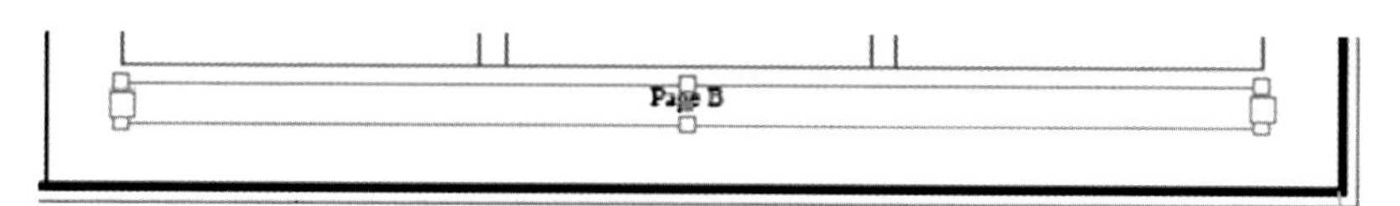

FIGURE 2.29

5 **Press the Delete/Backspace key to remove the frame.**

6 **Repeat Steps 4 and 5 on the header frame on the right master (the one containing the words "Sundae Times").**

You must Command/Control-Shift each frame before you can select it.

7 **Choose File>Place. Choose st_nameplate.eps from the file list in the Place dialog box, and then click Open.**

FIGURE 2.30

8 **When the "loaded" image-placement pointer appears, click in the upper-left corner of the live area (inside the margin guide) of the right master.**

The nameplate is placed. The little black triangle of the loaded pointer turns white when you get within snap distance of the margin guides. (The snap distance is set in the Guides Preferences dialog box.)

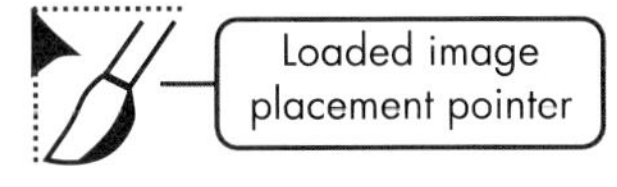

FIGURE 2.31

9 **In the Control palette, change the upper-left position of the image you just placed to X: 0.5 in, Y: 0.5 in.**

Remember to set the proxy-reference point to the upper-left corner.

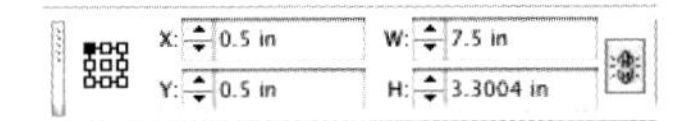

FIGURE 2.32

10 Deselect the graphic.

11 Choose File>Place. Choose st_masthead.eps from the file list, and then click Open.

12 When the image-placement pointer appears, click the lower part of the first column on the left page.

13 Use the Control palette to adjust the position of the lower-left corner of the image to X: 0.5 in, Y: 10.25 in.

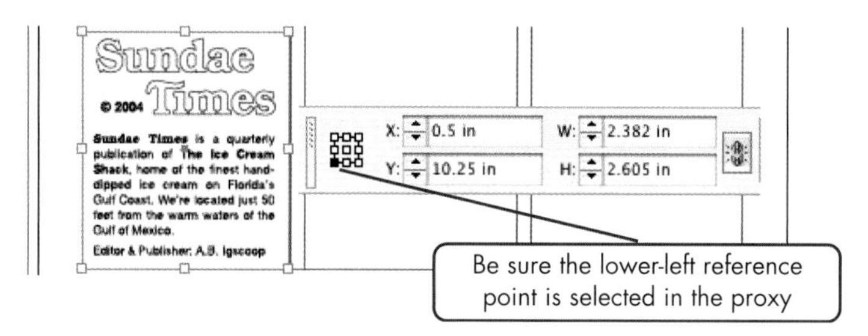

FIGURE 2.33

14 Save your changes, and leave the document open for the next exercise.

LESSON 6 Adding Document Pages

After constructing the necessary masters, you are ready to begin building your document. You can add new pages in several ways: clicking the page icon at the bottom of the Pages palette; choosing Insert Pages from the Pages palette Options menu; or dragging a master into the document pages section of the Pages palette. In the following exercises, you practice all these methods.

It is quite usual to apply a master to a range of pages, and then realize that the master needs some modification. You can modify the master, which applies the changes to all pages to which the master is applied, or you can modify features of a master on an individual page.

Apply and Edit Masters in Your Document

1 Continue working in the open newsletter_master.indd.

2 From the Pages palette Options menu, click Insert Pages. Insert 4 pages based on the A-Master after Page 1. Click OK.

3 In the Pages palette, click the right B-Nameplate master icon and drag it on top of the Page 1 icon. Release the mouse button.

Dragging a master icon on top of a page icon is one way to apply that master to the document page.

4 **Click the Page 2 icon (be certain only Page 2 is highlighted) and Option/Alt-click the left B-Nameplate master icon to apply it to Page 2.**

The correct masters are now applied to the pages in your document. Your Pages palette shows you at a glance what masters are applied to the document pages. You can double-click each page in the Pages palette and examine the document page to check your work.

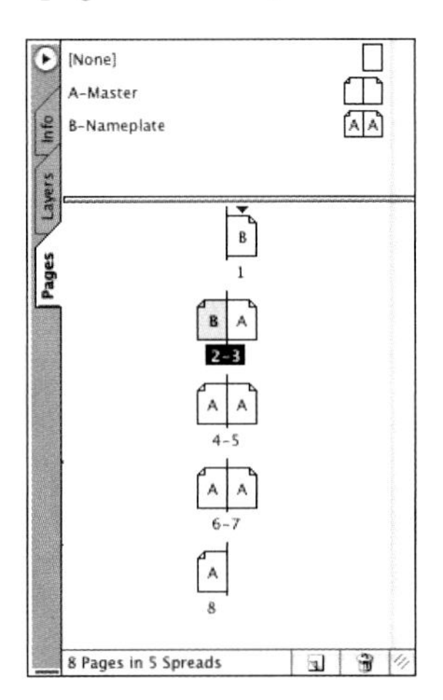

FIGURE 2.34

5 **Double-click the left B-Nameplate master icon.**

The B-Nameplate master opens.

6 **Click the Rectangle Frame tool in the Tools palette. Draw a frame with the following dimensions, with the upper-left proxy-reference point selected in the Control palette:**

X: 3.0556 in	**W: 4.9444 in**
Y: 0.75 in	**H: 9.5 in**

7 **Choose Object>Content>Text.**

8 **Choose View>Hide Guides.**

9 **Double-click the Page 2 icon in the Pages palette.**

The changes you made to the B-Nameplate master page are reflected on all pages to which that master was applied.

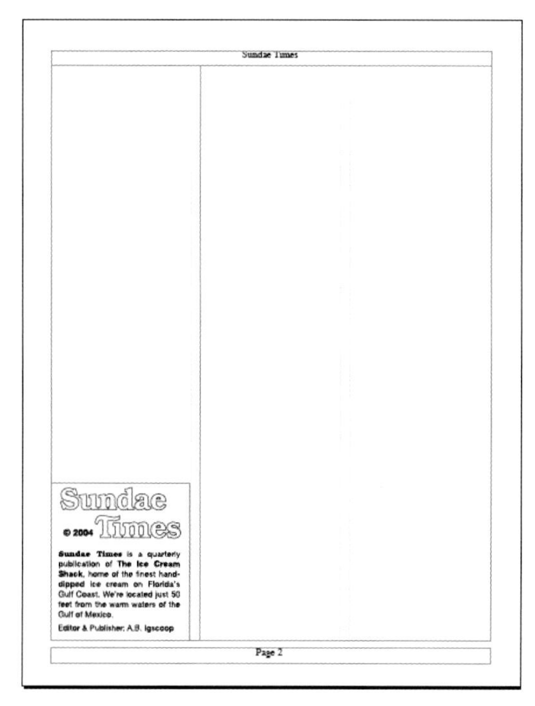

FIGURE 2.35

10 **Save the document as "newsletter.indd" and leave it open for the next exercise.**

Override Master Elements

1 **Continue working in the open document.**

2 **Double-click the Page 2 icon in the Pages palette.**

3 **Choose the Selection tool in the Tools palette. Press Command/Control-Shift, and click the frame that you added to the B-Master in the previous exercise.**

Pressing Command/Control-Shift allows you to access the master frame.

4 **Adjust the height of this frame to 7 inches (the Y dimension in the Control palette).**

5 **Apply the left B-Nameplate master to Page 2.**

The original 9.5-inch master page frame is applied beneath the frame you just altered (which should be selected). Although you can reapply a master to a page that is already based on that master, doing so simply places the master elements underneath the other elements on the page. It doesn't undo any changes you made to the document page. If you removed any master elements from the page, though, reapplying the same master brings them back.

6 **Display the Pages palette Options menu.**

The Remove All Local Overrides option is grayed out and unavailable. You reapplied the B-Nameplate master after altering the selected frame, so that frame is no longer regarded as a master element.

7 **Press Delete/Backspace to delete the altered frame.**

8 **Press Command/Control-Shift and click the frame from the reapplied master.**

9 **Adjust the frame height to 8 inches (the Y dimension in the Control palette).**

10 **From the Pages palette Options menu, choose Remove Selected Local Overrides.**

All master elements return to their original specifications.

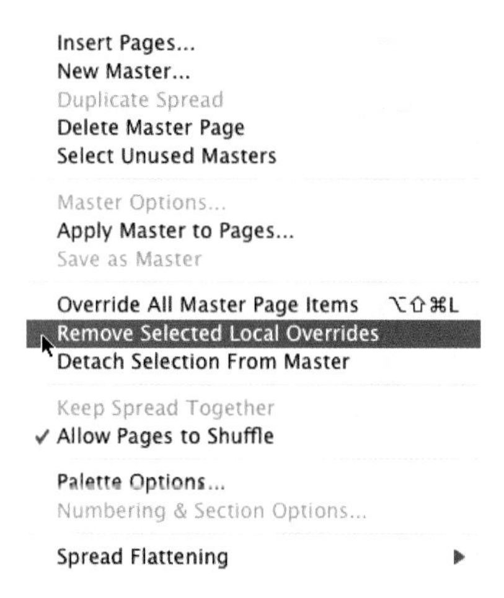

FIGURE 2.36

11 **Save your changes and close the document.**

To Extend Your Knowledge...

USE PLACEHOLDER FRAMES TO MANAGE TEXT AND GRAPHICS

When you know your document will have specific areas for text or graphics, it is a good idea to create placeholder frames on your master. In the previous exercise, you did this for an "editorial" block in the newsletter; other typical uses might be for real estate publications or car dealerships, where layouts contain one specified area for a photo and another for text below it.

SUMMARY

In this project, you learned that a document includes numerous elements. You learned how to set preferences and use masters to make document creation faster, easier, and more accurate. You learned that preferences can be defined to affect all future documents, or they can be defined solely for a specific document.

You learned to open and save pages in a variety of ways, leading to better overall control of the document-creation process. You also learned how to create templates that cannot be accidentally altered. When you created spreads, you learned the anatomy of pages and documents, including margins, gutters, body, and bleed area. You learned how to create running heads and to insert automatically incrementing page numbers in running feet.

Finally, you learned to create masters and apply them to document pages. You experimented with altering a master page, and discovered what happens when master elements are altered on a document page.

KEY TERMS

Absolute numbering
Baseline grid
Body area
Column guide
Document grid
Document page
Document preferences
Em
Font subset
Footer
Glyph
Header
Leading
Live area
Margin
Margin guide
Master
Page
Pica
Placeholder
Running foot
Running head
Section numbering
Slug area
Spine
Template
Tool tips
Universal preferences
Version Cue

CHECKING CONCEPTS AND TERMS

MULTIPLE CHOICE

Circle the letter of the correct answer for each of the following questions:

1. What advantage does a universal preference provide?
   a. It allows you to establish a parameter for a document from anywhere in the document.
   b. It allows you to set up a parameter that is specific to the document you are working on.
   c. It allows you to affect parameters for all future documents.
   d. It allows you to import text from a variety of word processors.

2. In InDesign, what constitutes a spread?
   a. A single page or pages that abut one another.
   b. A page with a tint area that goes off the edge of the page.
   c. The point where two pages join, otherwise known as a spine.
   d. Pages that mirror one another.

3. What is a master?
   a. A person who is an expert at using InDesign.
   b. A group of preferences that control a page.
   c. A page, taken as a whole.
   d. A page upon which other pages are built.

4. What is absolute numbering?
   a. Applying page numbers manually to a document page.
   b. Applying page numbers to a document page using a master.
   c. In the Pages palette, a display showing the pages' actual numbers.
   d. In the Pages palette, a display showing the pages' numbers, consecutively numbered, beginning with "1."

5. What is a font subset?
   a. Only a portion of fonts with many characters.
   b. A combination of type styles, such as Helvetica Regular, Bold, Italic, and Bold Italic.
   c. A designated portion of the alphabet, such as numbers or punctuation.
   d. A major grouping of fonts, such as serif, sans serif, or script.

6. What is the baseline grid?
   a. A grid system for the placement of type.
   b. A grid system that originates at the bottom of the page.
   c. A system that, by default, increments every 1/8 inch.
   d. A system of horizontal and vertical rules that overrides the document grid.

7. What is a document template?
   a. An overlay that allows you to trace illustrations.
   b. A system of grids and guides.
   c. A spread upon which other spreads are based.
   d. A document upon which other documents are based.

8. What two areas appear outside the normal document page?
   a. The bleed and slug.
   b. The gutter and guides.
   c. The slug and gutter.
   d. The headers and footers.

9. Of the following, which are not standard InDesign page sizes?

a. Letter and Legal.

b. Letter-Half and Tabloid

c. Compact Disk and A4

d. Envelope and Business Card

10. What is a running foot?

a. Text that overflows the page.

b. An image that extends beyond the bottom of the page.

c. Information at the bottom of the page, below the body of text and images.

d. Information at the top of the page, above the body of text and images.

SCREEN ID

Identify the indicated areas from the list below:

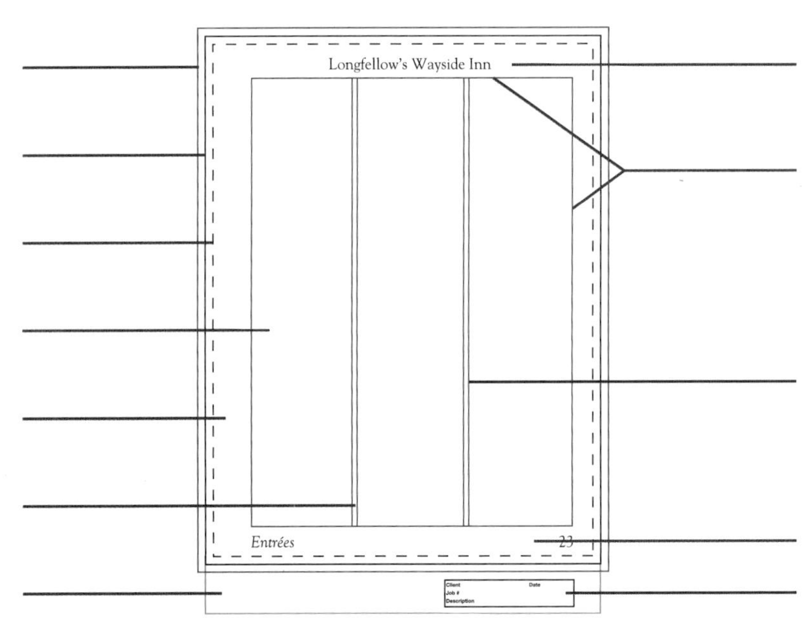

FIGURE 2.37

a. Bleed

b. Body Area

c. Column Guides

d. Gutters

e. Live Area

f. Margin Guides

g. Margins

h. Document Page

i. Running Foot (Footer)

j. Running Head (Header)

k. Slug

l. Slug Area

DISCUSSION QUESTIONS

1. In this project, you learned to set a number of preferences. Discuss the pros and cons of being able to do this.

2. Masters take some time to set up, but they are used extensively. Why would you take the time to set up masters? What options exist for ensuring consistency within and between documents?

3. Of the methods you worked with in this project, which ones do you think are most important to building and controlling documents?

SKILL DRILL

Skill Drills reinforce project skills. Each skill reinforced is the same, or nearly the same, as a skill presented in the lessons. Detailed instructions are provided in a step-by-step format. You can work through one or more exercises in any order.

1. Set Grid and Guide Preferences

The preferences you already set (or left at their defaults) are acceptable for many projects, but you might want to change some of the standard settings to accommodate different types of documents or personal preferences. For example, people with certain types of color-blindness might choose to change the display colors of the grids and guides.

1. Create a new Letter-size document with Portrait orientation. Accept the default settings.
2. Choose View>Show Document Grid.

   Your pasteboard fills with gray horizontal and vertical lines in two thicknesses. The heavier lines are one inch apart and the lighter lines are 1/8 inch apart.
3. Choose Preferences>Grids. Click the Color menu.

   This menu shows you the variety of colors you can use for the gridlines. The light gray grid probably won't conflict with elements you will place on it, so leave the color as it is.
4. Change the Horizontal and Vertical Subdivisions fields to "4".

   This value places a line every 1/4 inch instead of every 1/8 inch, making the grid less busy.
5. Choose the Rectangle Frame tool in the Tools palette. Using the grid as a reference, begin at X: 1 in, Y: 1 in, and drag a frame 2.75 in wide and 4 in high.

   Even with the grids in place, it is difficult to draw the frame accurately.
6. Choose View>Snap to Document Grid. Draw another frame of the same dimensions beginning at X: 4 in, Y: 1 in.

   Note how much easier it is to draw the frame accurately when the Snap feature is activated.

7. Try to drag one of the frames a little bit.

   The "magnetism" of the guides does not allow you to drag objects to make minor adjustments. You can, however, type in new dimensions or use the Arrow keys to move a frame a small distance.

8. From the Preferences dialog box, choose the Guides and Pasteboard preference. Change the Guide Options Snap-to Zone to "4".

   This changes the "magnetism" of the guides, so objects will snap to them when they are within 4 pixels, instead of 2 pixels.

9. Drag the frame again.

   Notice how much easier it is to position it in small increments.

10. Close the document without saving.

2. Build a Document with Structure

As a graphic designer, you must consider a number of specifications when creating documents for print. One of the most common documents you will create is the six-panel brochure, similar to the gebrochure.indd document you worked on earlier in this project. To allow for paper thickness and inaccurate folding machines, the panels in a six-panel brochure are of unequal widths — the panel that folds into the others is noticeably narrower.

1. Create a new 8.5 by 11-inch document with a Landscape orientation and no Facing Pages. Apply 0.25-in margins, a Bleed of 0.125 in on all sides, and a 2-in Slug at the bottom.

2. Drag vertical guides onto the page. Position them at 3.625 and 7.3125 inches.

   These guides are positioned where the brochure is designed to fold on the "cover" side of the brochure. The front cover will be positioned on the panel farthest to the right.

3. Drag additional vertical guides to 3.375, 3.875, 7.0625, and 7.5625 inches.

   These guides create the margins inside the brochure. The outside margins were created when you originally defined the page size.

4. Drag a new page from the Masters section into the Document section of the Pages palette.

5. Drag vertical guides to 3.4375, 3.6875, 3.9375, 7.125, 7.375, and 7.625 inches.

   These guides comprise the inside panels of the brochure.

6. Save the document to your WIP_02 folder as "structure.indd". Close the document

3. Create the Framework of a Manual

Most instructional manuals are designed to be distributed in binders. They are usually printed on only one side of the page. When creating such a document, which is often reproduced on a photocopier, you need to consider the space taken up by the bindings and the limitations of most photocopiers. On the other hand, you do not need to worry about bleed, which most copiers cannot accommodate.

1. Create a new, Letter-size document with Portrait orientation and a Master Text Frame, with no Facing Pages. Set the Top and Right Margins to 0.5 in, and the Bottom and Left Margins to 0.75 in.

   The clearance on the left side of the page accommodates the width of the bindings, and the space on the bottom allows for the running foot (footer).

2. In the Pages palette, double-click the A-Master.
3. Choose the Type tool in the Tools palette, and drag a text frame of the following dimensions:

   X: 0.75 in W: 7.25 in
   Y: 10.5 in H: 0.25 in

   If you can't drag to these exact dimensions, make your final adjustments in the Control palette.

4. Within the text frame, type "Instruction Manual", and then press Shift-Tab.

   This command inserts a right-margin tab.

5. Choose Type>Insert Special Character>Auto Page Number.

   An incrementing page number is inserted on each page to which this master is applied.

6. Double-click the visible document page.
7. Command/Control-Shift-click the text frame containing the page number. Press Delete/Backspace to delete the page number from the first page.
8. From the Pages palette Options menu, choose Insert Pages. Insert 5 pages after Page 1, accepting the default of A-Master.
9. Check the pages you inserted to verify that the information from the master was included.
10. Save the file as "manual.indd". Close the file.

4. Create a CD Card Template

When you send your documents to a printer, you will most likely save them to some type of removable media. This could be a CD, Zip drive, Jaz drive, or some other medium. In this Skill Drill, you create the master for a Zip drive label, which is more than adequate for submission of most brochures and ads.

1. Create a new custom landscape document, 8.25 by 3.9375 inches. Master Text Frame and Facing Pages should not be selected. Set the Columns to "1" and set all Margins to "0".
2. Drag horizontal guides to 0.25 in, 3.75 in, 4 in, and 4.25 in.
3. Drag vertical guides to 0.25 in and 3.6875 in.
4. Choose View>Lock Guides, so you will not accidentally move the guides.
5. Choose the Type tool and draw a text frame with a Width of 3.9375 inches and a Height of 0.25 inch.
6. Choose the Rotation tool, and rotate the text frame –90°.
7. With the proxy-reference point in the upper left, position the text frame at X: 4 in, Y: 0 in.

8. Choose Object>Lock Position so this frame will not move.
9. Create a new text frames as follows: X: 0.25 in, Y: 0.25 in, W: 3.5 in, H: 3.4375 in.
10. Hold down the Option/Alt key and the Shift key and drag the frame to X: 4.25 in, which will duplicate the frame in the new position.
11. Save the file to your WIP_02 folder as an InDesign template named "cd_card.indt". Close the file.

CHALLENGE

Challenge exercises expand on, or are somewhat related to, skills presented in the lessons. Each exercise provides a brief introduction, followed by instructions presented in a numbered-step format that are not as detailed as those in the Skill Drill exercises. You should complete the challenge exercises in the order provided.

1. Create the Basics for a Magazine Article

You work for a magazine publisher. You were asked to assemble a six-page article and its associated ads. Your magazine uses a standard page size of 8.25 by 10.5 inches. It is a perfect-bound publication, so you need to make the inside margin about 1/16 inch wider than the outside margin. This food and lifestyle magazine uses both two-column and three-column formats; the two-column format occupies the first page of an article, and the three-column format is used on succeeding pages.

1. Create a new document of the appropriate size, using a three-column format for the basic page. Choose the Facing Pages and Master Text Frame options. Set the Top and Outside margins to 0.5 in, the Bottom Margin to 0.75 in, and the Inside Margin to 0.5625 in. Use a standard 0.125-in Bleed. A Slug is unnecessary.
2. In the General pane of the Preferences dialog box, set the Page Numbering to Section Numbering. In the Units & Increments pane, set the Ruler Units Origin menu to Page.
3. Set up a running foot for both masters at Y: 9.875 in, with the magazine name "*Lifestyle Images*" at the inside margin, and the automatic page number at the outside margin. Use the margin tab (Shift-Tab) to flush the text to the right-hand margin.
4. Create a new 2-page master that is not based on another master.
5. Set the Number of Columns in the new B-Master to "2".
6. You will only use the right-hand page. Use the Rectangle Frame tool to create a frame that extends from the spine to the edge of the right bleed area, 5.75 in high.

   This frame will hold the article's main photo.
7. Insert a text frame at Y: 9.875 in, with the automatic page number centered in the frame.
8. Save the document as "lifestyle.indd". Leave it open for the next exercise.

2. Expand Your Magazine Article

Now that the base layout for the magazine article is set up, you can add some more details before handing it off to a layout specialist who will insert text and ads.

1. Double-click the first page in the open document to return to the document section of your Pages palette.
2. Adjust the page numbering to begin at Page 15.
3. Apply the B-Master to document Page 1.
4. Choose the Selection tool and Command/Control-Shift-click the frame on Page 15.
5. Place the photo eathealthy.tif in the frame on Page 15.
6. Add five more pages to the document. Base the pages on A-Master.

   The document is ready to hand off to a page-layout specialist.
7. Save the file and close it.

3. Build a Newsletter Template

One of the most-used marketing devices is the "bill-stuffer." Every month, when you're presented with a bill to pay, many companies include information about themselves or simply some handy tips — sometimes recipes — that will give their customers the "warm fuzzies" while they are making out their checks. In this exercise, you create a template for such a stuffer.

1. Create a new, custom landscape, 2-page document, 7 in by 5.5 in, with 2 Columns with 0.5-in Gutters. The Top, Left, and Right Margins should be 0.25 in, the Bottom Margins should be 0.375 in, and the Bleed 0.125 in. Facing Pages should be unchecked. Master Text Frame should be checked.
2. Draw a text frame: X: 0.25 in, Y: 5.25 in, W: 3 in, and H: 0.175 in.
3. Type "Month" and "Good Health", and then insert a margin tab to flush "Good Health" to the right margin.
4. Drag a copy of this frame to X: 3.75 in, Y: 5.25 in.
5. Transpose the words, so "Month" is to the outside of the page.
6. Click Page 1 in the Pages palette.
7. Place the file goodhealth.indd at X: 3.75 in, Y: 0.25 in.
8. Save a template as goodhealth.indt to your WIP_02 folder. Close the file.

PORTFOLIO BUILDER

Design a Yearbook Layout

You are the designer for American Yearbook Corporation — a company that produces yearbooks for many high schools in the United States. This year, the company wants to present at least two design options when it approaches its clients. The yearbooks will include the following:

- Feature pages that include one large and two small photographs, plus descriptive text, of school events held that year.
- Faculty pages, department-by-department, featuring the department chair, with a blurb about the department, and two lines for each teacher (name, degree, and college attended).
- Underclass pages, containing 48 pictures per page, with space for each student's name.
- Senior pages, containing 12–20 pictures per page, with space for each student's name and activities over their school career.
- The first page in each of these sections should have room for the title of the section.
- The underclass photos should be substantially smaller than those of the seniors.

You need to design a project that includes masters for each of these page types, so the final product can be assembled quickly and easily.

The specifications for the yearbook are as follows:

Trim size: 9 × 12 in.	Live area: 8 × 11 in.
Margins: 0.5 in. (all four edges)	Bleed allowance: None

LEVEL 1

PROJECT 3

Working with Text

OBJECTIVES

In this project, you learn how to

- Set text frame properties
- Edit text
- Enter and format text
- Use OpenType and special characters
- Format paragraphs
- Set tabs
- Import and export text files
- Thread text across multiple frames

WHY WOULD I DO THIS?

Text makes up approximately 70–80% of printed matter, so it is vital to learn to handle it well. You observed in Project 2 that many of InDesign's preferences help you set text efficiently and effectively.

Text in InDesign is always contained in frames. You can create a text frame with the Type tool or any of the frame-creation tools, or InDesign can create the frame for you when you place text into your document. A text frame is identified by an ***in port*** at the upper left and an ***out port*** at the lower right of the frame. These ports indicate whether the text in a frame is part of a stream coming from or going to other frames in the document; text that flows into another frame is indicated by a blue arrow in the frame's out port. If there is too much text to fit in a frame (or in a text stream that extends across several frames), a red plus sign (+) appears in the out port of the last frame in the text stream.

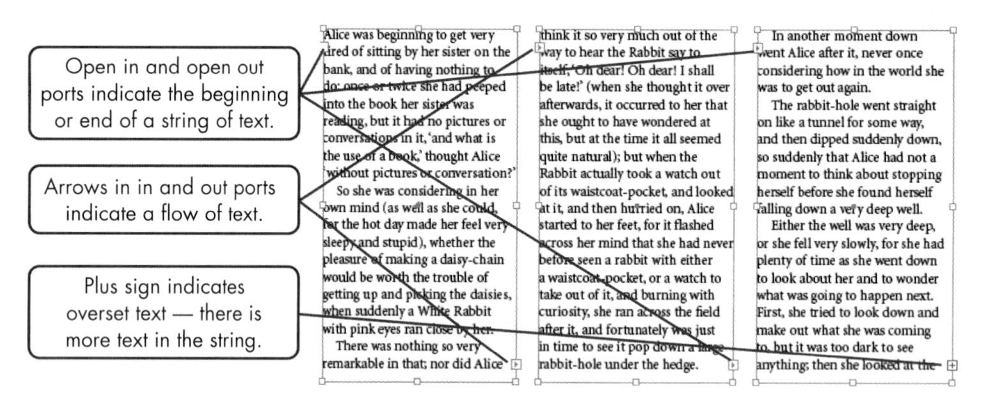

FIGURE 3.1

The Type tool is used to insert text into a frame or to edit text. You can use the Selection tool, the Transform palette, or the Control palette to position and size a text frame. To change the shape of a frame, you can use the Direct Selection tool (sometimes in conjunction with elements of the Pen tool), or you can make alterations through the Object>Transform dialog box. You can also resize a frame and the text size within it using the Selection tool, the Transform palette, or the Transform menu's Scale function.

There are many typefaces available for setting the text in your documents. Typefaces are organized by font family and style. A ***font family*** contains all the styles and weights in a specific typeface design. ***Font styles*** are design variants, with the exception of weights; they include Roman, Oldstyle, Display, Italic, and some fonts even have an Ornaments variant. Most professionally designed typefaces have a number of ***weights***, such as Light, Book, Medium, Semibold, and Bold.

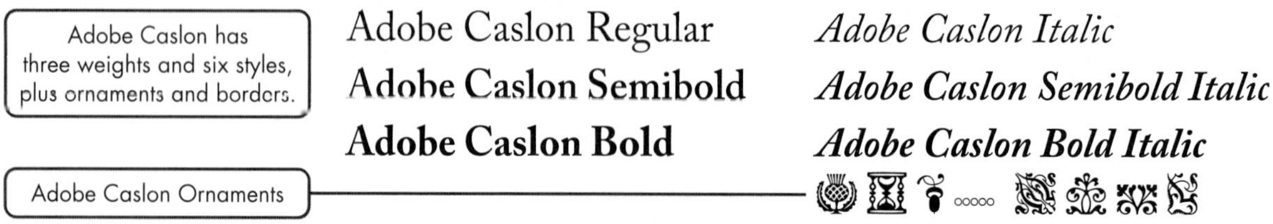

Adobe Caslon has three weights and six styles, plus ornaments and borders.

Adobe Caslon Regular — *Adobe Caslon Italic*

Adobe Caslon Semibold — ***Adobe Caslon Semibold Italic***

Adobe Caslon Bold — ***Adobe Caslon Bold Italic***

Adobe Caslon Ornaments

FIGURE 3.2

Once you have decided on a typeface for your text, you can also specify the ***font size***, which is the height of a typeface measured in ***points*** (a point is 1/72 inch). This distance refers not only to the visible size of the character, but also includes the distance from the bottom of the descender to the clearance allowance above the ascender. A ***descender*** is the part of a letter that extends below the baseline. An ***ascender*** is the part of a lower-case letter that extends above the x-height.

FIGURE 3.3

As you learned in Project 2, leading is the space between lines of type, and it is measured in points. Proper leading values ensure the readability of the text. Optimal leading values vary, depending on the design of the typeface and the content of the document. Typefaces with wider characters or large x-height (refer to Figure 3.3) require more leading than do narrower typefaces. Pages of solid text (a novel, for example) benefit from more leading than reference material (such as dictionary listings). Traditional designers and typographers indicate the desired type size and leading combination with notations such as "10/14 Helvetica Narrow." This statement, read as "ten over fourteen Helvetica Narrow," indicates that type should be set in 10-pt Helvetica Narrow using 14-pt leading. The figure below illustrates how much easier it is to read 10/12 Times Roman (left) than 10/12 ITC Bookman (right), which has wider characters and a taller x-height.

Down, down, down. Would the fall never come to an end? "I wonder how many miles I've fallen by this time?" she said aloud. "I must be getting somewhere near the centre of the earth. Let me see: that would be four thousand miles down, I think—" (for, you see, Alice had learnt several things of this sort in her lessons in the schoolroom, and

Down, down, down. Would the fall never come to an end? "I wonder how many miles I've fallen by this time?" she said aloud. "I must be getting somewhere near the centre of the earth. Let me see: that would be four thousand miles down, I think—" (for, you see, Alice

FIGURE 3.4

InDesign fully supports the features of OpenType fonts, jointly developed by Adobe Systems and Microsoft. You can use a single ***OpenType*** font on either Windows or Macintosh computers; each can contain as many as 65,000 glyphs (characters). Three OpenType font families are included with InDesign: Adobe Caflisch Script Pro, Adobe Caslon Pro, and Adobe Garamond Pro. If these fonts have not already been installed on your computer, you should install them now. (The Kozuka fonts are Japanese and are not needed for the material in this book.) There are also PDF type specimen documents within each font's folder. These documents show which characters are included in each font, and are handy references.

In the past, if you wanted to take advantage of the richness of typography, you were required to purchase more than one version of the same font. For example, if you wanted to use small caps, you had to purchase a font that includes small caps, in addition to the standard uppercase and lowercase. You might need yet another font for oldstyle numbers, fractions, ligatures, swash characters, or ornaments. In InDesign, using OpenType fonts, you can view specific glyphs, and even design custom glyph sets, which can include glyphs from more than one font, allowing you greater versatility, while reducing the need to purchase many fonts of the same family.

In formats other than OpenType, the Macintosh character set was different from the Windows character set. For example, standard ligatures were included for the Macintosh, but not for Windows; standard fractions were included under Windows, but not on the Macintosh. In addition, the same characters were accessed using different character codes on the two systems. For example, the bullet (•) is character 113 on the Macintosh and character 149 under Windows using PostScript or TrueType fonts. With OpenType, this cross-platform incompatibility no longer exists.

InDesign allows you to automate or to manually control virtually every function that applies to the look, feel, and placement of type. Not only can you manage the appearance of individual characters, but also the look of entire paragraphs. You can adjust paragraph alignment, indentations, spacing above and below paragraphs, drop caps, hyphenation and justification, and rules (lines) above and below paragraphs. You can force a specified number of lines in a paragraph to stay together — or even force an entire paragraph to remain together on a column or a page. You work with all these features as you progress through this project.

Type makes up the majority of most publications, which makes Project 3 one of the most important projects in this book. As you work through these lessons, you become familiar with using InDesign's tools to manage type. When you have finished the project, you will be well prepared to perform the basic functions involved in the production of text.

VISUAL SUMMARY

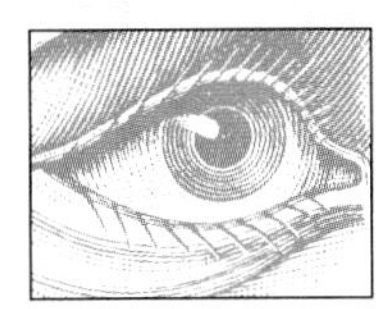

All text is inserted into frames, so it is important to understand how to control frames. You can use the Text Frame Options dialog box to specify information about columns, text inset, the position of the first baseline, and how the text is justified vertically within the frame.

Text Frame Options

Columns
Number: 1 Gutter: 0.1667 i
Width: 4 in
Fixed Column Width

OK
Cancel
Preview

Inset Spacing
Top: 0 in Left: 0 in
Bottom: 0 in Right: 0 in

First Baseline
Offset: Ascent Min: 0 in

Vertical Justification
Align: Top
Paragraph Spacing Limit: 0 in

Ignore Text Wrap

FIGURE 3.5

After you enter text into a frame, you usually need to edit it. You can cut, copy, paste, and move text, as well as modify its properties. When you begin to work with text, however, it often seems to have a mind of its own. This is usually because of hidden characters, special characters, and various spacing options that are assigned to the text. To gain greater control over your documents, you can make these hidden characters visible.

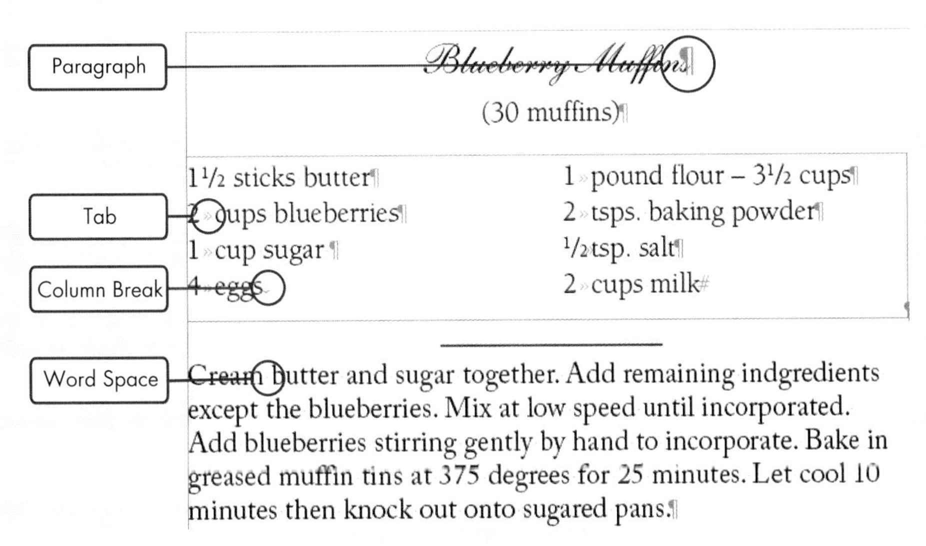

FIGURE 3.6

You can format text using either the Control palette or the Character palette. Although you can adjust most text characteristics using either palette, there are more functions available through the Character palette's Options menu. The Character palette, however, is less convenient to use; the Control palette is always available, so you will probably use it most often.

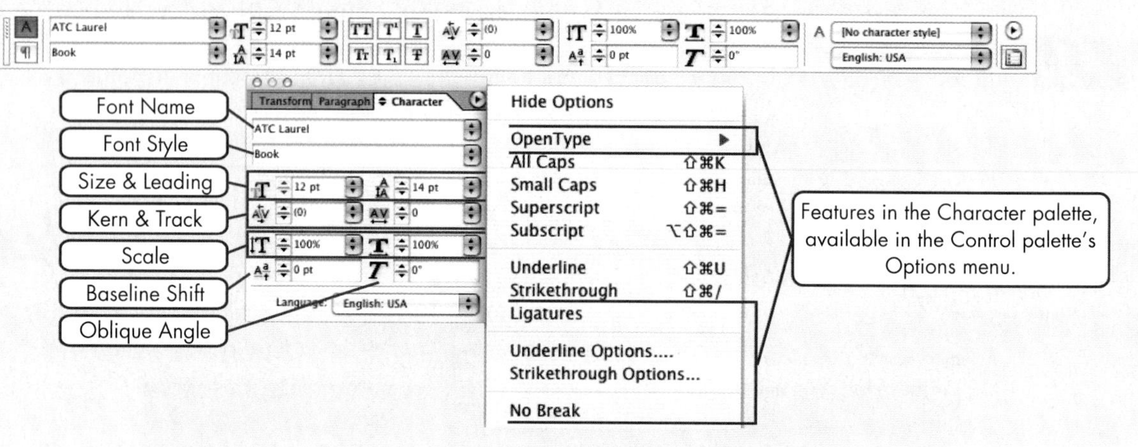

FIGURE 3.7

You can format entire paragraphs using either the Paragraph palette or the Control palette. As is the case with character formatting, the Paragraph palette is more powerful but less convenient; it allows you to define many features that function behind the scenes.

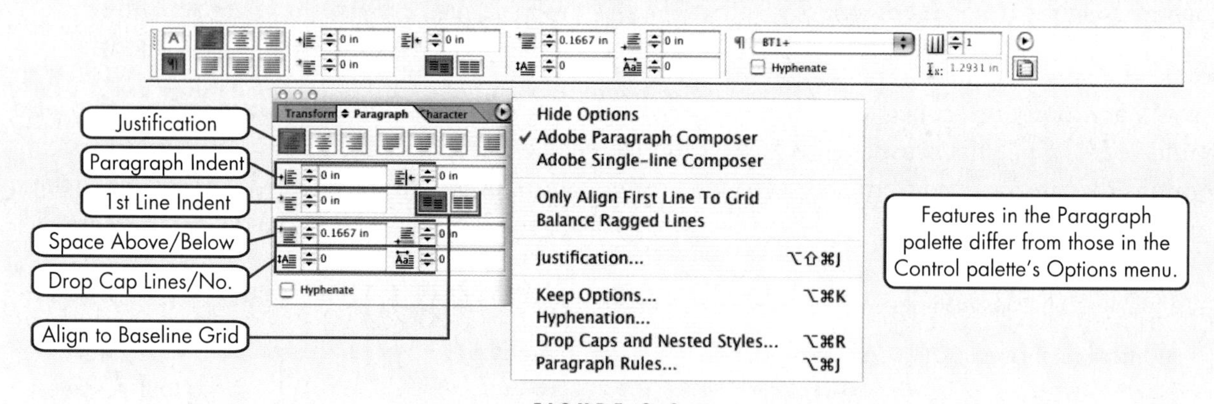

FIGURE 3.8

As we mentioned earlier, OpenType gives you access to up to 65,000 characters per font. In InDesign, you have access to all characters that have been designed into the font through the OpenType and Glyphs submenus.

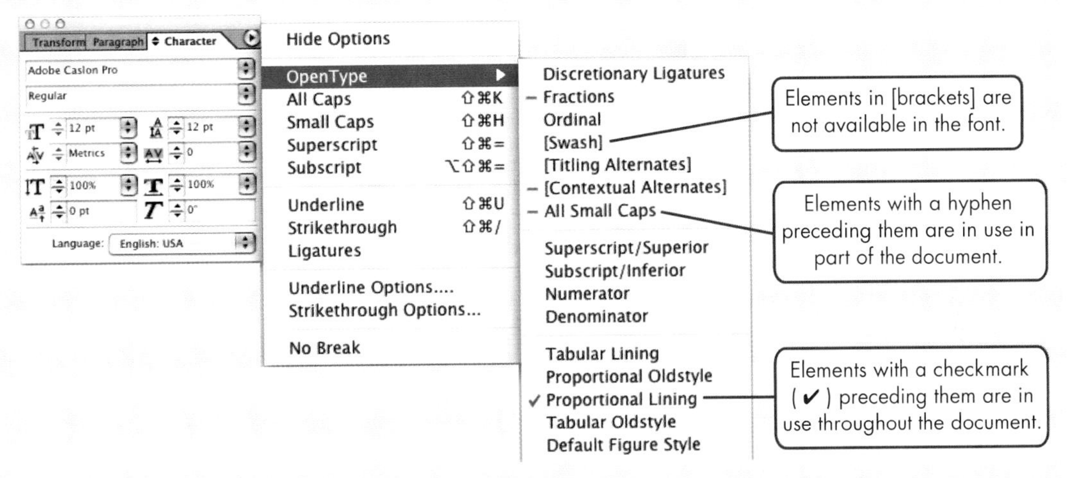

FIGURE 3.9

LESSON 1 Setting Text Frame Properties

The most basic element for working with text is the text frame. All text in your InDesign documents must be placed within text frames. You can generate a text frame by dragging with the Type tool, or you can create a text frame with the Frame tool and then click the Type tool inside the frame. Once the frame is created, you can set its properties from the Text Frame Options dialog box. In the following exercise, you become familiar with a number of text frame characteristics.

Create a Text Frame and Set Its Properties

1. **Create a new Letter-size document. Save it as "textwork.indd" in your WIP_03 folder.**

2. **Choose View>Show Text Threads.**

   This command allows you to see how the text flows between frames. You can also press Command-Option-Y (Macintosh) or Control-Alt-Y (Windows) to make text threads visible.

3. **Choose the Type tool in the Tools palette. Beginning at X: 1 in, Y: 1 in, drag a text frame 3 in wide and 3.5 in high.**

   You can refer to ruler positions, or check the Info palette or Control palette, as you drag this frame. If you want to tweak it, you can do so using the Control palette or the Transform palette (Window>Transform).

FIGURE 3.10

4 **With the Type tool positioned in the frame you created, choose Type>Fill with Placeholder Text.**

The frame fills with Greeked (dummy) text. It is traditional to set such text when creating page layouts at the beginning of the design stage. The dummy text generator is available whenever a text frame is selected.

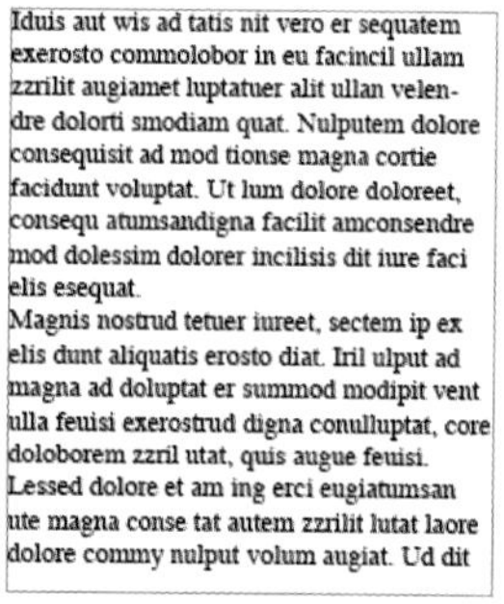

Iduis aut wis ad tatis nit vero er sequatem exerosto commolobor in eu facincil ullam zzrilit augiamet luptatuer alit ullan velen-dre dolorti smodiam quat. Nulputem dolore consequisit ad mod tionse magna cortie facidunt voluptat. Ut lum dolore doloreet, consequ atumsandigna facilit amconsendre mod dolessim dolorer incilisis dit iure faci elis esequat.
Magnis nostrud tetuer iureet, sectem ip ex elis dunt aliquatis erosto diat. Iril ulput ad magna ad doluptat er summod modipit vent ulla feuisi exerostrud digna conulluptat, core doloborem zzril utat, quis augue feuisi.
Lessed dolore et am ing erci eugiatumsan ute magna conse tat autem zzrilit lutat laore dolore commy nulput volum augiat. Ud dit

FIGURE 3.11

5 **Choose Object>Text Frame Options.**

You can also press Command/Control-B to open the Text Frame Options dialog box.

6 **Change all four Inset Spacing fields to "6 pt". Click OK.**

If you check the Preview box (below the Cancel button), you can see the effect of your actions in "real time." In Project 2, you selected inches as your Units preference, so InDesign automatically converts the 6-pt inset to its equivalent in inches (0.0833 in). The text insets 6 points from all sides of the frame. The bottom inset refers to distance between the baseline of the last line of text and the edge of the frame. In addition, the overset symbol (the red "+") appears, indicating that there is additional text that can be flowed to another text frame. You should inset text if you plan to apply a stroke (border) to the text frame.

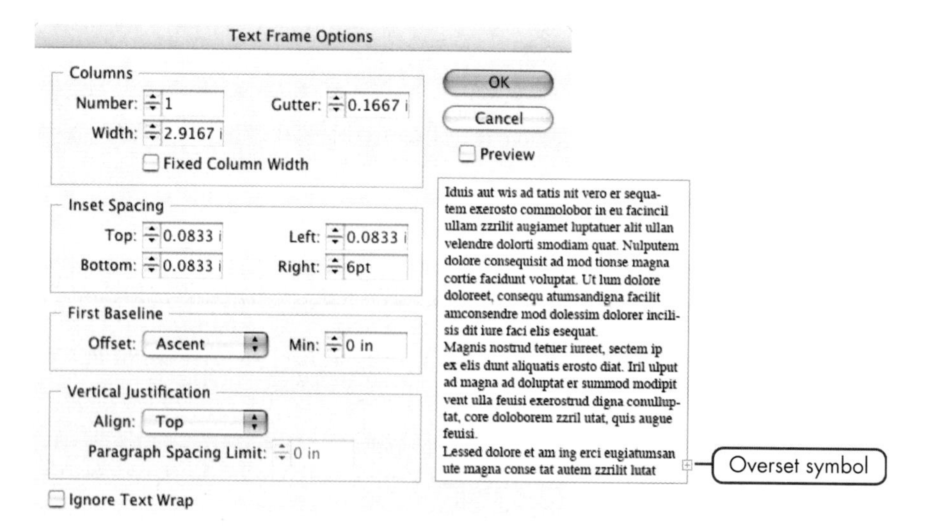

FIGURE 3.12

7 **Click the overset symbol with the Selection tool.**

The cursor changes to a loaded-text icon.

8 **Use the loaded-text icon to drag a new text frame next to the existing text frame.**

The overset type flows into the new text frame, which does not have the same frame insets as the original text frame.

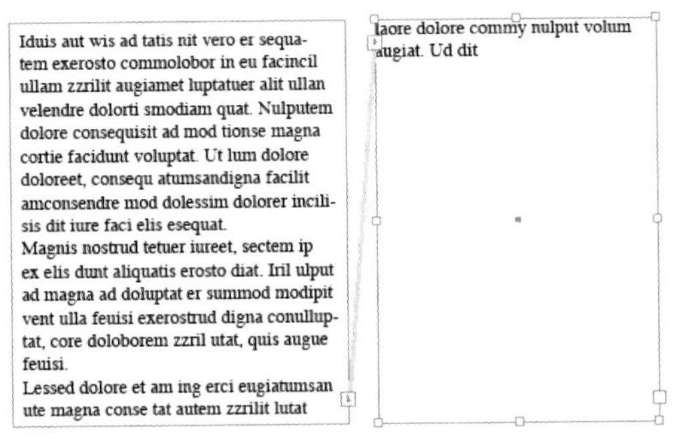

FIGURE 3.13

9 **With the second text frame selected, choose Object>Text Frame Options. From the First Baseline Offset menu, choose Fixed. Leave the Minimum field set to 0 in.**

The baseline of the first line of text in the second frame now rests on the top of the text frame. This option sets a fixed distance between the baseline of the first line and the top inset value defined for the frame.

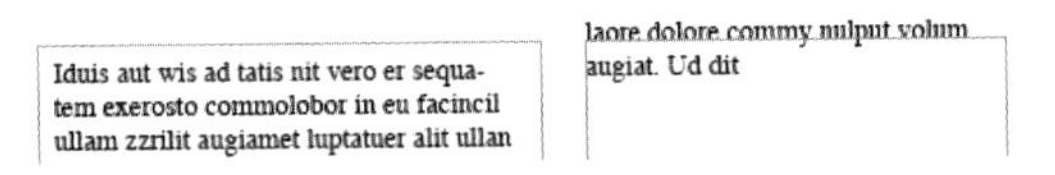

FIGURE 3.14

In the figure below, the inset value was set to zero, so you can easily see the effects of each of the baseline options.

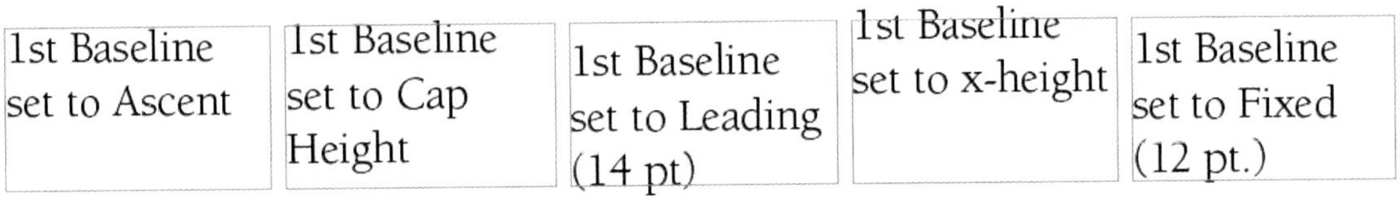

1st Baseline set to Ascent

1st Baseline set to Cap Height

1st Baseline set to Leading (14 pt)

1st Baseline set to x-height

1st Baseline set to Fixed (12 pt.)

FIGURE 3.15

10 **In the Text Frame Options dialog box, set the Align menu in the Vertical Justification area to Justify. When the Paragraph Spacing Limit menu becomes active, leave it set to 0 in. Click OK.**

The baseline of the last line of text justifies to the bottom margin of the text frame. Any descenders appear below the text frame. If your second text frame has three or more lines, there is equal spacing between every baseline. The other values in the justification menu set the type to the Top, Center, and Bottom positions in the frame.

FIGURE 3.16

11 **Save your changes and close the file.**

To Extend Your Knowledge...

MANAGING TEXT WITH TEXT FRAME PROPERTIES

In most cases, you will accept InDesign's default text frame options, with no Inset Spacing, First Baseline Offset to the Ascender value, and Vertical Justification set to the Top. There will be times, however, when a particular project requires vertical justification for all text. To avoid having to set each text frame individually, you can choose Object>Text Frame Options with no frame selected. Once you set the parameters, all subsequent text frames within that document follow those parameters. If you set the text frame options with no document open, the parameters apply to all future documents, until you reset the options with no document open.

LESSON 2 Editing Text

There are many reasons why you might want to edit text. A primary reason is that you want to correct spelling, as well as grammatical or typographical errors. You may also edit text to improve its appearance, or to make it fit the text frame. Many — if not most — edits occur when a client changes text, or when an editor makes corrections. When you become comfortable with InDesign's editing tools, you will be able to quickly and easily perform text edits, leaving more time to work with design and page-layout functions.

Edit Text

1 **Open edit_text.indd from the Project_03 folder.**

2 **Choose Type>Show Hidden Characters.**

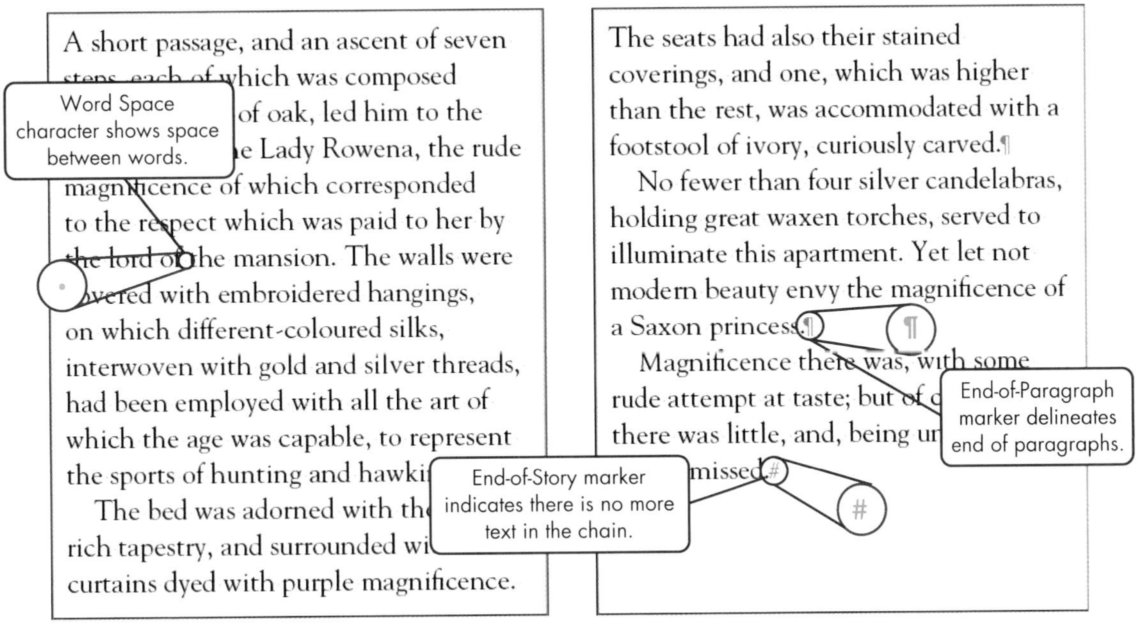

FIGURE 3.17

Special formatting characters, such as spaces and end-of-paragraph markers, become visible on the page.

3 **In the fifth line, double-click the word "magnificence".**

The word is selected. This is a useful method for selecting an entire word if you need to change it or correct a ***typo*** (typographical error). If the Triple Click to Select a Line option is activated in the Text pane of the Preferences dialog box, three clicks selects an entire line and four clicks selects an entire paragraph. If the option is turned off, three clicks selects the entire paragraph.

4 **Choose Edit>Cut to cut the selected word, and then press Delete/Backspace.**

The word is cut from the layout and saved on the InDesign clipboard. You can also press Command/Control-X to cut selected text. Double-clicking a word does not select the space (or punctuation mark) following the word. You must manually remove the extra space and/or punctuation.

5 **In the first paragraph, place the cursor in the last line of text, immediately before the period. Press the Spacebar, and then choose Edit>Paste.**

The content of the clipboard (the word that you cut in Step 4) is pasted into the last line. You can also press Command/Control-V to paste text.

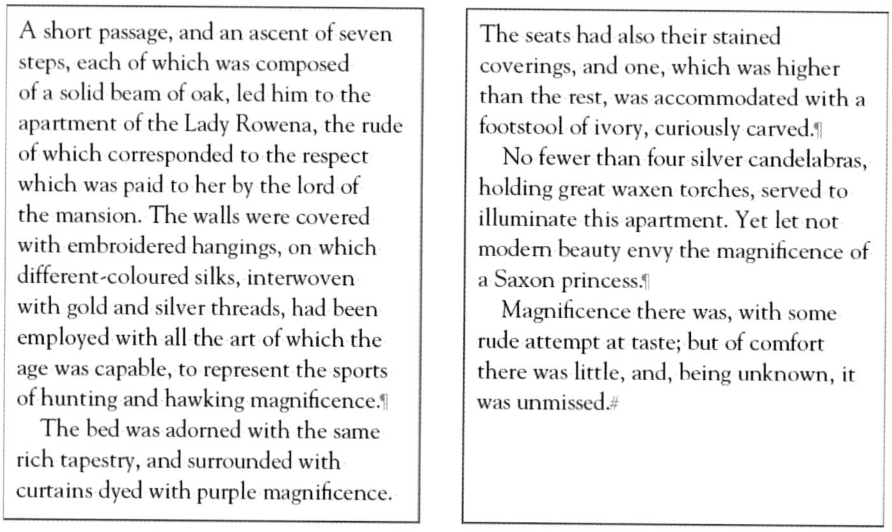

A short passage, and an ascent of seven steps, each of which was composed of a solid beam of oak, led him to the apartment of the Lady Rowena, the rude of which corresponded to the respect which was paid to her by the lord of the mansion. The walls were covered with embroidered hangings, on which different-coloured silks, interwoven with gold and silver threads, had been employed with all the art of which the age was capable, to represent the sports of hunting and hawking magnificence.¶
The bed was adorned with the same rich tapestry, and surrounded with curtains dyed with purple magnificence.

The seats had also their stained coverings, and one, which was higher than the rest, was accommodated with a footstool of ivory, curiously carved.¶
No fewer than four silver candelabras, holding great waxen torches, served to illuminate this apartment. Yet let not modern beauty envy the magnificence of a Saxon princess.¶
Magnificence there was, with some rude attempt at taste; but of comfort there was little, and, being unknown, it was unmissed.#

FIGURE 3.18

6 **At the beginning of the second paragraph in the first text frame, place the cursor immediately before the word "The". Choose Type>Insert Break Character>Frame Break.**

All of the text following the break point is forced into the next frame. You can also press Shift-Enter (the Enter key on the numeric keypad) to insert a frame break.

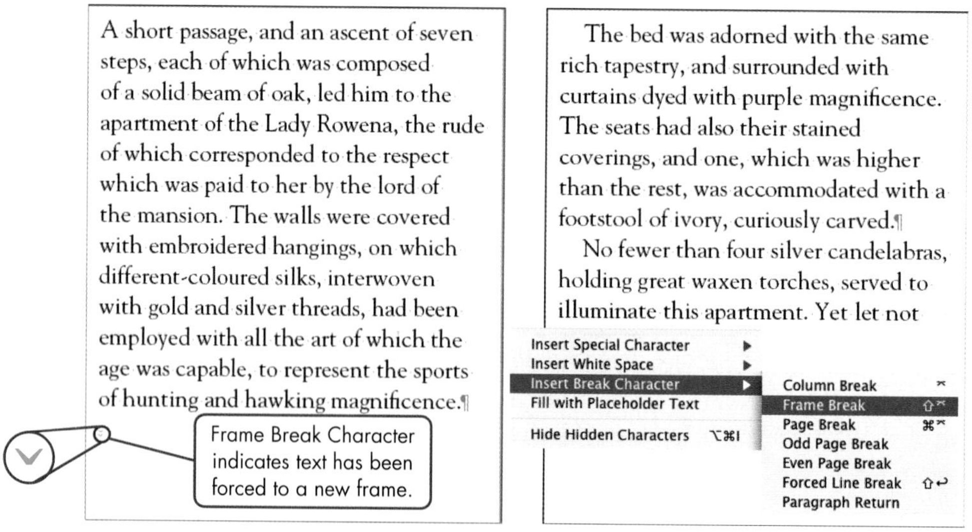

A short passage, and an ascent of seven steps, each of which was composed of a solid beam of oak, led him to the apartment of the Lady Rowena, the rude of which corresponded to the respect which was paid to her by the lord of the mansion. The walls were covered with embroidered hangings, on which different-coloured silks, interwoven with gold and silver threads, had been employed with all the art of which the age was capable, to represent the sports of hunting and hawking magnificence.¶

Frame Break Character indicates text has been forced to a new frame.

The bed was adorned with the same rich tapestry, and surrounded with curtains dyed with purple magnificence. The seats had also their stained coverings, and one, which was higher than the rest, was accommodated with a footstool of ivory, curiously carved.¶
No fewer than four silver candelabras, holding great waxen torches, served to illuminate this apartment. Yet let not

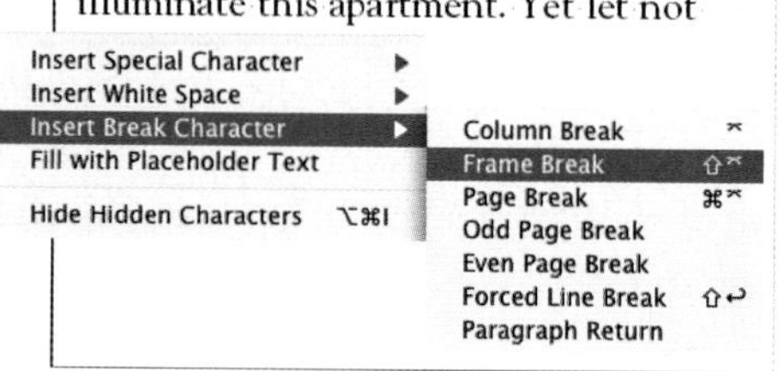

FIGURE 3.19

7 **Save the file in your WIP_03 folder and close it.**

To Extend Your Knowledge...

INSERTING BREAK CHARACTERS

You can insert a variety of break characters. You can access the Insert Break Character menu from the Type menu or by Control/right-clicking.

Type of Break	Keyboard Shortcut	Action
Column Break	Numeric Keypad Enter	Move text to the next column, or to the next linked text frame
Frame Break	Shift-Numeric Keypad Enter	Move text to the next linked text frame
Page Break	Command/Control-Numeric Keypad Enter	Move text to the next page.
Odd Page Break	None (available from menu only)	Force text to the next odd-numbered (right-hand) page
Even Page Break	None (available from menu only)	Force text to the next even-numbered (left-hand) page
Forced Line Break (Soft Return)	Shift-Return/Enter	Force a line break without starting a new paragraph
Paragraph Return	Return/Enter	Start a new paragraph

LESSON 3 Entering and Formatting Text

Much of what you will do in InDesign revolves around entering and formatting text. In an ideal world, you would receive all text in electronic form (such as a word-processing file) that is ready to place and format. More realistically, however, you will often manually type text into your InDesign pages. You will enter headlines and captions, set up program books with innumerable business-card ads, create stationery packages and custom forms (for which text is almost always entered by the person creating the pages), and sometimes type entire articles.

Regardless of whether you place text from an external file or type it directly into InDesign, you will need to format it after it is entered. Formatting can involve the basic assignment of character attributes, or zooming in on words and character combinations to fine-tune tracking and kerning. Effective formatting marks the difference between a competent page-layout artist and a master.

Enter and Format Text

1 **Create a new Letter-size document using the default margins. The Facing Pages and Master Text Frame options should not be checked.**

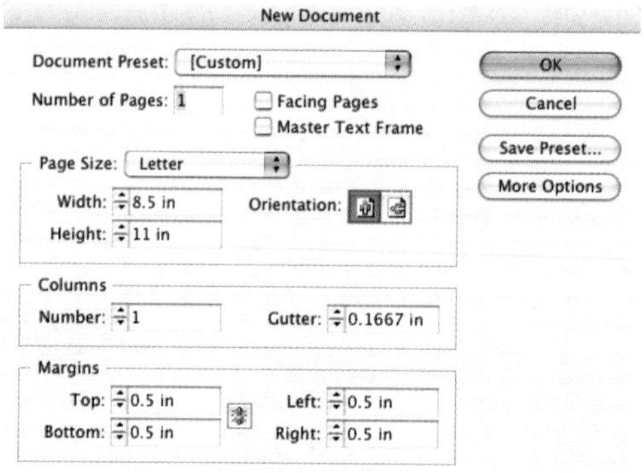

FIGURE 3.20

2 **Choose Type>Show Hidden Characters.**

If the menu offers the Hide Hidden Characters option instead, the hidden characters are already visible in your document. You can also toggle the visibility of hidden characters with the keyboard shortcut Command-Option-I (Macintosh) or Control-Alt-I (Windows).

3 **Choose View>Show Frame Edges.**

If the menu offers the Hide Frame Edges option instead, the frame edges are already visible in your document.

4 **Choose the Type tool in the Tools palette. Drag to create a text frame on the page's live area.**

You can access the Type tool by pressing the "T" key.

5 **Set the Control palette's proxy-reference point to the upper-left square. Change to the Selection tool. Enter the following values in the Control palette to position and size the text frame exactly: X: 0.5 in, Y: 0.5 in, W: 3.5 in, H: 3 in.**

By default, the proxy-reference point is set to the center. If you accidentally enter a frame's specifications with the proxy-reference point set to the center, you can simply select the upper-left proxy-reference point and re-enter the X and Y values. (You don't need to adjust the W and H values, because the size of the frame is unaffected by the proxy-reference point.)

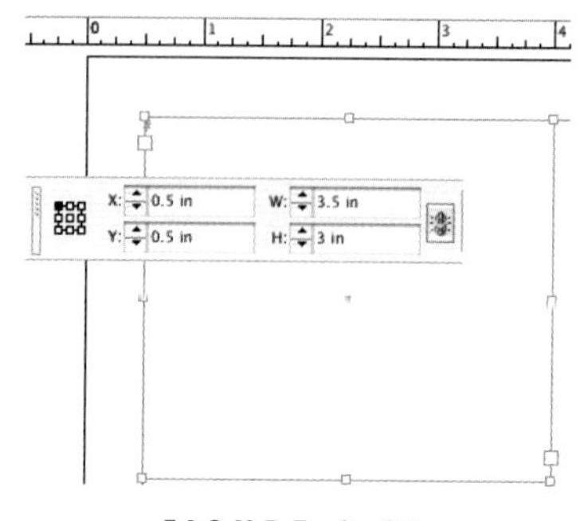

FIGURE 3.21

6 **Use the Type tool to click in the text frame and type "Alice's Adventures In Wonderland".**

7 **Select all the text with the Type tool. Use the Character Control palette to change the typeface to 36-pt ATC Oak Bold.**

FIGURE 3.22

8 **Place the insertion point just before the word "Adventures" (but after the space following "Alice's"). Press Shift-Return/Enter to insert a forced line break (soft return). Enter another soft return immediately before the word "Wonderland."**

A soft return forces the following text to the next line without creating a new paragraph. In this case, we needed to force the word "Adventures" to a new line to remove the hyphen. Typically, capitalized words and words in headlines should not be hyphenated.

9 **Select all the text, and enter "–20" in the Tracking field of the Character Control palette.**

As you remember from Project 2, tracking affects the overall character spacing between all characters selected. Negative tracking values tighten spacing, and positive values loosen it. You should track entire paragraphs rather than a single line within a paragraph to give your documents an even "color." Lines that are tracked too tightly appear dark in comparison to the rest of the page; lines that are tracked too loosely appear light.

10 **Place the cursor between the "W" and "o" and enter "–30" in the Kerning field. Kern any other letters that look poorly spaced.**

Kerning affects the spacing between individual characters. Be critical when you look at character spacing. A common typographer's trick is to "kern to white space" — in other words, to achieve an even amount of white space between each pair of letters. Character shape affects the visual amount of spacing. Don't forget to kern both sides of the apostrophe.

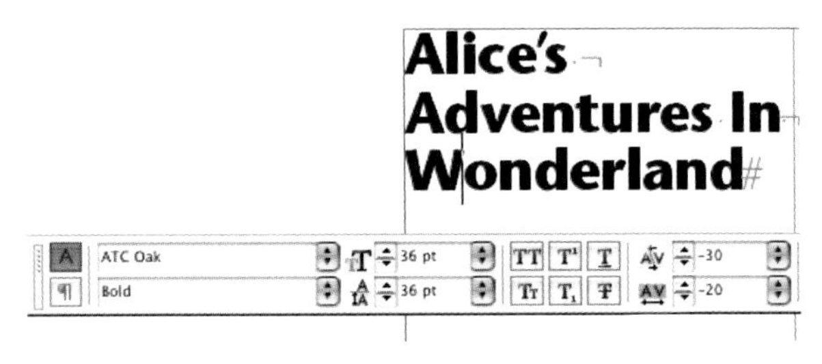

FIGURE 3.23

11 **Switch to the Selection tool. Move the text frame to the right side of the page.**

12 **Save the document as "working_text.indd" in your WIP_03 folder. Leave it open for the next exercise.**

Place and Format Text from a File

1 **In the open working_text.indd, create a new text frame with a Width of and Height of 2 inches. Position the new frame at X: 4.5 in, Y: 3.5 in.**

2 **Use the Type tool to click in the text frame. Choose File>Place to open the Place dialog box.**

You can also press Command/Control-D to access the Place dialog box.

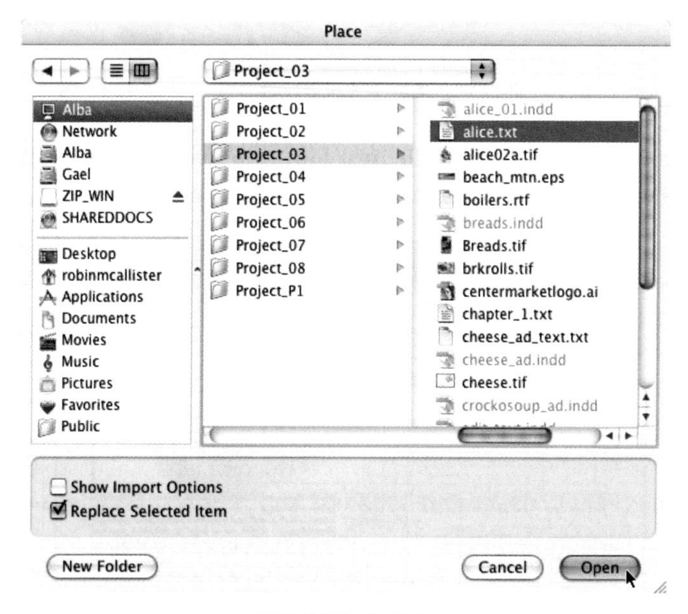

FIGURE 3.24

3 **Choose alice.txt from the file list. Make sure the Show Import Options box is not selected. Click OK.**

4 **With the Type tool still active in the frame, choose Edit>Select All to select all the text.**

Alternately, you could press Command/Control-A with the Type tool active in the frame to select all the text.

5 **From the Character Control palette, format the text as 12-pt ATC Laurel Book with 14-pt Leading.**

The red overset-text icon appears in the lower right of the text frame. This icon indicates that the text frame is not large enough to display all the text in the story.

6 **Hold down the Command/Control key, and then single-click the edge of the frame to select it. Drag the lower-right corner of the text frame to resize it so all the text fits within the frame. Release the Command/Control key.**

Holding down the Command/Control key temporarily switches to the Selection tool. Releasing the key reverts to the Type tool.

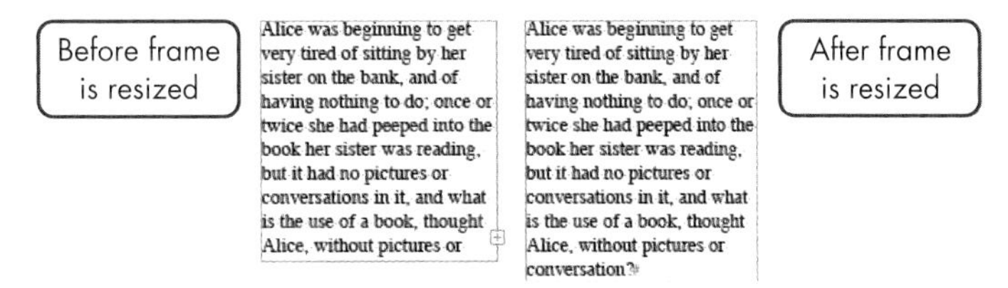

FIGURE 3.25

7 **Double-click the word "bank" in the first sentence. Type "fence".**

The selected text is replaced by the word "fence."

8 **Select the first word, "Alice". In the Character Control palette, select the Small Caps text style.**

The lowercase letters become small capitals, but the capital letter is unaffected.

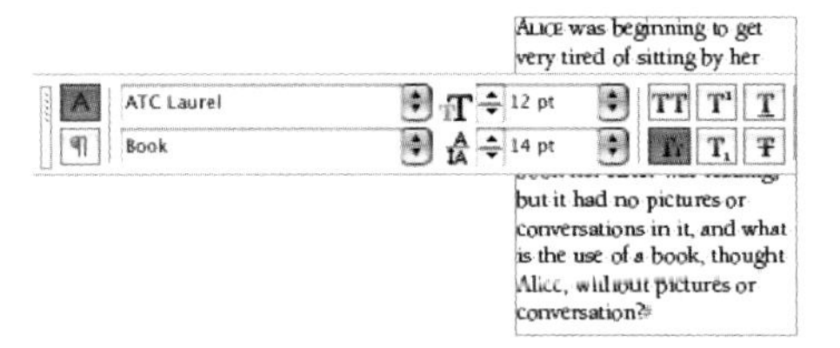

FIGURE 3.26

9 **Save your changes and leave the document open for the next exercise.**

To Extend Your Knowledge...

WORKING WITH TEXT FROM FILES

When you have only a few words to type into a document, it's easy to key them in yourself. When you have longer documents, files that contain numeric or technical data, or documents that include legal or medical terms, you should ask your client to provide the text files. This is the best way to avoid errors.

When you accept files from clients, however, you may open the Pandora's box of poor formatting. Either way, accepting text files from your clients gives you more time to make the document look good, without having to concern yourself with what it says.

LESSON 4 Using Special Characters and OpenType

Features such as small caps can be created in any typeface — but there's a considerable difference between true (or "cut") small caps and small caps that have been "faked" by simply reducing the size of the capital letters. Typically, PostScript and TrueType fonts offer "Expert" font sets to extend their typefaces, but having to switch fonts for small caps or oldstyle numerals is both time-consuming and expensive.

As OpenType becomes more common, better typography will evolve because special glyphs, such as small caps, will be readily accessible. Users will be able to access true small caps, build fractions, use ligatures across both platforms, and use swash caps and oldstyle numbers.

In this lesson, you learn to format with both PostScript/TrueType and with OpenType fonts. You discover that working with OpenType is easier, and it produces better results than the workarounds necessary with PostScript or TrueType technology.

Format "Fake" Small Caps

1 **In the open document, create a large text frame that extends the entire width of the page between the margins.**

2 **In 72-pt ATC Pine Normal, type two lowercase "x" characters. Use the Character Control palette to style the second "x" as a small cap.**

Typically, a small cap is the x-height of the font. You will use the "x" characters you typed to arrive at the correct percentage for a small cap.

3 **In the Text pane of the Preferences dialog box (accessed from the InDesign>Edit menu), change the Small Cap Size field to 60%.**

This setting needs to be adjusted manually for every different typeface so the small cap character is the same size as the lowercase "x." For the ATC Pine Normal typeface, the correct setting is 60%. You can see in the document window that creating a small cap in this manner distorts the letterform. The heavy stroke of the small cap "x" is noticeably lighter than that of the lowercase "x."

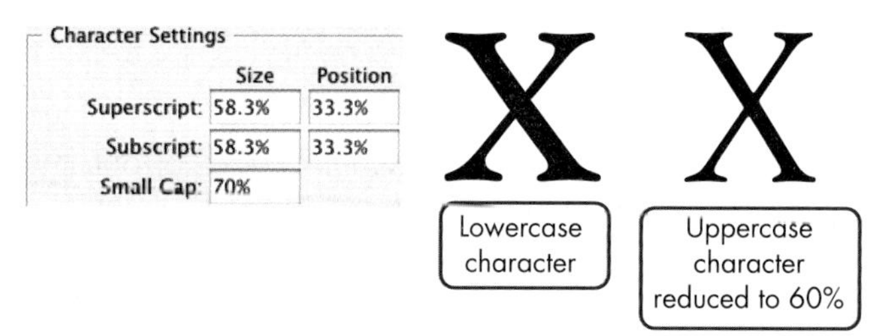

FIGURE 3.27

4 **On the line below these characters, type three more lowercase "x" characters. Style the first two as ATC Laurel Book and the third as ATC Laurel Medium. Style the last two characters as small caps.**

The lowercase "x" is considerably larger than the two characters styled as small caps. Obviously, the same preference setting does not work for both ATC Pine and ATC Laurel. This indicates that you should not use both fonts with small caps in the same document. If you did, you would need to manually alter one of them (use the Control palette to scale the type horizontally and vertically).

5 **Return to the Text pane of the Preferences dialog box. Change the Small Cap Size field to 68%.**

This is the appropriate setting for the ATC Laurel font. The percentage is greater, so the ATC Laurel small cap does not look nearly as distorted, as does the ATC Pine small cap. Notice that the ATC Laurel Medium small cap almost exactly matches the boldness of the lowercase "x" in ATC Laurel Book. For typefaces that have "intermediate" weights (such as Medium and Semibold), you can often use a slightly bolder font to create ***faux*** (fake) small caps that approximate the appearance of characters of a lighter weight. For example, when Medium is reduced in size, it is often approximately the weight of Book.

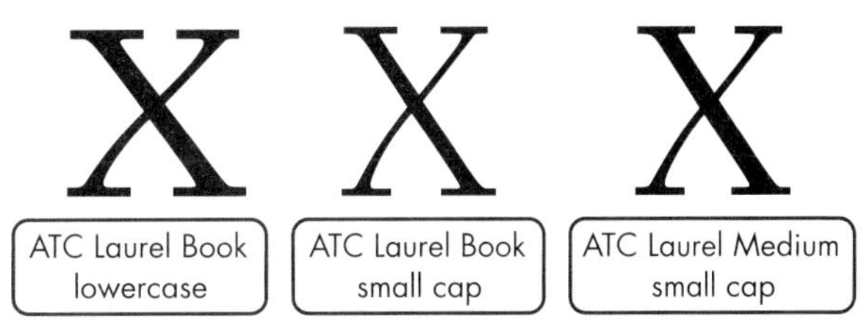

FIGURE 3.28

6 **Change the Font of the ATC Pine characters to Adobe Caslon Pro Regular.**

The small cap is slightly larger and heavier than the lowercase "x." If you adjust the small-cap size in the Preferences dialog box, nothing happens, because this is an OpenType font with a true small cap glyph. No setup is required to use OpenType small caps, unlike their PostScript and TrueType counterparts.

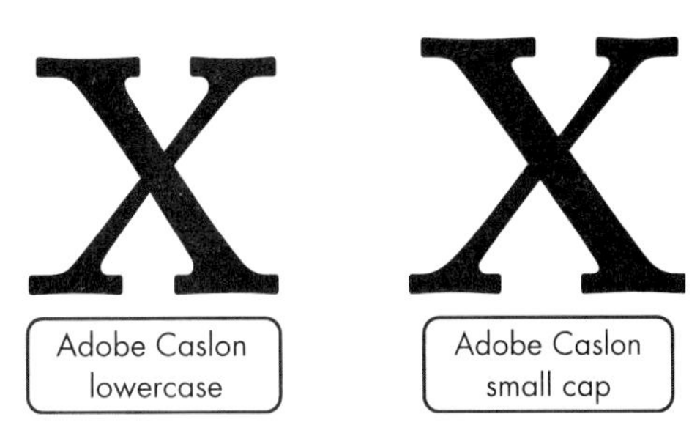

FIGURE 3.29

7 **Save your changes and keep the file open.**

Work with Special Characters

1 **In the open working_text.indd, insert the text cursor after the word "Wonderland" in the headline frame.**

2 **Press Return/Enter.**

This inserts a paragraph return, also called a hard return.

3 **Change the Font to ATC Oak Normal, 12/15. Set the Tracking to 0.**

Remember that 12/15 means Font Size of 12 over Leading of 15. No text is currently selected, so these settings apply to any text that you type.

4 **Choose Type>Insert Special Character. Choose Em Dash from the menu that appears.**

An em dash appears at the text-insertion point. You can use this menu to add a variety of special characters to your document. You can use the similar Type>Insert White Space menu to add different types of spaces.

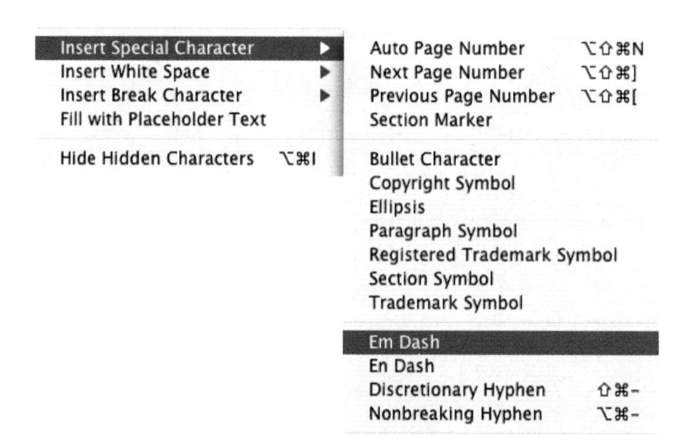

FIGURE 3.30

5 **Type "by Lewis Carroll", and then press Shift-Return/Enter.**

The resulting line break (soft return) begins a new line of text without creating a new paragraph. This allows paragraph formatting to apply to both lines, even if only one line is selected.

6 **Choose Type>Insert Special Character>Copyright Symbol, and then type [space] "[Public Domain]".**

FIGURE 3.31

7 **Save your changes and close the file.**

Use Fractions and Glyphs

1 **Open breads.indd from the Project_03 folder. Navigate to the Page 40–41 spread.**

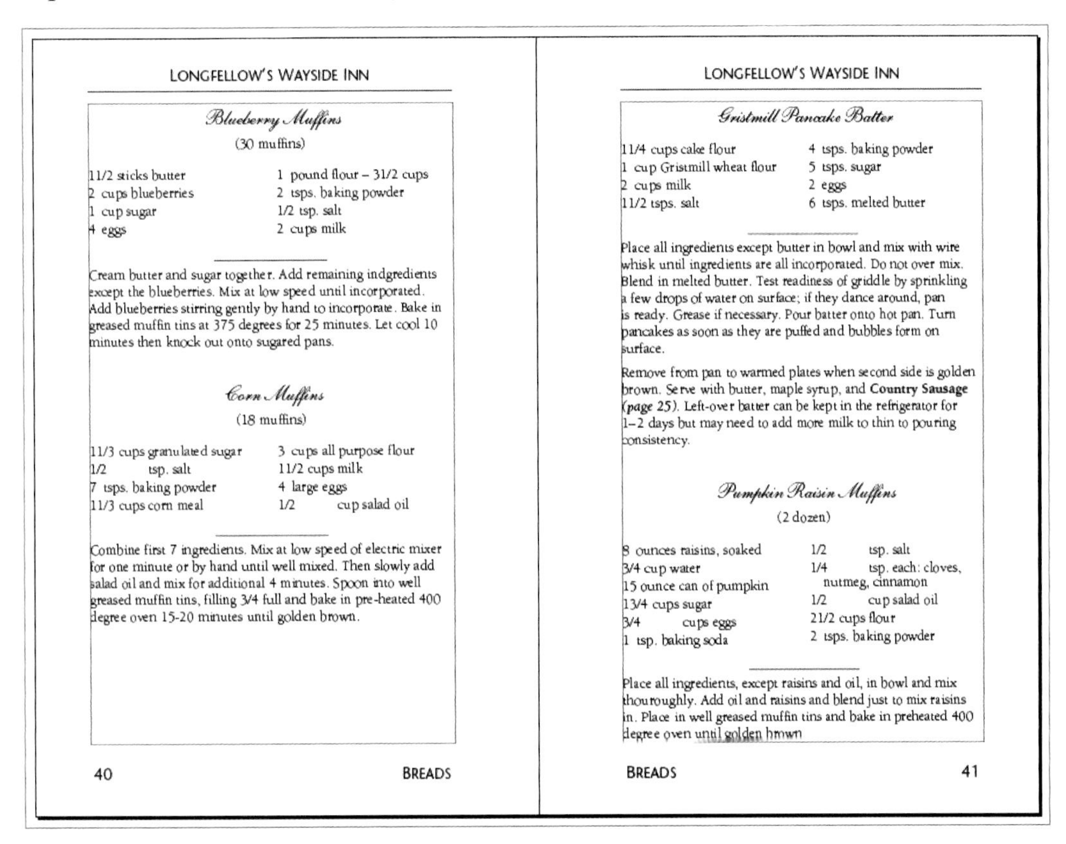

LONGFELLOW'S WAYSIDE INN

Blueberry Muffins

(30 muffins)

11/2 sticks butter
2 cups blueberries
1 cup sugar
4 eggs

1 pound flour – 31/2 cups
2 tsps. baking powder
1/2 tsp. salt
2 cups milk

Cream butter and sugar together. Add remaining indgredients except the blueberries. Mix at low speed until incorporated. Add blueberries stirring gently by hand to incorporate. Bake in greased muffin tins at 375 degrees for 25 minutes. Let cool 10 minutes then knock out onto sugared pans.

Corn Muffins

(18 muffins)

11/3 cups granulated sugar
1/2 tsp. salt
7 tsps. baking powder
11/3 cups corn meal

3 cups all purpose flour
11/2 cups milk
4 large eggs
1/2 cup salad oil

Combine first 7 ingredients. Mix at low speed of electric mixer for one minute or by hand until well mixed. Then slowly add salad oil and mix for additional 4 minutes. Spoon into well greased muffin tins, filling 3/4 full and bake in pre-heated 400 degree oven 15-20 minutes until golden brown.

40 BREADS

LONGFELLOW'S WAYSIDE INN

Gristmill Pancake Batter

11/4 cups cake flour
1 cup Gristmill wheat flour
2 cups milk
11/2 tsps. salt

4 tsps. baking powder
5 tsps. sugar
2 eggs
6 tsps. melted butter

Place all ingredients except butter in bowl and mix with wire whisk until ingredients are all incorporated. Do not over mix. Blend in melted butter. Test readiness of griddle by sprinkling a few drops of water on surface; if they dance around, pan is ready. Grease if necessary. Pour batter onto hot pan. Turn pancakes as soon as they are puffed and bubbles form on surface.

Remove from pan to warmed plates when second side is golden brown. Serve with butter, maple syrup, and **Country Sausage** (*page 25*). Left-over batter can be kept in the refrigerator for 1–2 days but may need to add more milk to thin to pouring consistency.

Pumpkin Raisin Muffins

(2 dozen)

8 ounces raisins, soaked
3/4 cup water
15 ounce can of pumpkin
13/4 cups sugar
3/4 cups eggs
1 tsp. baking soda

1/2 tsp. salt
1/4 tsp. each: cloves, nutmeg, cinnamon
1/2 cup salad oil
21/2 cups flour
2 tsps. baking powder

Place all ingredients, except raisins and oil, in bowl and mix thouroughly. Add oil and raisins and blend just to mix raisins in. Place in well greased muffin tins and bake in preheated 400 degree oven until golden brown

BREADS 41

FIGURE 3.32

2 **In the Text pane of the Preferences dialog box, set the Superscript fields to 60% Size and 30% Position. Set the Subscript fields to 60% Size and 0% Position. Leave the Small Cap Size field at 85%. Click OK.**

Many recipes include fractions, none of which are part of the standard Macintosh character set, and only certain fractions are included in standard Windows sets. These superscript and subscript settings allow you to create fractions with a numerator at the proper height and a denominator on the baseline.

Character Settings

	Size	Position
Superscript:	60%	30%
Subscript:	60%	0%
Small Cap:	85%	

FIGURE 3.33

3 **In the first ingredient of the Blueberry Muffins recipe, highlight the second "1" and style it as a Superscript. Highlight the "2" and style it as a Subscript. Copy and paste the fraction to the other fractions in the recipe.**

This process could be time-consuming if you had to repeat it for the entire cookbook. For common ***case fractions,*** such as 1/4, 1/2, and 3/4, Windows users can instead type (respectively) Alt-0188, Alt-0189, and Alt-0190 (using the numeric keypad). Some recipes call for measurements of 1/3 cup (which is not in the standard character set), however, so you are generally better off using piece fractions. As the name implies, ***piece fractions*** are pieced together from numerators, a fraction slash, and denominators for consistency.

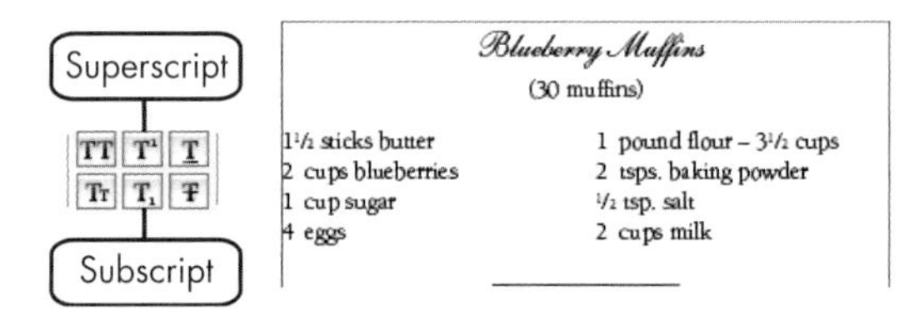

FIGURE 3.34

4 **Select all the text in the Corn Muffins recipe and change it to Adobe Caslon Pro Regular.**

Adobe Caslon Pro is an OpenType font, so it either has each fraction built in (as a case fraction), or it can automatically generate the piece fraction to match the exact appearance of a case fraction.

5 **Turn off the superscript and subscript that you previously applied to the fractions in the recipe.**

6 **Select each of the fractions in this recipe. From the Control palette Options menu, choose OpenType>Fractions.**

You can see in this one recipe how easy it is to create good-looking fractions in OpenType. Now you're ready to convert the rest of the section to OpenType.

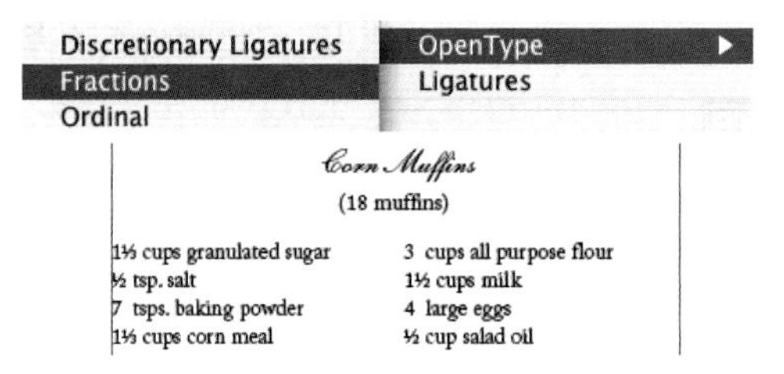

FIGURE 3.35

7 **Select all the text (excluding the recipe names, running head, and running feet) in the document and change it to Adobe Caslon Pro.**

8 **Create all fractions within the recipes as piece fractions, choosing OpenType>Fractions from the Control palette Options menu. Leave the fractions in the text as whole-number fractions, as shown below.**

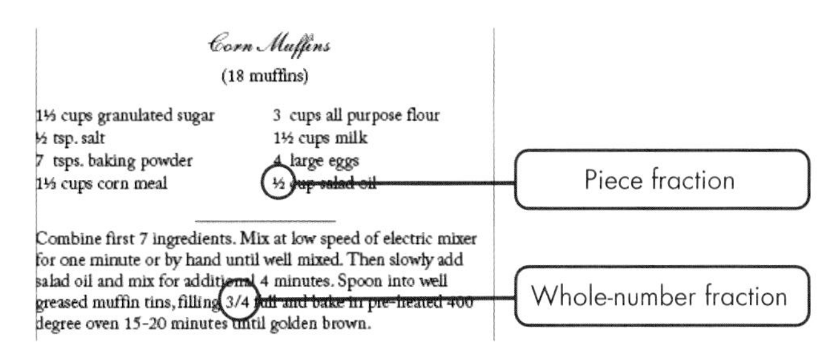

FIGURE 3.36

9 **Style the type that appears bold in the text as Semibold, rather than Bold.**

Bold is too heavy for this application. Applying the Semibold style provides a gentler transition.

10 **Place your text cursor in the space directly above the Corn Muffins recipe. Choose Type>Glyphs (the font should be Adobe Caslon Pro). Click Ornaments to display only the ornament selections.**

You could review all the glyphs in the font, but it is much simpler to view only the choices you really want to see.

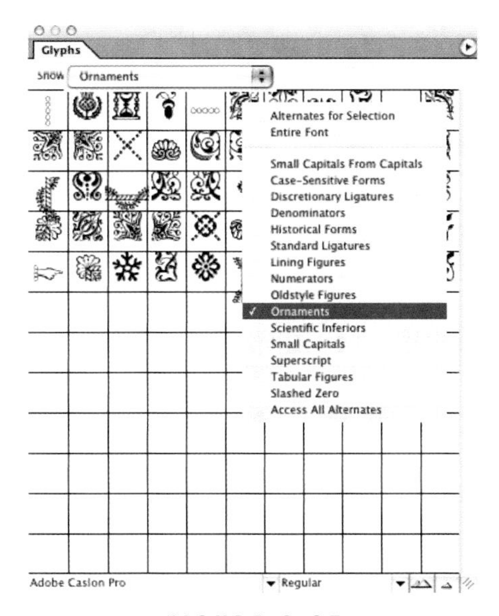

FIGURE 3.37

11 **Double-click the fourth ornament in the first row to select it. In the Control palette, shift the Baseline of the ornament to –8 pt.**

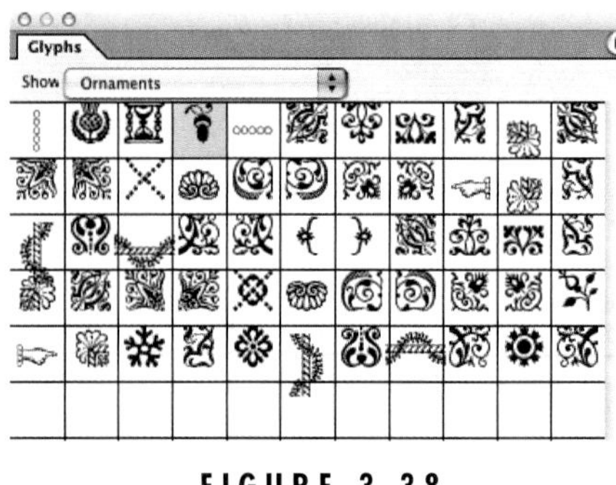

FIGURE 3.38

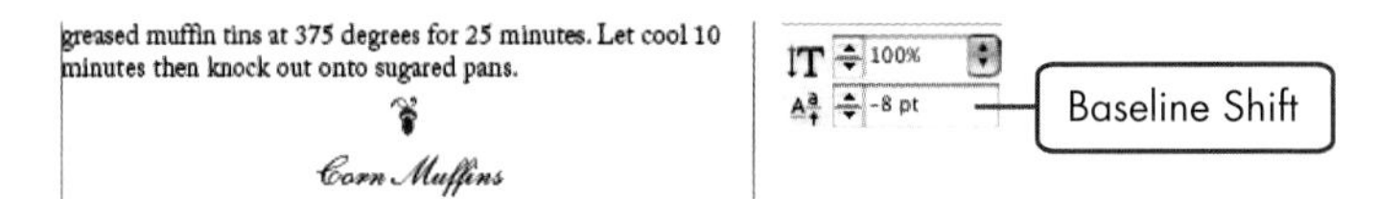

greased muffin tins at 375 degrees for 25 minutes. Let cool 10
minutes then knock out onto sugared pans.
Corn Muffins
100%
-8 pt
Baseline Shift

FIGURE 3.39

12 **Repeat Steps 10–11 to insert the same ornament above the Pumpkin Raisin Muffins recipe on Page 41.**

13 **Save your changes and close the file.**

To Extend Your Knowledge...

MORE ON FRACTIONS

There are two types of fractions that you may need to use when working in InDesign. A case fraction is a single glyph that is accessed through the Glyphs palette or with a keystroke. A piece fraction is one that you piece together using a numerator, a fraction slash, and a denominator. The image below illustrates the similarity in appearance of case (left) and piece (right) fractions.

$^{1}/_{3}$ $^{23}/_{64}$

FIGURE 3.40

A fraction slash has a different angle from a standard slash (called a ***solidus***). You can access a fraction slash on a Macintosh by pressing Option-Shift-1; it is not available in the Windows character set unless you are using an OpenType font.

LESSON 5 Formatting Paragraphs

While the appearance and style applied to text influence the tone and type color of a page, the formatting applied to entire paragraphs affects how your page looks and reads. Paragraph formatting can include text alignment, indents, spacing above and below paragraphs, drop caps, hyphenation and justification, widow and orphan control, and paragraph rules (lines).

The manner in which text is ***aligned*** affects its readability. For the most part, it is easier to read left-aligned text that has an unjustified right margin. This alignment maintains even spacing between words, and it allows your eye to return to the same place on the margin at every new line. Right-aligned text is often used when a caption appears to the left of an image; the text being read is short, and the lack of a consistent point of origin for each line in not overly taxing on the eyes. Centered text is used for invitations and short blurbs, in addition to headlines; it should not be used for long passages of text. Justified text, where text is forced flush to both margins, used to be the norm. Modern design opts for even word spacing as an aid to readability; however, when lines are long enough (as in books) justified text can be managed so it is easy to read, with no unsightly holes between words.

The King and Queen of Hearts were seated on their throne when they arrived, with a great crowd assembled about them — all sorts of little birds and beasts, as well as the whole pack of cards: the Knave was standing before them, in chains, with a soldier on each side to guard him; and near the King was the White Rabbit, with a trumpet in one hand, and a scroll of parchment in the other.
The King and Queen of Hearts were seated on their throne when they arrived, with a great crowd assembled about them — all sorts of little birds and beasts, as well as the whole pack of cards: the Knave was standing before them, in chains, with a soldier on each side to guard him; and near the King was the White Rabbit, with a trumpet in one hand, and a scroll of parchment in the other.
Left-aligned text
Right-aligned text
Justified text
Centered text
The King and Queen of Hearts were seated on their throne when they arrived, with a great crowd assembled about them — all sorts of little birds and beasts, as well as the whole pack of cards: the Knave was standing before them, in chains, with a soldier on each side to guard him; and near the King was the White Rabbit, with a trumpet in one hand, and a scroll of parchment in the other.
The King and Queen of Hearts were seated on their throne when they arrived, with a great crowd assembled about them — all sorts of little birds and beasts, as well as the whole pack of cards: the Knave was standing before them, in chains, with a soldier on each side to guard him; and near the King was the White Rabbit, with a trumpet in one hand, and a scroll of parchment in the other.

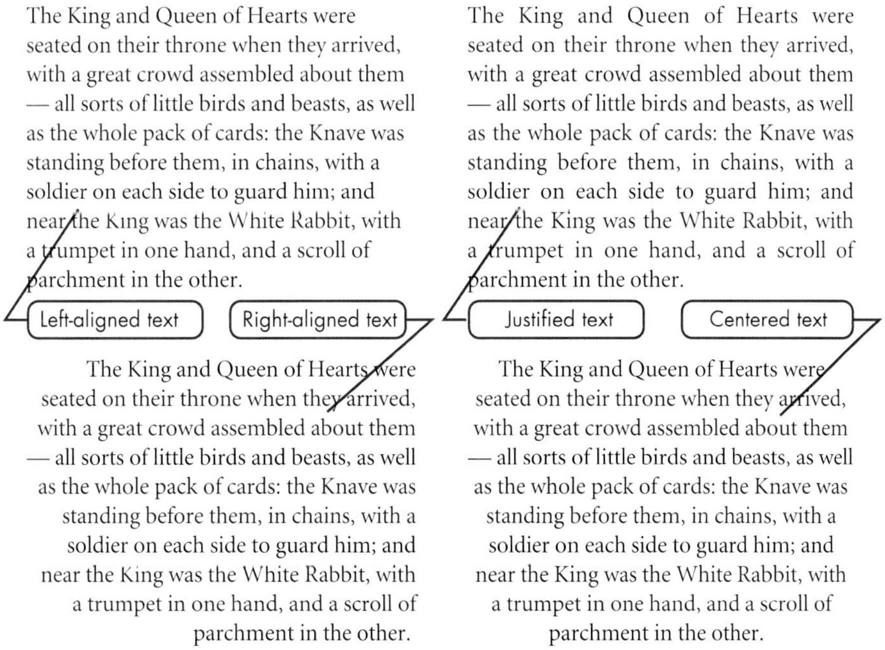

FIGURE 3.41

Format an Ad

1 **With no document open, check the Apply Leading to Entire Paragraphs box in the Text Preferences pane. Click OK.**

When this box is checked, leading values apply to the entire paragraph in which the cursor is positioned. If it is not checked, leading applies only to the line in which the cursor is placed, or to those specific lines in which text is highlighted.

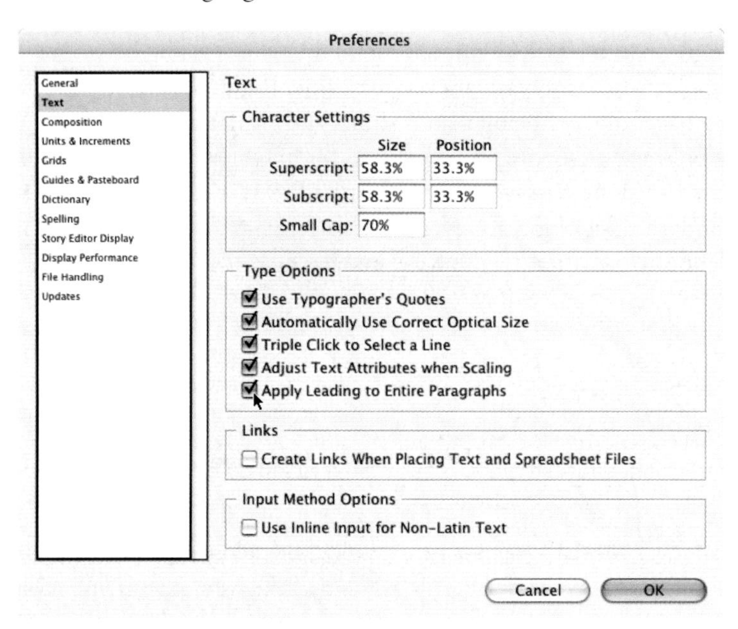

FIGURE 3.42

2 **Open crockosoup_ad.indd from the Project_03 folder.**

When you worked on a similar ad in Project 1, the text was preformatted for you. In this exercise, you apply formats on your own.

FIGURE 3.43

3 **Select all the text in the top text frame. Style it as ATC Laurel Bold Italic, 30/33. Adjust the Kerning and Tracking until you are satisfied with the settings.**

In Figure 3.40, the Tracking was set to –5; the "jo" and "oy" combinations in "Enjoy" and the "fo" combination in "comfortable" were kerned –20, –40, and –70, respectively.

4 **Select all the text in the frame containing body text. Style it as ATC Laurel Book, 10/12.**

5 **Choose Window>Type & Tables>Paragraph.**

The Paragraph palette appears. You can directly access the Paragraph palette by pressing Command-Option-T (Macintosh) or Control-Alt-T (Windows).

6 **From the Paragraph palette Options menu, choose Adobe Paragraph Composer.**

Adobe Paragraph Composer is an advanced text-justification engine that reviews all lines in the paragraph, and then makes line-break decisions based on established hyphenation and justification standards. You can use this feature when you want the best overall fit for the document. For the times when you want to make your own design-based decisions, you should use the Adobe Single-Line Composer. InDesign defaults to using the Paragraph Composer.

7 **With hidden characters showing (Type>Show Hidden Characters), select the second through the last paragraphs of body text. Use the Paragraph palette to assign a First-Line Indent of 1 pica (1p).**

Your measurements are set to inches, so InDesign automatically translates the 1-pica setting into its equivalent in inches.

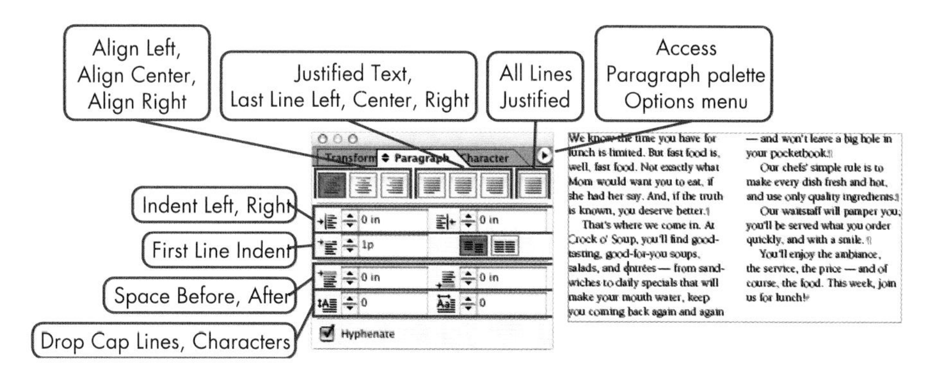

FIGURE 3.44

8 **Click the cursor in the first paragraph. Use the Paragraph palette to assign a 2-Line Drop Cap for a single character.**

If you wish, you can apply a color from the Swatches palette to the drop-cap character by selecting the character with the text cursor, opening the Swatches palette, and clicking the color of your choice.

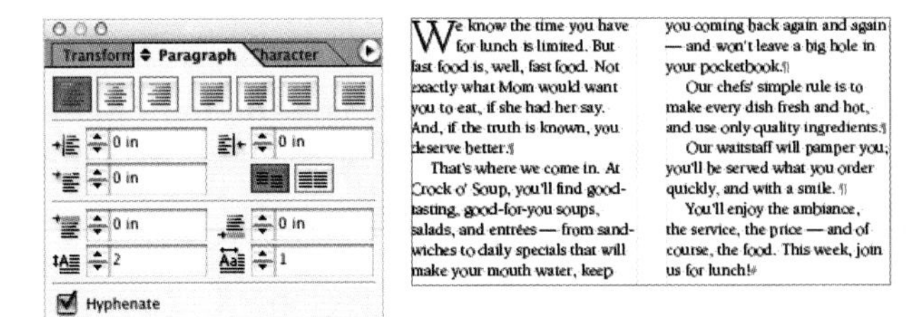

FIGURE 3.45

9 **Select all the paragraphs in this two-column text frame. In the Paragraph palette, select Justify, Last Line Left (the fourth alignment icon).**

Type is usually easier to read when it is left aligned. Some people, however, prefer the squared-off look of justified text. Notice that some of the lines have a lot of space between the words, making the line look space-heavy.

10 **In the second paragraph, three lines in a row end with hyphens. Place the cursor in front of the word "salad." Choose Type>Insert Special Character>Discretionary Hyphen.**

A ***discretionary hyphen*** placed at the beginning of a word prevents that word from hyphenating. When the word "salad" is forced to the next line, that line appears space-heavy, but it's still an improvement over the "ladder" formed by three hyphens in a row. You can also insert a discretionary hyphen by pressing Command/Control-Shift-Hyphen.

11 **Triple-click the words "Crock O' Soup" in the third text frame. Style it as 24-pt ATC Oak Bold, and center it in the frame.**

12 **Select the last line (containing the address and phone number). Style it as ATC Oak Normal, 10/15, Centered.**

13 **Use the Type>Insert Special Character menu to insert bullet characters that are centered in the spaces between "Row" and "Culloden", and between the zip code and phone number.**

You can also press Option/Alt-8 to create a bullet character.

14 **Click outside the text frame and press the "W" key to view your finished ad. You can also click the Preview Mode icon at the bottom right of the Tools palette.**

You can toggle in and out of Preview mode by pressing the "W" key. This command works regardless of which tool is active. If the Type tool is active, however, you need to make sure no text frame is active.

FIGURE 3.46

15 **Save the file in your WIP_03 folder and close it.**

Format an Invoice

1 **Open invoice.indd from the Project_03 folder.**

Invoice Nº: 536
Please Retain this Document for your Records
Sold To: Date: 2/12/2002
Design Works LLC The Computer Store
109 Too Darned Cold Lane 127 Icicle Road
St. Paul, MN 55387 Minneapolis, MN 55401
(651) 555-7799(612) 555-1784
Item Nº Description Price Quantity Ext.
8528 Power Macintosh G4 867MHz $2495.00 1
$2495.00
8942 Apple Studio Display 17″ LCD $995.00 1
$995.00
7230 Apple iPod MP3 player $399.00 1 $399.00
2732 Harmon-Kardon SoundSticks $299.00 1
$299.00
Subtotal: $4188.00
MN State Sales Tax @ 6.5%: $272.22
TOTAL DUE $4460.22
Terms: 2/10, Net 30.
All invoices are due and payable upon receipt, unless other payment terms have been arranged in advance and are stipulated. In no event shall credit be extended for more than thirty (30) days. Delivery of product(s) is F.O.B. Minneapolis, MN.

FIGURE 3.47

2 **Choose Type>Show Hidden Characters.**

Take a moment to see how the document is put together. In its current state, it looks messy, but you can fix that. You can use the Character and Paragraph palettes or the Character and Paragraph options in the Control palette to make the necessary adjustments. The keyboard shortcut to show hidden characters is Command-Option-I or Control-Alt-I.

3 **Select the word "Invoice" in the first line. Use the Character Control palette to change the Size to 30 pt with Automatic Leading.**

4 **Select "No 536". Change the Size to 8 pt.**

Notice that text with a smaller point size in the same line always remains on the baseline.

5 **Select the entire second line and set it at 8/10.**

6 **Click the cursor in the first line. Use the Paragraph Control palette to set the Space After to 9 pt.**

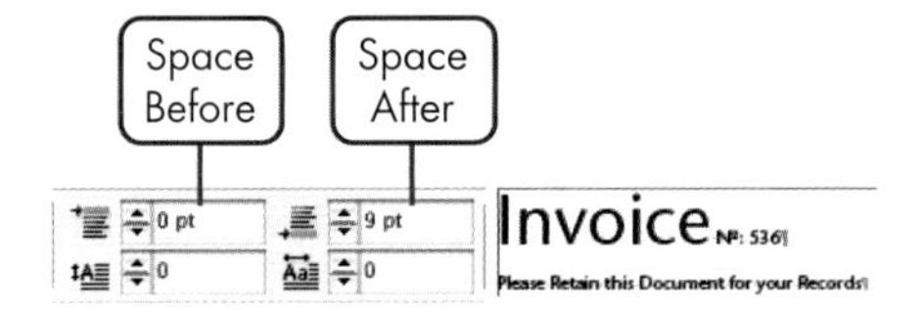

FIGURE 3.48

7 **Save the file as "invoice.indd" in your WIP_03 folder. Leave it open for the next exercise.**

Create Shaded Headings

1 **In the open invoice.indd, place the cursor in the second line. Choose Paragraph Rules from the Paragraph palette Options menu or the Paragraph Control palette Options menu. Check the Preview box if it is not already selected.**

You can also access the Paragraph Rules dialog box by pressing Command-Option-J/Control-Alt-J. When the Preview box is selected, any settings you define in the Paragraph Rules dialog box are immediately visible in your document.

2 **Choose Rule Above in the menu at the top left. Check the Rule On box. Set a 14-pt Weight, and set the Color to Black.**

The text is also black, so you can't see it anymore.

3 **In the Paragraph Rules dialog box, set the Tint field to 20%. Set the Offset field to –4 pt. Click OK.**

The Tint setting changes the line to gray. You can control the vertical position of a rule with the offset.

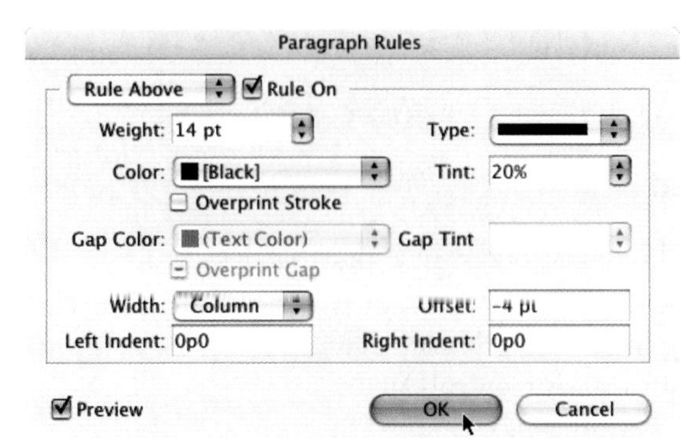

FIGURE 3.49

4 In the Paragraph Control palette, set the Space After to 15 pt.

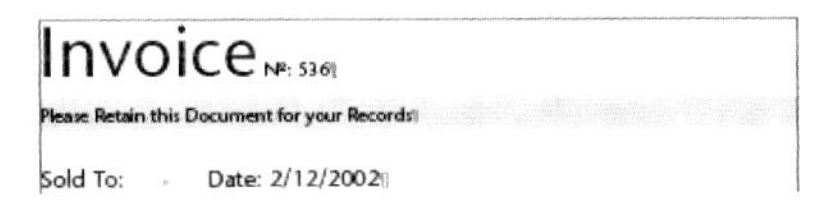

FIGURE 3.50

5 Select the line starting with "Item N°" and apply the same shaded rule that you applied in Steps 2–3.

6 Set the Space Before to 15 pt, and the Space After to 9 pt.

7 Place the cursor in the "Subtotal:" line. Set the Space Before to 9 pt. Apply a gray-shaded rule similar to the two rules you already made.

8 Place the cursor in the "TOTAL DUE" line. Apply a shaded rule with a Tint value of 40%.

9 Style the "Terms" line 8/10, 15-pt Space Before, 18-pt Space After, with a 1-pt rule below, Text Color, 11-pt Offset, and Left and Right Indents of 9p0. Click OK.

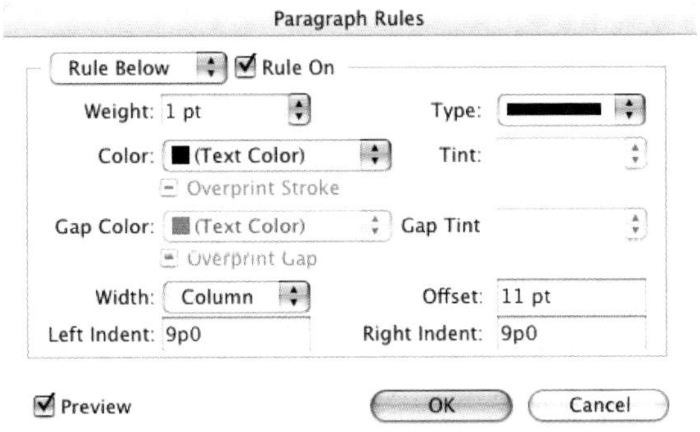

Paragraph Rules
Rule Below
Rule On
Weight: 1 pt
Type:
Color: (Text Color)
Tint:
Overprint Stroke
Gap Color: (Text Color)
Gap Tint
Overprint Gap
Width: Column
Offset: 11 pt
Left Indent: 9p0
Right Indent: 9p0
Preview
OK
Cancel

FIGURE 3.51

10 Click the Center icon to center the line of text.

11 Style the last paragraph as 8/10, Justified, with the Last Line Flushed Left.

12 Save your changes, and leave the file open for the next exercise.

To Extend Your Knowledge...

SAVE THE FORMATTING FOR INDESIGN

When you're creating text in a word processor, there is a real temptation to attempt to "format" the document you are typing by adding spaces for paragraph indents or even pressing the tab key several times to "align" columns. Unfortunately, when you place the text in InDesign, you must remove all the extraneous elements introduced by the word processor.

Another blunder often introduced when typing text is double-spacing between lines. As you have seen, adding space above and below paragraphs is quick and easy — and you can control the interline spacing to make text fit an area. Double spaces, similar to extra tabs, should be removed before you begin formatting a document in InDesign.

LESSON 6 Setting Tabs

Tabs constitute a very common type element. They are used to align columns of text that are not contained in a table. It's important to use tabs correctly — know when to use them, and when not to use them. For example, many people mistakenly use the Spacebar to align text, resulting in wavy, unprofessional-looking columns; instead, they should use tabs to accurately align text in a column to ensure the same indent in every line. Many beginners mistakenly use tabs to indent paragraphs, but it's better to define indentations as a paragraph characteristic.

You can access the Tabs palette by choosing Type>Tabs. If you're working on a text frame at the time you activate the Tabs palette, the palette is automatically positioned directly above the active frame. You can manually position the Tabs palette at the top of a frame by first selecting the frame, and then clicking the magnet icon at the right edge of the palette, or by clicking the magnet icon when the Type tool is in the frame. This feature does not work when the text frame is positioned at the page margins.

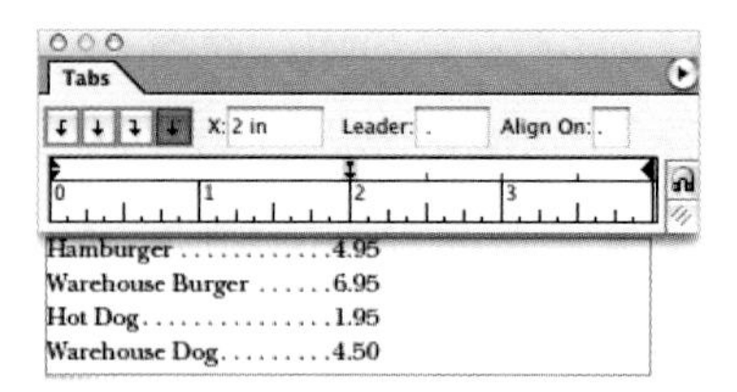

FIGURE 3.52

Tabs may align left, center, right, or to a defined character (the decimal, or period, is the default). A ***tab leader*** is a series of characters that follows a tab marker and ends at another character. For example, a page number in a table of contents might be preceded by a line of periods. You can leave the tab leader blank, or you can define it as any combination of characters (including spaces).

When you first begin typing, you needn't worry about precise tab settings. In the preliminary stages of design, you can set tabs at approximate positions. InDesign makes it easy to reposition the tabs later in the process, with interactive tab settings that allow you to see the effects of your changes immediately.

Apply Tabs

1 **In the open invoice.indd, activate the Selection tool. Choose Type>Tabs to display the Tabs palette. Click the magnet icon at the right side of the Tabs palette.**

Clicking the magnet icon precisely positions the palette over the selected text. If there is insufficient room for the Tabs palette above the frame, the palette will not position itself. You can also access the Tabs palette by pressing Command/Control-Shift-T.

2 **Select the five lines of text beginning with "Sold To".**

3 **Click the Right-Justified tab icon, and then click in the clear area above the ruler tick marks.**

This action sets an initial tab.

4 **Drag the tab marker until the X value reads 27p.**

When the cursor is positioned over the ruler tick marks, it turns into a hand, which allows you to scroll the ruler. When the cursor is positioned in the blank area above the ruler marks, it changes into an arrow pointer you can use to set tabs. Notice the vertical black line that appears on the page when you drag a tab marker along the tab ruler; this is an excellent visual aid for placing tabs.

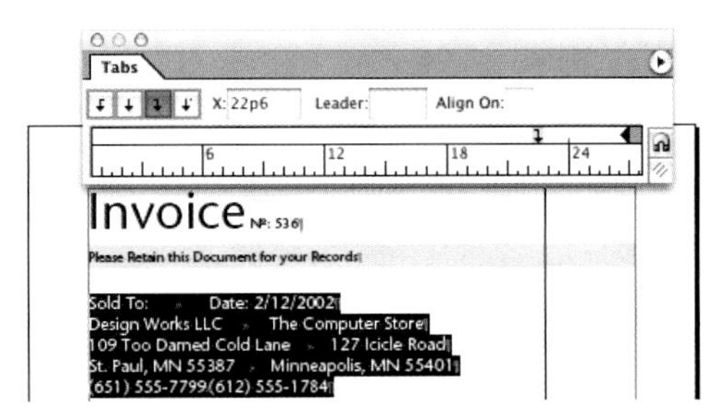

FIGURE 3.53

5 **Select the next five lines of text, beginning with "Item Nº." Use the Tabs palette to set Left tabs at 3p6 and 21p0, and Decimal tabs at 18p0 and 25p0.**

The decimal points in the list of prices are now precisely aligned with one another. To position tabs, you can click the tab markers in the palette and drag, or click anywhere in the clear area above the ruler tick marks and type the tab positions in the X field.

6 **The shaded "Item" heading needs some refinement. Click anywhere in this line. Click the tab marker over the word "Price." Click the Align-Center tab icon to convert it to a Centered tab. Set the tab to 17p6.**

7 **Click the tab marker over the word "Quantity." Change it to a Centered tab, and position it over the values in the column.**

If you wish, you can change the word "Quantity" to the more space-efficient "Qty." to improve the appearance of this header.

8 **Right-align the tab for the word "Ext." and adjust its position visually.**

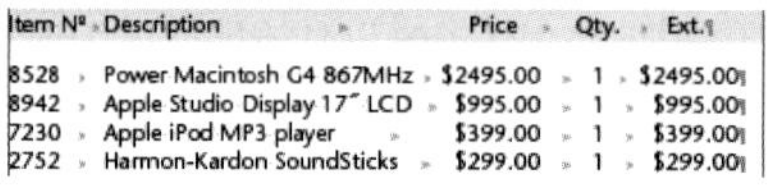

Item Nº	Description	Price	Qty.	Ext.
8528	Power Macintosh G4 867MHz	$2495.00	1	$2495.00
8942	Apple Studio Display 17" LCD	$995.00	1	$995.00
7230	Apple iPod MP3 player	$399.00	1	$399.00
2752	Harmon-Kardon SoundSticks	$299.00	1	$299.00

FIGURE 3.54

9 **Select the Subtotal, Tax, and Total lines. Set a Decimal tab at 25p0. Type a tab character before the dollar amounts on each line.**

Subtotal:	$4188.00
MN State Sales Tax @ 6.5%:	$272.22
TOTAL DUE	$4460.22

FIGURE 3.55

10 **Save your changes and close the document.**

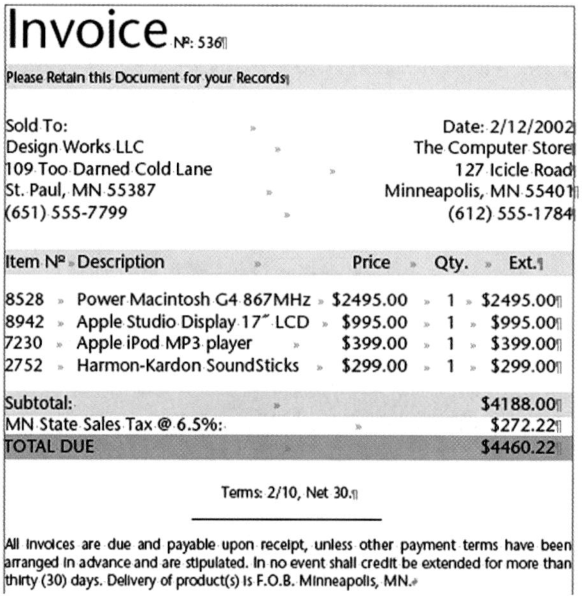

Invoice Nº: 536

Please Retain this Document for your Records

Sold To: Date: 2/12/2002
Design Works LLC The Computer Store
109 Too Darned Cold Lane 127 Icicle Road
St. Paul, MN 55387 Minneapolis, MN 55401
(651) 555-7799 (612) 555-1784

Item Nº	Description	Price	Qty.	Ext.
8528	Power Macintosh G4 867MHz	$2495.00	1	$2495.00
8942	Apple Studio Display 17" LCD	$995.00	1	$995.00
7230	Apple iPod MP3 player	$399.00	1	$399.00
2752	Harmon-Kardon SoundSticks	$299.00	1	$299.00

Subtotal:	$4188.00
MN State Sales Tax @ 6.5%:	$272.22
TOTAL DUE	$4460.22

Terms: 2/10, Net 30.

All invoices are due and payable upon receipt, unless other payment terms have been arranged in advance and are stipulated. In no event shall credit be extended for more than thirty (30) days. Delivery of product(s) is F.O.B. Minneapolis, MN.

FIGURE 3.56

To Extend Your Knowledge...

POSITIONING ELEMENTS FOR EASY REFERENCE

Tabbed items, such as those you just entered, make it easy for readers to identify similar grouped subjects, such as item numbers, descriptions, and price. In the exercise you performed, each item was on its own line. If an item description must go on a second line, you should press Shift-Return/Enter after you have entered all the data on the first line. You can either tab to the appropriate column, or you can create an Indent to Here command at the beginning tabular column in the first line of the description. When tabular elements contain a great deal of text, it is usually better to use tables, which are discussed in *Essentials for Design: InDesign Level 2.*

LESSON 7 Importing, Exporting, and Threading Text

It is very unusual for designers to type the bulk of a text-heavy document (such as a newsletter, magazine, or brochure) directly into an InDesign file. In most cases, you import the copy from files created in a word-processing program, such as Microsoft Word. InDesign has import filters for a variety of other text formats, including Microsoft Excel, Rich Text Format (RTF), Adobe InCopy, InDesign Tagged Text, and even raw text. You can define import options when you place a text file. These options vary, depending upon the nature of the file you are importing.

Microsoft Word Import Options

Include
☑ Table of Contents Text ☑ Footnotes and Endnotes
☑ Index Text

Formatting
☑ Use Typographer's Quotes
☐ Remove Text and Table Formatting
Convert Tables To: Unformatted Tables
Manual Page Breaks: Preserve Page Breaks

OK
Cancel

FIGURE 3.57

When you import text from an external file, you can place a ***link*** that allows the text in the InDesign document to be dynamically updated if the external text file is ever changed. For some data, such as price lists, this can be a very valuable feature. If major changes are made to a file after it has been linked, however, it can wreak havoc with your InDesign document. You should update linked text files with caution.

As you have seen in this and other projects, sometimes text does not fit in a frame and becomes overset. In most cases, you cannot resolve the problem simply by resizing the frame or the type. Instead, the solution is to link several frames together so the text can ***thread*** from one to another. It's a simple matter to link overset text to another frame; you first click the out port (the red "+" sign at the lower right of the frame) with the Selection tool. Then, when the cursor changes to a loaded-text icon, you can either drag the icon to form a new text frame, or you can simply click an existing frame to link the text.

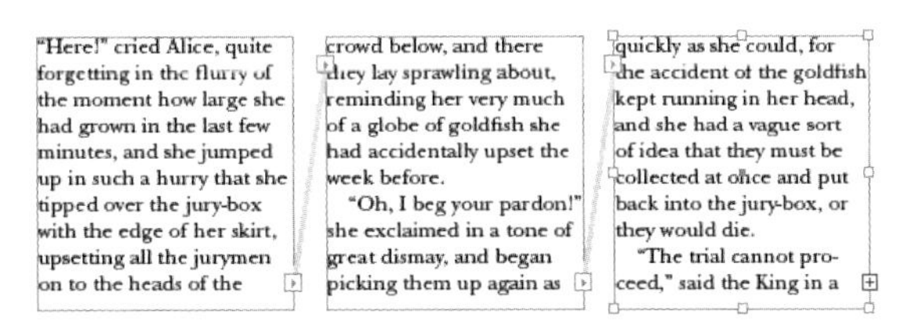

"Here!" cried Alice, quite forgetting in the flurry of the moment how large she had grown in the last few minutes, and she jumped up in such a hurry that she tipped over the jury-box with the edge of her skirt, upsetting all the jurymen on to the heads of the
crowd below, and there they lay sprawling about, reminding her very much of a globe of goldfish she had accidentally upset the week before.
"Oh, I beg your pardon!" she exclaimed in a tone of great dismay, and began picking them up again as
quickly as she could, for the accident of the goldfish kept running in her head, and she had a vague sort of idea that they must be collected at once and put back into the jury-box, or they would die.
"The trial cannot proceed," said the King in a

FIGURE 3.58

You can also export text in several formats, including Adobe InDesign Tagged Text, Rich Text, Text Only, and XML. Adobe InDesign Tagged Text can be imported into other InDesign files. Rich Text is compatible with Microsoft applications and with Macintosh OS X. Text-only is plain unformatted text that can be opened with nearly any application. Text formatted as XML (eXtensible Markup Language) is data structured for customized applications; the code looks similar to HTML, and can be used for Web or networked data-management solutions.

Place (Import) Text

1 **Open alice_01.indd from the Project_03 folder.**

2 **Choose the Type tool, hold down the mouse button, and drag a text frame to the following dimensions: X: 3p0, Y: 36 pt, W: 45p0, H: 216 pt.**

If you prefer, you can draw a text frame anywhere you prefer, switch to the Selection tool, click the frame, and adjust the dimensions in the Transform palette or the Control palette. Remember that the proxy-reference point must be set to the top left for this method to work correctly.

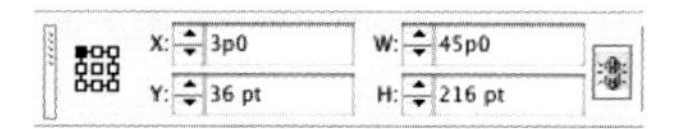

FIGURE 3.59

3 **Choose File>Place and choose the chapter_1.txt file. Make sure the Show Import Options and Replace Selected Item boxes are checked.**

In the preview at the right of the dialog box, it appears as though the "text" contains a lot of code. This is because the file you're placing is an InDesign Tagged Text file.

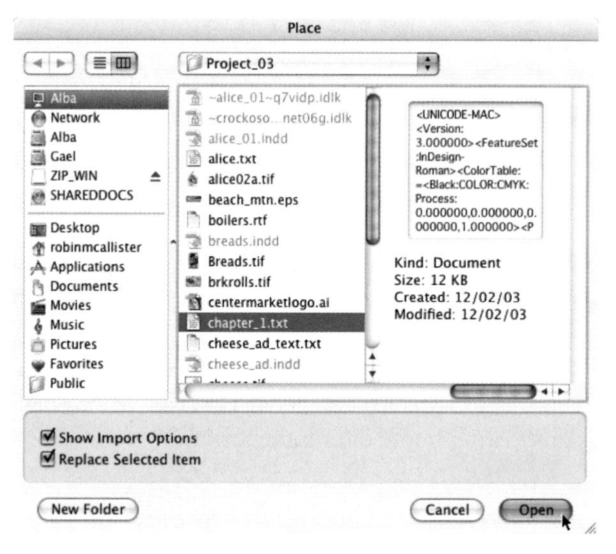

FIGURE 3.60

4 **Click Open.**

The InDesign Tagged Text Import Options dialog box appears.

5 **Check the Use Typographer's Quotes box, and set the Resolve Text Style Conflicts Using menu to the Tagged File Definitions option. Make sure the Show List of Problem Tags before Place box is checked. Click OK.**

Showing a list of problem tags is useful in case they have been entered improperly. A ***tag*** is instructional code, such as **<B>** to indicate that the following text should be bold. It can also include information that will affect several elements, such as font, style, and color. Such information is called styles, and is discussed in Project 6.

Adobe InDesign Tagged Text Import Options

Formatting
- [x] Use Typographer's Quotes
- [ ] Remove Text Formatting

Resolve Text Style Conflicts Using: Tagged File De...

OK
Cancel

- [x] Show List of Problem Tags before Place

FIGURE 3.61

The placed text flows into the text frame. The out port of the frame displays a red "+", indicating that there is more text than can fit in the frame.

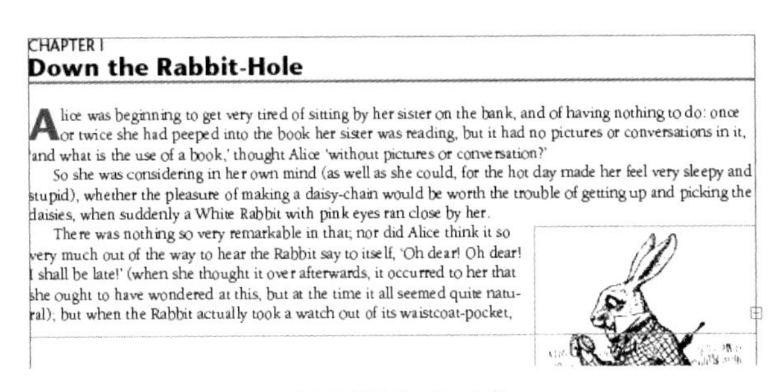

CHAPTER I

Down the Rabbit-Hole

Alice was beginning to get very tired of sitting by her sister on the bank, and of having nothing to do: once or twice she had peeped into the book her sister was reading, but it had no pictures or conversations in it, 'and what is the use of a book,' thought Alice 'without pictures or conversation?'

So she was considering in her own mind (as well as she could, for the hot day made her feel very sleepy and stupid), whether the pleasure of making a daisy-chain would be worth the trouble of getting up and picking the daisies, when suddenly a White Rabbit with pink eyes ran close by her.

There was nothing so very remarkable in that; nor did Alice think it so very much out of the way to hear the Rabbit say to itself, 'Oh dear! Oh dear! I shall be late!' (when she thought it over afterwards, it occurred to her that she ought to have wondered at this, but at the time it all seemed quite natural); but when the Rabbit actually took a watch out of its waistcoat-pocket,

FIGURE 3.62

6 **Save the file in your WIP_03 folder. Leave it open for the next exercise.**

Thread Text

1 **Continue in the open alice_01.indd.**

2 **Click the out port with the Selection tool. When the cursor changes to a loaded-text icon, drag a text frame with the following dimensions: X: 3p0, Y: 264 pt, W: 20p0, H: 492 pt.**

When you release the mouse button, the text fills the frame. Once again, the out port indicates that there is still additional text to place. Remember, you can use the Control palette to adjust the size of the frame to the exact dimensions.

3 **Click the out port and drag another text frame as follows: X: 24p0, Y: 264 pt, W: 24p0, H: 492 pt.**

When you release the mouse button, text fills the frame. Use the Control palette to adjust the size of the frame to match the specifications, if necessary.

4 **Select all text in the story. Choose Optical Kerning from the Control palette's Kerning menu.**

You can click your mouse in any of these threaded frames and choose Edit>Select All (or press Command/Control-A) to select all the text without having to drag the cursor through all three frames.

5 **Save the document and leave it open for the next exercise.**

Export Text

1. **Continue in the open alice_01.indd.**

2. **Click the Type tool inside any of the text frames.**

   The text is threaded through all the frames, so all the text in the document will be exported. If the text were not threaded, only the text in the frame in which the Type tool was clicked would be exported.

3. **Choose File>Export>Adobe InDesign Tagged Text.**

   The Adobe InDesign Tagged Text format allows you to import text into any InDesign document with all text attributes pre-defined.

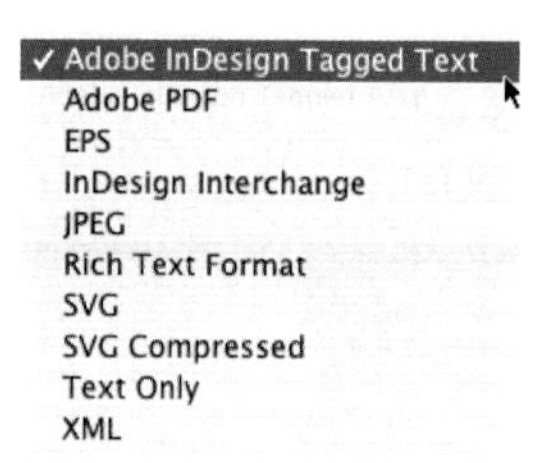

FIGURE 3.63

4. **Export the file to your WIP_03 folder as "alice_01_tagged.txt".**

   Once the export is complete, you can open the file in a word processor to see how the applied formatting attributes look.

5. **Save the file and close it.**

CAREERS IN DESIGN

SPACE AND TYPOGRAPHY IN DESIGN

When designing documents — from business cards to posters, and brochures to books — you regularly face the challenge of creating impressive spatial relationships and effectively using type in your documents. You must balance clients' requests against the principles of good document design — which are (occasionally) diametrically opposed.

As you review each document you create, look at it with a creative designer's eye, as well as a practical designer's eye. Your creative eye knows that if you design a six-panel brochure that will be displayed in a rack alongside other brochures, you should place eye-catching information in the top one-third of the document, so it can be easily seen and appreciated. Your practical side needs to choose the correct paper size for each job, so you don't throw away money as you throw away excess paper.

Within each document, leave adequate room for margins and fold, and assign enough white space so the reader can easily understand the information, whether it's text or graphics. When images are too large, they can overpower a page; when images are too small, they can become completely ineffective, depending upon the nature of the document and the image. Balance in your documents — within the page and between facing pages — is always necessary.

Working with type is challenging; you want to find the perfect way to convey your message. You may need to research typefaces to ensure that they are appropriate for the tone of the document — and that there isn't another face to accomplish the task more effectively. On a document-by-document basis, experiment with kerning, tracking, and leading to ensure that readability and mood are both well served.

As you work in both print and Web documents, you will discover that each brings unique challenges to working with space and type, and you will likely view each new challenge as another opportunity to hone your skills. You will develop tricks and techniques to set your work apart from others', which will bring both personal and material rewards.

SUMMARY

In this project, you explored many of InDesign's tools for formatting text. You learned about the properties of text frames, including columns, insets, and first baselines. You learned how to format text and paragraphs, how to find and insert special characters, and how to exploit the advanced typographic features of OpenType. You explored various options for fitting text into frames, including enlarging the frame, linking frames, and editing the text itself.

When you use InDesign as a production tool, you will likely use most of the skills you learned in this project on a regular basis. Much of the work done in the printing and advertising industries involves working on documents such as those you worked on here. As you develop your skills, you will identify strategies that fit both the types of documents you work on and your personal working preferences. (You might, for example, want to keep the Character Control palette always available and use the floating Paragraph palette, so you'll have immediate access to both.) In addition, you'll develop your own collection of tricks that enable you to accomplish specific tasks quickly and easily.

KEY TERMS

- Adobe Paragraph Composer
- Alignment
- Ascender
- Baseline
- Break characters
- Case fraction
- Column break
- Decimal tab
- Descender
- Discretionary hyphen
- Drop cap
- Export
- Faux
- First baseline offset
- Font
- Font family
- Font size
- Font style
- Font weight
- Forced line break
- Hidden character
- Hyphenation
- In port
- Indent
- Inset
- Justification
- Ligature
- Line break
- Line spacing
- Link
- Negative leading
- Oldstyle
- OpenType
- Optical kerning
- Ornament
- Out port
- Overset text
- Overset-text icon
- Page break
- Piece fraction
- Point
- PostScript
- Ragged margin
- Rule
- Small cap
- Solid leading
- Solidus
- Space Above
- Space Below
- Special character
- Tab leader
- Tag
- Text frame
- Text inset
- Threaded text
- TrueType
- Typo/typographical error
- Vertical justification
- X-height

CHECKING CONCEPTS AND TERMS

MULTIPLE CHOICE

Circle the letter of the correct answer for each of the following questions.

1. When must text be placed in a frame?
   a. Only when it is imported.
   b. Only when there are images on the page.
   c. Only when you specify the font and size.
   d. Always.

2. If all the text does not fit in the frame, you can __________.
   a. enlarge the frame
   b. link to another frame
   c. edit the text
   d. Any of the above.

3. Which of the following functions can be accomplished with the Character palette?
   a. Linking text frames
   b. Establishing leading
   c. Adding color to text
   d. Defining drop caps

4. Which of the following functions can be accomplished from the Paragraph palette?
   a. Linking text frames
   b. Establishing leading
   c. Adding color to text
   d. Defining drop caps

5. Which of the following features is dependent upon the position of the baseline?
   a. Weight
   b. Size
   c. Leading
   d. Ascender

6. Which of these is a feature of OpenType?
   a. The same font can be used on Macintosh and Windows computers.
   b. They all have at least six weights.
   c. They were developed by Apple Computer.
   d. All of the above.

7. When would you want to link an external text file to an InDesign document?
   a. When using variable data, such as a price list.
   b. When creating a draft copy, so the edits automatically update.
   c. For articles such as a "Letter from the President."
   d. When the length of text is likely to change.

8. What is the purpose of tracking?
   a. To move pairs of characters closer together or farther apart.
   b. To adjust the overall letter space of a range of characters.
   c. To manage changes in an editing cycle.
   d. To establish line spacing.

9. How is text threaded?
   a. Using the Character Thread tool.
   b. Clicking a frame's out port before importing text.
   c. Clicking a frame's out port, then dragging a new text frame.
   d. Moving it from column to column.

10. When are paragraph rules applied?
    a. When the paragraph needs adjustment.
    b. When you create a document with many parts.
    c. When you need a line above or below a paragraph.
    d. When character rules are also in effect.

DISCUSSION QUESTIONS

1. You will often use imported text, rather than typing text directly into an InDesign layout. What are the advantages of this doing this? Consider both mechanical and workflow issues that might be affected.

2. What are the advantages or disadvantages of placing text in frames, as opposed to simply typing on the page, as you do in word-processing programs?

3. When formatting text, the most important factor is to ensure its readability. What affects readability? Expand your thinking beyond the text itself to include the medium on which it is presented. For example, what issues must be considered for text that will be printed in a magazine versus text that is viewed on a monitor, in a presentation, or on a billboard?

SKILL DRILL

Skill Drills reinforce project skills. Each skill reinforced is the same, or nearly the same, as a skill presented in the lessons. Detailed instructions are provided in a step-by-step format. You should work through these exercises in sequence.

1. Place and Flow Text

This is the beginning of a moderately complex page. You will often work on projects (such as this specification sheet) that are not particularly exciting, but are necessary for a company to sell its product. In many cases, you will be in tight copyfitting situations because the client has so much to say and only a limited space in which to say it. Work through the elements step-by-step, and you'll be surprised with what you can accomplish.

1. Create a new Letter-size document with a master text frame. Use the default margins.
2. Choose the Selection tool. While pressing Command/Control-Shift, click the text frame. Place the file named boilers.rtf. Accept the default placement options.
3. In the Control palette, change the Height of the text frame to 0.75 in.
4. Choose the Type tool in the Tools palette. Drag a new text frame the entire width of the text area, with a Height of 5.4 in. Choose Object>Text Frame Options (Command/Control-B), and create a 2-column frame with a default gutter. Position it at Y: 1.35 in.
5. Create two additional single-column frames as follows: X: 0.5 in, Y: 7 in, W: 5.33 in, H: 1.95 in, and X: 6 in, Y: 7 in, W: 2 in, H: 1.95 in.
6. Use the Selection tool to click the overset-text icon. Click the next text frame to flow the text into it. Continue to link the remaining frames in the same manner.
7. Save your file as "mbda_boilers.indd" and leave it open for the next exercise.

2. Style the Text

Now that your text is flowed, you need to style it and manipulate some of the text frames. You want the text to flow from frame-to-frame so it can be easily exported and repurposed, if necessary. That's why it was imported as a single file.

1. In the open file, use the Character Control palette to style the first line as 24-pt ATC Oak Bold with default Leading.
2. Style the second line as 18-pt Adobe Garamond Pro Semibold with 27-pt Leading.
3. In the second text frame, select all text from "1" through "hydronic heating systems."
4. Style the selected text as Adobe Garamond Pro Regular, 12/14.
5. From the Paragraph Control palette, set a Left Indent of 0.5 in and a First-Line Outdent of –0.5 in. Set a 7-pt Space After, and leave the text at the default Left Alignment.

6. Reset the First-Line Indent to 0 (zero) for the two paragraphs not preceded by numbers.
7. Assign a 3-Line Drop Cap to each paragraph that begins with a number. Change the numbers to ATC Oak Bold.

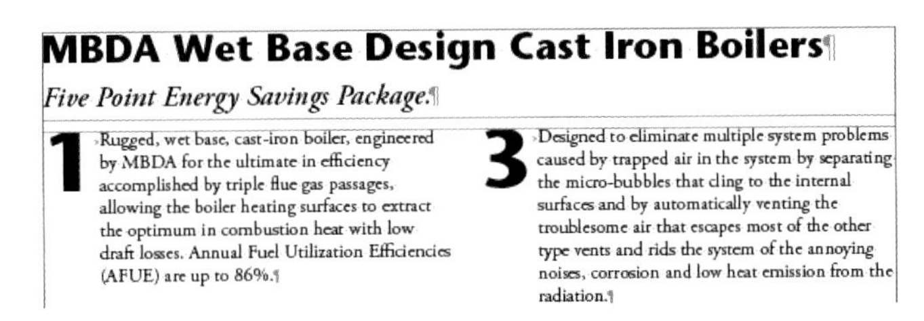

FIGURE 3.64

8. Place the text cursor in front of the line that begins with "Burner Capacities." Choose Type>Insert Break Character>Frame Break (Shift-Enter on the numeric keypad).

   The resulting frame break forces the remainder of the text to move into the next frame.
9. Save the file and leave it open for the next exercise.

3. Set Tabs and Rules

The next block of text is tabular data. The data is to be included in a box, and there isn't a great deal of extra space to work with. You should zoom in on this text as you make your adjustments.

1. In the open file, click the Type tool in the text frame and choose Object>Text Frame Options (Command/Control-B) to access the Text Frame Options dialog box. Assign a 4-pt Inset to all four sides.
2. Set the first line of text in this frame to ATC Oak Bold, 11/Auto, with 5.5-pt Space After.
3. Set the next three lines (from "Boiler," to "(ins.)L") as ATC Garamond Pro Semibold, 9/10, with 8-pt Space After.
4. Set the remaining lines of tabular text as ATC Garamond Pro Regular, 9/12, with no Space After.
5. Highlight all the tabbed text (both 9/10 Semibold text and 9/12 Regular text) and use the Tabs palette (Type>Tabs) to assign Centered tabs in the following positions: 0.222 in, 0.75 in, 1.35 in, 2 in, 2.5 in, 3 in, 3.5 in, 4 in, 4.5 in, and 5 in.
6. Assign a 1-pt rule with a 6-pt (0.0833 in) Offset below the three lines of Semibold text.

   These three lines of text comprise a single paragraph.
7. Select all of the text below the rule. Change the second and third tab markers to Decimal tabs, and adjust their positions until they appear correct to your eye.
8. Select the line that begins with an asterisk. Style it as ATC Oak Normal, 8/16. From the Character palette Options menu, select Underline Options. Check the Underline On box, set the Weight to 0.5 pt, and set the Offset to –9 pt.

9. Switch to the Selection tool. Click the frame, and then click the Default Fill & Stroke icon in the Tools palette.

   A 1-pt stroke is assigned to the frame.

10. Save the file and leave it open for the next exercise.

Burner Capacities – Ratings – Chimney Sizes – Dimensions

Boiler Model No.	D.O.E. Heating Capacity	IBR Burner Oil Inut GPH(1)	IBR Net Water Sq.Ft.	AFUE%	Chimney Size	Water Cont. (gal.)	Boiler Weight (lbs.)	Overall Length*	Boiler Length (ins.)
M-3	60.0	.50	348	84.6	8x8x15	3.55	209	24.81	13.18
M-4	86.0	.70	499	84.6	8x8x15	4.54	253	28.36	16.73
M-5	113.0	.95	655	84.6	8x8x15	5.52	297	31.55	20.67
M-6	138.0	1.15	800	84.6	8x8x15	6.49	341	34.69	23.81
M-7	164.0	1.40	951	84.6	8x8x15	7.49	385	38.24	27.36

*Overall length includes burner mounted.

FIGURE 3.65

4. Add Special Characters

Not all characters are easily accessed from the keyboard. In this section, you add characters (visible and invisible) using either keyboard shortcuts or elements from the Type menu.

1. In the final text frame of the open document, set the first line of text as ATC Oak Bold, 11/Auto, with a 3-pt Space After.
2. Select the rest of the text and style it as Adobe Garamond Pro Regular, 9/9.5, with a 2-pt Space After.
3. At the beginning of the "Boiler body" line, insert a bullet followed by an en space and an Indent to Here marker. You can access all of these characters by choosing Type>Insert Special Character or Type>Insert White Space.
4. Copy and paste these three characters in front of each paragraph in the frame.

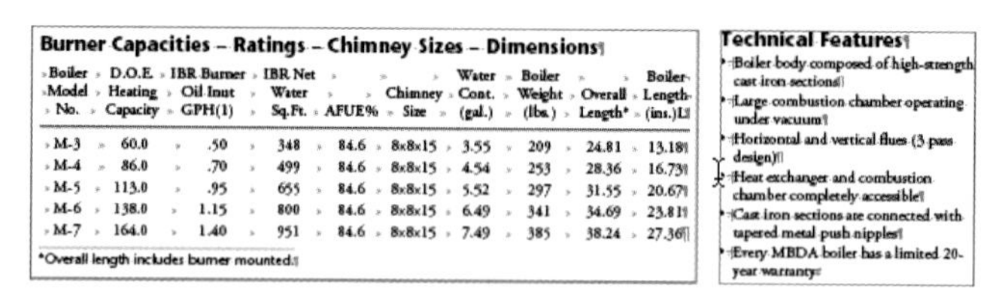

Burner Capacities – Ratings – Chimney Sizes – Dimensions

Boiler Model No.	D.O.E. Heating Capacity	IBR Burner Oil Inut GPH(1)	IBR Net Water Sq.Ft.	AFUE%	Chimney Size	Water Cont. (gal.)	Boiler Weight (lbs.)	Overall Length*	Boiler Length (ins.)
M-3	60.0	.50	348	84.6	8x8x15	3.55	209	24.81	13.18
M-4	86.0	.70	499	84.6	8x8x15	4.54	253	28.36	16.73
M-5	113.0	.95	655	84.6	8x8x15	5.52	297	31.55	20.67
M-6	138.0	1.15	800	84.6	8x8x15	6.49	341	34.69	23.81
M-7	164.0	1.40	951	84.6	8x8x15	7.49	385	38.24	27.36

*Overall length includes burner mounted.

Technical Features

- Boiler body composed of high-strength cast iron sections
- Large combustion chamber operating under vacuum
- Horizontal and vertical flues (3 pass design)
- Heat exchanger and combustion chamber completely accessible
- Cast iron sections are connected with tapered metal push nipples
- Every MBDA boiler has a limited 20-year warranty

FIGURE 3.66

5. In the Chimney Size column of the tabular chart, select one of the "x" characters. Choose Type>Glyphs. Scroll down until you see the multiplication symbol. Double-click the symbol to replace the "x."

FIGURE 3.67

6. Copy and paste the multiplication symbol to replace all the "x" characters in the column.
7. Save the file and leave it open for the next exercise.

5. Enter and Style Text

1. In the open document, create a text frame extending from the left margin to the right margin, and abutting the bottom margin.
2. On two lines, type the following:

    MBDA Thermal Design, Inc.
    3516 Hotspur Avenue • Duluth, MN 55803 • 218/555-8907 • www.mbdaheat.com

3. Center the two lines. Style the first as 27-pt ATC Oak Normal with a 12-pt Space Below.
4. Style the second line as ATC Oak Normal, 12/15.
5. Choose Object>Text Frame Options. Set the Align menu to Bottom.
6. Press "W" to view the document. Save the document and close it.

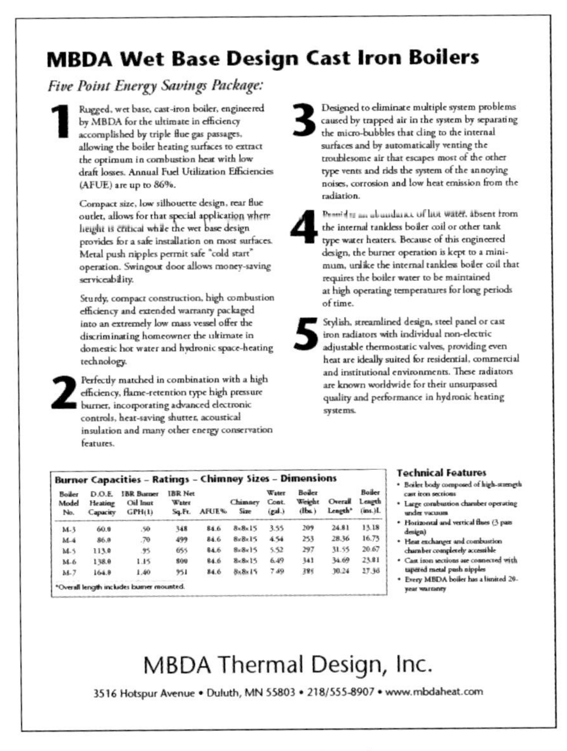

MBDA Wet Base Design Cast Iron Boilers

Five Point Energy Savings Package:

1 Rugged, wet base, cast-iron boiler, engineered by MBDA for the ultimate in efficiency accomplished by triple flue gas passages, allowing the boiler heating surfaces to extract the optimum in combustion heat with low draft losses. Annual Fuel Utilization Efficiencies (AFUE) are up to 86%.

Compact size, low silhouette design, rear flue outlet, allows for that special application where height is critical while the wet base design provides for a safe installation on most surfaces. Metal push nipples permit safe "cold start" operation. Swingout door allows money-saving serviceability.

Sturdy, compact construction, high combustion efficiency and extended warranty packaged into an extremely low mass vessel offer the discriminating homeowner the ultimate in domestic hot water and hydronic space-heating technology.

2 Perfectly matched in combination with a high efficiency, flame-retention type high pressure burner, incorporating advanced electronic controls, heat-saving shutter, acoustical insulation and many other energy conservation features.

3 Designed to eliminate multiple system problems caused by trapped air in the system by separating the micro-bubbles that cling to the internal surfaces and by automatically venting the troublesome air that escapes most of the other type vents and rids the system of the annoying noises, corrosion and low heat emission from the radiation.

4 Provides an abundance of hot water, absent from the internal tankless boiler coil or other tank type water heaters. Because of this engineered design, the burner operation is kept to a minimum, unlike the internal tankless boiler coil that requires the boiler water to be maintained at high operating temperatures for long periods of time.

5 Stylish, streamlined design, steel panel or cast iron radiators with individual non-electric adjustable thermostatic valves, providing even heat are ideally suited for residential, commercial and institutional environments. These radiators are known worldwide for their unsurpassed quality and performance in hydronic heating systems.

Burner Capacities – Ratings – Chimney Sizes – Dimensions

Boiler Model No.	D.O.E. Heating Capacity	IBR Burner Oil Inut GPH(1)	IBR Net Water Sq.Ft.	AFUE%	Chimney Size	Water Cont. (gal.)	Boiler Weight (lbs.)	Overall Length*	Boiler Length (ins.)L
M-3	60.0	.50	348	84.6	8×8×15	3.55	209	24.81	13.18
M-4	86.0	.70	499	84.6	8×8×15	4.54	253	28.36	16.73
M-5	113.0	.95	655	84.6	8×8×15	5.52	297	31.55	20.67
M-6	138.0	1.15	800	84.6	8×8×15	6.49	341	34.69	23.81
M-7	164.0	1.40	951	84.6	8×8×15	7.49	385	30.24	27.36

*Overall length includes burner mounted.

Technical Features
- Boiler body composed of high-strength cast iron sections
- Large combustion chamber operating under vacuum
- Horizontal and vertical flues (3 pass design)
- Heat exchanger and combustion chamber completely accessible
- Cast iron sections are connected with tapered metal push nipples
- Every MBDA boiler has a limited 20-year warranty

MBDA Thermal Design, Inc.

3516 Hotspur Avenue • Duluth, MN 55803 • 218/555-8907 • www.mbdaheat.com

FIGURE 3.68

CHALLENGE

Challenge exercises expand on, or are somewhat related to, skills presented in the lessons. Each exercise provides a brief introduction, followed by instructions presented in a numbered-step format that are not as detailed as those in the Skill Drill exercises. You should perform these exercises in order.

1. Place Text into the Ad Shell

Many design projects are simple one-page layouts that appear in a magazine or newspaper. The ad in this exercise uses images already placed on the page, as you might find when you work from comps created with placeholder text. The exercise focuses on text placement and formatting, using InDesign's built-in tools to complete the ad.

The ad in this project has some initial copy already typed in, but it's not formatted. The two required images are already placed exactly where the ad manager specified, and their position cannot be changed without approval. The ad designer set up some guidelines for specifying the position of text elements.

1. Open cheese_ad.indd from the Project_03 folder.

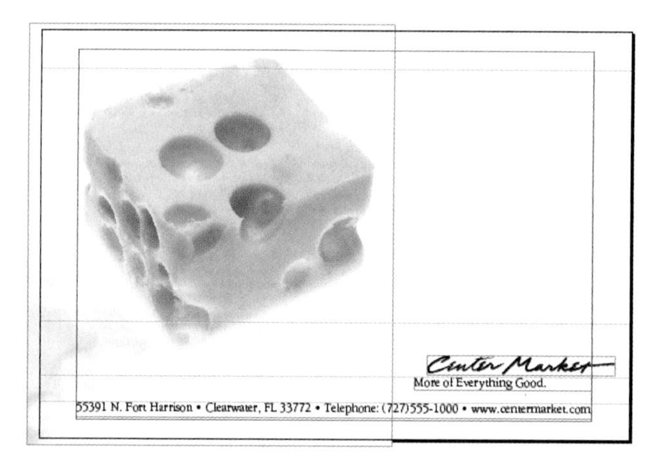

FIGURE 3.69

2. Place cheese_ad_text.txt.

   This is a plain text file, so it requires no import options; but make sure the Use Typographer's Quotes box is checked.

3. Position the file at the second horizontal guideline, 3.75 inches from the top edge of the page and the left margin.

   The text frame fills the width between the margin guides, and the red plus sign indicates overset text. The text wraps around the Center Market logo because the designer already applied a text wrap to the logo.

4. Save the file as "cheese_ad.indd" in your WIP_03 folder.

2. Format Ad Copy

1. In the open document, select all the text in the ad copy frame (the one you just placed). Change the Font to Adobe Garamond Pro Regular. Set the Alignment to Justify, Last Line Left.
2. Adjust the Width of the text frame to 3.25 in. Click the overset-text icon, and then drag another 3.25-in wide text frame that aligns to the right margin.

   This ensures that the text is easy to read. The line length, as the ad presently stands, is too wide to allow the eye to scan the text easily.
3. Select all the text and decrease the size until it fits the area comfortably.

   The art director specified that the type should be 9–11 pt.
4. Change the Leading from Auto (10.5 pt) to 11 pt.

   Even this small change makes a significant difference in how the text fits.
5. Use the Selection tool to drag the bottom of the left text frame up, until there are seven lines of text in the frame.
6. Examine the word spacing of the body copy (you may wish to zoom in a bit). Your evaluation is purely subjective. Select all the text, and then experiment with tracking values and the Optical/Metrics kerning options. Try tracking up to ± 10 units, paying attention to line breaks. The client wants the phrase "Every hour of every day" to remain together if possible. In addition, you want to avoid an extremely short last line of text.
7. If you end up with the single word "soul" on the last line, insert a soft return before the word "we" at the end of the first frame.

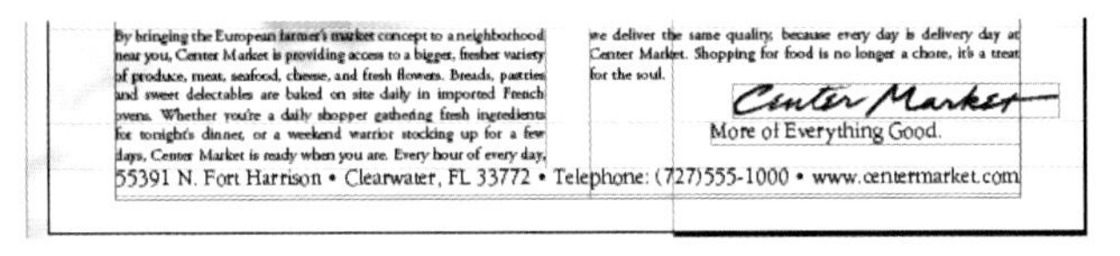

FIGURE 3.70

8. Save the file and continue to the next exercise.

3. Add and Format the Headline

For the headline, the art director's specifications indicate a typeface of Adobe Garamond Pro Regular, with a minimum size of 60 pt, a maximum of 84 pt, set tight. These settings will accommodate headlines of varying lengths. The headline is to be set flush to the right margin and shouldn't overly obscure the product shot.

1. In the open document, create a text frame. Type "Guess who's the Big Cheese in Cheeses?" in the frame.
2. Style the headline as Adobe Garamond Pro Regular, 60 pt, Flush Right.
3. Press Command/Control-Shift-> to enlarge the selected text. Keep pressing the keys until the headline wraps to three lines, and then oversets. When it oversets the text frame, press Command/Control-Shift-< to reduce the text size by two points.

4. Set the headline to a size that you think looks good, and doesn't crowd the body text.
5. The automatic leading value is too high for this headline. Experiment with solid, or even negative leading.

   Solid leading means that the leading value is the same as the point size of the type. ***Negative leading*** is a leading value that is smaller than the type size.
6. Kern and track the headline until you're satisfied with its appearance. Remember, the specification is to set the text tight.

   There should be no excess space between letters; they should almost — but not quite — touch one another. Pay as much attention to detail as you would if the art director were looking over your shoulder; in a real assignment, that could very well be the case.

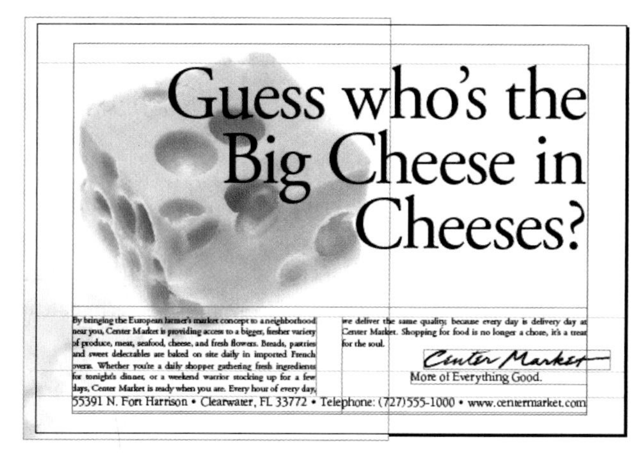

FIGURE 3.71

7. Save the file and keep it open for the next exercise.

4. Finish the Ad

All that remains is to format the information line and the line under the Center Market logo.

1. In the open document, use the Selection tool to verify that the info line at the bottom of the page is at X: 0.5 in and Y: 4.7779 in. If it is not at this position, move it.
2. Select all the text in this line. It is specified as 10-pt Adobe Garamond Pro Italic, centered, and tracked to fill the width of the margins. Begin by formatting it to the specified typeface and size, and then center it on the line.
3. Try force justifying the line, using the last of the justification icons.

   The result is a very space-heavy line.
4. Set the Alignment back to Centered. In the Tracking field, enter "25", and then press the Tab key to advance to the next field.

5. Press Shift-Tab to return to the Tracking field. Increase the value until the text fills the frame.

6. You are directed to change the specification of the numbers in this line to Oldstyle. Last-minute addition of information (from art directors or clients) is typical, although it can quickly become annoying. From the Character palette Options menu, choose OpenType>Proportional Oldstyle.

7. The oldstyle figures take up less space than the tabular lining figures (which are the default), so the line no longer fills the frame. Choose Optical Kerning to help balance the spacing of these characters.

   Optical kerning, which considers the shapes and point size of the letters and of applied kerning, is more effective when text is tracked to such a great extent.

8. Adjust tracking until the text fits. If you overset the text, just change the tracking back to the last value you used.

9. Select the text under the logo ("More of Everything Good"). If you can't select it because your body text frame covers it, change to the Selection tool and press Command/Control while clicking.

   The first click should select the body text frame and the second should select the line of text you want to edit.

10. Set the text as 10-pt Adobe Garamond Pro Regular, with Optical Kerning. Center it in the text frame.

11. Fit the entire ad within the document window. Examine the finished ad. Make any kerning changes you believe are necessary, especially in the headline.

FIGURE 3.72

12. Save your changes and close the file.

Your experience with creating this ad should demonstrate that there's a lot more to composing a layout than simply dropping text into a frame. Good composition is the result of paying attention to details, such as manually kerning large type when necessary, and experimenting with the tracking and automatic kerning options of complete lines and paragraphs. Don't overdo kerning; too much is worse than none at all. Even with all the fine-tuning, this ad-creation process should have been a relatively quick exercise.

PORTFOLIO BUILDER

Ice House Placemat

The Ice House is more than an ice cream stand — it has a full menu for the casual diner. The menu is presented as a letter-size placemat. The theme of the restaurant has always been casual and upbeat, with more than the occasional play on words. This year, the owner wants to use Adobe Caslon Pro as the primary typeface, but you can use a sans-serif face as an accent. Check the alternate characters and ligatures in Adobe Caslon as you make your character selection. You can introduce color, if you prefer.

The text file for the menu, icehouse.rtf, is included in the Project_03 folder. In addition to the menu items, the client needs to have his slogan, "Simply the Best," the words, "The Ice House," and phone number, "555-3086," included.

LEVEL 1

PROJECT 4

Working with Graphic Tools

OBJECTIVES

In this project, you learn how to

- Use primitive shapes
- Draw and constrain lines and frames
- Determine line and corner characteristics
- Draw with Bézier tools
- Add color to your documents
- Move objects in front of and behind one another
- Rotate, scale, and shear objects

WHY WOULD I DO THIS?

The content of any document includes only two elements: text and graphics. In Project 3, you learned how to create and format type. In this project, you learn how to create objects with InDesign's drawing tools, and discover how to modify objects with the transformation tools. In a future project, you explore how to import objects from outside sources, and place those objects in InDesign documents.

Objects created with InDesign drawing tools consist of two basic parts: a path and points. A ***path*** is any unbroken line or curve that describes a shape. An ***open path*** (such as a straight line) has a defined start and endpoint; a ***closed path*** (such as a circle) has no start and endpoints, but is still defined by points. A ***point*** is a position on a path that defines the direction, angle, and curve direction (if any) of the path it intersects. Points are also known as ***anchor points*** because they anchor the path's characteristics where they are set.

A ***stroke*** is the visible boundary of the path. A ***fill*** describes the content of a path. Both fills and strokes can be colored with numerous options, or set to None. Fills can be solid colors, tints of colors, graduated blends, or gradients.

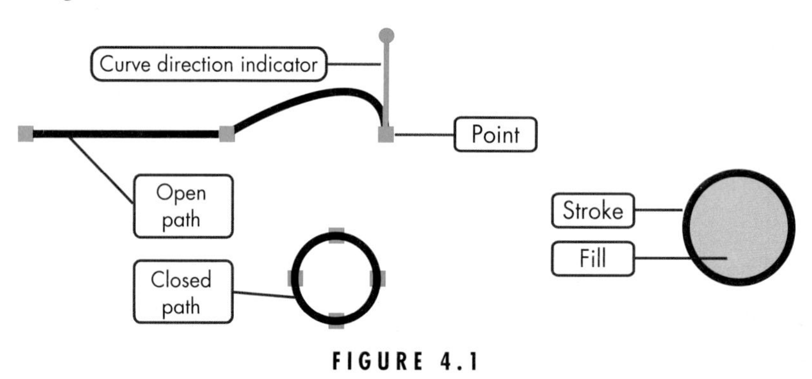

FIGURE 4.1

Every object, whether selected individually or as a group, has a ***bounding box*** that marks the extreme perimeter of the object. You can use the four corner handles, four side handles, and center point of the bounding box to modify the shape and size of the object. Dragging any of the corner handles scales an object both horizontally and vertically; dragging the left or right handle scales the object horizontally; and dragging the top or bottom handle scales the object vertically.

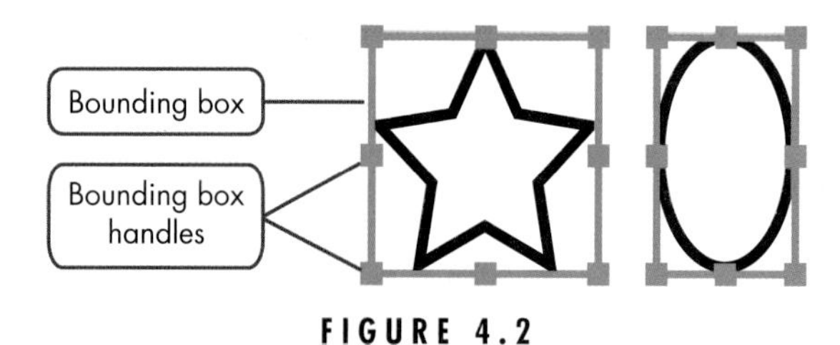

FIGURE 4.2

Color can be applied to an object's fill and stroke. We address the basics of selection and application of color in this project. An in-depth discussion of color, its application, and use are presented in *Essentials for Design: InDesign Level 2.*

InDesign supports three methods for creating (mixing) colors: CMYK, RGB, and L*a*b:

- ***CMYK*** is the color mode used in printing. It describes percentages of the subtractive primary inks — cyan, magenta, and yellow, with the addition of black. When none of the inks is applied, the result is white; when all of the inks are applied at full intensity, the result is a theoretical black.
- ***RGB*** is the color mode used in computer monitors, scanners, and the Web. It describes parts (up to 255) of the additive primary colors — red, green, and blue. When all of the colors are applied, the result is white; when none of the colors is applied, the result is black.
- ***L*a*b*** is a color mode that allows you to describe both RGB and CMYK colors using their hue, saturation, and value.
- InDesign also supports a number of spot color modes. ***Spot colors*** are pre-mixed inks. In the United States, the most common spot color mode is the ***PANTONE® color*** matching system.

Once you have created objects in an InDesign document, you can arrange and transform them in a variety of ways. You can use the Control palette, the Transform palette, the Arrange menu, or you can perform a number of functions interactively using the Selection and Direct Selection tools. Objects can be grouped, so several objects can be treated as a single object; you can apply attributes to the group, and the modification affect all of the objects in the group simultaneously.

VISUAL SUMMARY

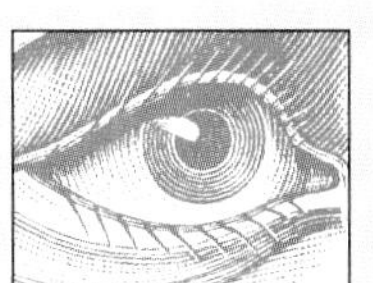

Text needs to be placed into frames, but graphic elements created in InDesign do not, because graphics are frames by themselves. You can create objects ranging from very simple to quite complex. InDesign includes six tools for drawing lines and objects: the Line, Pen, Pencil, Frame, Shape, and Scissors tools. Variations of these tools are located in pop-up menus that appear when you click the active tool and hold down the mouse button for a moment. For example, the Rectangle, Ellipse, and Polygon shape tools are all found under the same tool icon, which defaults to the Rectangle tool. Any of the three tools can be on top, so we refer to them collectively as the ***shape tools***. The object drawing tools are shown in Figure 4.3.

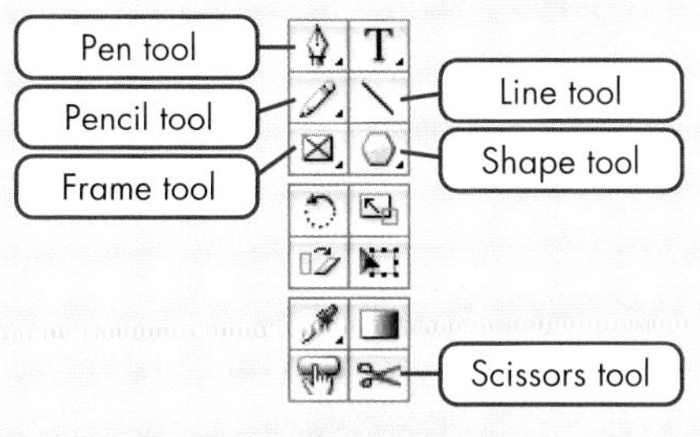

FIGURE 4.3

A straight line is the simplest of all InDesign objects. You can draw a line with the Line tool by clicking the beginning point and dragging to the endpoint. To create a line that changes direction, either obliquely or with curves, the best tool to use is the Pen tool. Clicking point-to-point produces sharp angles; clicking and dragging produces curves. The Pencil tool can be used for freehand drawing or sketching, but is not particularly useful for detailed illustration.

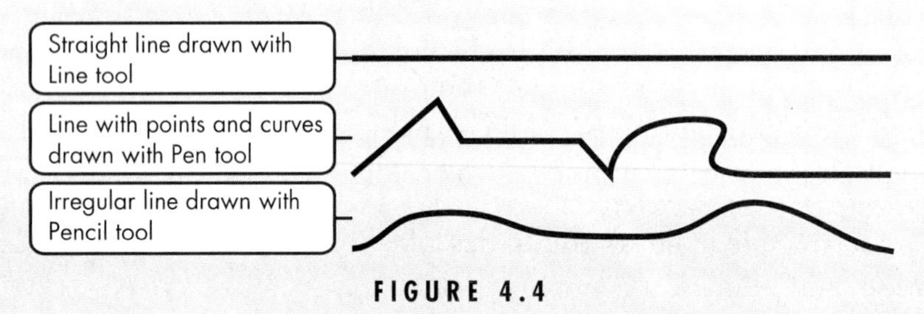

FIGURE 4.4

Standard predefined shapes, such as rectangles, ellipses, and polygons, are often called ***primitives***. You can use the frame tools and shape tools to draw primitive objects. Objects drawn with the frame tools (Rectangle Frame, Ellipse Frame, and Polygon Frame tools) are designed to hold images or type. Objects drawn with the corresponding shape tools are designed to be stand-alone objects, but may be converted to frames by clicking the Text tool in them, or selecting them when importing images. Shapes can be filled with colors or other images.

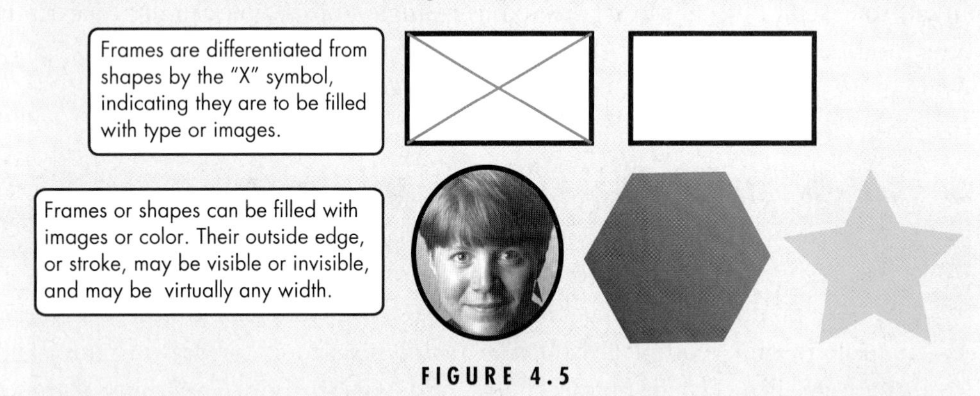

FIGURE 4.5

Irregular shapes are drawn with the Pen and Pencil tools. As is true with drawing lines (open paths), you have better control when drawing shapes (closed paths) when you use the Pen tool rather than the Pencil tool.

You can select from a number of color modes when choosing the colors to use in a document. If you are creating a document for print, you should use either spot colors or colors created in the CMYK (process) color mode. If you are creating a document that will be viewed on screen, such as a Web document, you should use RGB color and the restrictive Web-safe palette.

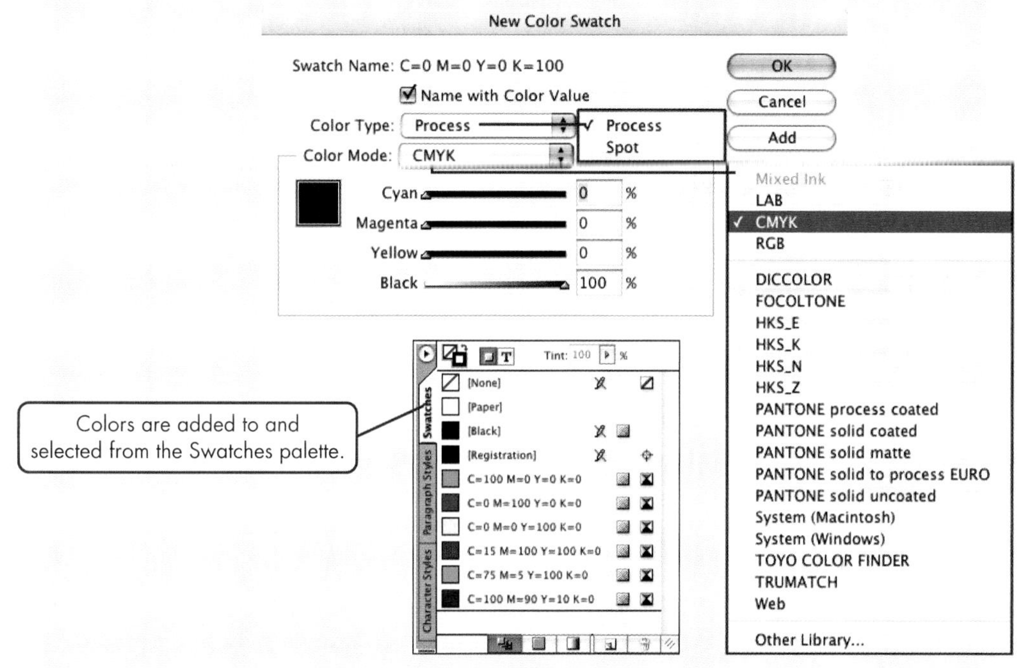

FIGURE 4.6

When you apply color to an object, you use the Tools palette to define the part of the object that will receive the color. Apply a fill to color the inside of the object; apply a stroke to color its outline. The default is a fill of none (the object has no background) and a stroke of black.

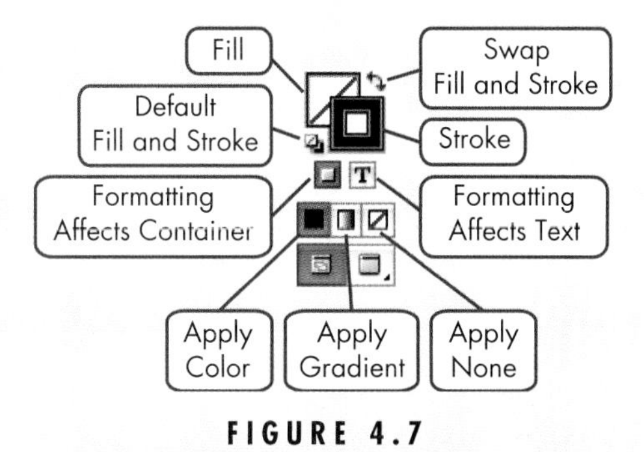

FIGURE 4.7

After an object is created, it can be manipulated (transformed). The ***transformation tools*** allow you to scale, rotate, shear, and flip objects using the Tools palette, Control palette, or Transform palette.

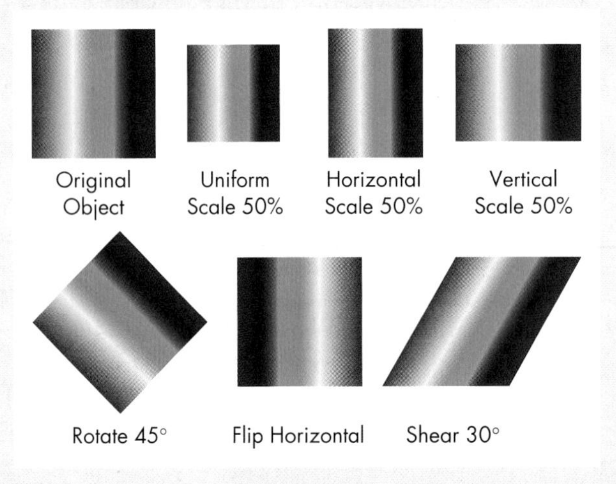

FIGURE 4.8

Sometimes it is important to maintain the ***stacking order*** of elements on a page (how elements are layered one on top of the others). Opaque backgrounds are usually at the bottom of the stacking order, and other objects are then layered on top. Another example is an object that must be placed on top of a photograph, but behind type. Objects normally stack in the order they were created, with the first object created at the bottom of the stacking order; but that may not be the order they should be displayed, back to front. You can use the Arrange menu to change the stacking order (bring an object to the front, send it to the back, bring it forward or send it backward one level) to achieve the desired effect in your InDesign document.

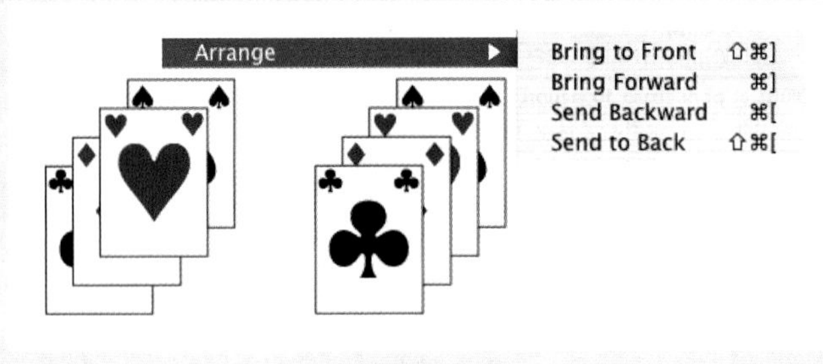

FIGURE 4.9

In addition to arranging elements three-dimensionally, you sometimes need to quickly align elements according to their centers, tops, or bottoms, or to distribute objects across a given space. While you can do this manually (measure each element and divide the space), an easier method is to use InDesign's built-in Align palette to align and distribute the items quickly and easily.

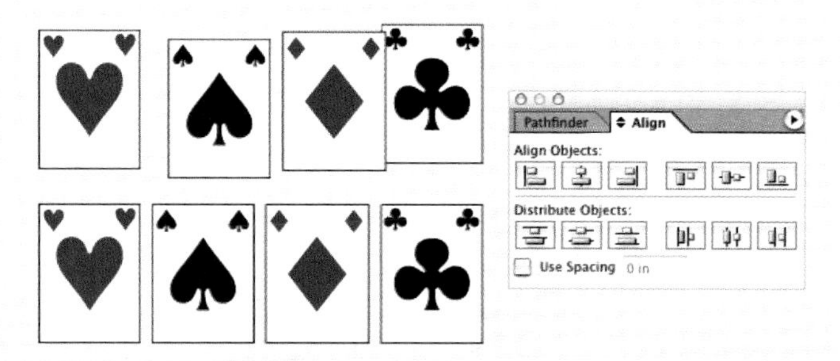

FIGURE 4.10

Now that you have been introduced to the techniques you can use to create images in InDesign, it's time to start using the tools. As you progress in this project, you integrate skills you learned in Projects 1 and 2 with new skills. We encourage you to stretch your imagination and build creatively upon these skills.

LESSON 1 Using Basic Shapes

Even though the basic shapes are called "primitives," they are very useful when creating graphics in InDesign. You will include lines and rectangles in virtually every document you create. When drawing with the Line, Rectangle, and Ellipse tools, you can use the Shift key to constrain the objects you create. When the Shift key is used in conjunction with the Line tool, lines are constrained to 45-degree increments; when used with the Rectangle and Ellipse tools, rectangles are constrained to squares, and ellipses to circles. Many of the features you use when creating lines can also be applied to the strokes of closed paths.

Use the Line Tool

1. **Create a new document using InDesign's default Size, Orientation, and Margins.**

2. **Click the Default Fill and Stroke icon in the Tools palette, and then choose the Line tool.**

   Refer to Figure 4.3 to locate the Line tool.

3. **Click the Line tool on the page and drag in several directions without holding any additional keys.**

   The tool creates a line wherever you move the cursor.

4 **Press the Shift key while you drag the Line tool.**

Pressing the Shift key constrains the line to 45-degree increments. The dragging becomes jerky and snaps to 45-degree angles as you drag up and down.

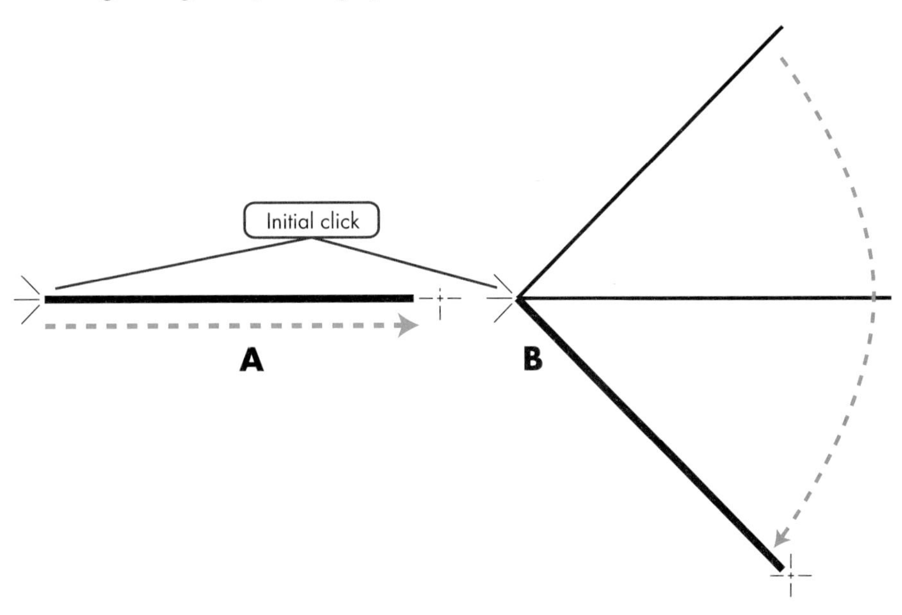

FIGURE 4.11

5 **Hold down the Shift key and drag the Line tool to the right about 2 inches from the initial click, then release the mouse button. Leave the line selected.**

Watch the Control palette or Info palette while you drag to check the length of the line. Holding down the Shift key constrains the Line tool to a straight line.

6 **Double-click the Line tool in the Tools palette.**

The Stroke palette opens.

7 **Use the Stroke palette Options menu to access Show Options, if they are not already visible.**

When you choose Show Options, you can access the Stroke Type and Endpoint options, such as arrows.

8 **Click the drop-down Weight menu and choose 3 pt. Click the Type menu and choose Dashed.**

When you choose Dashed, the Corners and Dash-and-Gap options become available.

9 **In the Corners section at the bottom of the palette, choose Adjust gaps and dashes from the list of options. Type "2 pt" in the first Dash box and "5 pt" in the first Gap box. Press Return/Enter to apply your entries.**

You have a 3-pt dashed line with 2-pt segments and 5-pt gaps.

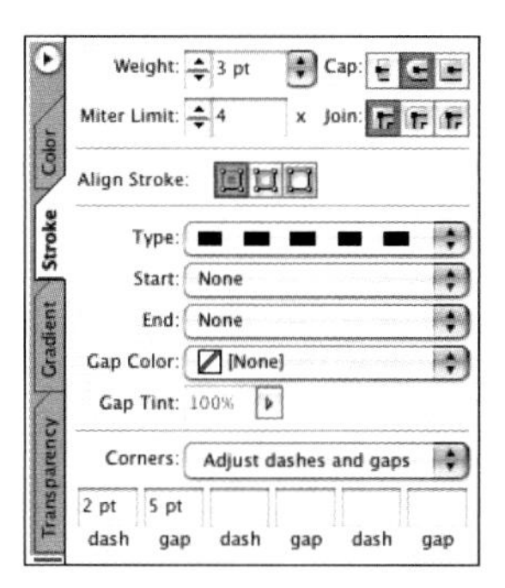

FIGURE 4.12

10 **Click the middle Cap option to choose Rounded End caps.**

Rounded end caps are applied to each of the dashed segments. They are considerably longer than the 2 points specified for square end caps.

FIGURE 4.13

11 **From the End menu in the Stroke palette, choose Curved.**

The right side of the line becomes a curved arrowhead.

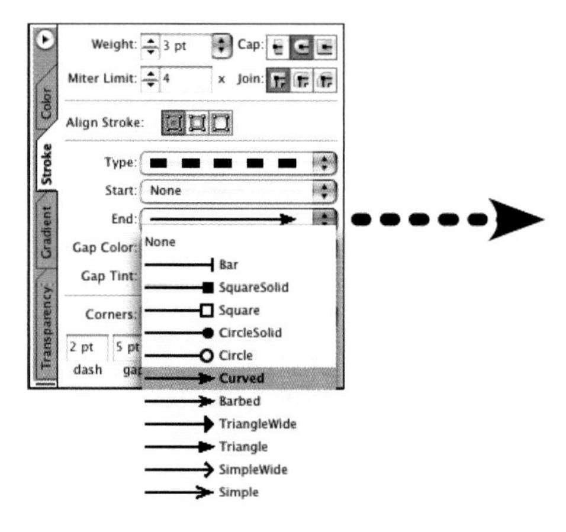

FIGURE 4.14

12 **Deselect the line.**

The stroke automatically resets to Weight of 1 pt, Cap to Butt, Type to Solid, and End to None.

13 **Save the document as "objects.indd". Leave it open for the next exercise.**

Draw Basic Shapes

1 **In the open document, choose the Ellipse tool from the Tools palette. Drag the cursor on the page.**

Note how the shape changes as the tool moves.

2 **Hold down the Shift key and draw a 1-inch circle on the page. Use the Selection tool to move the circle to the upper-left corner of the page. If necessary, adjust the size in the Control palette.**

Holding the Shift key while dragging constrains the ellipse to a circle. If you click the Constrain Proportions icon to the right of the Width and Height fields in the Control palette, you adjust both dimensions proportionally.

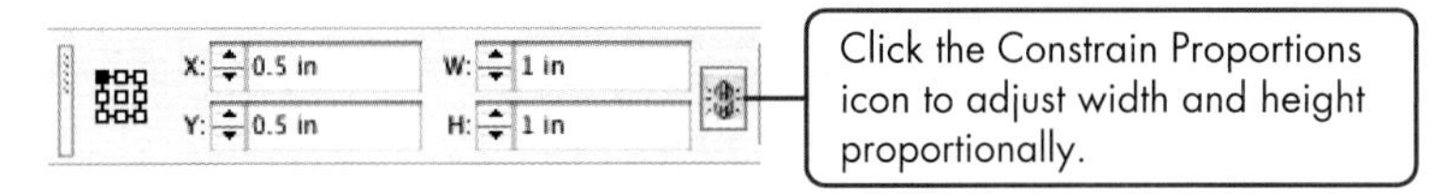

FIGURE 4.15

3 **Choose the Rectangle tool from the Tools palette. Click the cursor on the page and drag.**

Note how the rectangle can be created at any size or proportion.

4 **Hold down the Shift key while you draw a 1-inch square. Switch to the Selection tool and position it to the right of the circle.**

The Shift key constrains the rectangle to a square.

5 **Double-click the Polygon tool in the Tools palette.**

The Polygon Settings dialog box opens.

6 **In the Polygon Settings dialog box, set the Number of Sides to "8". Leave the Star Inset field at 0%. Click OK.**

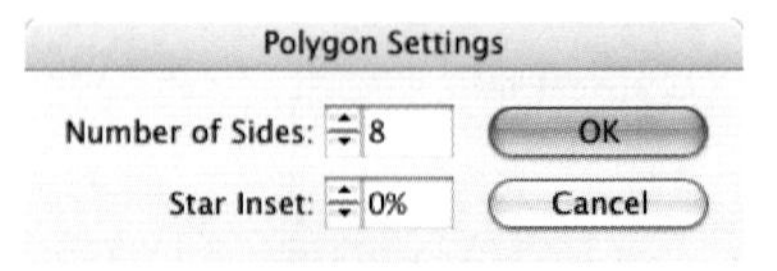

FIGURE 4.16

7 **With the Polygon tool selected, drag the cursor on the page.**

The polygon grows disproportionately as you drag the cursor.

8 **Hold down the Shift key while you drag the Polygon tool.**

The sides of the polygon are constrained to the same size.

9 **Draw a 1 × 1-in polygon. Move it to the right of the square. Deselect the polygon.**

Three objects should be lined up — the circle, square, and polygon.

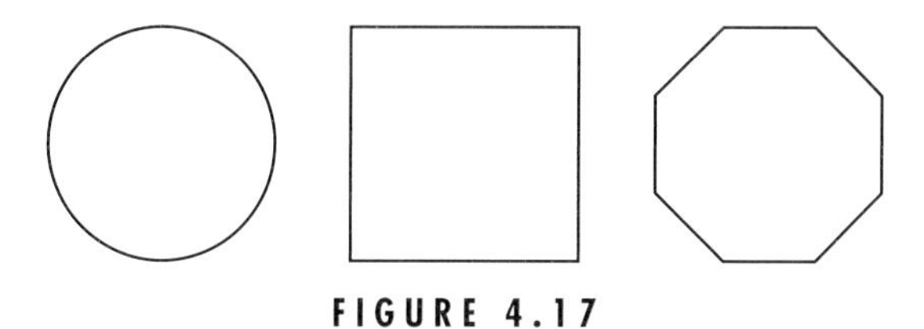

FIGURE 4.17

10 **Save the file and leave it open for the next exercise.**

To Extend Your Knowledge...

MORE ON PATHS

The Ellipse, Rectangle, and Polygon tools automatically create closed paths. The Line tool can only create linear, open paths. Closed paths can be broken with the Scissors tool. The Pen tool and the Pencil tool can be used to create either open or closed paths.

LESSON 2 Adding Color

Black-and-white images are suitable (and often required) for certain types of designs. A large percentage of designs used in advertising and on the Web, however, require the addition of color. Colors can be mixed using the CMYK, RGB, or L*a*b color mode in the Color palette. Colors can also be mixed and retained in the Swatches palette, where swatches from other color modes, such as PANTONE, can be selected and retained. (An in-depth discussion on color is included in *Essentials for Design: InDesign Level 2.*)

When you open the Swatches palette, you see ten default colors. The first four colors (None, Paper, Black, and Registration) cannot be deleted. Their names appear in brackets. The color of Paper can be changed to reflect the appearance of a document printed on paper colored other than white, but it will not add color to the actual document. The next three colors (Cyan, Magenta, and Yellow) are standard colors for the CMYK (process) color mode. The final three colors (Red, Green, and Blue) are the RGB equivalents to the CMYK color mode.

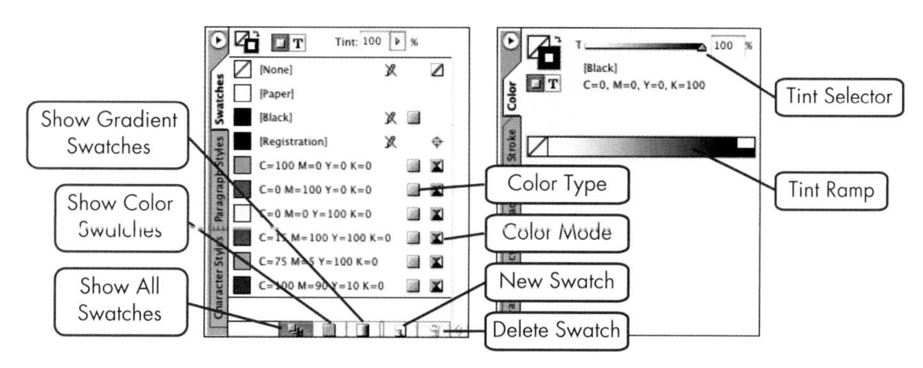

FIGURE 4.18

Prepare Color Swatches

1 **In the open objects.indd, open the Swatches and Color palettes.**

The Swatches palette is in the same palette bay as the Character Styles and Paragraph Styles palettes. The Color palette shares the palette bay with the Transparency, Gradient, and Stroke palettes.

2 **In the Swatches palette, hold down the Shift key while you click the bottom three swatches. Click the Delete Swatch icon.**

Holding the Shift key when selecting allows you to select multiple items. These three swatches approximate RGB colors, which are normally used for images that appear on monitors. Since InDesign is primarily used for creating documents for print, you don't need these three swatches.

3 **Click the Swatches palette Options icon. Choose New Color Swatch from the Options menu.**

4 **In the New Color Swatch dialog box, choose Spot as the Color Type, and choose PANTONE solid coated from the drop-down menu.**

The PANTONE dialog box appears.

PANTONE solid coated, PANTONE solid matte, and PANTONE solid uncoated are designed to show the effect of using coated, matte, and uncoated papers. Using the same color, such as PANTONE 341, in both coated and uncoated would require two separate color plates.

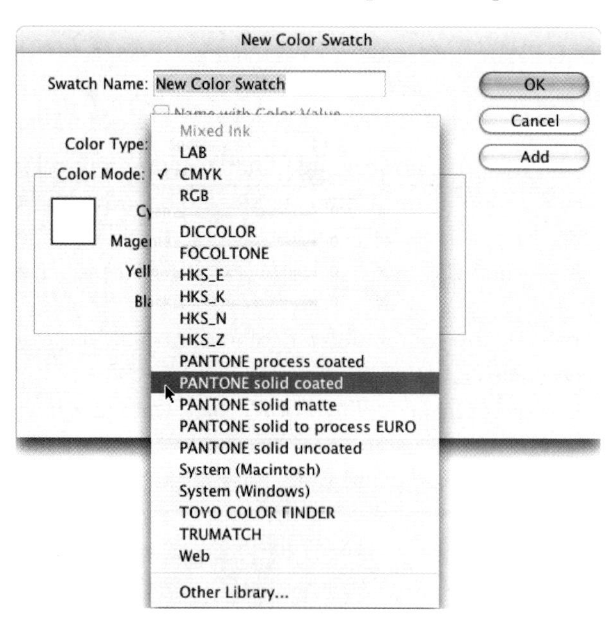

FIGURE 4.19

5 **Type "341" in the PANTONE dialog box. Click Add.**

PANTONE 341 C is assigned as the Swatch Name. The swatch is added to the palette. The New Color Swatch menu closes. Note the difference in the Color Type icon. In the graphics industry, PANTONE colors are generally referred to as ***PMS colors***. PANTONE 341 would be referred to as PMS 341. We refer to PANTONE colors as PMS colors in this book.

6 **Change the Color Mode to CMYK, and change the Color Type to Process. Name the swatch "Process 341". Click OK.**

The Process 341 swatch is added to the palette. You might choose to create a custom palette such as this if you had specific corporate colors that needed to be applied to different types of documents. For example, you might use the spot color for business cards, and use the process color for color brochures.

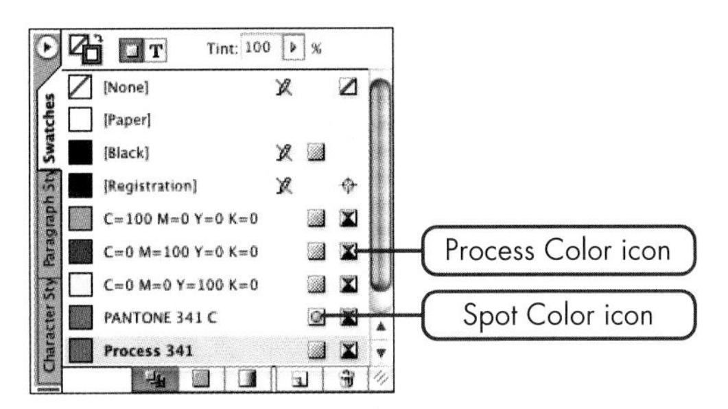

FIGURE 4.20

7 **Save the document and leave it open for the next exercise.**

Apply Color to Shapes

1 **In the open document, click the Fill icon in the Tools palette to bring it to the front of the Stroke icon, making the Fill icon active.**

2 **Use the Selection tool to click the circle. In the Swatches palette, click the Yellow swatch (C=0, M=0, Y=100, K=0).**

The circle is filled with yellow.

3 **Click the tab for the Stoke palette (or double-click the Line tool in the Tools palette). In the Weight pop-up menu, change the Weight to "4 pt". Press Return/Enter.**

4 **In the Tools palette, click the Stroke icon to make it active. Click the Process 341 swatch in the Swatches palette.**

Making the Stroke icon active allows you to apply color to the stroke of the object. The circle now has a 4-pt green border.

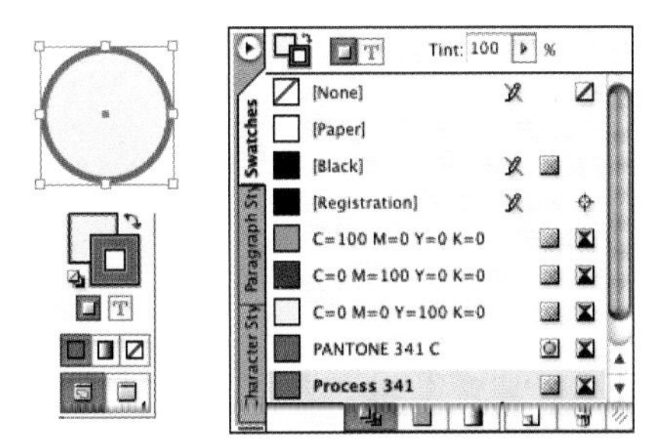

FIGURE 4.21

5 **Use the Selection tool to click the square. In the Swatches palette, make the Fill icon active. Click the Magenta swatch (C=0, M=100, Y=0, K=0).**

The square is filled with magenta. The Apply Color box also becomes magenta.

6 **In the Stroke palette, set the Weight to "6 pt". Set the Type to Dashed and enter "2 pt" in the first Dash box. Leave the Gap box blank.**

You now have a magenta square with a 6-pt dashed stroke, with 2-pt dashes alternating with 2-pt gaps.

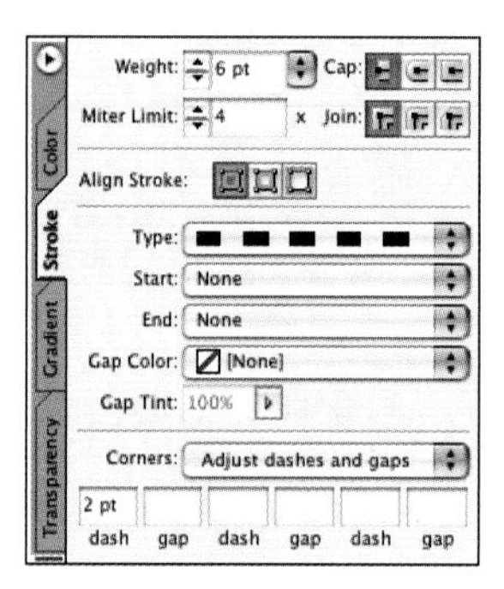

FIGURE 4.22

7 **Click the Stroke icon to make it active. Click the Cyan color swatch (C=100, M=0, Y=0, K=0).**

If necessary, zoom in to see that half the stroke extends inside the object and half extends outside. This is the default stroke alignment, and forms a ***trap*** — a condition where the stroke overprints the image beneath it, so there is no gap when the object is printed.

FIGURE 4.23

8 **Use the Selection tool to click the Cyan Stroke icon from either the Tools palette or the Swatches palette, and drag it to the center of the polygon.**

When you click the Stroke icon or Fill icon in either the Tools palette or the Swatches palette, it becomes the active icon in both palettes.

9 **Click the Magenta Fill icon and drag it to the edge of the polygon.**

This is an alternate method of filling the polygon with cyan and stroking it with magenta. Note that the polygon is not actively selected.

10 **Click the polygon to select it. In the Swatches palette, click the Fill icon to make it active. Type "50%" in the Tint dialog box. Deselect the polygon.**

The fill of the polygon changes to a 50% tint of cyan.

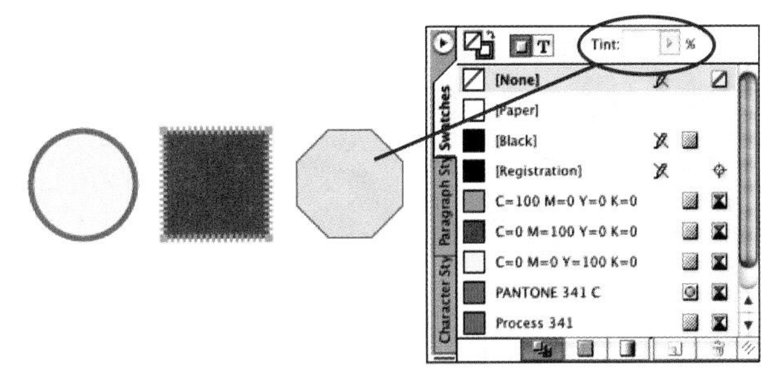

FIGURE 4.24

11 **Click anywhere on the page to deselect. Save your changes and leave the document open for the next exercise.**

To Extend Your Knowledge...

ABOUT TINTS

A ***tint*** is a lightened derivative of a solid ink color that is produced by creating a percentage of the color. You can use the Swatches palette to create tints. You can also create tints from ***process color builds*** (combinations of process inks), but the results are somewhat unpredictable. You should only create tints from spot colors and the four solid process colors.

THE "K" IN CMYK

Why use "K" for black in CMYK? Why not "B" for black? There are a number of answers to this question — and most of them are right. Black has long been considered the base, or "Key" color; hence, "K" for Key. Additionally, printers are often imprecise when they talk about color. Most call cyan "blue" and call magenta "red." To avoid confusion between "blue" and "black," the "K" refers to blacK. Take your pick from the reasons we use "K"; the one most nearly correct is "tradition."

SPECIFYING COLOR IN L*A*B

Even though it's possible to do so, we do not recommend using the L*a*b color mode in InDesign. Since L*a*b employs two color modes with different color spaces, all L*a*b colors do not display correctly on a computer monitor or in print. Just say "No" to using L*a*b color in InDesign.

LESSON 3 Creating and Applying Gradients

A ***gradient*** is a fill or blend consisting of two or more colors or tints that blend from one to another using the mathematics of the PostScript language. A gradient can be linear or radial. The most basic gradient blends from a single color to white.

You may have seen gradients that have distinct bands (called ***banding***) between color tones. There are only 100 possible steps in a printed gradient, from 0–100%. If any step is wider than approximately 0.05 inches, it is usually visible to the eye. Gradients prepared for display on monitors can include up to 255 steps.

Visible banding can occur because the gradient is too large for the available resolution of the device that imaged it, or the gradient doesn't contain enough levels. A 5-inch gradient from 0–100% black will not band, but a 5-inch gradient from 0–50% black will band because the ratio between the distance of each step would be greater than 0.05 inches, and the steps would be visible. PostScript Level 3 has resolved most banding problems, but many print providers still use PostScript Level 2 equipment; because of this inconsistency from one service provider to the next, you should be aware of the potential for banding in your printed documents.

Create and Apply a Simple Gradient

1 **With objects.indd still open, choose Black from the Swatches palette. Choose New Gradient Swatch from the Swatches palette Options menu.**

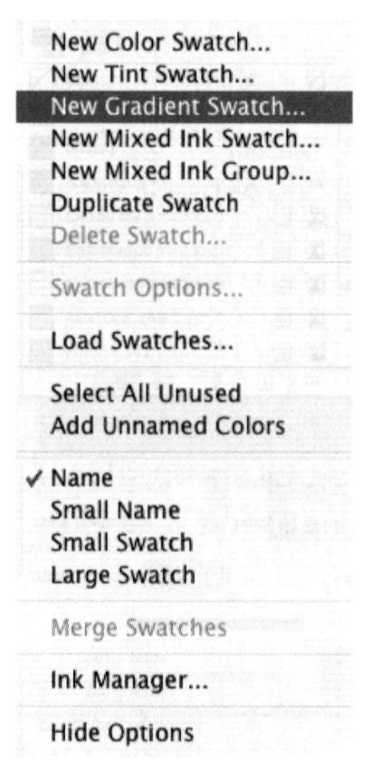

FIGURE 4.25

2 **Name the new swatch "Black to White".**

3 **Click the First Stop Color (leftmost) icon in the Gradient Ramp.**

4 **Leave the Type field as Linear.**

5 **Click the Black swatch in the swatch selector list and choose Swatches from the Stop Color menu.**

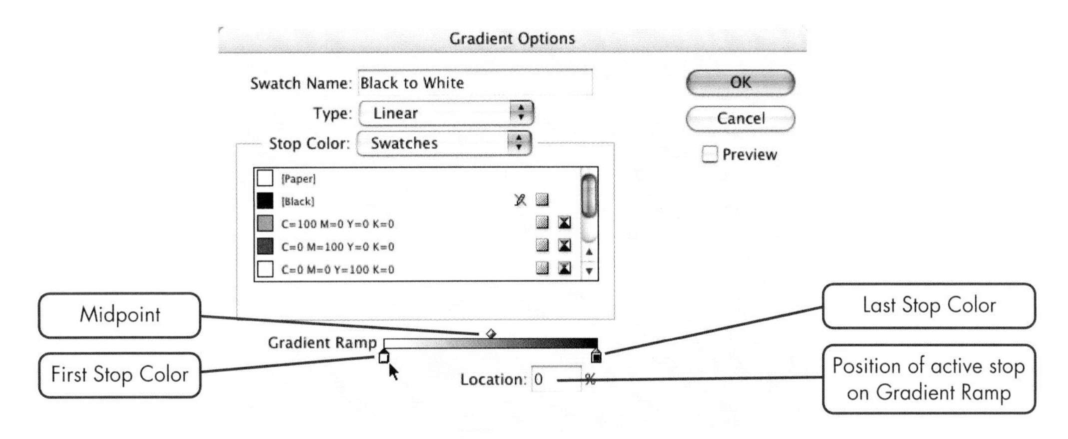

FIGURE 4.26

6 **Click the Last Stop Color icon (on the right end) in the Gradient Ramp. Choose Paper from the swatch selector list.**

7 **Click the Midpoint icon (shaped like a diamond) above the bar and move it to the left and right.**

Note how moving the midpoint (50% of each color) affects the appearance of the gradient. If the midpoint is moved to 70%, how does this affect the maximum length of the gradient? The 20% difference means the maximum length of the gradient will be 40% shorter (in order to avoid banding) because the length of each step in the 100% to 50% area of the black is increased. Many banding problems occur because of inattention to details such as this.

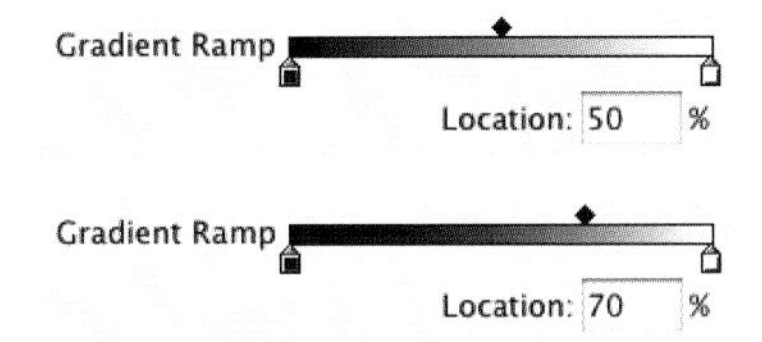

FIGURE 4.27

8 **When you are finished experimenting, reposition the Midpoint icon at 50%. Click OK.**

9 **Click the Fill icon to make it active, and choose the gradient in the Swatches palette, if it is not already selected.**

10 **Draw a rectangle.**

The gradient is automatically applied to the rectangle.

11 **Save the document and leave it open.**

Create a Three-Color Gradient

1 **In the open document, add two PANTONE solid-coated swatches to your Swatches palette: PANTONE 185 and PANTONE 286.**

2 **Choose New Gradient Swatch from the Swatches palette Options menu. Name the new swatch "Red, White & Blue".**

3 **Click the First Stop Color icon in the Gradient Ramp.**

4 **Leave the Type as Linear and set the Stop Color to Swatches.**

5 **Click PMS 185 as the color for this stop.**

6 **Click the Last Stop Color icon in the Gradient Ramp. Set it to PMS 286.**

7 **Click directly below the Gradient Ramp bar, beneath the Midpoint icon at 50%.**

A new stop is inserted at the point you clicked.

8 **Apply the Paper swatch to this stop. Click OK.**

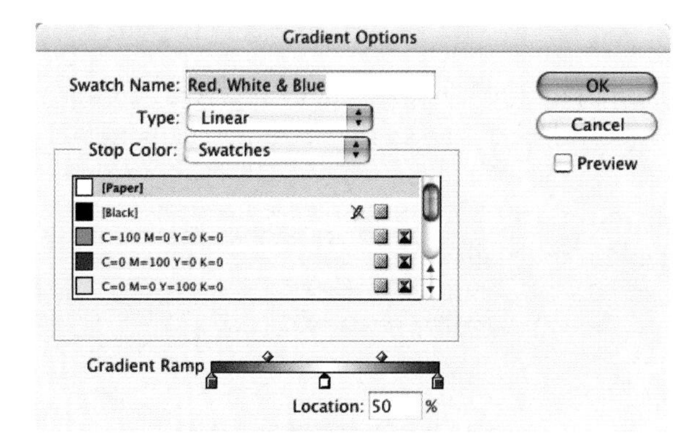

FIGURE 4.28

9 **Click the rectangle with the gradient you created in the previous exercise.**

The Fill color in the Tools palette reverts to the Black to White gradient.

10 **With the Fill active, click the Red, White & Blue gradient to apply it. Deselect the rectangle.**

The new gradient is applied to the rectangle.

11 **Save your changes and leave the document open for the next exercise.**

If you have problems...

If you mix color modes in gradients, InDesign converts all the colors to CMYK. Be sure to use only one color mode when creating a gradient — all spot, all CMYK, or all RGB colors.

Create CMYK Gradients

1 **In the open document, choose New Gradient Swatch from the Swatches palette Options menu. Name the gradient "Blue to Yellow".**

The middle stop you created in the previous exercise is still visible.

2 **Click the middle stop and drag it away from the Gradient Ramp.**

The stop is removed.

3 **Click the First Stop Color icon. Choose CMYK as the Stop Color. Assign the color as C:0, M:20, Y:100, K:0.**

Mixing a little magenta with pure yellow creates a richer yellow, which is especially useful when working with gradients.

4 **Click the Last Stop Color icon. With the Stop Color set to CMYK, assign the color as C:100, M:80, Y:0, K:0. Ensure that the midpoint remains at 50%. Click OK.**

Even though you created unnamed colors, you used them in a named gradient, so you can edit them later.

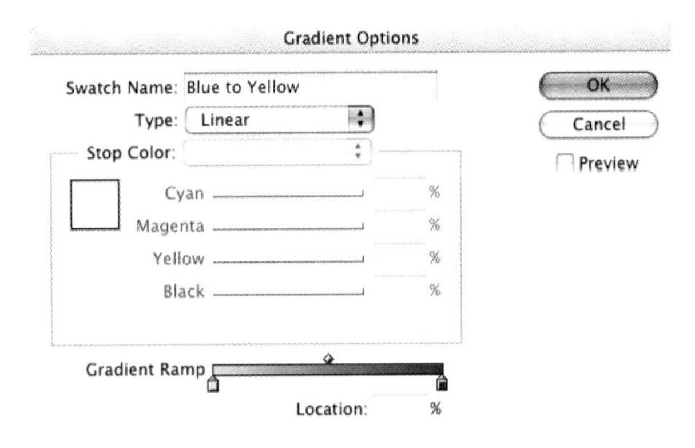

FIGURE 4.29

5 **Open the Gradient palette. Choose Show Options from the Gradient palette Options menu.**

The options may already be showing.

6 **Click the Reverse button to flip the stop colors. Drag the reversed swatch to the Swatches palette.**

The name does not match the direction of the gradient, which could be confusing. When you use this method to reverse a gradient, rather than rebuild it, it does not change the gradient definition, or its application to objects.

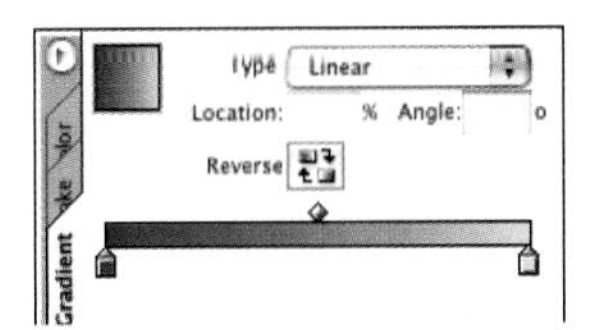

FIGURE 4.30

7 **Select the original Blue to Yellow swatch. Click the Delete Swatch icon.**

The swatch is deleted.

8 **Double-click the new gradient swatch and name the reversed swatch "Blue to Yellow". Click OK.**

9 **Apply the new gradient to the existing gradient rectangle, and then deselect the rectangle.**

10 **Double-click the Blue to Yellow swatch.**

The Gradient Options dialog box appears so you can edit the swatch.

11 **Change the Magenta value of the blue stop to 40%.**

The new value is applied to the object containing the gradient, even though the object was not selected. Before changing values of colors or gradients, be sure you want to apply those values to all objects in the document to which that color swatch is applied.

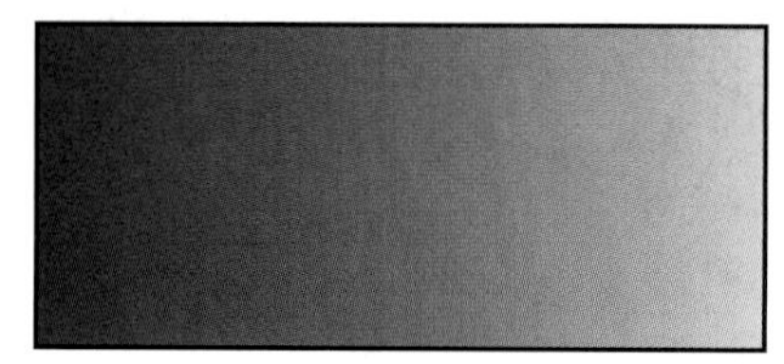

Original Blue to Yellow Gradient
(C:100, M:80/Y:100, M:40)

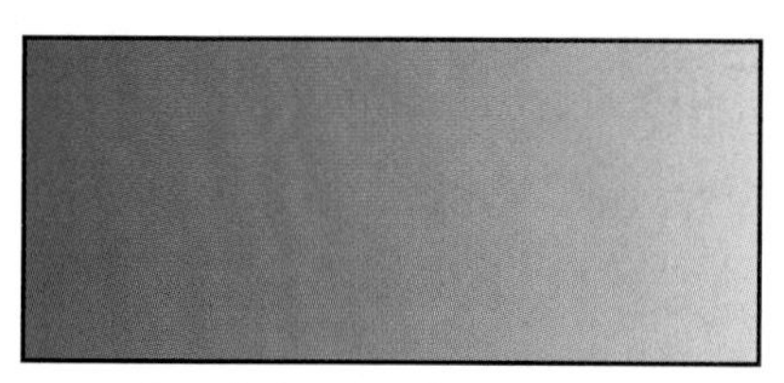

Altered Blue to Yellow Gradient
(C:100, M:40/Y:100, M:40)

FIGURE 4.31

12 **Save your changes and leave the file open for the next exercise.**

To Extend Your Knowledge...

WORK WITH YOUR SERVICE PROVIDER

Working with a number of color modes is fun and adds variety to your jobs. You need to remember, however, that process colors (CMYK) can create most of the colors you need. Adding a spot color adds another plate to the printing process — each color has its own printing plate — and every additional color results in increased printing costs.

While you can specify spot colors as Toyo, Trumatch, or Focoltone, remember that PANTONE is the de facto standard spot color mode in the United States. If you specify color using another system, your printer may not support it, and it may be regarded as a (very expensive) specialty item.

LESSON 4 Importing Color

In addition to creating colors in a document, you can import colors from other documents or from images you place. Importing colors can be useful when you need to match colors from other documents, or if you need to pull a color from an image.

If your clients use specific colors — perhaps for their logos — it is good practice to create a document (one per client) that contains a swatch palette populated with the colors used on a regular basis. It is usually best to include the PANTONE colors they use, in addition to colors mixed from the four process inks.

If you create multimedia pages for your clients, you should also store RGB and/or Web-safe approved colors in a document, so you can save time "mixing" those colors when you need them. Your productivity increases when you create client-specific or product-specific color documents, since the inks are already mixed, and the colors are already selected from the various libraries.

Import Colors

1. **Continue in the open objects.indd.**

2. **From the Swatches palette Options menu, choose Load Swatches.**

3. **Navigate to your Project_04 folder and choose fairisles.indd. Click Open.**

   The color PANTONE 116C is added to your palette. Faire Isles uses PMS 341 and 116 as its standard colors.

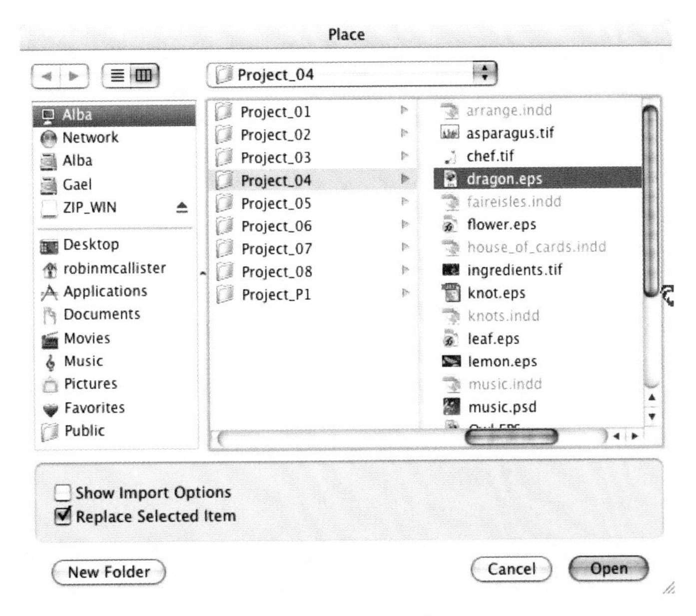

FIGURE 4.32

4. **Choose File>Place. From the Project_04 folder, double-click dragon.eps to import it.**

5 **When the loaded-image icon appears, click the page to place the image.**

The image imports, as well as its colors. You can match a headline or any other element to the imported colors from this image.

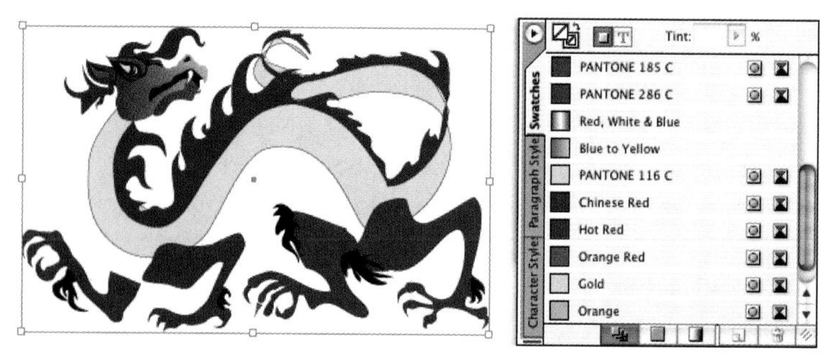

FIGURE 4.33

6 **Save your changes and close the file.**

To Extend Your Knowledge...

ALWAYS NAME COLORS

Whenever you create a process color, be sure to name it appropriately. If you create the color in the Swatches palette, InDesign names the color by defining its color values, such as C=100, M=50, Y=0, K=10. This is not the case when you create colors in the Color palette.

LESSON 5 Drawing with the Pen Tools

The Pen and Pencil tools create paths comprised of ***Bézier curves.*** These complex mathematical formulae are entered when you position points with the Pen tool or when you draw a free-form shape with the Pencil tool.

When the Pen tool is used, you simply click the pen tip on the page. This defines a point that becomes the beginning of your line. When you click a second time, you define a second point; the distance between these two points is a path. As long as the Pen tool remains active, you can add any number of points to create an unending path. To deselect a path, click an empty area of the page with the Selection tool, Direct Selection tool, Type tool, or any other drawing tool.

Each click of the Pen tool creates a new anchor point on the page. A single segment (path), which can be straight or curved, connects each pair of adjacent anchor points. Paths are categorized as open or closed. An open path has a separate beginning and endpoint; a closed path is continuous, and has no apparent beginning or end.

A ***corner point*** is an anchor point at which a path abruptly changes direction. It may connect two straight segments, two curved segments, or a straight and a curved segment. A ***smooth point*** gets its name from the shape of the curved segments that surround it; the segments are smooth in their flow and continuity as they extend from the point. The clearest identifying aspect of the smooth point is that it has two direction lines you can use to adjust both segments attached to the anchor point.

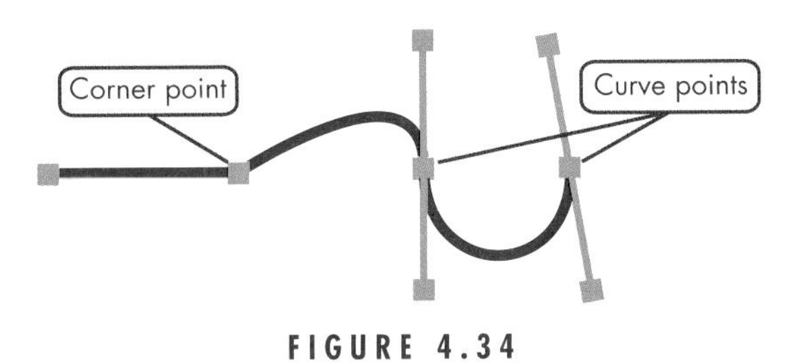

FIGURE 4.34

The tools in the Pen tool Options menu are used primarily for editing or modifying existing paths. Clicking a path with the Add Anchor Point tool adds a new point to the path. Clicking with the Delete Anchor Point tool removes an existing anchor point. Dragging an anchor point with the Convert Anchor Point tool changes the type of point; clicking a smooth point removes the curves from the segments, and dragging a corner point converts it to a smooth point.

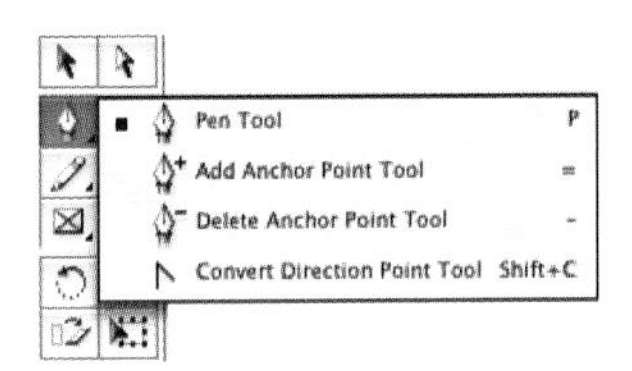

FIGURE 4.35

When you drag with the Pen tool, an icon at the lower right of the tool indicates the status of the drawing process. These symbols can be helpful when you are creating a complex object.

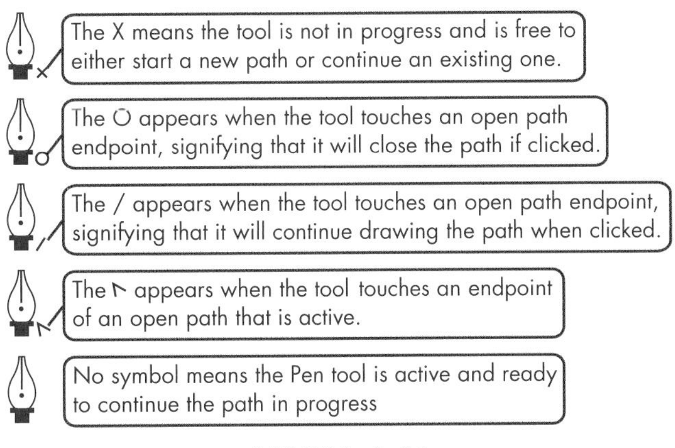

FIGURE 4.36

Draw with the Pen Tool

1 **Create a new Letter-size 1-Column document with 0.5-inch Margins all around.**

2 **Click the Default Fill and Stroke icon in the Tools palette.**

This sets the stroke to a black line and the fill to none. Alternately, you can press the "D" key to invoke the default fill and stroke.

3 **From the vertical ruler on the left of the screen, drag a guide to the 2-inch mark on the horizontal ruler on the top. Make certain that Snap to Guides is checked in the View menu.**

4 **Choose the Pen tool in the Tools palette. Near the top of the page, single-click the guide to create a beginning point. Move the cursor to the right about 4 inches, press the Shift key to constrain, and click again. Do not deselect the object.**

You created a single line segment. The guide will assist you in keeping the alignment straight when the final clicks are applied to create this object.

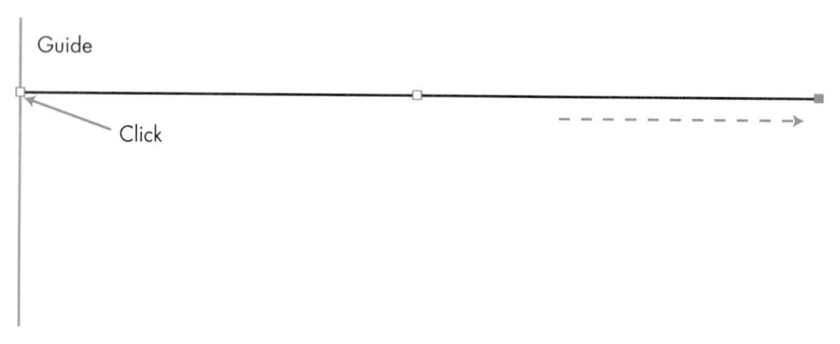

FIGURE 4.37

5 **Move the Pen tool cursor about 1 inch below the second point, hold down the Shift key, and click again to continue the path. Do not deselect.**

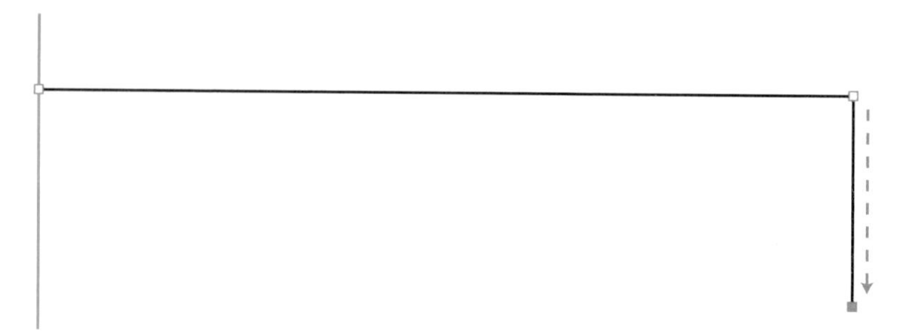

FIGURE 4.38

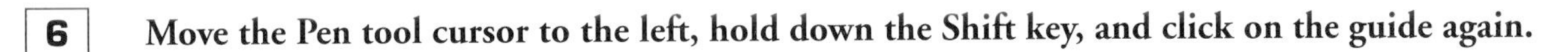

6 **Move the Pen tool cursor to the left, hold down the Shift key, and click on the guide again.**

The anchor point snaps to the guide, even if you didn't click in exactly the right place.

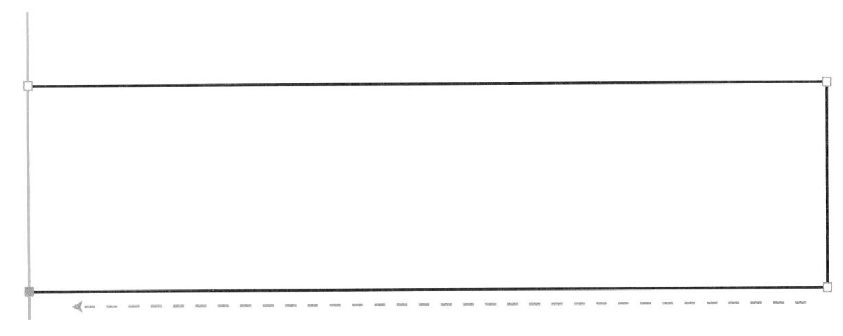

FIGURE 4.39

7 **Hold down the Shift key, move the Pen tool up, and click the beginning point.**

You created 4 × 1-inch rectangle from scratch.

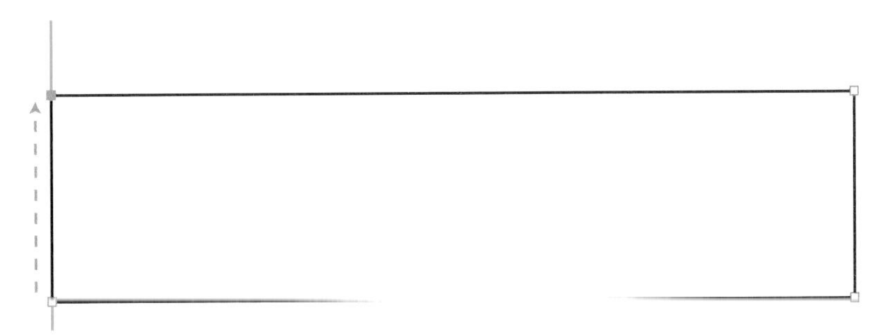

FIGURE 4.40

8 **Save the document as "pentool.indd" and leave it open for the next exercise.**

Create an Irregular-Shaped Object

1 **With pentool.indd open and the Pen tool active, click near the center of the page to create a beginning point. Move the cursor up and to the right, and then click again.**

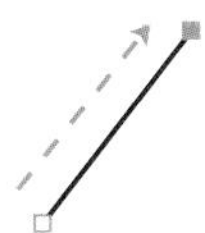

FIGURE 4.41

2 **Move the Pen tool down and to the right, below the beginning point, and click again.**

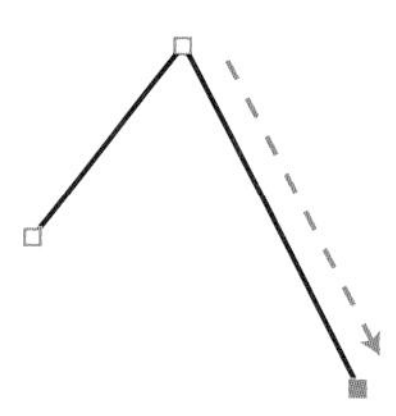

FIGURE 4.42

3 **Move the tool down and to the left, and click once more.**

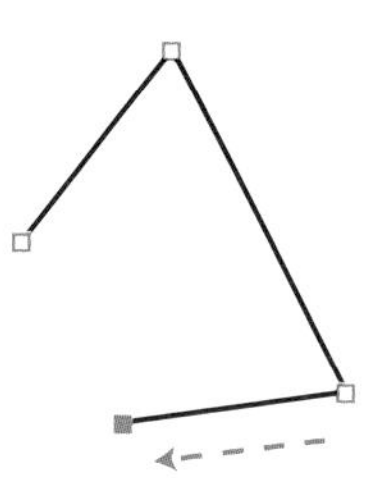

FIGUIRE 4.43

4 **Move the Pen tool up, and add a final click on the beginning point.**

As you approach the endpoint of the path, the "o" appears in the Pen tool tip, indicating that clicking will close the path. You created a free-form object without the constraint of the Shift key.

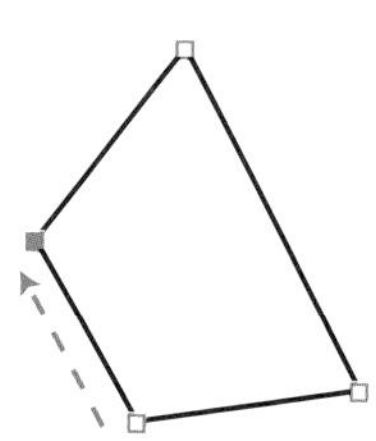

FIGURE 4.44

5 **Choose the Selection tool from the Tools palette.**

This action automatically selects the object you just drew. Notice the blue bounding box that surrounds the object. The bounding box tells you the object is selected.

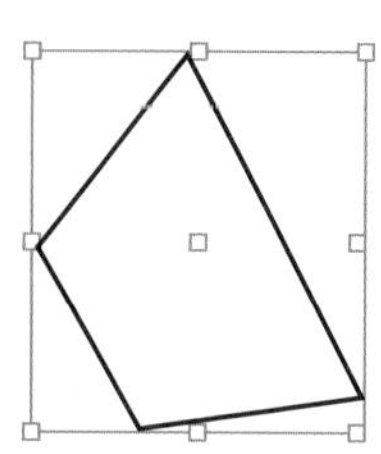

FIGURE 4.45

6 **Drag the right-middle handle on the bounding box to the right. Release the mouse button when the object is as wide as you want.**

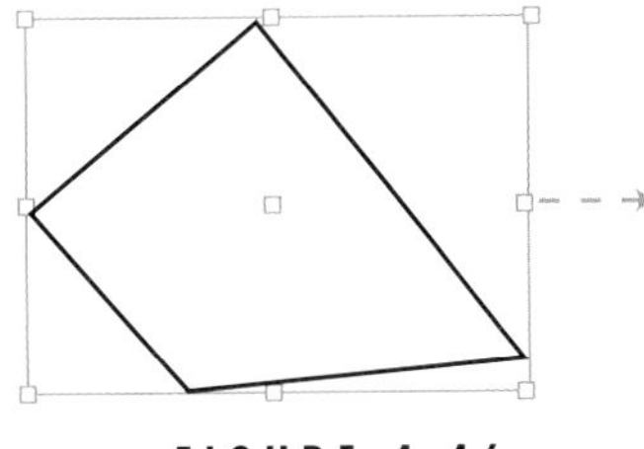

FIGURE 4.46

7 **Drag the bottom bounding box handle upward.**

The bounding box allows you to modify objects quickly and easily.

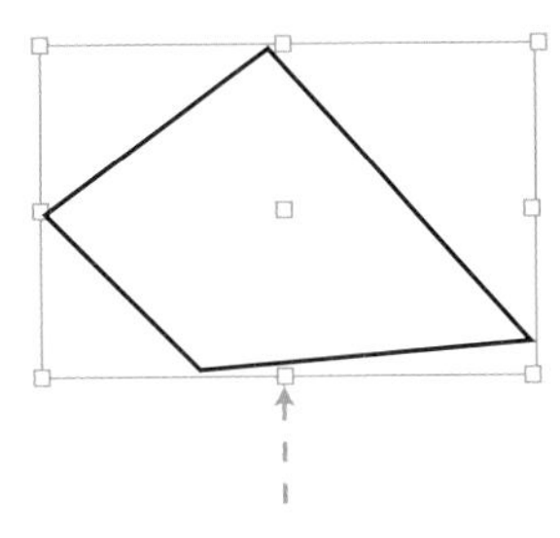

FIGURE 4.47

8 **Drag the bottom-right corner handle down to the right.**

When the corner handles are dragged without the Shift key, the object transforms with a free-form effect.

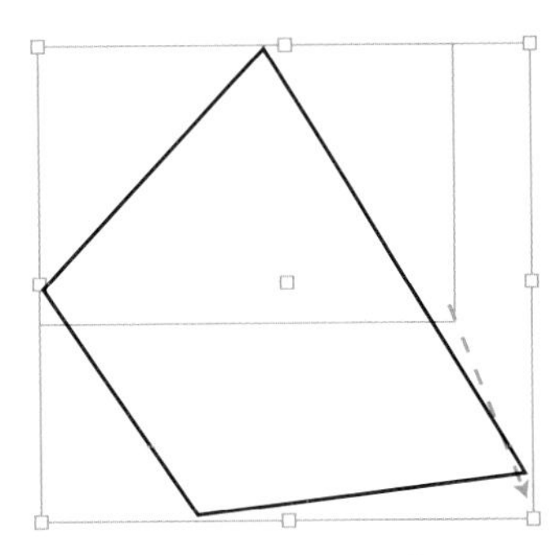

FIGURE 4.48

9 **Hold down the Shift key while you drag the bottom-right corner handle toward the upper-left corner of the bounding box.**

The object retains its proportions.

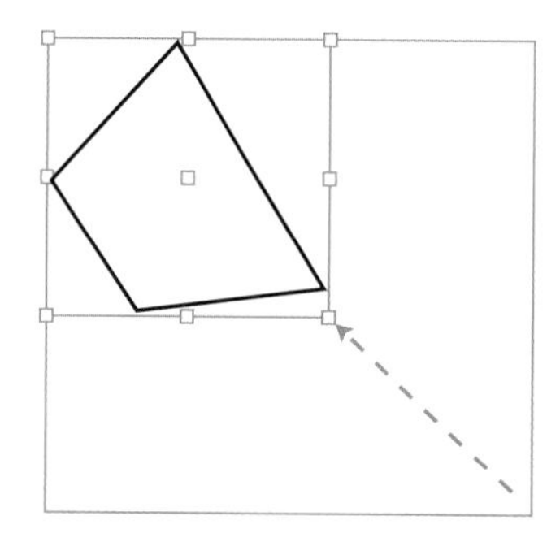

FIGURE 4.49

10 **Save your changes and keep the document open for the next exercise.**

Create Curved Segments

1 **With pentool.indd open, choose the Pen tool from the Tools palette. Click the cursor anywhere on the page. Move the cursor about one inch to the right. Hold down the Shift key and click again to create a line segment.**

2 **Click the Pen tool on the endpoint and drag out a direction line. Release the mouse button.**

You created a corner point and established the direction the line will take when you click the mouse again.

FIGURE 4.50

3 **Move the Pen tool cursor one inch farther to the right, hold down the Shift key and click. Release the Shift key, and drag diagonally on the page.**

You created a smooth point with a double control handle. If you click without dragging, you create a corner point with a direction line.

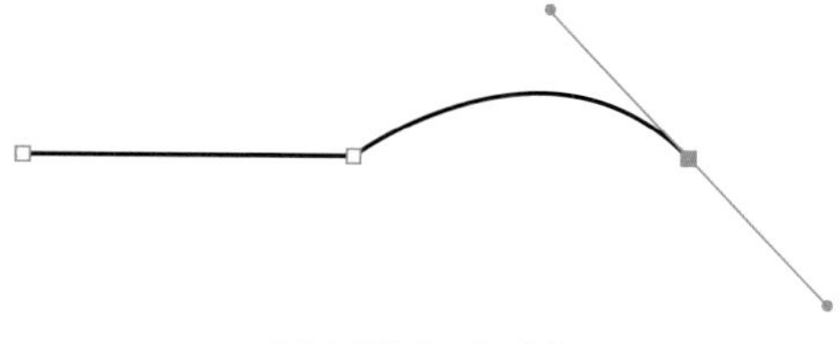

FIGURE 4.51

4 **Hold down the Shift key while you move the Pen tool an inch farther to the right. Single-click the Pen tool on the page to finalize the path.**

FIGURE 4.52

5 **Use the Direct Selection tool to click the second point. Drag the tip of the direction line to change the curve's shape.**

The direction line of the curved segment follows the corner point.

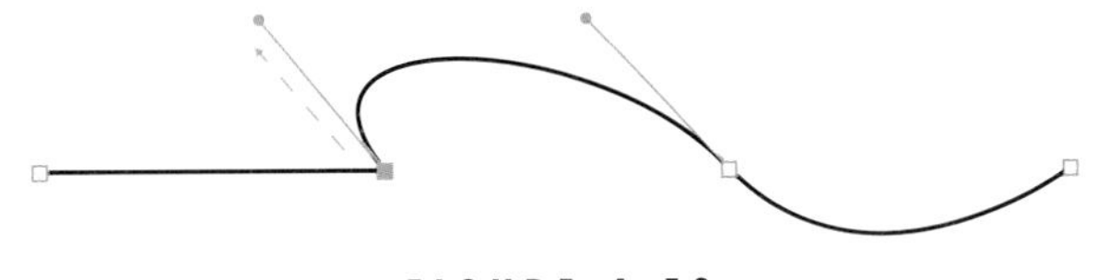

FIGURE 4.53

6 **Click the third point and drag either of the top handles to alter the curve.**

The curving segments on either side of the anchor point change as you drag.

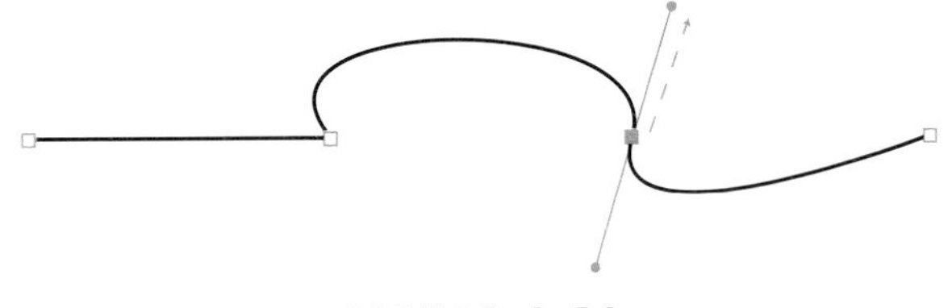

FIGURE 4.54

7 **Save your changes and leave the document open for the next exercise.**

Modify Shapes

It is common practice to modify a shape — sometimes radically — once it has been created. In addition to the Direct Selection tool, you can use the Add Anchor Point, Delete Anchor Point, and Convert Direction Point tools to modify existing shapes. These last three tools are located beneath the Pen tool icon in the Tools palette.

1 **Continue working in the open document.**

2 **Choose the Add Anchor Point tool from the Tools palette.**

3 **Click in the middle of the bottom stroke of the rectangle you created in a previous exercise.**

A new point is added to the path.

4 **Switch to the Direct Selection tool. Drag the new point down approximately one inch.**

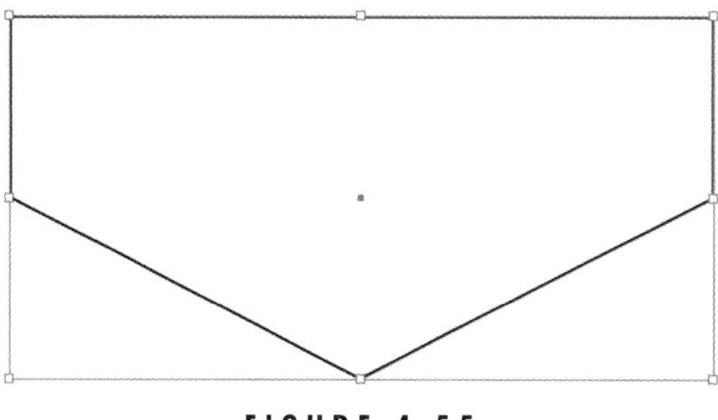

FIGURE 4.55

5 **Switch to the Convert Direction Point tool (one of the optional Pen tools). Drag the new point approximately 1.5 inches to the left.**

The corner point changes to a curve point. If you were to click one of the curve points, it would be converted to a corner point. You can directly access the Convert Direction Point tool by pressing Shift-C.

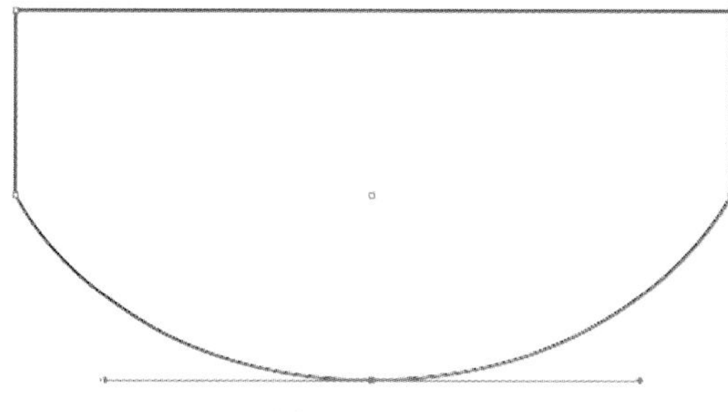

FIGURE 4.56

6 **Switch to the Delete Anchor Point tool. Click the point you just converted.**

The point is removed, and you are back to your original rectangle.

7 **Save your changes and close the document.**

To Extend Your Knowledge...

MIRRORING OBJECTS

You can use the bounding box to mirror objects. When you drag the selected handle toward and past the opposing handle, you change the horizontal or vertical appearance of the object. This is also known as ***reflecting*** or ***flipping*** the object.

THE PEN TOOL AND FILLS

When you use the Pen tool to draw a path, it's best to set the fill to None (which is the default), so it doesn't interfere with drawing. You can apply a fill to an open path — the fill jumps from the starting point to the last-clicked point as you draw.

LESSON 6 Using the Pencil Tool

The Pencil tool simulates freehand drawing. To use it, click a starting point and draw the desired shape. InDesign automatically creates numerous Bézier points and curves as you draw. When you are using the Pencil tool and you release the mouse button, the path ends, unlike a path drawn with the Pen tool. If a gap remains between the beginning and endpoints on the path, press the Option/Alt key to close the gap.

The Pencil tool is the default tool in the Tools palette, but two other tools reside below the Pencil tool — the Smooth tool and the Eraser tool. The Smooth tool removes unwanted raggedness from the paths in the drawing, while it retains the general shape of the object. The Smooth tool must be dragged along (not across) the part of a path that you want to smooth. Similar to its physical counterpart, you can drag the Eraser tool along the part of a path you want to remove.

Create a Freehand Drawing

1 **Open pencil_practice.indt from the Project_04 folder. Zoom to 150%.**

This file is a template you can use to practice drawing with the Pencil, Smooth, and Eraser tools. The flower image is on a locked layer beneath the layer you will work on, so you can't damage it. (You will learn about layers in *Essentials for Design: InDesign Level 2*.)

2 **Open the Stroke palette.**

On Windows systems and Macintosh OS 10.2, pressing the "F10" key toggles the Stroke palette.

3 **Double-click the Pencil tool.**

The Pencil Tool Preferences dialog box opens

4 **In the Tolerance area, set the Fidelity to 2 pixels and the Smoothness to 0%. Click OK.**

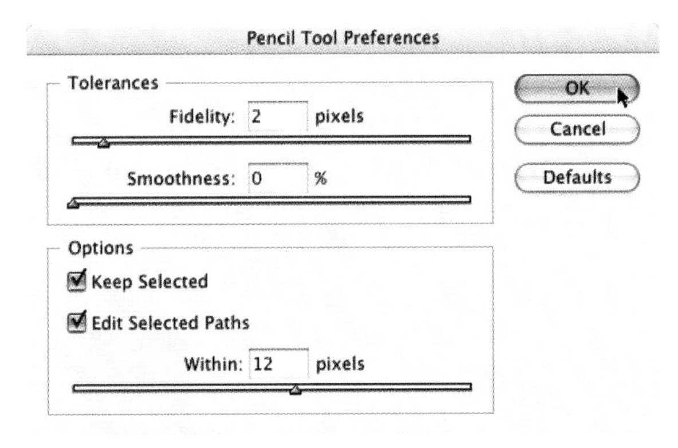

FIGURE 4.57

5 **Click the Default Fill and Stroke icon in the Tools palette.**

6 **Set the Stroke Weight to 1 pt.**

7 **Choose the Pencil tool from the Tools palette. Trace the star shape inside the flower. Press the Option/Alt key to complete the path, and then release the mouse button.**

A small circle appears to the right of the Pencil tool, indicating that the path will be closed.

FIGURE 4.58

8 **Fill the shape with Black. Deselect the shape.**

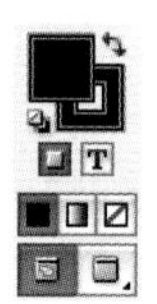

FIGURE 4.59

Drawing with a mouse is about as precise as drawing with a bar of soap, so don't be too concerned about the accuracy of your art. The goal is simply to learn how to use this tool.

9 **Return to a Fill of None. Use the Pencil tool to trace the white flower petals.**

10 **When the flower shape is complete, change the Fill to Paper and choose Object>Arrange>Send to Back.**

This command sends the flower behind the star shape.

11 **Deselect the object. Save the file as "flower.indd" and leave it open for the next exercise.**

Finish the Flower

1 **Continue using the Pencil tool in the open document.**

2 **For the outline of the flower, change the Stroke Weight to 12 pt. In the Pencil Tool Preferences dialog box, change the Edit Selected Paths Within value to 4 pixels. Trace the outline.**

If you start and stop while drawing the outline, you should stop on a rounded area, rather than a concave area.

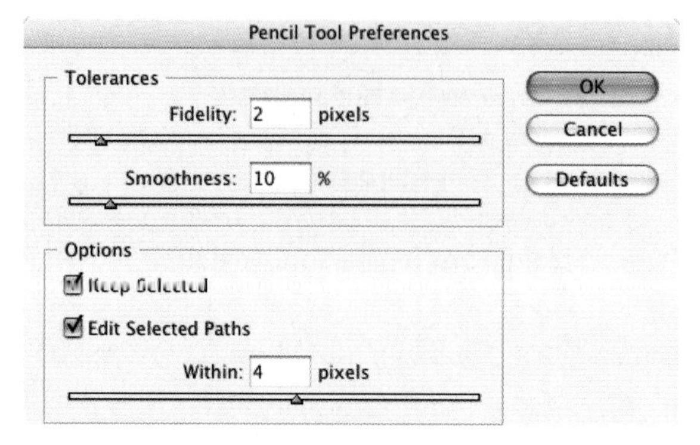

FIGURE 4.60

3 **Send the outline of the flower to the back and deselect.**

4 **Before drawing the stem, switch to a 1-pt Stroke Weight.**

The stem varies in width, so you need to outline it, and then fill it with black. Always draw with a fill of none; a colored fill makes it difficult to see what you are doing.

5 **When drawing the leaves, draw the white portion first, then outline with black. Send the black outlines to the back, as you did above.**

6 **If you make a mistake, switch to the Eraser tool and drag either across or along the length of the line.**

7 **Switch to the Pencil tool and begin re-tracing by clicking an endpoint.**

8 **When you finish the basic shapes, use the Selection tool to select a jagged line. Switch to the Smooth tool (one of the optional Pencil tools). Drag the Smooth tool along the jagged line. Do not rub across the line.**

You can press Command/Control to temporarily change to the Direct Selection tool to choose the next element to edit. Repeat as needed.

9 **Save the file as "flower.indd". Close the file.**

To Extend Your Knowledge...

CREATING GRAPHICS IN INDESIGN

Even though the tools in InDesign are very similar to the basic tool set in Illustrator and FreeHand, you should not use InDesign to create intensive illustrations. InDesign images cannot be imported into other applications, such as Microsoft Word or other page-layout applications.

THE PEN TOOL VS THE PENCIL

After completing the previous exercise, you probably realize that InDesign's Pencil tool is not designed to create quality drawings. If you must create artwork inside the program, the Pen tool is better suited for the job. The Pencil has its place, however, when you want to create a rough, hand-drawn illustration.

LESSON 7 Manipulating and Arranging Objects

Once an object is created, you may need to change its appearance — slightly or extensively. An object may need to be rotated a few degrees, mirrored, enlarged, or reduced. You may also need to change the stacking order of objects.

The Arrange feature in the Object menu allows you to rearrange the ***hierarchy*** (stacking order) of objects on a page. The four menu options save valuable time when moving objects forward and backward as necessary. Remember, the first item placed on the page is the lowest in the stacking order. The next item is placed on top of the first, and so on. At any time during development, you can use the Arrange menu to change the hierarchy of items in your InDesign documents.

The four commands in the Arrange menu are:

- ***Bring to Front*** moves all selected objects to the immediate front of all other objects, while retaining their stacking order relative to one another. (Command/Control-Shift-])
- ***Bring Forward*** moves all selected objects up one level in the stacking order. (Command/Control-])
- ***Send Backward*** moves all selected objects back one level in the stacking order. (Command/Control-[)
- ***Send to Back*** moves all selected objects to the immediate back of all other objects, while retaining their stacking order relative to one another. (Command/Control-Shift-[)

Transforming Objects

Enhancing an object by changing its size, rotation, or perspective is considered a transformation because the object's original state is altered. InDesign includes options for rotating, scaling, shearing (to obtain a simulation of perspective), and free transformation. Objects can be transformed using the Control palette, the Transform palette, or they can be manipulated manually with the transformation tools.

- The ***Rotate tool*** spins the selected object around the reference point.
- The ***Scale tool*** reduces or enlarges an object, either uniformly (proportionally) or non-uniformly.
- The ***Shear tool*** skews a selected object to make it appear as if it were being viewed from an angle.
- The ***Free Transform tool*** allows you to move, rotate, scale, shear, and reflect objects — all with the same tool.

If you want to resize a text frame, the Selection tool is the best tool for the job. InDesign remembers rotation and shear transformations applied to text frames. InDesign does not remember scaling of text frames, no matter how you accomplish the task. In addition, scaling text frames with the Transform palette or Scale tool always scales the text, which might not be the desired result. The Selection tool does not scale the text — it simply resizes the text frame.

InDesign remembers text frame transformations as they apply to the text in the frame. For example, if you use the Transform palette to scale a text frame to 150% in the X axis and 200% in the Y axis, the Transform palette reads 100% for both after the transformation. If you select the text with the Type tool and look at the Character palette or Control palette, the new point size and the percentage of horizontal scaling are indicated. We discourage the use of frame scaling for altering type sizes and shapes. Instead, use the Character palette and other more appropriate tools for these purposes.

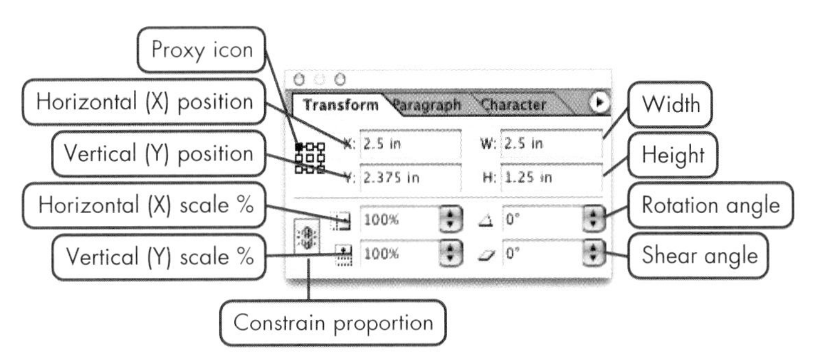

FIGURE 4.61

Arrange Objects

1 **Open arrange.indd from your Project_04 folder.**

This image appears to be a simple photo of some food; but if you open the Links palette, you see that there are actually three placed images in the document. You can use the Arrange options to enhance this photo and put all of the images in proper order.

FIGURE 4.62

2 **Use the Selection tool to click the picture of the food. Choose Object>Arrange>Send to Back.**

The food photo becomes the background image. You can now see the other two photos, as well as a headline. Examine the InDesign document carefully, and note the new stacking order: the waiter is now in front (he obscures part of the chef's skillet), the chef is next (her hair obscures some of the type), and the type is in the layer directly above the background photo.

3 **Use the Selection tool to click the waiter. Choose Object>Arrange>Send Backward.**

The stacking order changes again: the waiter moves back one layer, and the skillet is now in front of the waiter.

FIGURE 4.63

4 **Command/Control-click the type until the type frame is selected, and then choose Object>Arrange>Bring to Front.**

If you press Command-Option or Control-Alt and click, you can select the previous layer.

FIGURE 4.64

5 **Reposition the type however you prefer.**

6 **Choose File>Save As to save the file to your WIP_04 folder. Close the file.**

Transform Objects

1 **Open transform.indd from your Project_04 folder.**

You see three objects in the file: a red and yellow circle, a green and yellow square, and a cyan and blue polygon.

2 **Use the Selection tool to click the square. In the Control palette or the Transform palette, verify that the center proxy-reference point is active. In the Rotate field, enter "45". Press Return/Enter to apply the rotation.**

The square rotates 45 degrees on its center axis.

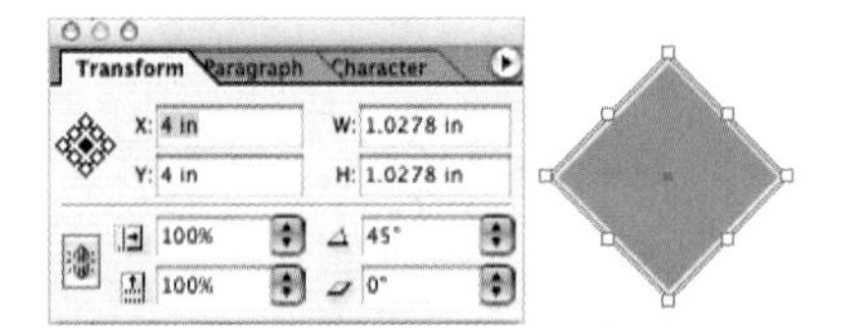

FIGURE 4.65

3 **Select the Polygon. Click the center-right proxy-reference point in the Transform palette. Choose the Rotate tool from the Tools palette. Drag the tool down on the left side of the polygon.**

The object rotates on the center-right axis.

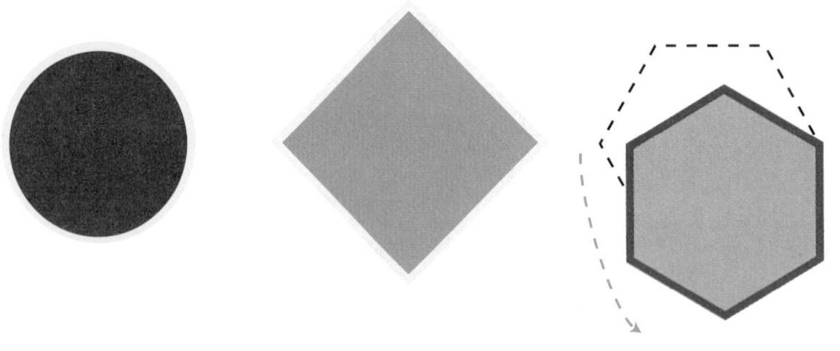

FIGURE 4.66

4 **Hold down the Shift key while you select all three objects. Click the Rotate tool in the Tools palette to see the reference point crosshair. Drag the crosshair to the right to relocate it manually.**

5 **Click the Rotate cursor to the left of the circle and drag downward.**

All three selected objects rotate as you drag.

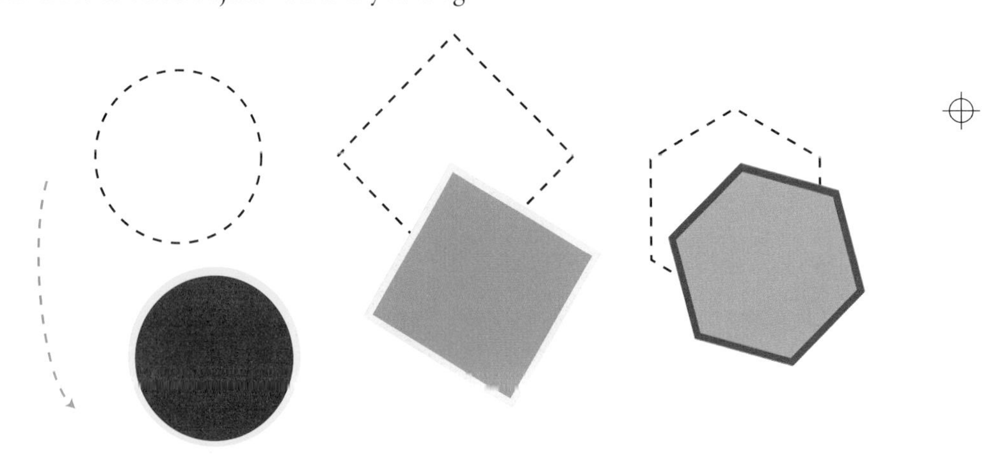

FIGURE 4.67

6 **With the three objects still selected, choose the Scale tool from the Tools palette. Drag the crosshair to the upper left of the area surrounding the three objects.**

7 **Hold down the Shift key while you click the page and drag the Scale tool cursor toward the crosshair. Stop at approximately 50% of the original size.**

Remember that the Shift key constrains the scale to uniform proportions. You must release the mouse button to check the actual size because the values don't change while you are using the tool.

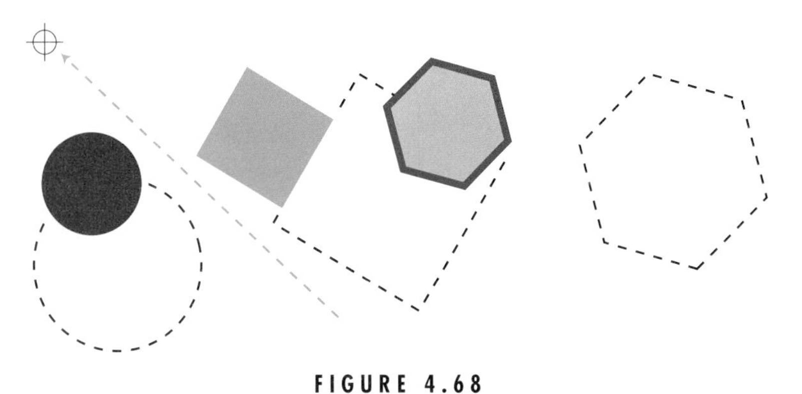

FIGURE 4.68

8 **In the Transform or Control palette, set the reference point as the center of the objects. In the Scale field, type "200" for the X percentage, and ensure that the Constrain Link icon is checked. Press Return/Enter to apply the transformation.**

The objects scale to approximately their original sizes.

FIGURE 4.69

9 **From the Transform palette Options menu, choose Flip Vertical.**

The three objects flip across a vertical axis at their combined center.

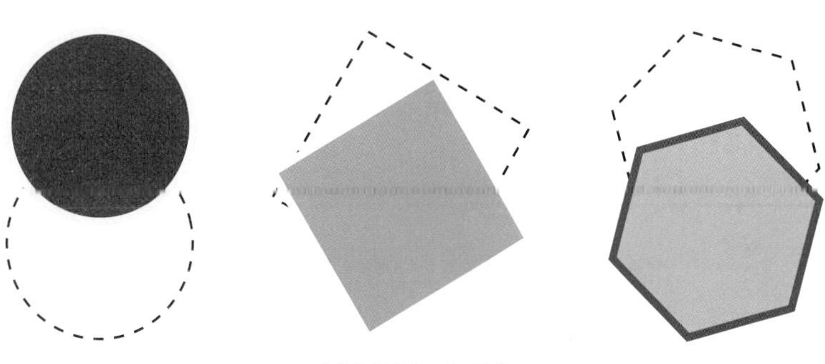

FIGURE 4.70

10 **Choose the Shear tool from the Tools palette. Drag the reference point crosshair to the upper-left corner of the area surrounding the polygon. Click the Shear tool near the bottom right of the polygon, and drag up and to the left.**

All three objects are sheared, giving them the appearance of perspective.

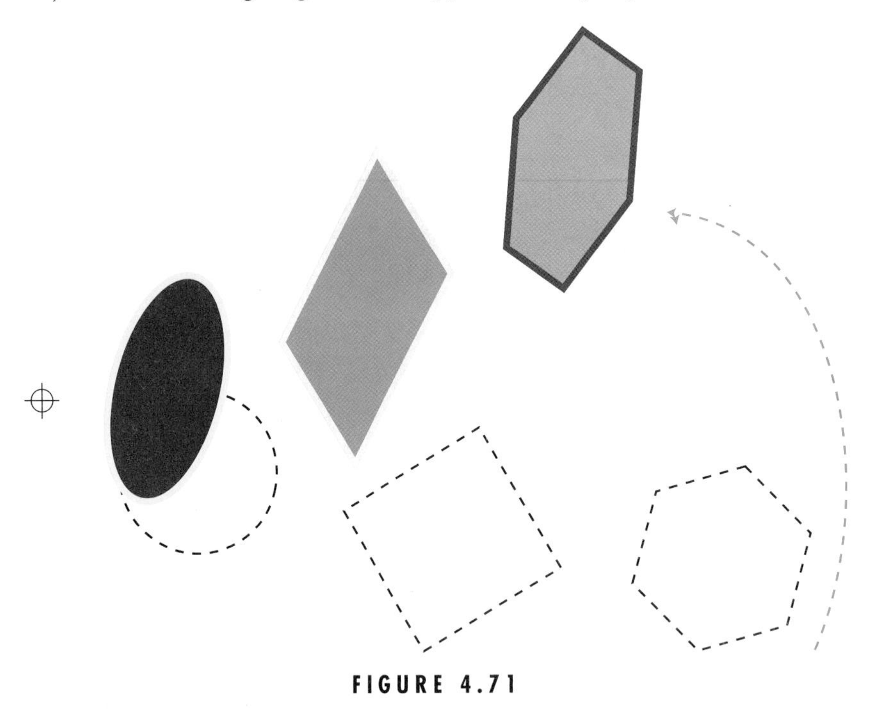

FIGURE 4.71

11 **Choose Window>Align.**

The Align palette opens. You can also press Shift-F7 to access the Align palette.

12 **Select all three objects. In the Align palette, choose Align Top Edges, and then choose Distribute Horizontal Centers.**

The objects align at the top and spread out, with even spaces between the centers, but not necessarily even spaces between the objects.

FIGURE 4.72

13 **Save the file as "transform.indd". Close the file.**

To Extend Your Knowledge...

ROTATING OBJECTS

In the Transform palette, positive numbers rotate objects toward the left (counterclockwise). To rotate an object clockwise, a negative sign must be placed in front of the number. For example, -45 rotates an object 45 degrees clockwise.

LESSON 8 Grouping and Duplicating Objects

You will often encounter situations when it is convenient to group multiple objects before performing transformations, or when you want to move multiple objects as a single unit. You may also want to copy an object without moving it, or duplicate an object (or group) at specific intervals (this is often done when setting up business cards for press). The Group function allows you to combine multiple objects (of any type) into a single larger object.

This feature is useful when you are working with art that requires precise positioning of several items, or when you need to copy, move, or transform a number of objects simultaneously. When you group objects, the resulting object is a frame with the group as the frame's content. The frame has a single bounding box that encloses the dimensions of the group. The shortcut command to group selected objects is Command/Control-G; Shift-Command/Control-G ungroups objects.

The Duplicate function replaces a copy-and-paste sequence with a single command. It offsets a copy of the selected object/s a few points away from the original. You can press Command-Option-Shift-D (Macintosh), or Control-Alt-Shift-D (Windows) to duplicate one or more selected objects.

The Step and Repeat function enables you to specify how many copies to make of one or more objects, and how the copies should be distributed across the page. You can press Command/Control-Shift-V to access the Step and Repeat dialog box.

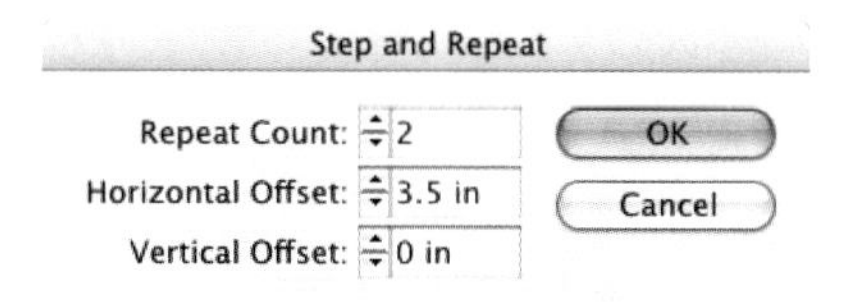

FIGURE 4.73

To place a copy of a selected object directly on top of the original, you can use the Paste in Place function to effectively clone an object. Press Command-Option-Shift-V (Macintosh) or Control-Alt-Shift-V (Windows) to invoke the Paste in Place function. You can also use the Step and Repeat function with horizontal and vertical offsets of "0" to achieve the same result as a Paste in Place.

Use Group and Step and Repeat Functions

1 **Open upickem.indd from the Project_04 folder.**

You see a business card with vertical orientation comprised of two frames: an image frame the width and depth of the card, and a text frame within the image frame.

FIGURE 4.74

2 **Choose the Selection tool from the Tools palette. Click the text frame, and then Shift-click the image frame.**

Both frames are selected. As an alternative, you can drag a selection box that intersects both frames.

3 **Choose Object>Group (Command/Control-G) to group the two frames.**

The grouped object is the size of a business card. The inner page dimensions allow you to print four cards across and three down. The cards will be printed 12 per sheet (also called "12-up").

4 **To create the print layout, select the card group, and then choose Edit>Step and Repeat. Choose a Repeat Count of 3 and a Horizontal Offset of 2 in. Click OK.**

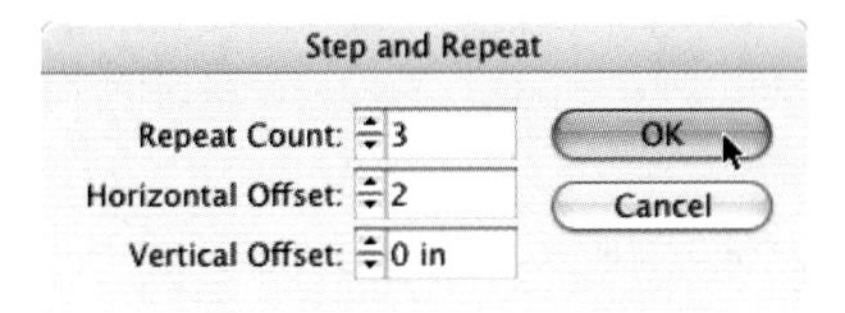

FIGURE 4.75

These settings give you four cards across (you already have one), repeated by the width of the business card.

FIGURE 4.76

5 **Press Command/Control-A to select all of the objects on the page. Choose Edit>Step and Repeat again. Set the Repeat Count to 2, the Horizontal Offset to 0 in, and the Vertical Offset to 3.5 in. Click OK.**

Your finished page should have 12 cards: 4 across and 3 down. If you achieve a different result, double-check your Step and Repeat settings.

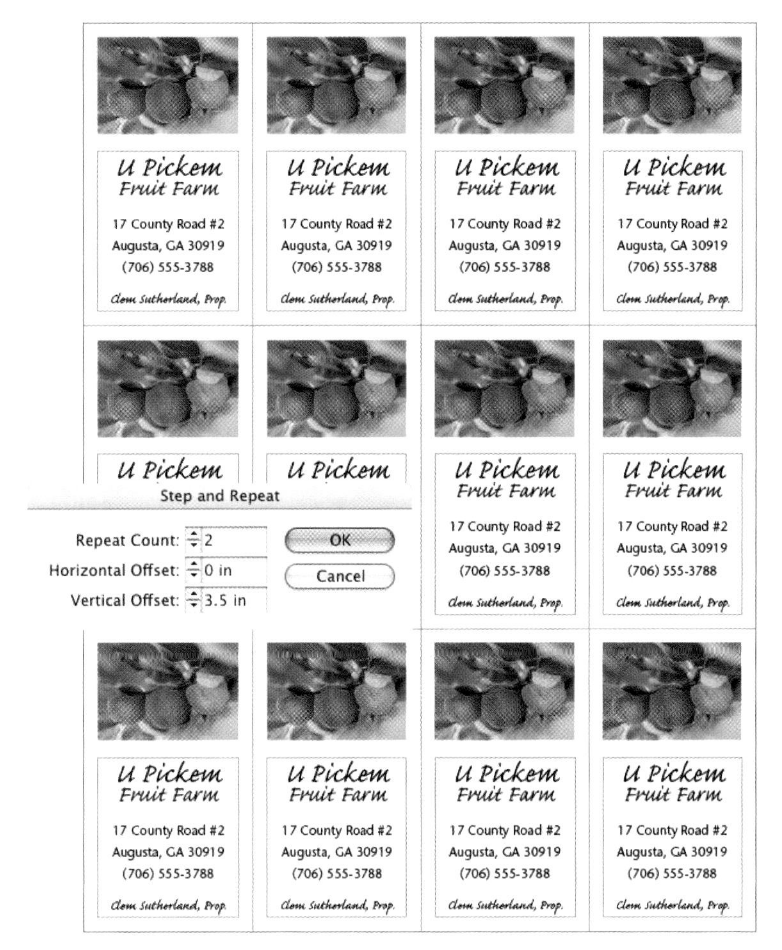

FIGURE 4.77

6 **Choose Save As to save the document to your WIP_04 folder. Close the document.**

When used in conjunction with the Group feature, the Step and Repeat function can save a significant amount of time as you build certain types of documents.

SUMMARY

In Project 4, you learned how to use InDesign's graphic object-creation tools. You discovered how to specify and apply color fills and strokes. You learned to draw Bézier paths and objects with the Pen tool, and to create primitive shapes. You learned how to apply strokes and fills to objects, and how to manipulate those objects using the transformation tools. You discovered how to align and distribute objects, as well as alter the stacking order of multiple objects in an image. You also learned the features and functions of InDesign's scaling tools, and learned how to group objects.

KEY TERMS

Align menu
Anchor point
Banding
Bézier curve
Bring Forward
Bring to Front
Closed path
CMYK
Constrain
Corner point
Distribute
Ellipse
Fill
Flip
Gradient
Group
Hierarchy
L*a*b color mode
Open path
PANTONE colors
Path
PMS colors
Primitive shapes
Process color build
Process color mode
Reflect
RGB color mode
Send Backward
Send to Back
Smooth point
Spot color
Stacking order
Step and Repeat
Stroke
Tint
Trap

CHECKING CONCEPTS AND TERMS

MULTIPLE CHOICE

Circle the letter of the correct answer for each of the following questions:

1. To constrain a path to 45-degree increments, you should _________.
   a. click the Constrain button
   b. drag the Pen tool
   c. hold down the Shift key
   d. choose the Stroke icon

2. Which tool is best for drawing straight lines?
   a. Pen tool
   b. Pencil tool
   c. Line tool
   d. Smooth tool

3. What are primitive shapes?
   a. Shapes that are predefined.
   b. Shapes that are rough sketches.
   c. Shapes made with the Pencil tool.
   d. Shapes made with the Pen tool.

4. What is a bounding box?
   a. The visible boundary of a path.
   b. The edge of where you can move an object.
   c. A position on a path that defines the path.
   d. A box that marks the perimeter of an object.

5. Which color mode should you use when designing for print?
   a. CMYK
   b. HSV
   c. L*a*b
   d. RGB

6. What is spot color?
   a. Any color applied to objects.
   b. The subtractive primary inks.
   c. A premixed ink color.
   d. An ink color selected from the Swatches palette.

7. What tool would you use to simulate perspective?
   a. Gradient tool
   b. Rotate tool
   c. Scale tool
   d. Shear tool

8. How do you manage the stacking order of objects?
   a. With the Align palette
   b. With the Arrange menu
   c. With the Direct Selection tool
   d. With the Transform tool

9. When should you create tints from process colors?
   a. When you need a lighter version of the color.
   b. When you need the most predictable results.
   c. When CMYK inks are not used.
   d. Never.

10. Which of the following gradients is acceptable?
    a. A gradient that extends the depth of a letter-size page.
    b. A gradient from a CMYK color to a spot color.
    c. A process color gradient.
    d. A 5-inch gradient from 50% to 100%.

DISCUSSION QUESTIONS

1. We discussed different color types in this project. Under what circumstances would you use spot color instead of process color? Discuss the pros and cons of both color types.

2. In addition to color types, there are color modes, such as CMYK, RGB. L*a*b, PANTONE, and others. What are the advantages of using these color modes and others within InDesign? When would you use each color mode?

3. Illustrations can be created in InDesign using a combination of tools. They can also be created in dedicated illustration programs, such as Adobe Illustrator or Macromedia FreeHand. Under what circumstances would you choose to create illustrations in a dedicated program, and when would you opt to create them in InDesign?

SKILL DRILL

Skill Drills reinforce project skills. Each skill reinforced is the same, or nearly the same, as a skill presented in the lessons. Detailed instructions are provided in a step-by-step format. You must perform Skill Drills 2–4 in order.

1. Create an Illustration with Primitives

Even though InDesign contains relatively robust illustration tools, you can often create the images you need using only primitive shapes and lines. In this exercise, you create a cartoon bear from primitive shapes.

1. Create a new Letter-size document. Accept the default settings.
2. Choose the Ellipse tool from the Tools palette. Draw a 1-inch circle. With the center proxy-reference point selected, position the circle at X: 4.25 in, Y: 3 in.
3. With the circle selected, change the Stroke to None, and the Fill to Black. In the Tint box of the Swatches palette, set the Tint to 50%. Drag this fill into the Swatches palette.
4. Draw a half-inch circle. Position it at X: 3.75 in, Y: 2.6 in. Apply the same Stroke and Fill from Step 3.
5. Choose the Selection tool from the Tools palette. Hold down the Option/Alt and Shift keys while you click the center point of the circle and drag it to X: 4.75 in.

   This action duplicates the circle.
6. Draw an ellipse as follows: W: 0.35 in, H: 0.5 in. Position the ellipse at X: 4.05 in, Y: 2.9 in. Apply a Stroke of None and a Fill of Paper.
7. Hold down the Shift-Option/Alt keys while you drag the ellipse to X: 4.45 in.

   This action duplicates the ellipse at the new X location, while maintaining its Y coordinate.
8. Draw a circle 0.28 in wide. Position it at X: 4.05 in, Y: 3 in. Apply a Stroke of None and a Fill of Black. Drag-duplicate the circle to X: 4.45.

   Remember to hold down the Shift-Option/Alt keys while you drag.
9. Create a black ellipse as follows: W: 0.38 in, H: 0.25 in, X: 4.25 in, Y: 3.1 in. Apply a Stroke of 50% Black.
10. Create an ellipse with a default Fill and Stroke, Width of 0.5 in, and Height of 0.28 in.
11. Use the Scissors tool to click the left and right handles of the bounding box. Change to the Selection tool, and drag the lower half of the ellipse to X: 4.25 in, Y: 3.3 in. Delete the unused top half.
12. Finally, click on the "ears" of the figure you created in Steps 4 and 5. Choose Object>Arrange>Send to Back, or press Command/Control-Shift-[.

13. Save the document as "skill_object.indd". Close the file.

FIGURE 4.78

2. Build a Color Palette

You can build your colors as you go along, but it is generally much more efficient to build your color palette in advance. In this exercise, you build the color palette that you will use in Skill Drill 3.

1. Open music.indd from the Project_04 folder.

   The musical notes and the background are on a locked layer.

2. Activate the Swatches palette and delete the three colors at the bottom of the pallet (Blue, Red, and Green).

   We will not use these colors. The more colors you have in a palette, the more difficult it is to work with.

3. From the Swatches palette Options menu, choose New Color Swatch. Change the Color Type to Spot and change the Color Mode to PANTONE solid coated.
4. In the New Color Swatch dialog box, type "116". Click the Add button.
5. In the New Color Swatch dialog box, type "R", scroll down, and click PANTONE Rhodamine Red C. Click Add.
6. In the New Color Swatch dialog box, type "O", and click PANTONE Orange 021 C. Click Add.
7. In the New Color Swatch dialog box, change the Color Mode to CMYK and the Color Type to Process. Be sure the Name with Color Value box is unchecked.

   We will use the abbreviations for Cyan, Magenta, Yellow, and Black.

8. Name the swatch "Dark Blue". Use the sliders or type the following values in the dialog boxes: C:100, M:85, Y:5, K:0. Click Add.
9. Change the Swatch Name to "Light Blue" and assign the colors C:70, M:45, Y:0, K:0. Click OK.
10. Save the document and leave it open for the next exercise.

3. Create a Gradient Swatch

In this exercise, you use your custom color palette to create the gradient swatch you use for the background in the next exercise. The gradient is made of the process colors you created in Skill Drill 2.

1. With music.indd open, choose New Gradient Swatch from the Swatches palette Options menu.
2. Name the swatch "Dark to Light Blue". Choose Linear as the Type.
3. Click the Left Color Stop in the Gradient Ramp. Choose Swatches as the Stop Color.
4. Click the Light Blue color swatch in the palette that appears.
5. Click the Right Color Stop, and then click the Dark Blue color swatch.
6. Click OK.
7. Save the document and leave it open for the next exercise.

4. Draw with the Pen Tool

This Skill Drill will help you gain confidence in your drawing abilities. It involves tracing moderately complex objects. You will likely want to tweak your work after you complete the final step of the exercise.

In case you are not familiar with musical notes, the G Clef is white, the eighth note is yellow, the sixteenth note is Rhodamine red, and the Cut Time symbol is orange.

1. In the open document, use the Pen tool to click the inside point where the ball on the bottom of the G Clef joins the stem. Do not drag.
2. At about 90 degrees, drag until the new drawing aligns with the template.
3. Go another 90 degrees, and drag again. Continue outlining the image. When you get to a straight line, single-click at each end.

   Fewer clicks are better than more.
4. When you finish with the G Clef, proceed to the eighth note. Start at the bottom left.
5. On the sixteenth note, begin at the top left. Consider the two flags as separate items, not joined elements.
6. Start at the top center of the Cut Time symbol.
7. When you're finished, use the Direct Selection tool to tweak your work.

   If you were sparing in the number of points you added, this may be the only tool you need to use.
8. When you color the musical symbols, assign the Fills and Strokes (left to right) as Paper, PMS 116, PMS Rubine Red, and PMS Orange 021.

   If you were to apply a Stroke of None, the images below might show through

9. Click the Pen tool on the top-left point of the rectangle. Hold down the Shift key and click the top-right point. Continue to hold the Shift key as you click each of the corners, and then click the top-left point again.

   When you click your beginning point, the path closes.

10. Fill the rectangle with the Dark to Light Blue gradient. Apply a Stroke of None.
11. In the Gradient palette, set the Angle to 90 degrees.
12. Press Command/Control-Shift-] to send the gradient rectangle to the back of the stacking order.
13. Save the document and close it.

FIGURE 4.79

CHALLENGE

Challenge exercises expand on, or are somewhat related to, skills presented in the lessons. Each exercise provides a brief introduction, followed by instructions presented in a numbered-step format that are not as detailed as those in the Skill Drill exercises. Complete these exercises in the order provided.

1. Prepare the Basics

You were assigned the task of preparing stationery for Erin Imports, an Irish import company. The client likes Celtic knotwork, and wants a knot included in the stationery design. You have an image of a knot that is acceptable, but it needs some modification before it can be used. You can use the InDesign drawing tools to trace the image and then apply modifications.

1. Open knots.indd from your Project_04 folder.

   In the middle of the page, you see a Celtic knot on a locked layer.

2. Remove all but the four standard colors (None, Paper, Black, Registration) and Cyan.

3. Add the two company colors: PMS 341 and PMS 116.
4. In the Stroke palette, set the Width to 4 pt, with Round Join and Round End caps.
5. Set the Stroke Color to PMS 116, and set the Fill to None.
6. Trace the knot.

   Here are some hints: (1) Use as few anchor points as possible. (2) There are four corner points in the knot. Simply click corner points, and drag curve points. (3) Remember, you can always go back and edit curves with the Direct Selection tool by re-dragging handles or moving anchor points.
7. Copy the knot you created. Choose Edit>Paste in Place.
8. Change the Stroke Weight to 8 pt, and change the color to PMS 341.
9. Send the copy backward one level.

   This creates a knot with an outline, since the paths automatically align with one another.
10. Group the two paths. Save the document as "erinimport.indd". Leave the file open for the next exercise.

2. Position the Knots

1. With erinimport.indd open, scale the grouped knot to 50%.
2. With the upper-left proxy-reference point selected, move the knot to X:0.5, Y:0.5.
3. Step and Repeat 7.5 inches Horizontal.
4. Select both knots. From the Transform palette Options menu, choose Flip Horizontal.
5. Step and Repeat 10 inches Vertical.
6. Flip Vertical.

   The basic page is complete.
7. In any typeface you prefer, enter the company's name and location, centered in a text frame, as follows:

   Erin Imports
   2305 Cabernet Way, Healdsburg, CA 95448
   707/555-3746 • www.erinimports.com
8. Position the address information near the top of the page. Select the text frame and the two knots.
9. In the Align palette, distribute the horizontal space between the centers of the elements.

10. In the Layers palette, click the visibility icon (the eyeball) in front of Layer 1 to hide your tracing layer.

11. Save the document. Leave it open for the next exercise.

FIGURE 4.80

3. Build the Business Cards

1. With erinimports.indd open, copy the upper-left grouped knot.
2. Create a second page in the Pages palette and paste the knot on the page.
3. Create a 3.5 × 2-in text frame at X:0.75 in, Y:0.5 in. Add your address information. Add your name to the business card. Establish the position of the text in the frame by adjusting the inset spacing in the Text Frame Options menu (Command/Control-B).
4. Uniformly scale the knot to approximately 180%. Position the knot on the business card.

   It doesn't look very good.

5. With the proxy-reference point set to the center, rotate the knot 90 degrees. If you can't click the knot, it's because it is behind the text frame. Command-click (Macintosh) or Control-click (Windows) to access the knot frame.

   Command/Control-click allows you to access a frame that is covered by another frame.

6. Style the type however you prefer, keeping it consistent with the letterhead.
7. Group the items. Step and Repeat once 3.5 inches Horizontal.
8. In the Control palette, select the left-center proxy-reference point. Draw a horizontal line with a 0.5-pt Stroke as follows: X: 0.25 in, Y: 2.5 in, L: 0.4 in. Color the line registration so it prints on both printing plates.
9. Step and Repeat the line 7.6 inches Horizontal, using the center proxy-reference point.
10. Select all four objects. Step and Repeat them 4 times Vertical, with 2-in Offsets. Reselect the top two lines and Step and Repeat them –2 inches Vertical.

    These actions set the vertical cutting spaces between the cards.

11. Set up the vertical cut marks similarly. Remember, they should not touch the cards.
12. Save the file and close it.

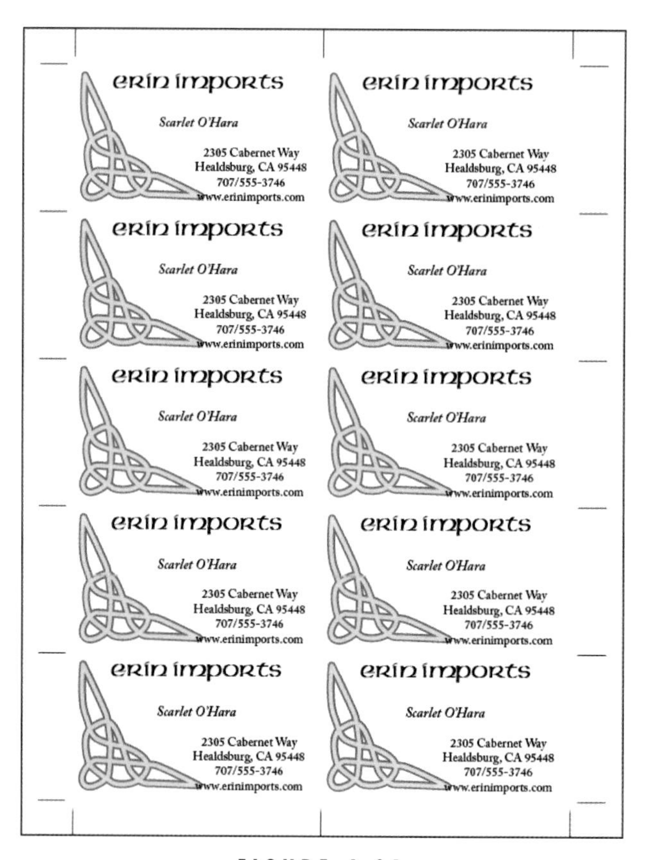

FIGURE 4.81

4. Support the Arts T-Shirt

You will seldom hear that InDesign is the "right" application for producing complex pieces of art. InDesign may, however, be the only application you have available, or the art you want to produce may be needed only in an InDesign document. In this Challenge, you use the Pen and Pencil tools to produce a "Support the Arts" illustration, and then add type. The design could be used on a poster, or reduced for other applications.

1. Create a 1-Column Letter-size page with 0.5 in Margins, no Facing Pages, and no master text frame.
2. Use the Pen tool to draw the outline of an open book that fits within the page.
3. On the edges where pages would cascade down, use the Pencil tool to draw some rough vertical lines.
4. Use the Pen tool to draw a human-like figure. Use a circle for the head. Place the figure in the middle of the book.
5. Using primitive shapes, draw a sign.
6. Convey the message, "Education Needs The Arts."
7. Add the colors of your choice.
8. Save your design as "art_tee.indd".

FIGURE 4.82

PORTFOLIO BUILDER

Spam Stopper Logo

Info Management developed a new product called Spam Stopper that reduces the amount of spam that filters in through your e-mail. Spam Stopper gives you almost complete control over what is filtered out, and it can "learn" what you consider spam. To keep costs down, the product is only available over the Internet as a downloadable file.

Your assignment is to use type elements and InDesign's graphics to create a catchy logo. You should create at least three unique ideas for presentation to the company's management. Some ideas you may wish to consider include:

- Use of the international "No" symbol
- Incorporating a stop sign (8-sided polygon)
- Replacing letters with graphic symbols

Let your imagination run. Remember, there is no "right" solution.

Your assignment is to use type elements and InDesign's graphics to create a catchy logo. You should create at least three unique ideas for presentation to the company's management.

LEVEL 1

PROJECT 5

Working with Images

OBJECTIVES

In this project, you learn how to

- Work with image frames
- Understand image formats
- Understand image resolution
- Place, scale, and position images
- Link and embed images
- Scale and crop images
- Use borders to frame images

WHY WOULD I DO THIS?

As you know, documents combine text and graphic images to convey an idea or a message. Although you can create basic shapes and Bézier curves in InDesign, you should generate complex artwork and detailed illustrations in software designed for that purpose. Likewise, you should prepare photographic images scanned from photo prints or slides, or captured with a digital camera, with an application designed to manipulate such images. You can import these images into InDesign and position, crop, scale, and place them on the page with text and graphic elements created with the InDesign drawing tools.

Placing images and graphics into an InDesign layout is a relatively straightforward process. Deciding what to place, however, is a far more complex matter. The terminology used to refer to graphics and images can be confusing — perhaps more so than any other aspect of publishing. In this project, you review the terms most often used in the graphics industry, define them, and discuss how and when they are used in relation to InDesign.

You work primarily with three types of images: vector graphics (drawings), raster images (often photographs), and line art. Each type of image has specific advantages and drawbacks, depending on its intended use. You can explore this topic in depth in the Companion Series book, *Color Companion*, published by Prentice Hall.

Vector Graphics

Most of the drawing elements on a page, including those you create with InDesign's drawing tools, can be described as a series of vectors (mathematical descriptors). This type of graphic is ***resolution independent***; you can freely scale a vector with no resolution degradation because it adopts its resolution from the output device when the graphic is printed. You can save vector art in a file format associated with the application used to create the file (for example, Adobe Illustrator or Macromedia FreeHand format), or in a common interchange format called ***Encapsulated PostScript*** (***EPS***).

Raster Images

While vector art is composed of mathematical descriptors of a series of lines and geometric shapes, a raster-art file is made up of a grid of individual ***rasters*** (also called ***bits*** or ***pixels***) placed in rows and columns (called a ***bitmap***). The word pixel is a contraction of "picture element" (also known as a ***pel*** in some industries). A raster is a scan pattern (as in the electron beam in a cathode-ray tube) in which an area is scanned from side to side in lines from top to bottom, or a pattern of closely spaced rows of dots that form the image on a cathode-ray tube (as in a television or computer display).

Each pixel is a tiny square of color, and thousands of adjacent pixels in different colors and shades create the illusion of smooth, continuous tone. In contrast to vector files, which are resolution independent, raster files are ***resolution dependent*** — they receive their resolution at the time of input (scanning or capture with a digital camera). A raster file specifies the number of pixels it contains. If the image is enlarged, the pixels enlarge to fill the extra space, reducing the resolution. This makes the image appear ***pixelated*** (course and jagged). Raster files for print are generally saved in TIFF or EPS formats; for the Web, raster files are generally saved in the JPEG format, and sometimes GIF.

Line Art

Line art is a special kind of raster image made entirely of 100% solid areas. The pixels in a line-art image have only two options: they can be all black or all white. Line-art images are sometimes called bitmap, bi-level, or one-bit images. Scanned pen drawings, signatures, and printed text all represent this type of line art.

Resolution

Image resolution refers to how many pixels per inch (ppi, for input devices and monitors) or dots per inch (dpi, for imaging devices) are contained in the raster graphic. Every pixel is one block of color. When each block or pixel is very small, it blends with the pixels surrounding it to smoothly form the shapes, coloring, and shading in the image. It's important to understand when and how to adjust resolution when preparing graphics for import into InDesign. It is best not to perform gross enlargements or reductions in InDesign, because it can destroy the quality of the image or create longer processing times.

In general, a higher resolution results in a cleaner, smoother appearance; but higher resolution is not always better. The most important consideration is to match image resolution to the requirements of the output device. If you are preparing a graphic for output on a screen for a Web page, you should set its resolution at 72 ppi because monitors typically have resolutions of 72 ppi (Macintosh) and 96 ppi (Windows). Desktop printers reproduce images by applying tiny amounts of ink or toner onto paper; typical resolution is 600–1,200 dpi. High-end imagesetters are capable of printing at resolutions from 1,600–4,000 lpi (lines per inch) or more.

When we discuss resolution, we speak in terms of pixels per inch (ppi), dots per inch (dpi), lines per inch (lpi) and sometimes spots per inch (spi).

- ***Pixels per inch (ppi).*** The number of pixels in one horizontal or vertical inch of a digital raster file.
- ***Lines per inch (lpi).*** The number of halftone dots produced in a horizontal or vertical linear inch by a high-resolution imagesetter to simulate the appearance of continuous-tone color.
- ***Dots per inch (dpi)*** or ***spots per inch (spi).*** The number of dots produced by an output device in a single line of output. It is sometimes incorrectly used interchangeably with pixels per inch.

When reproducing a photograph on a printing press, the image must be converted into different-sized dots that fool the eye into believing that it sees continuous tones. The result of this conversion process is a ***halftone image***; light tones are represented by small halftone dots; dark tones are represented by large halftone dots.

Graphics File Formats

You can import a number of graphic file formats into InDesign, but some of them should be avoided. If you remember that InDesign is designed for print production, you will automatically know which formats you should and should not import.

- PDF, a self-contained format that includes all raster and vector data — even fonts — imports and prints well. It is the native format of Adobe Acrobat.
- Vector formats that work well include Adobe Illustrator (ai) from version 5.5 and later, and Encapsulated PostScript (eps). Desktop Color Separation (dcs), a subset of EPS, can also be used, but it is less popular. Generally speaking, EPS is the standard format.
- Acceptable raster formats include Adobe Photoshop (psd) from version 4.0 and later, and ***TIFF*** (Tagged Image File Format, also called tif), which is the de facto standard for raster images. ***JPEG*** (Joint Photographers Expert Group) can be used, but may degrade the image, since it uses a "lossy" compression method; it is better for Web images.
- Web formats, such as JPEG, GIF, and PNG, should not be used. Platform-specific formats, such as BMP, PCX, WMF (Windows) or PICT (Macintosh), should be avoided. Scitex CT format, once popular in high-end prepress workflows, is rarely used anymore.

There will undoubtedly be occasions when you receive a graphic file that's in one of the "not recommended" formats. You can usually open it in an application such as Photoshop, Illustrator, FreeHand, or CorelDraw, and then save it in one of the preferred formats.

VISUAL SUMMARY

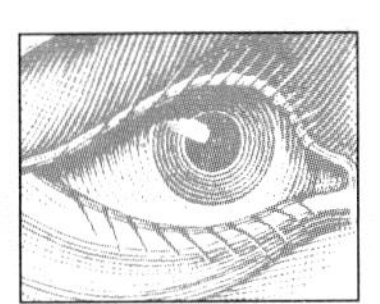

Images do not need a pre-prepared frame because they create a frame that matches their bounding box when they are imported. They are, in most ways, treated similarly to objects you create in InDesign using the shape tools or Bézier tools; in fact, shapes can be converted to frames and frames to shapes. The frame tools (Rectangle Frame, Ellipse Frame, and Polygon Frame tools) are located opposite the shape tools in the Tools palette.

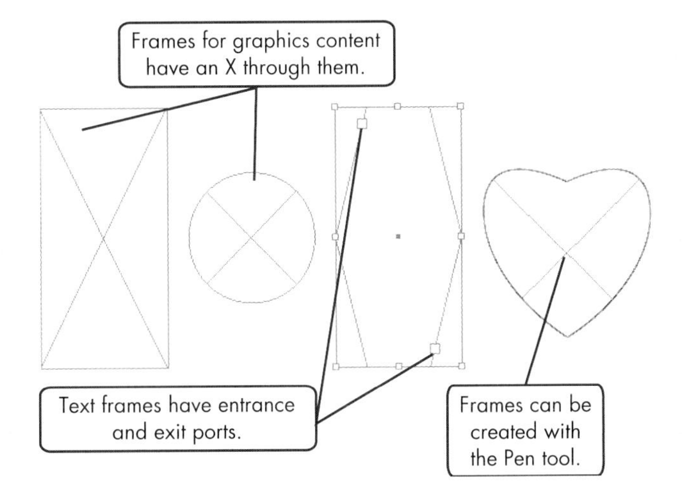

FIGURE 5.1

You manipulate frames in the same way as shapes. A frame's content can be manipulated separately from the frame itself — you can move it around inside the frame and even resize it within the frame. The frame ***crops*** (removes from vision) any part of an image that is outside the frame's boundary. To move a graphic around within a frame, you can click a graphic with the Direct Selection tool and reposition it, or use the Object>Fitting menu options.

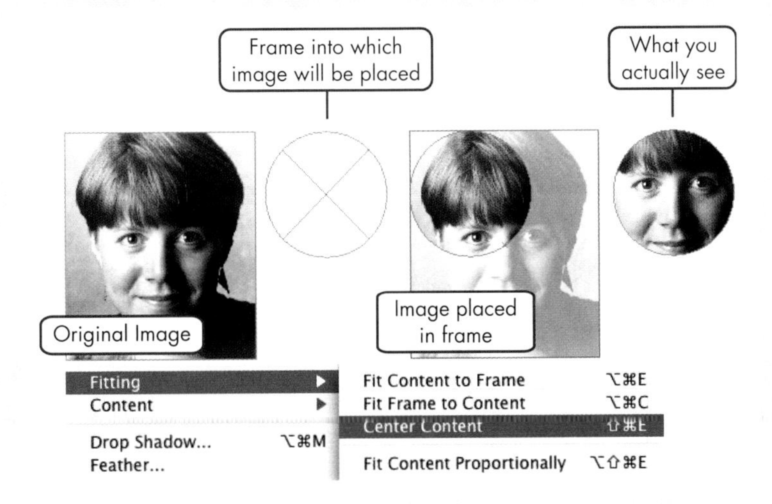

FIGURE 5.2

Graphic files can be linked or embedded. Linking is the preferred solution to managing graphic files because it controls the size of the InDesign file and allows you to edit the original file — automatically updating each instance of the image in a document. Files under 48K are automatically embedded, but you can manually embed a file if necessary. The Links palette gives you access to information about the status of the link and about the file itself.

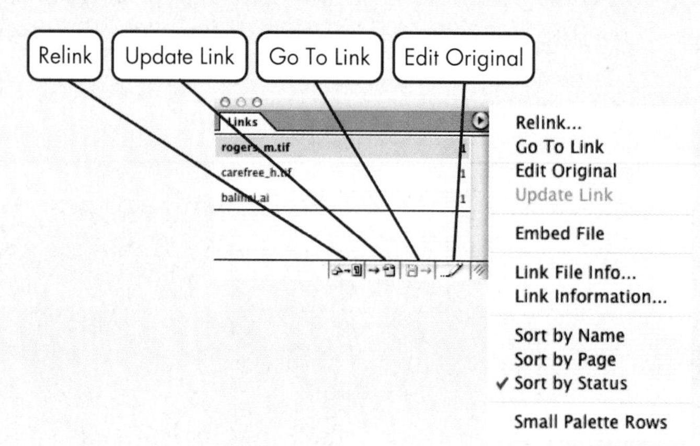

FIGURE 5.3

InDesign allows you to create custom strokes and borders for frames. You can create strokes based on stripes, dashes, or dots. You cannot combine dashes and dots in a single custom stroke.

In addition to adjusting the frame and its content, you can wrap text around either a graphic frame or around its content. This technique is often used, especially when the image is irregularly shaped and silhouetted from its background. Wrapping text around images adds variety to documents, and is especially useful in ads and magazine articles, where there is substantial interaction between images and type.

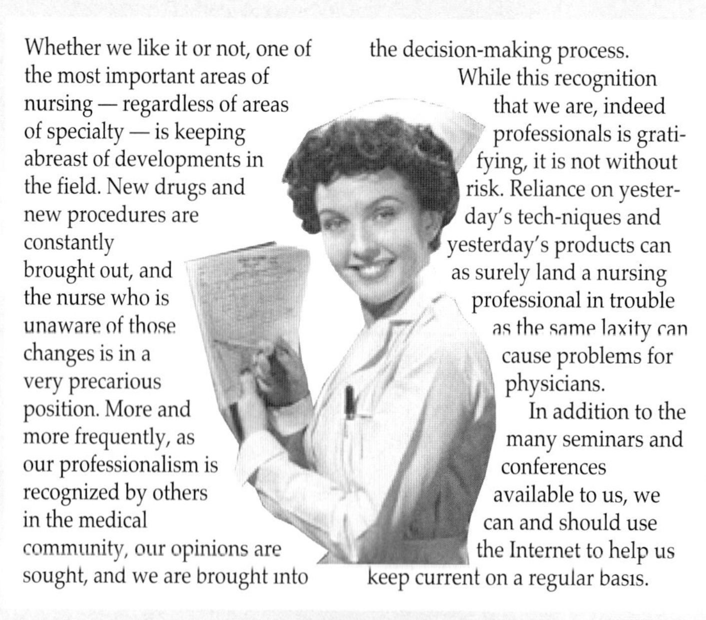

Whether we like it or not, one of the most important areas of nursing — regardless of areas of specialty — is keeping abreast of developments in the field. New drugs and new procedures are constantly brought out, and the nurse who is unaware of those changes is in a very precarious position. More and more frequently, as our professionalism is recognized by others in the medical community, our opinions are sought, and we are brought into the decision-making process.
While this recognition that we are, indeed professionals is gratifying, it is not without risk. Reliance on yesterday's tech-niques and yesterday's products can as surely land a nursing professional in trouble as the same laxity can cause problems for physicians.
In addition to the many seminars and conferences available to us, we can and should use the Internet to help us keep current on a regular basis.

FIGURE 5.4

LESSON 1 Working with Frames

Every element within InDesign is contained in a frame, which is typically created with one of the three frame tools. Any shape automatically converts to a frame if it is selected when you place text or graphics. When you create a frame with the frame tools, it is created with no stroke, and defaults to a graphic frame. You can apply a stroke and fill to your frames, just as you apply them to shapes.

You can cut and paste other frames or objects created in InDesign into a frame, or you can place graphics created in other programs into the frame. Once the object is placed in the frame, you can move it around, resize it (in conjunction with or independent of the frame itself), or crop it so just a portion of the image shows. You can place objects in frames of any shape.

Work with Frames

1 **Create a new Letter-size document. Use the default parameters.**

2 **Choose the Ellipse from the Tools palette. Draw a 1-in circle. Color the circle with a Red Fill and a Yellow Stroke.**

3 **Switch to the Rectangle tool. Draw a 2 × 1-in rectangle with a Cyan Fill and a Green Stroke.**

4 **Switch to the Polygon tool. Draw a 6-sided symmetrical polygon, with a 1-in Height, a Yellow Fill, and a Red Stroke.**

You have three objects to work with and place inside the frames you create later.

5 **Select all three objects. Use the Stroke palette to set their Stroke Weights to 2 pt.**

FIGURE 5.5

6 **Click and hold the Frame tool icon to access its pop-up menu. Choose the Ellipse Frame tool. Drag the cursor to create a 2 × 4-in oval frame.**

7 **Draw frames of the same size with the Rectangle Frame and Polygon Frame tools.**

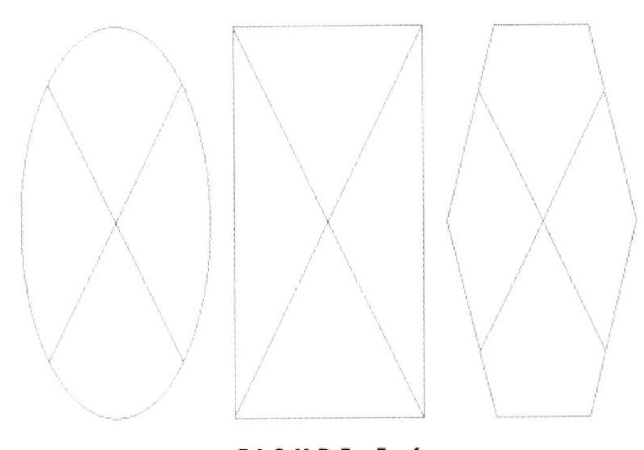

FIGURE 5.6

8 **Select the circle object you drew earlier and cut it (Edit>Cut or Command/Control-X). Click the oval frame and choose Edit>Paste Into to paste the circle inside the oval frame.**

You can also press Command-Option-V (Macintosh) or Control-Alt-V (Windows) to paste an object.

A frame can act as a mask for any graphical content it contains. A ***mask*** is used to hide parts of an image and show others. Anything outside the mask doesn't show.

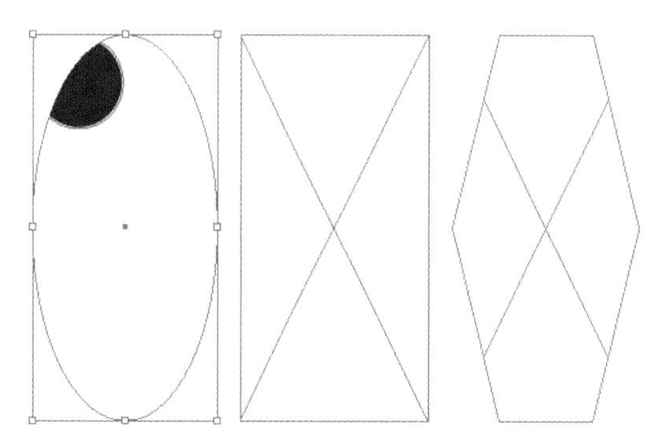

FIGURE 5.7

9 **Use the Direct Selection tool to click the circle and move it around inside the oval frame.**

The Direct Selection tool allows you to position objects inside frames.

10 **Use the Selection tool to click the ellipse frame. Choose Object>Fitting>Center Content.**

The circle moves to the exact center of the frame, centered horizontally and vertically. You can also access the Fitting options through the contextual menus. When you click a frame, Control-click (Macintosh) or right-click (Windows) to access the contextual menu.

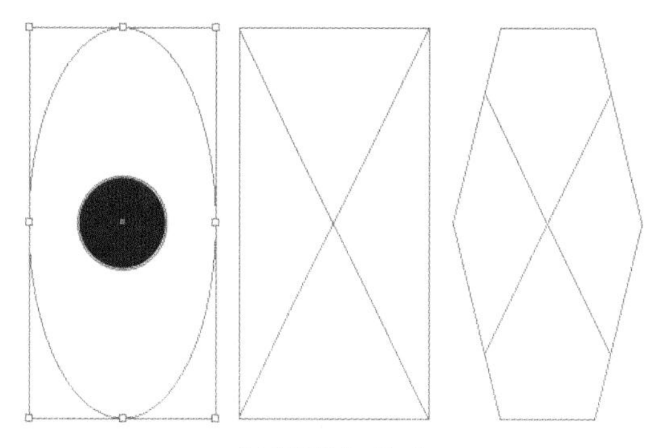

FIGURE 5.8

11 **Hold down the Shift key while you click the control handles on the bounding box of the oval frame and reduce the size of the frame to approximately 1.25 in, surrounding the circle.**

You can use one or more of the control handles to resize the frame.

12 **In the Tools palette, click the Fill box to make it active. In the Swatches palette, click the Cyan swatch to color the oval frame.**

The color of the frame appears behind the circle.

13 **Select the polygon object and choose Edit>Cut to cut it. Select the Rectangle frame and choose Edit>Paste Into to place the polygon inside the frame. Click the center of the frame with the Direct Selection tool and move the frame to center the object.**

If you click the edges of the frame with the Direct Selection tool, you resize the frame.

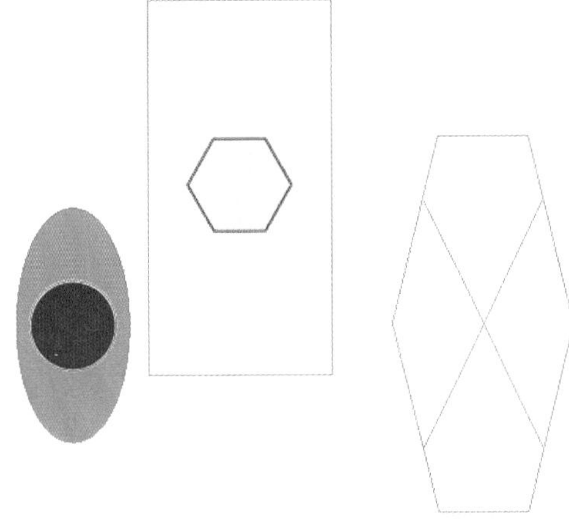

FIGURE 5.9

14 **Save the document as "frames.indd". Leave it open for the next exercise.**

Fit Frames and Content

1 **With frames.indd open, use the Selection tool to select the rectangular frame. Choose Object>Fitting>Fit Frame to Content.**

The frame shrinks to conform to the edges of the polygon.

2 **Fill the rectangle with Cyan and apply a 4-pt Green Stroke.**

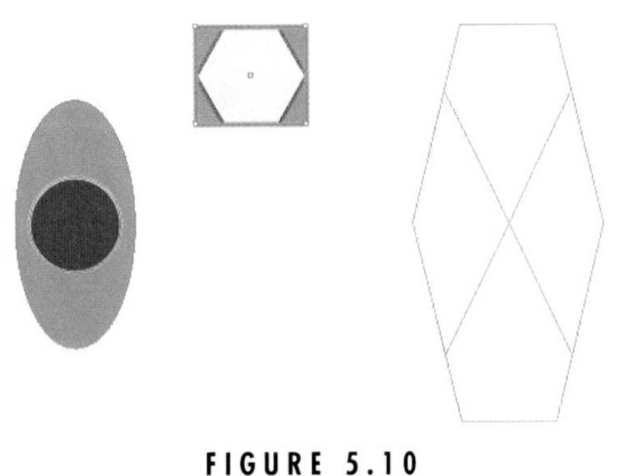

FIGURE 5.10

3 **Use the Selection tool to select the rectangle, and then cut it. Paste the rectangle into the polygon frame.**

4 **Control/right-click to access the contextual menu, and choose Fitting>Fit Content to Frame.**

The rectangle fills the entire bounding box area of the polygon.

5 **Select the ellipse frame containing the circle. Choose Edit>Cut. Use the Direct Selection tool to click the rectangle in the polygon frame. Paste the ellipse and its content into the rectangle.**

This "nests" the elliptical frame inside the rectangle; the rectangle is now a frame because an object is pasted inside it, and the rectangle is still inside the polygon frame. The elliptical frame is the same color as the rectangle. Note the position of the frame in Figure 5.11.

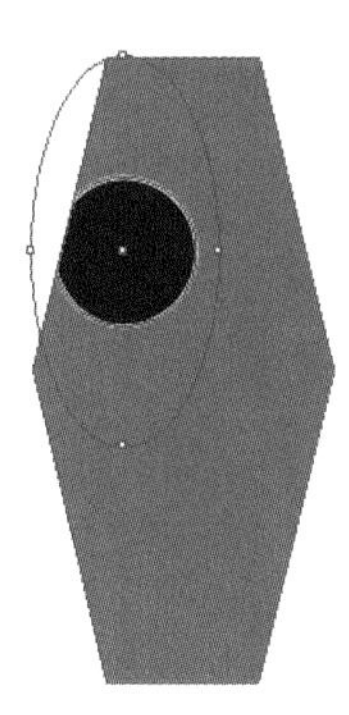

FIGURE 5.11

6 **Save your changes. Close the file.**

To Extend Your Knowledge...

COMBINED VECTOR AND RASTER IMAGES

Vector-based programs can incorporate raster images into illustrations. For example, many of the screen captures in this book were annotated with arrows and text after importing the raster screen-capture file into Adobe Illustrator, where the raster image became another element in the drawing.

With raster-based programs such as Photoshop, you use vector tools to manipulate a raster image, and you can add layers of vector shapes to the image. Depending on the format the file is saved under, these vector shapes can remain vectors, or they can be converted to rasters.

LESSON 2 Placing and Positioning Images

As you create documents, you will discover that a substantial portion of the content will be imported graphics — either raster or vector. Unless you have created the images specifically for use in a particular document, you will undoubtedly need to manipulate the images within InDesign.

Vector graphics, such as EPS files, are resolution-independent, so they can be enlarged or reduced almost infinitely with no degradation of quality; however, enlarging an image excessively may cause problems when the file is printed. If you need to enlarge or reduce a vector image to less than 50% or greater than 200%, you should scale the image in its originating program.

Resolution-dependent raster files, on the other hand, deteriorate if they are enlarged. Of course, the amount you can enlarge a raster image depends upon its resolution; as a rule of thumb, however, you should enlarge a raster image no more than 10%. Greater enlargements result in pixelation — sometimes referred to as "jaggies." You can reduce raster images the same amount as you can reduce a vector image without degradation of quality.

Place and Position Images

1 **Create a new Letter-size document, and accept the default settings.**

2 **Choose File>Place. Choose academy.eps from the file list. Click the Open button.**

Windows users can click the Show Preview button to view a thumbnail of each file. The preview automatically shows on the Macintosh when you click an image. The cursor changes to a loaded-graphic icon, which marks where the upper-left corner of the graphic will be placed.

FIGURE 5.12

3 **Click the loaded-graphic icon near the top-left margin.**

The image is an EPS file, so a low-resolution proxy (preview) image of the graphic appears at 100% of the image size.

4 **Use the Selection tool to drag the image to the upper-left corner of the page until it "snaps" to the margin guides.**

The Selection tool moves the bounding frame and the image it contains.

5 **Choose the Zoom tool from the Tools palette. Drag a marquee around the placed graphic to enlarge the view.**

Even though this is a vector graphic, it looks terrible when enlarged because the image on the screen is a low-resolution raster thumbnail. When the page is printed, however, the image looks crisp because the actual PostScript vector data is sent to the printer with all the adjustments made to the proxy image in InDesign.

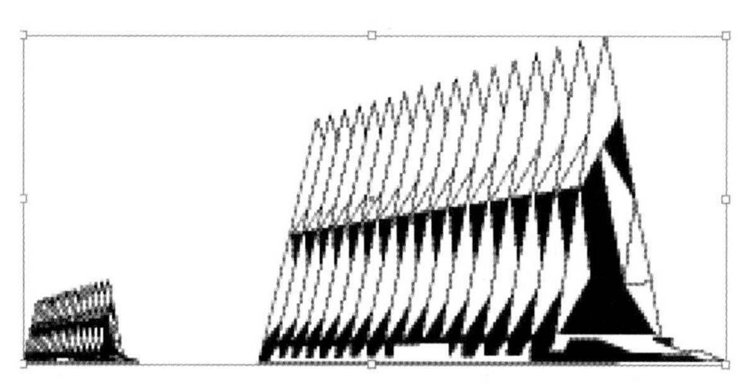

FIGURE 5.13

6 **Control/right-click the graphic. Choose High Quality Display from the Display Performance sub-menu.**

This command instructs InDesign to render a high-resolution preview from the PostScript data in the file, which noticeably improves the preview quality. Using this display mode can significantly slow down your system if you have multiple placed EPS files. You can turn this feature on or off in the Display Performance sub-menu, or you can set the display quality in InDesign's Preferences dialog box.

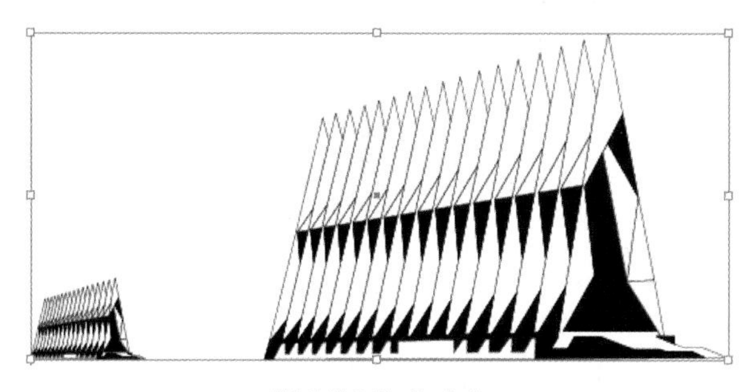

FIGURE 5.14

7 **Type "100" in the Zoom Percent box at the lower left of the window.**

You return to 100% magnification.

8 **Press the "V" key to switch to the Selection tool. Deselect the image.**

You should always deselect any selected items when placing images or text. If a frame is selected when you place an image or text, the new content replaces the existing content of the frame.

9 **Choose File>Place. Choose the file named ballroll.eps. Click Open.**

You can also press Command/Control-D to access the Place dialog box.

10 When the loaded-graphics icon appears, click the top margin at the center of the page. Drag a frame across to the right margin and down to 3.25 inches on the vertical ruler.

FIGURE 5.15

11 Save the document as "picture_practice.indd" in your WIP_05 folder. Leave it open.

Place Graphics within Frames

1 Continue in the open picture_practice.indd.

2 Choose the Rectangle Frame tool in the Tools palette. Drag the tool to create a frame under the academy.eps image. With the upper-left reference point selected in the proxy, set the frame as follows: X: 0.5 in, Y: 3.5 in, W: 4 in, H: 2.75 in.

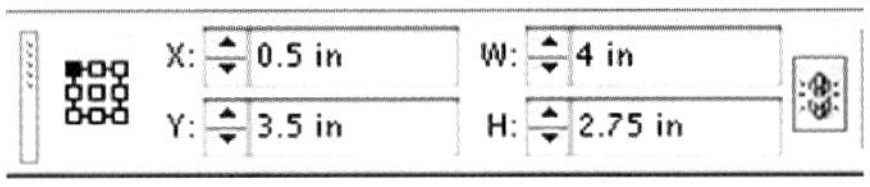

X: 0.5 in W: 4 in
Y: 3.5 in H: 2.75 in

FIGURE 5.16

3 Leave the frame selected and choose File>Place. Choose farmer.tif to import. Be sure the Replace Selected Item box is checked.

The image is smaller than the frame; it could be enlarged to fill the frame, since the enlargement would be less than 10%, or the frame could be reduced to fit the image.

4 Switch to the Selection tool. Resize the frame by dragging the bottom-right corner point up and to the left until it touches the edge of the image. Deselect the frame.

FIGURE 5.17

5 **Choose the Rectangle tool in the Tools palette. To the right of the farmer, drag a shape that is 1.5 inches wide and 3.25 inches high. If your rectangle does not have a black stroke, click the Default Fill and Stroke icon in the Tools palette.**

At this point, the rectangle is a graphic element, but you can use it as a frame. Remember, a graphic element receives a 1-pt black stroke by default, and the stroke prints.

6 **With the rectangle selected, place flowers2.tif.**

The image appears in the rectangle automatically. The rectangle is now a frame because it contains an image. Note that this new frame retains the black stroke. Graphic elements that are converted to frames retain their original fill and stroke attributes.

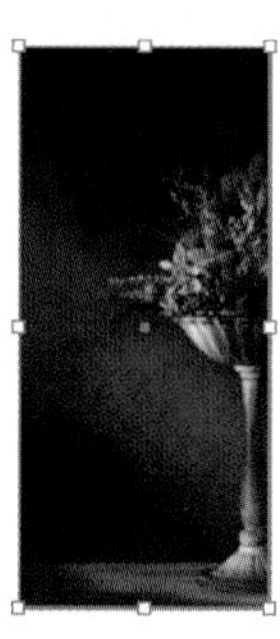

FIGURE 5.18

7 **Press Command/Control-Z to undo the placement of the flowers.**

You see the loaded pointer, and the rectangle is still selected.

8 **Press and hold the Command/Control key to temporarily switch to the Selection tool. Click a blank area on the page to deselect the rectangle, and then release the Command/Control key to switch back to the loaded pointer. Move the pointer over the rectangle and watch it change.**

InDesign detects when you move a loaded pointer over any potential container. The new pointer appears enclosed in parentheses, indicating that you moved it over a container of some sort.

FIGURE 5.19

9 **Single-click to place the flowers in the rectangle.**

The rectangle converts to a frame. It is smaller than the imported image. You could manually enlarge the frame, but you have automated tools to accomplish the task.

10 **Change to the Direct Selection tool. Click and hold on the image.**

You can see the rest of the photo, as it extends beyond the frame. This is particularly useful if you are going to move the photo around in the frame to show a specific element. When you click an image with the Direct Selection tool, its bounding box appears in brown.

FIGURE 5.20

11 **Control/right-click the image. Choose Fitting>Fit Frame to Content.**

The frame enlarges to perfectly fit the image. You could also use the keyboard shortcut Command-Option-C (Macintosh) or Control-Alt-C (Windows).

12 **Save the file. Leave it open for the next exercise.**

To Extend Your Knowledge...

USE THE FITTING SHORTCUTS

The following shortcuts will speed up your workflow when you place graphics in frames:

Function	Macintosh	Windows
Fit Content to Frame	Command-Option-E	Control-Alt-E
Fit Frame to Content	Command-Option-C	Control-Alt-C
Center Content	Command-Shift-E	Control-Shift-E
Fit Content Proportionally	Command-Option-Shift-E	Control-Alt-Shift-E

LESSON 3 Linking vs. Embedding Images

It is important to understand how InDesign places image files because managing imported graphics ensures that the file prints correctly. Placing a graphic imports the image onto the InDesign page, but it does not automatically copy the graphic into the InDesign file (known as ***embedding*** the file) unless the file size is smaller than 48K (kilobytes). For anything larger, InDesign utilizes a technique known as ***linking*** to store and display a preview of the image on the page, and to store the location of the original graphic. When the file is printed, InDesign locates the original graphic, applies the positioning, cropping, and scaling that you applied to the preview, and sends the adjusted file to the output device in place of the preview.

Linking allows you to position, crop, and scale graphics alongside page elements without significantly increasing the document's file size. It is also a convenient mechanism for modifying the original graphic; changes in the original file are applied to every instance of the graphic in your InDesign document. If you move, rename, or delete a linked graphic file, you see a warning message the next time you open or print your InDesign document. InDesign also alerts you of graphics that have been changed since you first placed them.

For the most part, you will work with linked graphics. While it may seem as though it's more efficient to simply embed the graphics, doing so can make the document file unmanageably large. Embedded graphics are listed in the Links palette, but InDesign does not track the status of the original file after the graphic is embedded.

Manage and Update Image Links

1 **Continue in the open picture_practice.indd. Choose Window>Links.**

The Links palette opens. You can see the name of each graphic file, along with the page number on which the graphic is placed (at the right). If no symbol appears between the name and page number, the graphic is linked and ready for output.

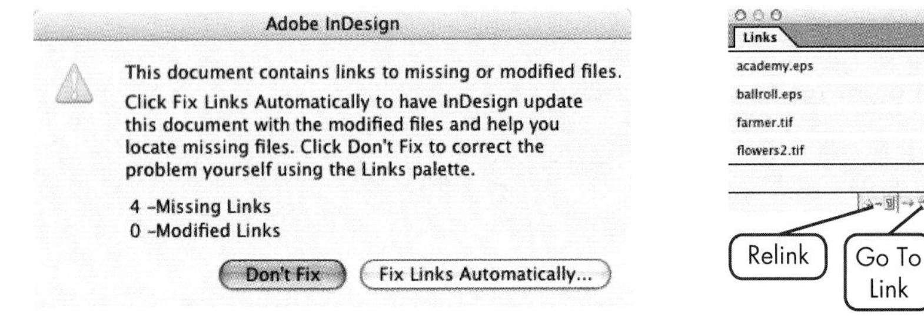

FIGURE 5.21

For demonstration purposes, you're going to break the links.

2 **Save and close picture_practice.indd.**

3 **Locate the Project_05 folder and delete the following files: academy.eps, ballroll.eps, farmer.tif, and flowers2.tif. Copy the Links folder in your Project_05 folder to your WIP_05 folder. If you have been working from the Resource CD-ROM, remove the CD from your drive.**

The Links folder contains copies of these graphic files, but flowers2.tif is renamed as flowers_new.tif. The files are not in their original location, so the links are now "broken."

4 **Reopen picture_practice.indd.**

You receive a warning that there are missing links. If the Links palette is visible, it shows that linked images are missing (see Figure 5.22). The red question mark symbol indicates that InDesign can't find the files for these graphics. They must be relinked.

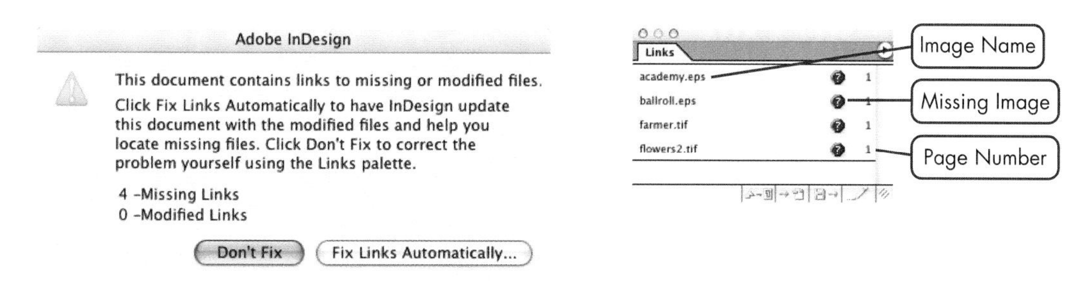

FIGURE 5.22

5 **Click Don't Fix to dismiss the warning.**

6 **Choose academy.eps in the Links list. Click the Relink button (on the far left at the bottom of the palette). Navigate to the Links folder you copied to your WIP_05 folder, choose academy.eps, and then click Open.**

After you locate the first graphic in a set of unlinked files, you can easily relink all the other graphics that reside in that location without browsing to their location.

7 **Choose ballroll.eps and click the Relink button. Choose farmer.tif and click the Relink button.**

8 **Choose flowers2.tif and click the Relink button. Choose flowers_new.tif, and click OK. A dialog box appears. Click Yes.**

All the broken links are resolved.

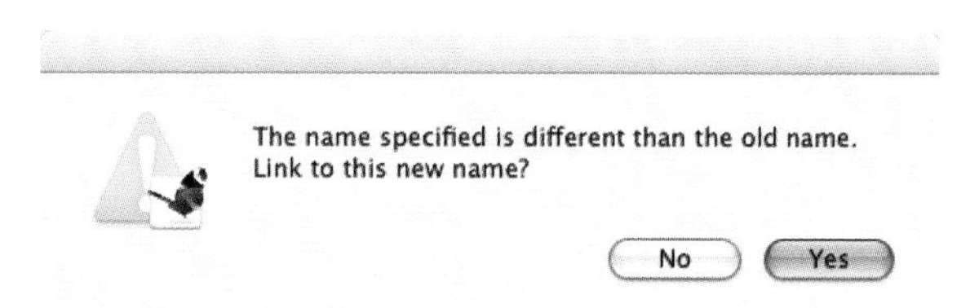

FIGURE 5.23

9 **Save the document. Keep it open for the next exercise.**

Embed Placed Graphics

1. **In the open document, choose flowers_new.tif in the Links palette.**

2. **In the Links palette Options menu, choose Embed File.**

   The graphic file is copied into the InDesign document. It is no longer a linked file, but the graphic name remains in the Links palette with a small symbol showing that it is now embedded.

   If you alter the original file and need to incorporate the change, you must either delete and re-create the image, or select the image in the document, choose Unembed from the Links palette Options menu, and direct InDesign to relink to the new file.

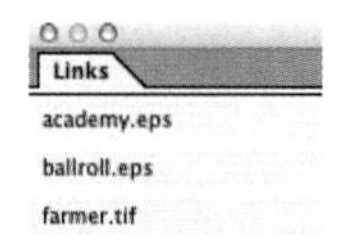

FIGURE 5.24

3. **Save your changes. Close the file.**

To Extend Your Knowledge...

EXTENDED LINKING

Another kind of broken link occurs when the original graphic has been modified and resaved in the original program. The link must be updated to display and print the latest version of the graphic. The exclamation point symbol indicates that a graphic has been edited. You can update modified links by clicking the Update Link button on the Links palette.

Locating and relinking graphics can be time-consuming. Be careful not to rename or move graphics after you link them to an InDesign file. Do not delete placed graphic files; the InDesign document won't print correctly without them. Always send copies of the graphic files with the document for output. Packaging files for output is discussed in detail in Project 8.

EDITING LINKED IMAGES

If you have a placed file in a document, and the program used to create the file is installed on your computer, you can select the file name in the Links palette and click the Edit Original button to edit the file in its original program. After you save the file, the new version is automatically updated in the InDesign document. If you update the graphic by pressing Command-Option or Control-Alt and double-click the image, the new version is also automatically updated. If you enlarged the image in the original program, however, you must manually adjust the size of the frame in InDesign.

LESSON 4 Scaling and Cropping Images

Placed images are imported at the full size at which they were created in their native application. During page composition, however, that size may not fit your page layout. InDesign provides several ways to reduce or enlarge imported graphics to suit any design requirements. Remember that vector graphics may be scaled to any percentage larger or smaller without concern for resolution and print quality; resolution-dependent raster graphics, however, must contain a sufficient number of pixels per inch to print at the resolution and scaling percentage chosen in the document. For each raster image, you should check the resolution against the scaling percentage assigned in InDesign to ensure it is still within acceptable parameters. If not, you should resample the raster image (change its resolution), or rescan it in the original application and update it in InDesign before output.

Another way to control the appearance of placed images on the page is to crop them. Cropping essentially draws a frame beyond which the image is masked; areas that are masked don't display or print. Cropping can occur automatically if an image is placed into a small or irregular-shaped frame. You can also crop images by reducing the frame size after placing an image. You can combine scaling and cropping to manipulate imported images and blend them with other InDesign elements.

Create a Newspaper Ad

1. **Create a new single-sided document with a 4.125-in Width and a 5-in Height. Set all Margins to 0 (zero), and use 1 Column.**

2. **Choose File>Place (or press Command/Control-D) and select the file named bluestraw.eps. The Show Import Options box should be unchecked.**

3. **Position the loaded-graphics icon in the lower third of the page. Single-click (don't drag) to place the image.**

FIGURE 5.25

4 **With the image still selected, go to the Control or Transform palette. With the Constrain Link icon active, enter "40%" for the Width.**

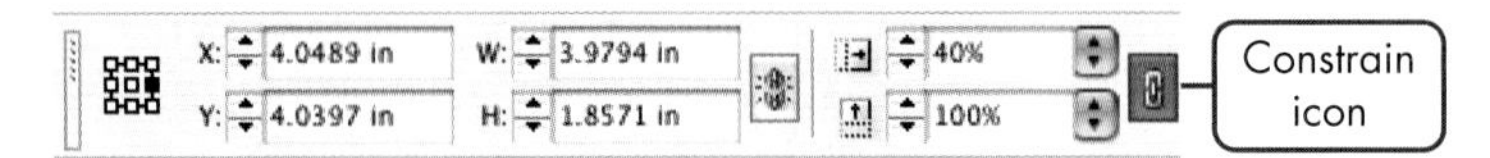

FIGURE 5.26

5 **Position the graphic in the lower-right corner, but not at the edge of the page. Deselect the image.**

FIGURE 5.27

6 **Place the image named dining.tif near the upper-left corner of the page.**

The photo is much too large for the page. You need to scale and crop it to fit.

FIGURE 5.28

7 **Scale this raster graphic to fill the ad area. Hold down the Command/Control and Shift keys and drag the Selection tool until the image fills the page. The bottom of the image should be at the bottom of the page**

If you click the lower-left reference point in the proxy, the image should be positioned at X:0 in, Y:5 in, with a width of 4.125 in.

FIGURE 5.29

8 **Use the Selection tool to click the top-center handle of the frame. Drag the frame edge until the top of the frame is at the top of the page.**

This effectively crops the image. Scaled Frame Content shows 100% in the palette, regardless of how much the frame and its content are scaled; but if you select the content with the Direct Selection tool, the true scaling percentage is shown.

FIGURE 5.30

9 **Change to the Selection tool. Choose Object>Arrange>Send to Back, and then deselect the image.**

10 **Save the document as "ad.indd". Leave it open for the next exercise.**

Add and Manipulate Images

1 **Continue in the open document. Place the image named vday.eps. Click the loaded-graphics icon to the left of the Blue Strawberry logo.**

FIGURE 5.31

2 **Use the Selection tool to click the lower-right control handle of the frame and drag it up and to the left until the frame is about 1.5 inches wide.**

Look at the Control palette to verify the width.

3 **With the graphic still selected, choose Object>Fitting>Fit Content Proportionally. Deselect the frame.**

FIGURE 5.32

4 **Choose the Rotate tool in the Tools palette. Click the cursor outside the bottom-right corner and drag counterclockwise until the Transform palette indicates approximately 20° Rotation.**

5 **Switch to the Selection tool. Reposition the Valentine's Day image if necessary, then deselect it.**

When using the Rotate, Scale, or Skew tool, click and hold the tool for a moment to view a live preview of the transformation. If you move the tool away immediately, you see the outline instead of the content.

FIGURE 5.33

6 **Place the image named vday_head.eps in the upper center of the ad. Use the center proxy-reference point to adjust the position to X: 2.0625 in, Y: 1.33 in.**

The finished ad should resemble Figure 5.34.

FIGURE 5.34

7 **Save your changes. Close the document.**

To Extend Your Knowledge...

PERFORMING EXTENSIVE TRANSFORMATIONS

You can make some transformations in InDesign, but significant transformations — even with vector images — should be completed in the original drawing or image-management program before placing the image. It is best to avoid enlarging raster graphics more than 10%. Do not rotate rasters in InDesign; doing so may deteriorate the image, and it definitely impacts print speed.

LESSON 5 Framing Images with Borders

Depending on the layout, some images require borders. With InDesign, the frame container itself, or another frame, can provide the border. You can add borders to rectangular, circular, or irregular-shaped graphic containers using the Stroke and Swatches palettes.

You should apply a border to an image when you want it to stand out from the background. Borders also tend to cover up imperfections that occur when two dissimilar colors abut one another. Borders also allow subtle images to stand out on the page.

When you create a border for a frame, the safest color to work with is black because the frame overlaps the image by 50% of the weight of the border. If, for example, you create a thick light blue border, the sky in your image may look fine; but if the lower part of the photo includes grass, you may have a section of the border that is darker than the rest, progressing to the light blue color that you want.

FIGURE 5.35

Create Borders for Imported Graphics

1 **Open picture_practice.indd from your WIP_05 folder.**

2 **Adjust the view so the academy.eps image is visible. Select the frame's handles with the Selection tool and resize the frame so it is slightly larger than the image itself. Choose Object>Fitting>Center Content.**

The image shifts to the horizontal and vertical center of the frame.

3 **With the frame still selected, click the Stroke box in the Tools palette, and then click the Default Fill and Stroke icon.**

A black stroke is applied to the frame border.

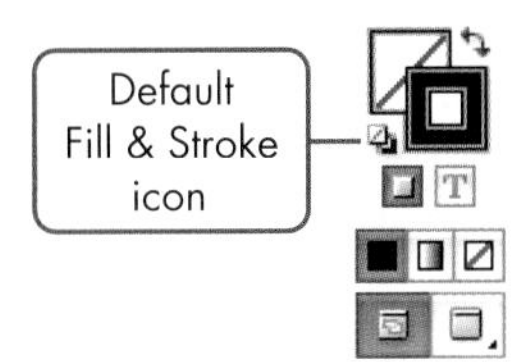

FIGURE 5.36

4 **Display the Stroke palette. From the Stroke palette Options menu, choose Show Options to display the entire palette. Choose 5 pt from the Weight menu. Choose Solid from the Type menu, if it is not already selected.**

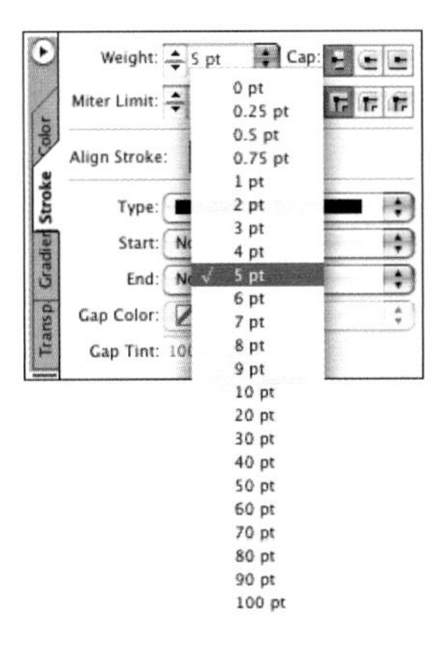

FIGURE 5.37

5 **Use the Selection tools to choose the ballroll.eps graphic. Choose Stroke in the Swatches palette, and then click the Black swatch.**

6 **In the Stroke palette, change the Weight of this frame to 2 pt.**

7 **Choose Object>Corner Effects. First check Preview, and then change the Effect to Fancy in the pop-up menu. Enter "0.5 in" in the Size field. Click OK. Deselect the image.**

The frame does not appear to change until you enter a reasonably large value in the Size field.

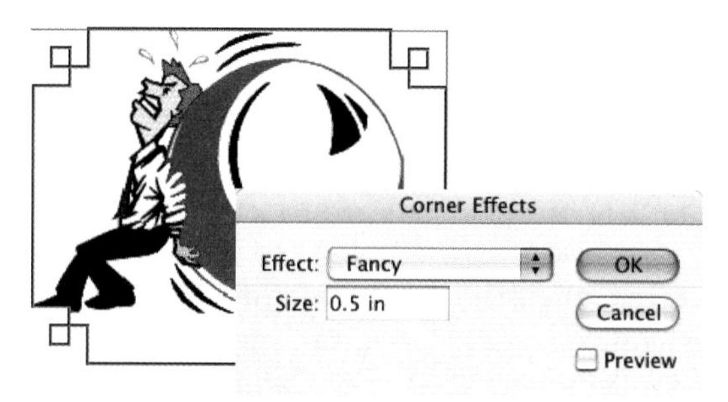

FIGURE 5.38

8 **Use the Selection tools to choose the farmer.tif image. Choose Black for the Stroke Color of this frame and assign a 10-pt Weight. Access the Color palette. Enter "50" in the Percentage field. Press Return/Enter.**

You assigned a 10-pt black border, tinted to 50%.

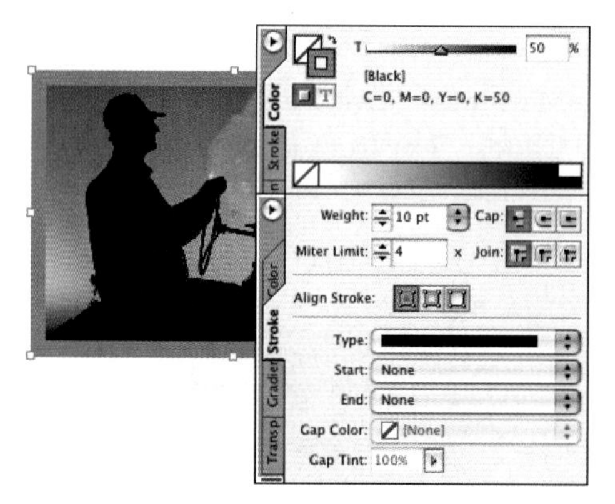

FIGURE 5.39

9 **Choose Object>Corner Effects. In the Effect field, chose Rounded. Enter "0.25 in" in the Size field. Click OK and deselect.**

10 **Save the file. Leave it open for the next exercise.**

Create Custom Strokes

1 **Continue in the open document. Below the farmer image, create a rectangular frame with a 4.125-in Width and 5-in Height in the empty space on the page.**

If there isn't enough room, move the images above; it's okay if they overlap. You're going to create a custom stroke for this frame, then import a version of the ad you created earlier into the frame.

2 **Open the Stroke palette. Choose Stroke Styles from the Options menu.**

You can create custom stroke styles in this menu. It comes pre-loaded with seven styles that you will find in the standard Stroke palette. You can create a new stroke from scratch, or you can base your custom stroke on a pre-existing stroke.

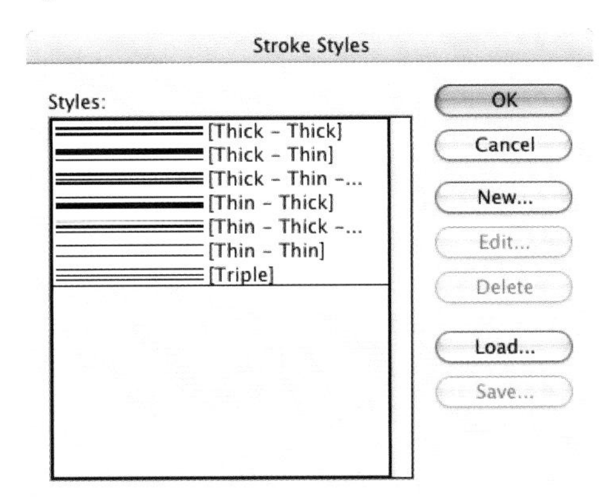

FIGURE 5.40

3 **Click the top stroke [Thick – Thick], and click the New button.**

The New Stroke Style menu appears, and allows you to name your new stroke. It is currently named "Thick – Thick copy." You have the option of creating a stroke consisting of stripes, dashes, or dots.

4 **Name the new stroke "Thick-Thin-Thin-Thick". Leave the Type defined as Stripe.**

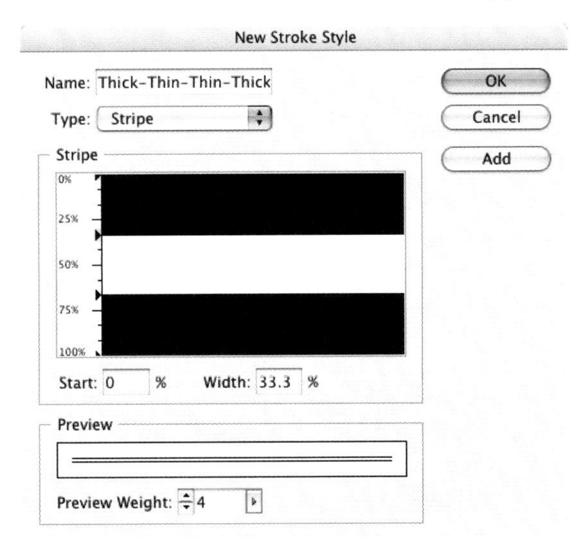

FIGURE 5.41

5 **Click the triangle that starts at 0 and change its Width to 25%.**

If you choose to type the value in the box, press the Tab key to apply the change. Do not press Return/Enter; doing so would accept all values and save the new stroke style.

6 **Click the triangle that starts at 66%. Change its Width to 25% and its Start position to 75%.**

You must change the width first; otherwise, you get an error message telling you that a width of 33% won't fit between 75% and 100%.

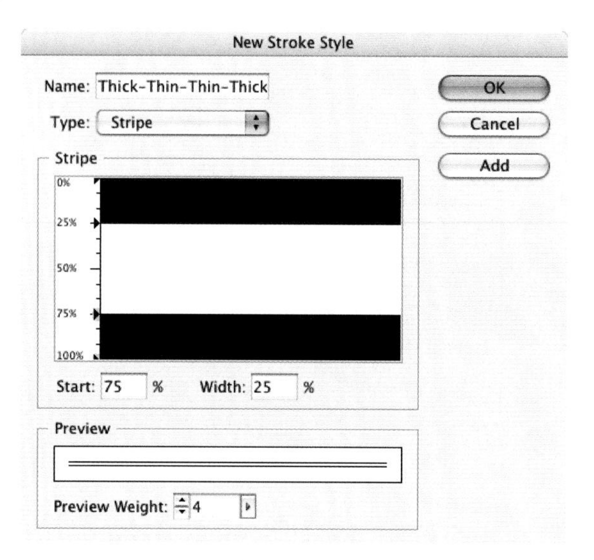

FIGURE 5.42

7 **Click your mouse at approximately the 35% position. Specify another stripe with a Start position of 35% and a Width of 10%.**

You created another, narrower stripe.

8 **Create another 10% stripe at a Start position of 55%.**

9 **Change the Preview Weight to 18 pt.**

A Preview Weight smaller than this is too narrow to display this stroke.

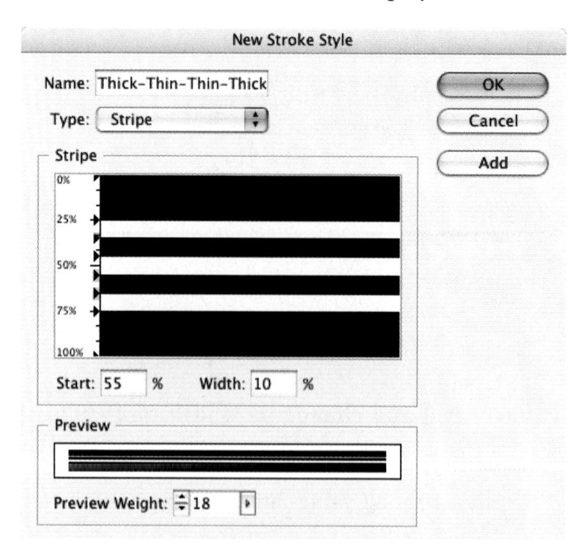

FIGURE 5.43

10 **Click OK to add the stroke to the palette. Click OK on the Stroke Styles palette.**

The stroke is now available from the Stroke palette. It is the last item in the palette.

11 **Use the Selection tool to click the frame you created in Step 1. Assign the new stroke to the frame. Apply a Weight of 18 pt and a Color of Black. Assign a Gap Color of Paper.**

12 **With the frame still selected, place the file vday_ad.pdf. Center it in the frame.**

FIGURE 5.44

13 **Save your changes. Close the file.**

LESSON 6 Wrapping Text Around Simple Objects

Wrapping text around simple objects, such as frames, is a straightforward process. It is a bit more complicated to wrap text around shapes within frames. Wrapped text is used to create many designs, so we introduce the feature here. In this lesson, we discuss simple text wraps. Complex text wraps are discussed in *Essentials for Design: InDesign Level 2.*

When text is wrapped around an image, you must take into consideration both the effect on readability and the overall appearance of the text and images on the page. When wrapping to an irregular image, it is especially important to establish offsets that are large enough to create a discernable space between the text and the image. You also need to look at the size of the image relative to the width of the column. It is often better to simply stop the text wrap above an image, and then restart it again below the image, rather than have a very narrow column of text that becomes difficult to read.

Compare the text wraps around the berry on the left and the berry on the right in Figure 5.45. Graphically, the wrap on the right is more attractive because both sides are nearly equal. Notice how bad the narrow column of type on the extreme left appears.

The Strawberry Festival is looked forward to each year as the harbinger of summer in the rural com- munity of West Alfalfa, Florida. Visitors come from around the state to participate in the
event and to crown the year's Strawberry Queen. The festival includes agricultural exhibits (Biggest Berry, Most Perfect Berry, and Tasti- est Berry) and contests that pit one person against another, such as the Strawberry
Sundae-eating contest and the Strawberry Fling. Also featured is top- name entertain- ment, which plays for the Strawberry Jam from noon to 9PM each day of the festival. The Festival began in 1933, and has been a recurring tradition ever since.

FIGURE 5.45

Wrap Text Around Frames

1 **Open the document named textwrap.indd.**

Text and images were already inserted into this document. When you look closely at the page, you see that the images are placed on top of the text.

2 **Choose Window>Type & Tables>Text Wrap.**

The Text Wrap palette opens.

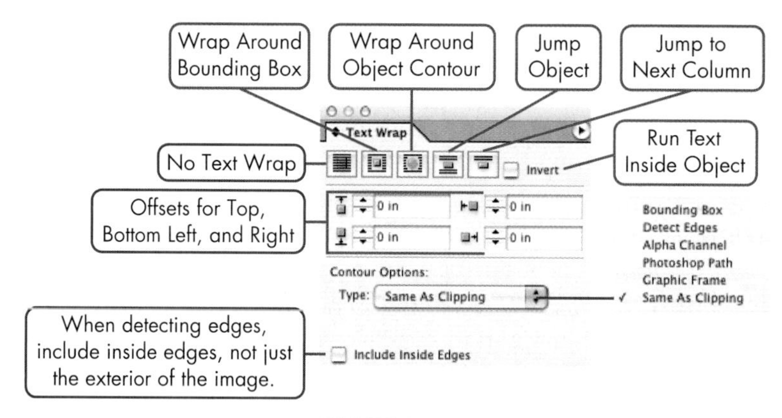

FIGURE 5.46

3 **Use the Selection tool to click the Alice illustration in the left column, and then click the Wrap Around Bounding Box icon.**

The text wraps around the bounding box of the frame. Since the bounding box is wider than the image, the type looks fine.

4 **Click the Alice illustration between columns 2 and 3, and then click the Wrap Around Bounding Box icon.**

The text wrap is fine on the left, but too close on the right.

5 **In the Right Offset box, specify "0.125 in".**

This adjusts the offset, and improves the appearance of the type.

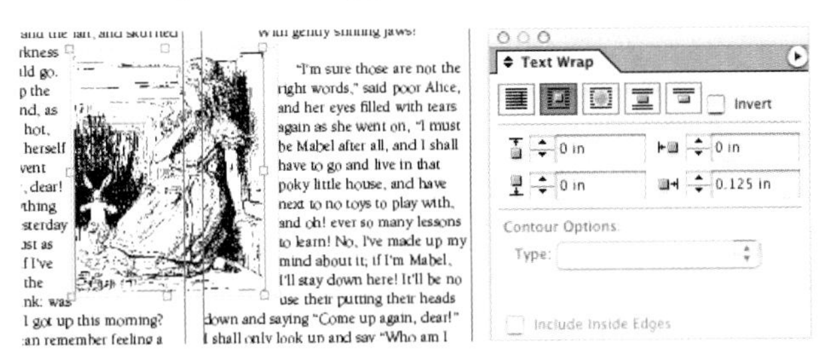

FIGURE 5.47

6 **Return to the Alice illustration in the first column. Click the image, and then change the wrap to Wrap Around Object Shape.**

7 **Change the Top Offset to "0.13 in".**

You can only set the Top offset. The wrap is equal all around.

8 **Set the Contour Options Type to Detect Edges.**

The type wraps, and part of it goes under the text frame.

9 **Click the image frame and send the image to the back (choose Object>Arrange>Send to Back or press Command/Control-Shift-[).**

The contoured wrap becomes visible.

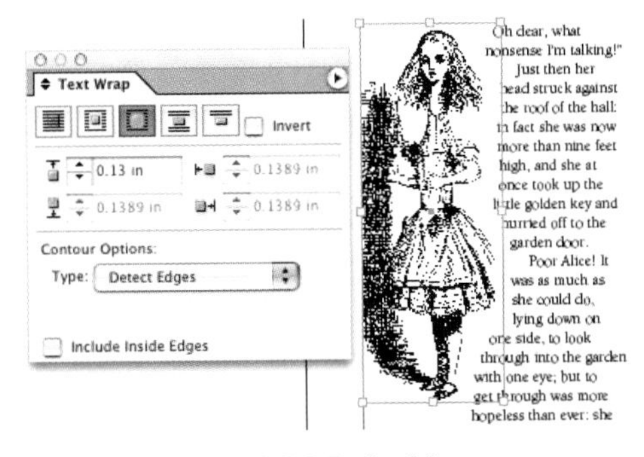

FIGURE 5.48

10 **Choose Save As to save the file to your WIP_05 folder. Use the same file name. Close the file.**

CAREERS IN DESIGN

USING STOCK IMAGES

When you think of the graphic arts, the first thing that comes to mind is images (graphics). As you have discovered, there is far more to graphic design than drawing or taking photographs. The graphic designer combines text and images in a pleasing manner to create a variety of products. If you don't create the images yourself, however, where do they come from?

The traditional answer is to hire an illustrator or photographer to create the images for you. For much of the work you will do, however, custom artwork and photography is prohibitively expensive. An acceptable alternative is to use stock files. You can find stock illustrations, photographs, sounds, and even video clips on virtually any subject — if you look hard enough.

Stock images are good for both the creator of the image (and the agency, if one is used) and the client. The creator benefits from the sale of his images to each and every client; the client pays a substantially lower fee than that of commissioned work. There are two basic types of stock images, each with unique advantages for the client:

- ***Rights-managed*** images form the more traditional method of acquiring stock images for use in publications. When you purchase rights to use an image, the fee you pay is based on a combination of the intended use, number of copies you will distribute, time frame for use, and the level of exclusivity for the time frame contracted.
- ***Royalty-free*** images, for all intents and purposes, give purchasers unlimited use of the images. The one-time fee is usually based on the resolution of the image. The down side of using a royalty-free image is that there is no restriction on its use — your competitor across the street could use an image identical to the one you built your entire campaign around.

You can purchase images on an individual basis, or in collections; sometimes they are bundled with other software — be sure to read the license. Other sources offer a subscription-based structure, in which you pay for access to the stock library for a specified period. During that period, you can use any file in the subscription collection without paying additional fees. If you use a large number of stock images, this method could be far less expensive than paying for individual royalty-free images.

When necessary, you can purchase the right to manipulate an image. While royalty-free files usually carry no restrictions, rights-managed files may. The license you receive specifies what you can do with the image.

You can usually download the low-resolution preview image and include it in comps; this way, you can present several ideas to your client before incurring substantial expense. You cannot download a preview image and use it for publication — modified or not. To do so is considered theft.

SUMMARY

In Project 5, you learned how to create and manage frames and their contents. You learned about image formats, and discovered when each format should be used. You also learned when it is acceptable to enlarge graphics in InDesign, and when you should edit images in their originating programs before placing them in your InDesign documents. You learned how to place images, as well as how to scale and position them within their respective frames. You explored the differences between linking images to a document and embedding images within it, and the benefits and pitfalls associated with both practices. You learned a number of ways to scale images, and how to use frames to crop the parts of an image you do not want to display. Finally, you learned how to apply borders to images, as well as create custom borders.

KEY TERMS

Bit
Bitmap
BMP
Border
Continuous tone
Crop
Desktop color separation
Dots per inch (dpi)
Encapsulated PostScript (EPS)
GIF
Halftone
Joint Photographic Expert Group (JPEG/JPG)
Line art
Lines per inch (lpi)
Linking
PCX
PDF
PCIT
Pixel
Pixels per inch (ppi)
Proxy image
Raster image
Resolution
Sample
Scitex CT
Screen ruling
Spots per inch (spi)
Tagged Image File Format (TIFF/TIF)
WMF

CHECKING CONCEPTS AND TERMS

MULTIPLE CHOICE

Circle the letter of the correct answer for each of the following questions.

1. Which of the following best describes vector art.
   a. It should be created at the resolution of the output device.
   b. It is resolution dependent.
   c. It is resolution independent.
   d. It is often saved in JPEG format.

2. Which of the following best describes raster art?
   a. It should be created at the resolution of the output device.
   b. It is resolution dependent.
   c. It is resolution independent.
   d. It is often saved in JPEG format.

3. Which of the following is an example of a raster image?
   a. A black-and-white line drawing
   b. An illustration drawn in Illustrator
   c. A photograph
   d. An object created in InDesign

4. Why is understanding resolution important when creating images?
   a. You should always create images at the highest possible resolution.
   b. You should match the resolution to the output device.
   c. Bad resolution affects the image's color.
   d. You can use unlimited scaling on raster images.

5. How do you apply a border to an object?
   a. Use the Border palette.
   b. Use the Stroke palette.
   c. Use the Stroke Styles palette.
   d. Use the Line tool.

6. What is a halftone?
   a. An image that uses only 0–50% or 50–100% of the color palette.
   b. A continuous-color original photograph.
   c. An image that is only black and white.
   d. A conversion of a photograph into dots.

7. What graphics file format is usually associated with vector images?
   a. TIFF
   b. EPS
   c. JPEG
   d. PDF

8. What happens when you move a linked graphic?
   a. It becomes unlinked.
   b. InDesign tracks the changed position.
   c. The image has to be re-created.
   d. Nothing.

9. What happens when you crop an image?
   a. The cropped portion is visible.
   b. The cropped portion is not visible.
   c. The frame is enlarged.
   d. Two images can be placed in the same frame.

10. How do you modify a graphic image?
    a. Use any of the transformation tools.
    b. Use a transformation tool after clicking it with the Direct Selection tool.
    c. Use the Object>Content menu.
    d. Use the Pen tool.

DISCUSSION QUESTIONS

1. In this project, you learned that extensive graphic transformations should not be made in InDesign. Why should you make extensive graphic transformations in the originating programs instead of making them within the page-layout program?

2. You discovered that linking graphics to your InDesign documents can lead to difficulties. Discuss the benefits and liabilities of both methods of introducing graphics (linking and embedding).

SKILL DRILL

Skill Drills reinforce project skills. Each skill reinforced is the same, or nearly the same, as a skill presented in the lessons. Detailed instructions are provided in a step-by-step format. You should complete these exercises in order.

1. Create a Catalog Cover

Your client, Premier Products, produces catalogs for corporate employee programs. The winter catalog appropriately features gifts for the holidays, in addition to a number of items people might want to purchase for themselves. In the following Skill Drills, you compose the cover and inside front cover for this year's catalog. We placed a couple of initial items to help you get started.

1. Open premier_catalog.indd from your Project_05 folder. Be sure you are on Page 1.

   Some text is in place, but you will create frames and import images. Notice that the text frame in the upper right is irregularly shaped. It was created with the Pen tool.
2. Create a new rectangular frame that fills the entire page, including bleed area.
3. Fill the frame with the graduated tint swatch labeled Light Gradient. Set it as a Linear gradient at a –35° Angle in the Gradient palette.
4. Use the Selection tool to select the frame containing the gradient. Place holiday_cover.tif.
5. With the frame still selected, Choose Object>Arrange>Send to Back to send the frame to the back.

   You could also use the keyboard shortcut Command/Control-Shift-[.
6. Center the image in the frame. Choose Object>Fitting>Center Content.

   It sits too high in the frame, but it's centered horizontally.
7. Use the Direct Selection tool to select the image. Set the Y position to 2.75 in, with one of the upper proxy-reference handles selected.
8. Save the document to your WIP_05 folder. Leave it open for the next Skill Drill.

2. Convey the Main Offer

1. In the upper-right corner, create a new frame at X: 5.5 in, Y: –0.125 in (the top of the bleed area). Extend the frame to the right-hand bleed area, with a Height of 2.6 in.
2. With the frame active, place the palmy_beach.tif photo.
3. Send the frame to the back. Choose Object>Arrange>Bring Forward, or press Command/Control-] to bring it forward one level.
4. Click the image with the Direct Selection tool and change its X and Y percentages to 75%. Drag the image around until the two people are visible in the frame.
5. With the Direct Selection tool active, click the lower-left anchor point of the frame, and drag it up and to the right until the image disappears from below and to the left of the arrow.

6. Change to the Selection tool and click the frame containing the "Save 50%" offer.
7. Choose Edit>Step and Repeat.
8. Step and Repeat the object one time, with Horizontal and Vertical Offsets of –0.0139.
9. Change the Color of the new frame to None.
10. Change to the Type tool. Select the type in the frame. Change the Color of the type to Paper.
11. Save the document. Leave it open for the next Skill Drill.

FIGURE 5.49

3. Deliver the Message

1. In the open document, go to Page 2.
2. Create a rectangular frame in the upper right. Choose File>Place and place the image vp.tif. Be sure the Replace Selected Item box is checked.
3. Control/right-click to access the contextual menu. Choose Fitting>Fit Frame to Content.
4. With the upper-right proxy-reference point selected, reposition the frame at X: 7.75 in, Y: 1.3 in.
5. Choose Window>Type & Tables>Text Wrap.

   The Text Wrap dialog box appears. You can also press Command-Option-W (Macintosh) or Control-Alt-W (Windows) to open the Text Wrap dialog box.

6. In the Text Wrap dialog box, click the Wrap Around Bounding Box button and set the Left Offset to 0.125 in.
7. In the Tools palette, click the Default Fill and Stroke icon to apply a 1-pt Black Stroke to the frame.
8. Create a new rectangular frame with a Stroke of None. Place the frame below the word "Sincerely".

   This frame is for the signature.

9. Place the signature, vpsig.ai. If necessary, adjust the size of the frame. Use the Direct Selection tool to move the signature to an appropriate position within the frame.
10. Use the Direct Selection tool to click the "I Agree" frame.

    This is placed as an in-line graphic, but it can be edited.
11. Choose Object>Corner Effects. Choose an Effect of Rounded and a Size of 0.08 in.
12. Save the document. Leave it open for the next Skill Drill.

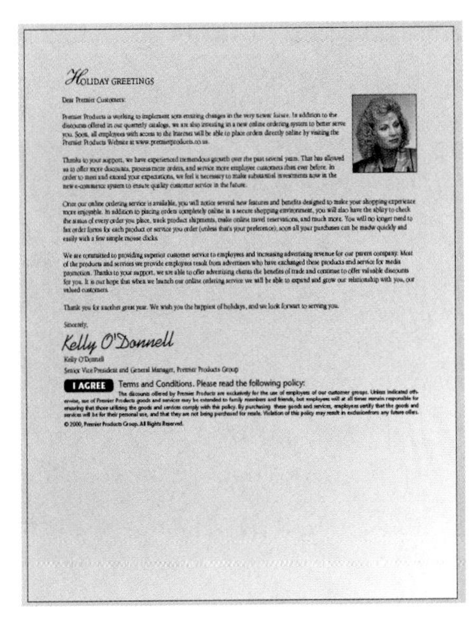

HOLIDAY GREETINGS

Dear Premier Customers:

Premier Products is working to implement some exciting changes in the very near future. In addition to the discounts offered in our quarterly catalogs, we are also investing in a new online ordering system to better serve you. Soon, all employees with access to the Internet will be able to place orders directly online by visiting the Premier Products Website at www.premierproducts.co.us.

Thanks to your support, we have experienced tremendous growth over the past several years. That has allowed us to offer more discounts, process more orders, and service more employee customers than ever before. In order to meet and exceed your expectations, we feel it necessary to make substantial investments now in the new e-commerce system to ensure quality customer service in the future.

Once our online ordering service is available, you will notice several new features and benefits designed to make your shopping experience more enjoyable. In addition to placing orders completely online in a secure shopping environment, you will also have the ability to check the status of every order you place, track product shipments, make online travel reservations, and much more. You will no longer need to fax order forms for each product or service you order (unless that's your preference); soon all your purchases can be madw quickly and easily with a few simple mouse clicks.

We are committed to providing superior customer service to employees and increasing advertising revenue for our parent company. Most of the products and services we provide employees result from advertisers who have exchanged these products and service for media promotion. Thanks to your support, we are able to offer advertising clients the benefits of trade and continue to offer valuable discounts for you. It is our hope that when we launch our online ordering service we will be able to expand and grow our relationship with you, our valued customers.

Thank you for another great year. We wish you the happiest of holidays, and we look forward to serving you.

Sincerely,

Kelly O'Donnell

Kelly O'Donnell

Senior Vice President and General Manager, Premier Products Group

I AGREE Terms and Conditions. Please read the following policy:

The discounts offered by Premier Products are exclusively for the use of employees of our customer groups. Unless indicated otherwise, use of Premier Products goods and services may be extended to family members and friends, but employees will at all times remain responsible for ensuring that those utilizing the goods and services comply with the policy. By purchasing these goods and services, employees certify that the goods and services will be for their personal use, and that they are not being purchased for resale. Violation of this policy may result in exclusionfrom any future offers.

© 2000, Premier Products Group. All Rights Reserved.

FIGURE 5.50

4. Complete the Base Page

1. Continue on Page 2 in the open document.
2. Place bg_pattern.tif at X: 0.5 in, Y: 0.5 in.
3. Use the Selection tool to click in the lower-right corner of the frame. Reduce the size to a 7.5-in Width and 10-in Height.
4. With the Stroke active, apply a 1-pt Black Stroke in the Stroke palette.
5. Choose Object>Arrange>Send to Back.

   The image disappears. You can also press Command/Control-Shift-[to send an item to the back.
6. With the image still selected, choose Object>Arrange>Bring Forward or press Command/Control-] to bring the image forward one level. Deselect the image.
7. With the upper-left proxy-reference point active in the Control palette, create a new frame as follows: X: 0.75 in, Y: 7.8 in, W: 3.35 in, H: 2.5 in.
8. Step and Repeat the frame one time, 3.65 in Horizontal.
9. Save the file. Leave it open for the Challenge exercises.

CHALLENGE

Challenge exercises expand on, or are somewhat related to, skills presented in the lessons. Each exercise provides a brief introduction, followed by instructions presented in a numbered-step format that are not as detailed as those in the Skill Drill exercises. Complete these exercises in order.

1. Build the Makeovers Ad

1. Continue in the open document. Select the left ad frame and place makeover_shell.eps.
2. Deselect the frame. Place makeover_logo.eps. Position it in the upper-left of the frame, aligned with the margin of the type below.
3. Create a 1.2-in square with a Stroke of Black.
4. Place the image makeover.tif into the square.
5. With the frame still selected, double-click the Rotate tool. Apply a Rotation of 45°. The Rotate Content box should not be checked.
6. Reduce the size of the imported image until both women's faces show in the frame. Use the Direct Selection tool to position the faces in the frame. Be sure no background shows through.
7. Using the center proxy-reference point, position the image at X: 3.1025 in, Y: 9.225 in.
8. Create a square with a 0.1675-in Width. Rotate the square 45°. Apply a Fill of Purple and Stroke of None. Position it at X: 3.1025 in, Y: 8.15 in.
9. Select the frame of the ad and apply a 2-pt Purple Stroke.
10. Apply a Beveled Corner effect with a Size of 0.1667 in.
11. Save the file. Leave it open for the next Challenge.

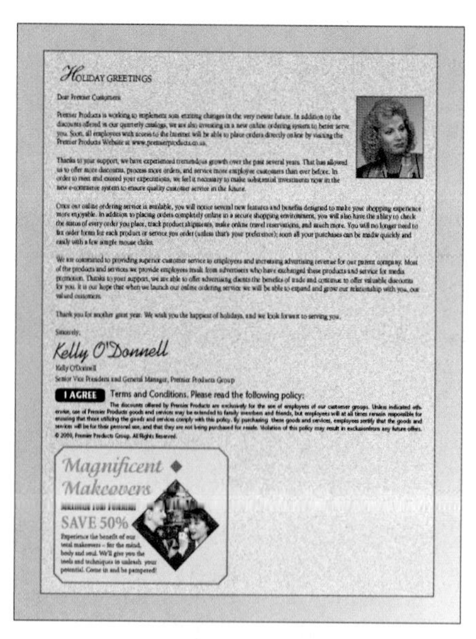

FIGURE 5.51

2. Build the Molly Malloy's Ad

1. Continue in the open document. Select the right frame and import m_malloy_shell.eps. Deselect.
2. Place m_malloy_logo.eps. Position it in the upper right of the ad. Deselect.
3. Place couple_dining.tif. Position it in the upper left of the ad. Deselect.
4. Place surfnturf.tif. Position it in the lower right of the ad. Deselect.
5. Adjust the frames and their contents so they appear attractive and well balanced.
6. Access the Stroke Styles menu and create a new dashed style. The pattern Length should be 0.333 inches, the Corners should adjust both Dashes and Gaps, and the Cap should be Round. Name the style "Dash-Dot".
7. Set the first dash to Start at 0 inches, with a Length of 0.125 inches.
8. Set another dash to Start at .2216 inches and extend for 0 inches.
9. Select the ad frame and apply the Dash-Dot stroke style, with a 3-pt Width.
10. Save your changes. Close the document.

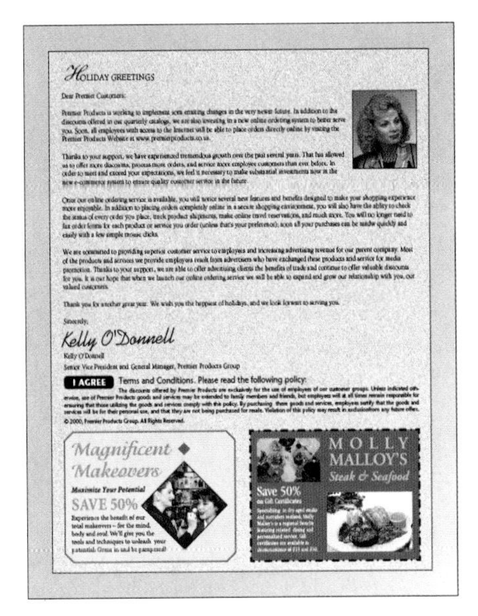

FIGURE 5.52

PORTFOLIO BUILDER

Create Posters for a Play

Your local repertory theatre, in conjunction with local high schools, is presenting performances of William Shakespeare's *Romeo and Juliet* and its modern-day sequel, *West Side Story.* Your task is to create two tabloid-size posters that tie the two plays together. You may decide to use similar scenes from the plays, such as the balcony scenes, or you might find a way to portray the animosity between the Montagues and Capulets, and the Americans of European heritage and the immigrant Puerto Ricans.

Since you are working with a not-for-profit organization, the budget does not allow you to purchase images or hire a photographer. You can use any images for which you have rights, or you can search the Web for free images to incorporate into the posters. The more graphic the images are, the better.

One requirement for the *West Side Story* poster is that it contain the following information, with all names of equal size:

Book by ARTHUR LAURENTS
Music by LEONARD BERNSTEIN
Lyrics by STEPHEN SONDHEIM
Entire Original Production Directed and Choreographed by JEROME ROBBINS

Don't forget to include the name (and logo) of the theatre, its address, and phone number.

LEVEL 1

PROJECT 6

Working with Character and Paragraph Styles

OBJECTIVES

In this project, you learn how to

- Create and assign character styles
- Create and assign paragraph styles
- Create styles based on one another
- Edit styles
- Build style sheets
- Apply styles to your document

WHY WOULD I DO THIS?

When you worked on Project 3, you discovered that formatting text can be somewhat time-consuming. Imagine creating a book such as this one, or a textbook with many similar tables or numbered lists. You would spend a great deal of time formatting text, and have less time for the more creative aspects of page layout.

Styles allow you to format characters, words, or entire paragraphs with a single click or keystroke, eliminating the need to apply each attribute individually. You can also edit styles and apply the changes throughout the document quickly and easily. If, for example, a designer decided to change the paragraph indents in a document from one pica to one pica, six points, as well as change the font from Adobe Garamond Pro to Adobe Jenson Pro. The designer could simply modify the styles applied to the paragraph indents and font, and the changes would be made automatically.

A primary purpose of creating documents using styles is to provide separate realms for editorial and design. ***Editorial*** determines the hierarchy of document — the relative importance of elements. Design determines the appearance of a document — type style, indents, and similar aspects.

You can create character and paragraph styles by formatting a text selection or paragraph, and then using that formatted text to create a named style in the Character Styles or Paragraph Styles palette. As an alternative, you can create the styles before you place text in a paragraph. You can also import styles from word-processing documents or from other InDesign documents. Later, you can apply the named styles to other paragraphs or text elements by selecting the desired style from the appropriate palette, or by using keyboard shortcuts. The process of creating styles is almost identical to creating character or paragraph attributes. The difference is that you can apply the style to paragraphs other than the one you are working in.

Styles can contain predefined settings for almost any available attribute. Character styles may include font, size, color, and other character attributes — even scaling and OpenType characters. Paragraph styles may include character attributes, plus any information available from the Paragraph palette, including alignment, tabs, and rules. Character styles may be based on other character styles, and paragraph styles may be based on other paragraph styles.

Styles are used to their best advantage when working with long text-intensive documents that include recurring editorial elements, such as headlines, subheads, captions, and so forth. Styles are very valuable when several people work concurrently on documents, such as books with multiple chapters, each of which is being written by a different author. They are also effective in documents with specific recurring stylistic requirements, such as catalogs. In cases such as these, styles ensure consistency in text and paragraph formatting throughout a publication. Styles also guarantee that similar editorial elements are treated with design consistency throughout the document.

You should always assign descriptive names to both character styles and paragraph styles. In many cases, character styles or paragraph styles are based on other styles, and have a very close relationship to those styles. For example, you may assign the style name "Body Text," or simply "BT" to body text. The first paragraph following a subhead may have no paragraph indent, so you might describe it as "BT_1." The first paragraph in a chapter may have no paragraph indent, and have a drop cap, so you might want to call it "BT_Chap," or "BT_Dcap." A character style may be red and small caps, but otherwise identical to BT, and you might name it "BT_RedSC."

To apply a character style, you must highlight the characters affected and click the character style in the palette, or press the key (or keys) to which you assigned the shortcut. To apply a paragraph style, place the cursor in the paragraph (or highlight a number of paragraphs) and click the paragraph style in the palette, or press the shortcut key/s.

As you learn how to build and apply styles, you might at first think, "this is doing things the hard way." After you have worked on a number of longer documents, however, you will undoubtedly come to appreciate their value.

Text documents can be created in Microsoft Word; they can be tagged with InDesign's proprietary format, Adobe InDesign Tagged Text; they can be RTF (Rich Text Format) files; and they can be simply raw text. If they are Word or Tagged Text files, you can apply styles in the word-processing program in which they were created.

If a style is defined in the word-processing program, the definition is imported with the file. Keep in mind that InDesign's style definitions override imported definitions. For example, if Body Text is defined in Word as Minion Regular, 12/14, that is how it will be styled in InDesign, *unless* InDesign has already defined the Body Text style. If InDesign defines Body Text as Adobe Garamond Pro, 11/13, that definition overrides the Word definition.

VISUAL SUMMARY

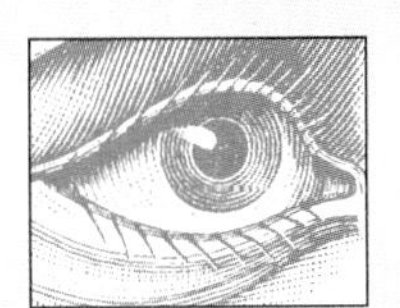

Creating styles is no different than tagging text and paragraphs on an individual basis, except that you create the attributes for many paragraphs or characters at one time; however, you don't want to go overboard when creating styles. For example, there is little point in creating a character style that simply changes a single word to italic; that's one operation, regardless of how you do it. On the other hand, if you're going to change from Garamond Book to Garamond Bold Italic, small caps, colored blue, that's a substantial savings in keystrokes and mouse clicks, if you will use that style several times. Similarly, if you have one paragraph that is indented from both margins, there is no point in creating an "Indent Both" paragraph style — but if you have several of those paragraphs, a style will prove very useful.

It may be helpful to consider a character style as the primary building block of all elements in a document. The Character Styles Options menu offers a number of choices. If you choose New Style, there is a series of options available in a list to the left of the New Character Style dialog: General, Basic

Character Formats, Advanced Character Formats, Character Color, OpenType Features, Underline Options, and Strikethrough Options (see Figure 6.1). Character styles are most useful when you need to make only a few changes (such as formatting the first phrase of a paragraph in a different font, weight, and color), but otherwise maintain the underlying paragraph attributes.

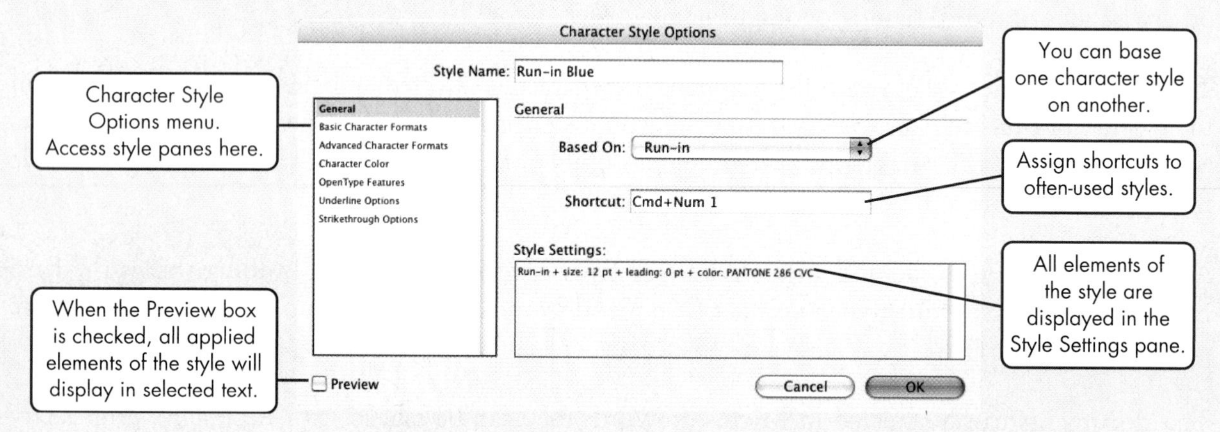

FIGURE 6.1

You can assign character attributes using the Character Styles palette, as if you were applying the attributes directly to highlighted text using the Control palette or the Character palette. To apply the attributes, highlight the text, and then click the character style.

If an element of a character style is left blank, it assumes that characteristics from the style of the characters to which it is applied. Where there are check box options, a "–" symbol (Macintosh) or a square within the check box (Windows) indicates that the character style picks up the attribute from the underlying paragraph. A checkmark indicates that the attribute will be applied to the characters selected, and a blank check box indicates that the attribute will be removed from the characters to which the style is applied.

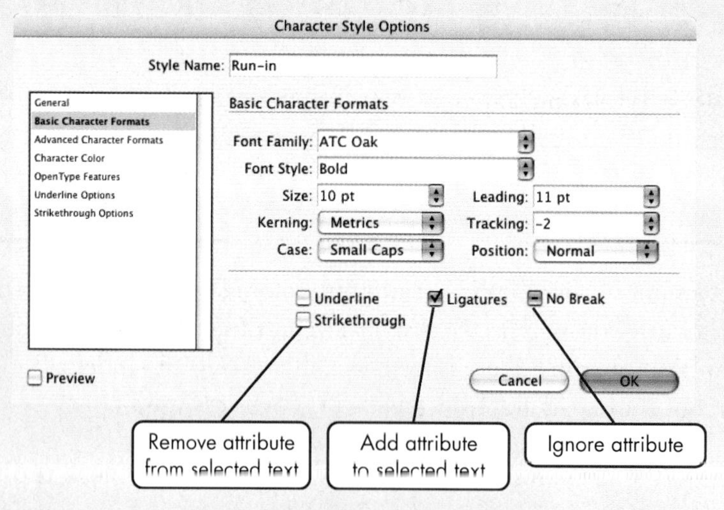

FIGURE 6.2

Similar to character styles, each paragraph style needs a distinctive name. A paragraph style may have the same name as a character style, and this is often desirable for easy cross-reference. As with character styles, paragraph styles may be assigned keyboard equivalents. For convenience, or to maintain a relationship between styles, you can base a paragraph style on another paragraph style that has similar character style, leading, or indents. If text is typed directly into InDesign, the Next Style feature is very powerful. For example, let's say an H2 style (second-level headline) is followed by a BT1 (first body text paragraph), followed by BT paragraphs. If the Next Style box were checked, the operator would simply select H2, type the headline and press Return/Enter to change to BT1, type the text and press Return/Enter to change to BT, and type in the BT style.

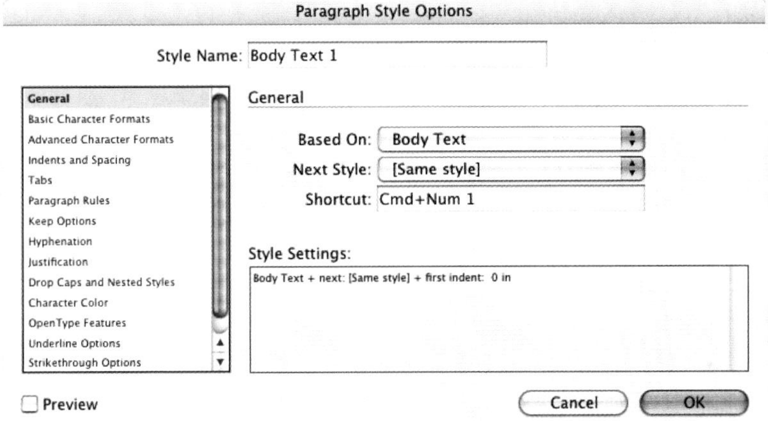

FIGURE 6.3

As in the Character Styles dialog box, the Basic Character Formats of the Paragraph Styles dialog box enable you to set the basic and advanced character formats, character color, OpenType features, as well as underlining and strikethrough options. The difference is that the applied paragraph style affects the entire paragraph, instead of only the characters or words you selected.

Very little of the content presented in this project will be new to you — except finding out how easy it is to format a document once you define your styles.

LESSON 1 Assigning Character Styles

You should create character styles when you have recurring character-related formatting issues — usually those that involve changing more than one stylistic component of the text. For example, you may want a run-in headline that is boldface and blue, or you may want to use more advanced features and reference a foreign language for a passage of text to ensure proper hyphenation and spelling.

Character styles pick up the characteristics of the underlying text. If the text is manually formatted as 9/11 Adobe Garamond Pro, Black — or formatted using a paragraph style — that is the "starting point" of the character style. You can change as many character-based parameters as you wish: you can change the typeface, size, or leading; you can make the text small caps, or change its color; if the typeface specified in the character style is an OpenType font, you can choose to use oldstyle numerals.

Character styles also give you the option to deselect a specification. For example, if the underlying text or paragraph style specifies oldstyle numerals, but you don't want to use oldstyle numerals, you can specify that oldstyle characters should not be used; instead, the default setting of lining characters should be used.

Each character style needs a distinctive name. Since they will usually interact with paragraph styles, they could reasonably have a name linked to a paragraph style. For example, if you have a paragraph style named "Body Text 1," and you want to style the first phrase of that paragraph in a different font and color, you might name the character style "Body Text 1 Run-in." Character styles may be assigned keyboard equivalents for fast application. The shortcuts must include a number from the numeric keypad; one or more of the Command, Option, or Shift keys (Macintosh); or Control, Alt, or Shift keys (Windows).

Build Character Styles

In this exercise, you build a complete ***style sheet*** that contains all of the settings for a new character style. In a later exercise, you build style sheets for paragraph styles, as well.

1. **Open working_with_style.indd from the Project_06 folder.**

   If the document does not open to the first page (the first line is "Chapter II"), double-click the Page 1 icon in the Pages palette to go to Page 1.

2. **If it is not already open, open the Character Styles palette from Window>Type & Tables>Character Styles.**

   You can also use the keyboard shortcut, Shift-F11.

3. **Choose New Character Style from the Character Styles Options menu.**

As an alternative, you can click the Create New Style icon at the bottom of the Character Styles palette to automatically create a new character style based on the [No Character Style] definition.

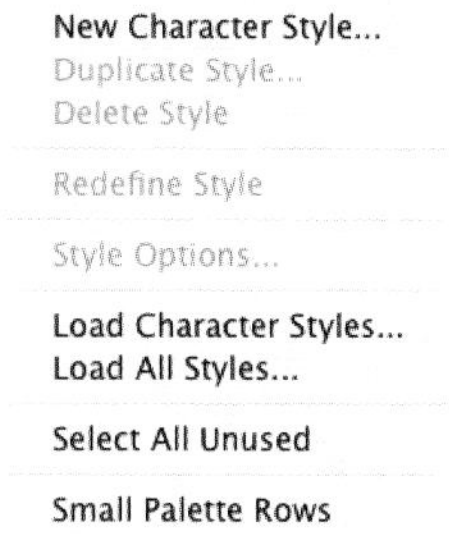

New Character Style...
Duplicate Style...
Delete Style
Redefine Style
Style Options...
Load Character Styles...
Load All Styles...
Select All Unused
Small Palette Rows

FIGURE 6.4

4 **Type "Run-in Blue" in the Style Name field. Place the cursor in the Shortcut field and press Command/Control-1 (on the numeric keypad) to assign the shortcut.**

If you are working under Windows, Num Lock must be turned on.

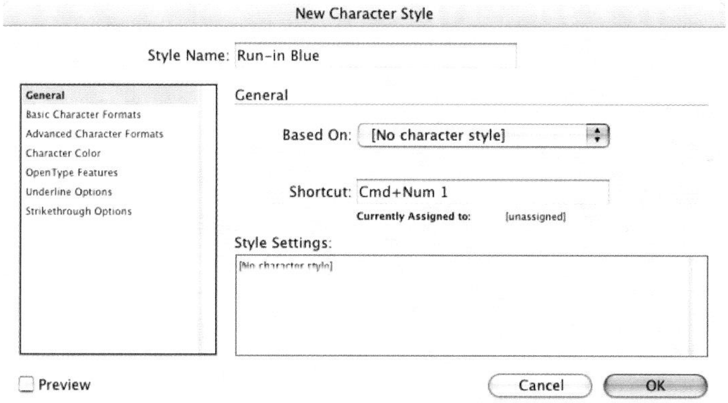

New Character Style
Style Name: Run-in Blue
General
Basic Character Formats
Advanced Character Formats
Character Color
OpenType Features
Underline Options
Strikethrough Options
General
Based On: [No character style]
Shortcut: Cmd+Num 1
Currently Assigned to: [unassigned]
Style Settings:
[No character style]
Preview
Cancel OK

FIGURE 6.5

5 **Click Basic Character Formats in the list on the left. Define the format as ATC Oak Bold, 12 pt.**

Undefined elements, such as leading, kerning, tracking, case, and position, are picked up from the paragraph, as are the four check box options at the bottom of the dialog box.

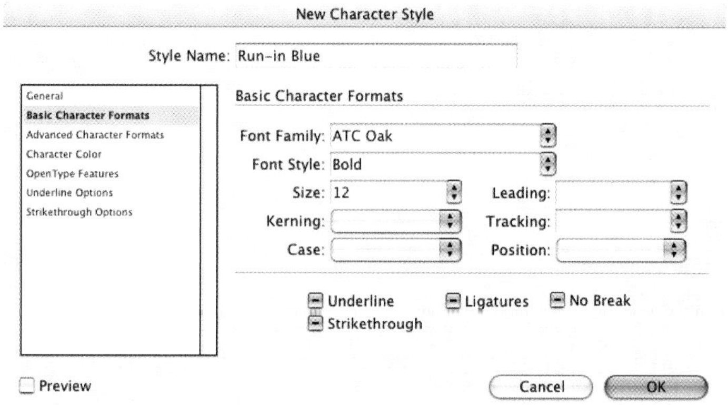

New Character Style
Style Name: Run-in Blue
General
Basic Character Formats
Advanced Character Formats
Character Color
OpenType Features
Underline Options
Strikethrough Options
Basic Character Formats
Font Family: ATC Oak
Font Style: Bold
Size: 12 Leading:
Kerning: Tracking:
Case: Position:
Underline Ligatures No Break
Strikethrough
Preview
Cancel OK

FIGURE 6.6

6 **Click Character Color in the list on the left. With the Fill icon active, click PANTONE 286 CVC to assign this color.**

The Fill icon is now filled with the color you assigned to this character style.

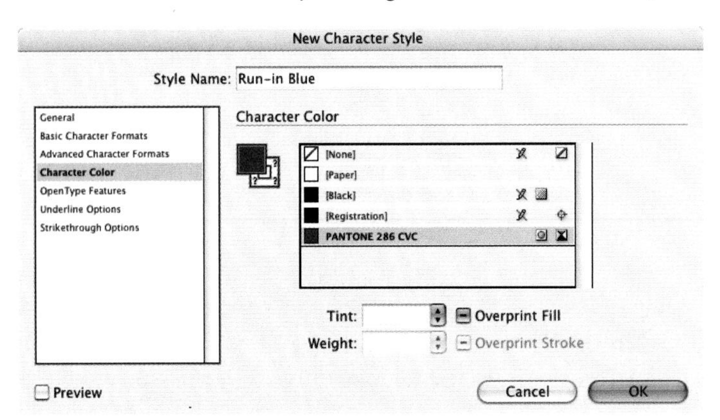

FIGURE 6.7

7 **Return to the General pane.**

Note that the Style Settings box displays all the options you selected for this character style. Click OK to add the style to the Character Styles palette. You apply this style later in the project.

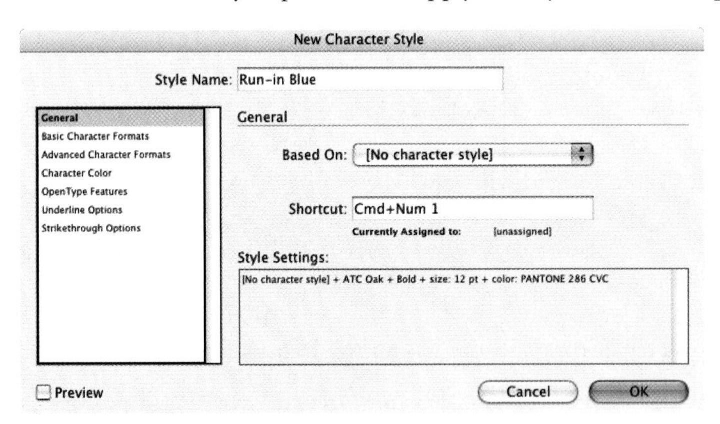

FIGURE 6.8

8 **Click OK to accept the character style.**

9 **Choose File>Save As and save the document to your WIP_06 folder as "alice_02.indd". Leave it open for the next exercise.**

To Extend Your Knowledge...

HYPHENATION LADDERS

If you allow too many hyphens to be used in a row, the appearance called a "ladder" occurs, which is very distracting. Many publishing standards set this number at two or three. Advertising standards usually allow no more than one (and that with caution).

LESSON 2 Creating Paragraph Styles

As you work with InDesign, you will create many more paragraph styles than character styles, because there are more recurring standard paragraphs in documents than those that contain exceptions to which you would assign a character style. Paragraph styles define the appearance of the style, which may have been assigned in a word-processing program.

A paragraph style can contain the same information as a character style, but it usually contains much more. In fact, it can contain all the specifications that can be assigned through the Paragraph or Paragraph Styles palette. Similar to character styles, each paragraph style needs a distinctive name. You can assign keyboard shortcuts, following the same parameters as assigning shortcuts to character styles. If you are creating associated character and paragraph styles, you might consider assigning the character style the Option/Alt-numeric keypad number, and the paragraph style the Command/Control-numeric keypad number, to make it easier to remember them.

As we said earlier, the Next Style feature is very powerful if text is typed directly into InDesign. For example, if an H2 style (second level headline) is followed by a BT1 (first body text paragraph), which is followed by the BT paragraph style, the operator would simply select H2, type the headline and press Return/Enter to change to BT1, type the text and press Return/Enter to change to BT, and continue typing in the BT style.

The ***Keep options*** are sometimes thought of as widow and orphan control. A ***widow*** is an objectionably short line at the end of a paragraph or headline, such as only one word on the line. An ***orphan*** is a word or a line of type that is left by itself at the end of a page or column, such as leaving the heading of a new section as the last line on a page, and the supporting text starting on the top of the following page. At least two lines of a paragraph should remain together in running text. There are, however, some types of text (such as headlines, and bulleted or numbered lists) that should keep all lines in the paragraph together whenever practical. Some paragraphs, such as headlines, should remain with the paragraph that follows.

Paragraph styles can specify that the paragraph can start anywhere (the default), or the style can force a paragraph to begin on the next column or threaded frame. Styles can force paragraphs to the next page, the next odd page, or the next even page. Using the Keep options usually results in uneven columns, so it's often better to eliminate widows and orphans with tracking, editing, or adjustments to word spacing.

You can turn automatic hyphenation on or off and stipulate the length (in number of characters) of the shortest word that is allowed to hyphenate. In addition, you can stipulate the number of hyphens that can appear sequentially. The ***hyphenation zone*** determines how close to the end of a line the text must come before a hyphen is inserted. This specification only applies to text that is not justified to both margins, and when the Adobe Single-Line Composer is used. Hyphenation is inserted only if the previous word ends before the hyphenation zone begins, and there is an acceptable hyphenation point within the word. A hyphenation zone of zero means there is no zone, and InDesign hyphenates according to all other hyphenation criteria. Choose the Adobe Single-Line Composer when you want absolute control over your documents; use Adobe Paragraph Composer for the best automatic setting.

Create the Body Text Paragraph Style

1 **If it is not already open, open the alice_02.indd file.**

Nothing should be selected in the document.

2 **Click the Paragraph Styles palette's tab to activate it. If the tab is not visible, choose Window>Type & Tables>Paragraph Styles.**

InDesign's Type & Tables menu indicates the keyboard shortcut for Character Styles is Shift-F11, and for Paragraph Styles is F11. These shortcuts do not work on Macintosh version 10.3.

3 **Click the New Paragraph Style icon at the bottom of the Paragraph Styles menu, and then double-click the Paragraph Style 1 style.**

The General pane appears.

4 **In the Style Name field, type "Body Text". Click once in the Shortcut field and press Command/Control-2 (from the numeric keypad) to assign it as the shortcut.**

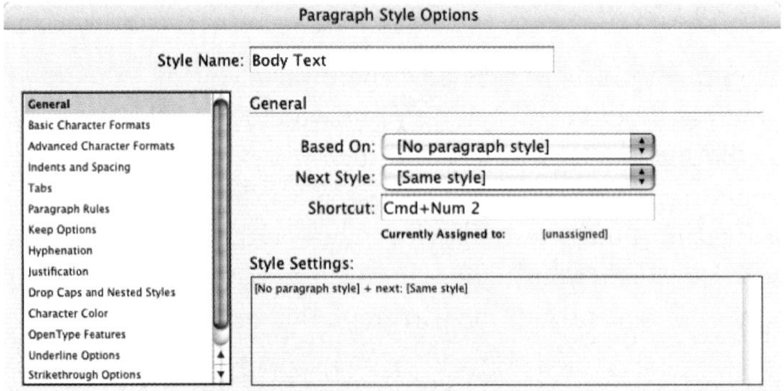

FIGURE 6.9

5 **In the Basic Character Formats pane, choose Adobe Caslon Pro, Regular, 12 pt, with a Leading of 15 pt (12/15), and choose Metrics Kerning. The Ligatures box should be checked.**

This is an OpenType font, so you know that both Macintosh and Windows support ligatures. If it were not OpenType, ligatures would exist on the Macintosh, but not on Windows, since they are not part of the standard Windows character set.

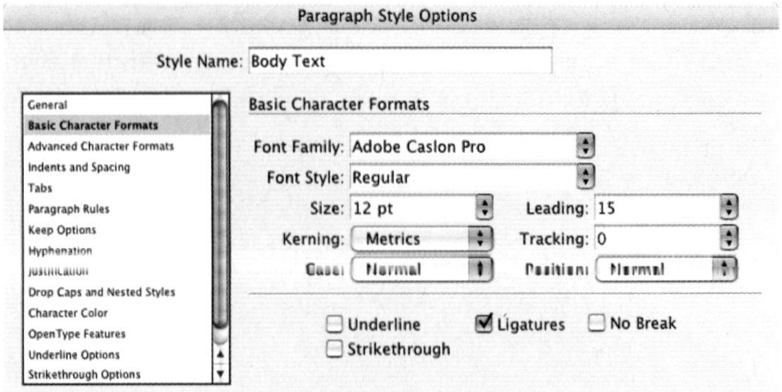

FIGURE 6.10

6 **In the Indents and Spacing pane, set Alignment to Left Justify and First Line Indent to 1p6. Leave everything else at 0 (zero). Leave Align to Grid set at None.**

The Balance Ragged Lines box should only be checked when the object paragraphs are short, such as headlines or callouts.

Paragraph Style Options
Style Name: Body Text
General
Basic Character Formats
Advanced Character Formats
Indents and Spacing
Tabs
Paragraph Rules
Keep Options
Hyphenation
Justification
Drop Caps and Nested Styles
Character Color
OpenType Features
Underline Options
Strikethrough Options
Indents and Spacing
Alignment: Left Justify
Balance Ragged Lines
Left Indent: 0p0
First Line Indent: 1p6
Right Indent: 0p0
Space Before: 0 pt
Space After: 0 pt
Align to Grid: None

FIGURE 6.11

7 **In the Keep Options pane, check the Keep Lines Together box, and accept the default of 2 for both Start and End Lines.**

Keeping at least two lines together at the end or beginning of a column or page creates a much more professional-looking document than allowing a single line to begin or end a paragraph.

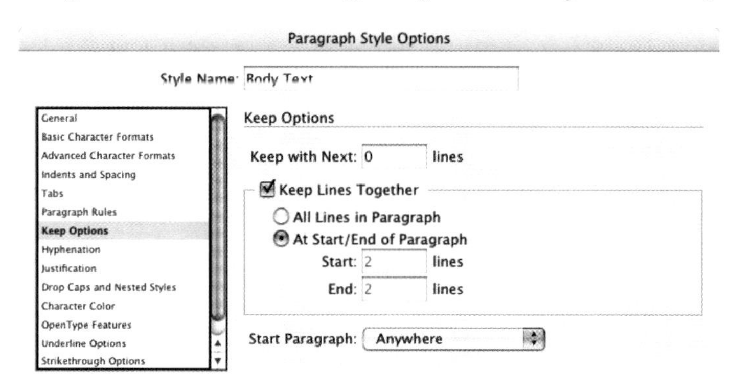

FIGURE 6.12

8 **In the Hyphenation panel, uncheck Hyphenate Capitalized Words.**

Paragraph Style Options
Style Name: Body Text
General
Basic Character Formats
Advanced Character Formats
Indents and Spacing
Tabs
Paragraph Rules
Keep Options
Hyphenation
Justification
Drop Caps and Nested Styles
Character Color
OpenType Features
Underline Options
Strikethrough Options
Hyphenation
Hyphenate
Words with at Least: 7 letters
After First: 3 letters
Before Last: 3 letters
Hyphen Limit: 2 hyphens
Hyphenation Zone: 3p0
Better Spacing
Fewer Hyphens
Hyphenate Capitalized Words

FIGURE 6.13

9 **From the Character Color pane, accept the default Character Color of Black.**

10 **Return to the General pane, and then click OK.**

Note the information in the Style Settings field. Your style is now saved for future use.

11 **Save your changes. Leave the document open for the next exercise.**

Create the Chapter Number Style

1 **In the open document, choose New Style from the Paragraph Styles Options menu.**

Be certain you click [No Paragraph Style] before you create your new style; otherwise, you may inadvertently include unwanted elements in your new style.

2 **Name the style "Chapter Number". Do not assign a shortcut.**

3 **Choose Basic Character Formats from the list on the left. Assign ATC Oak Bold, 12/15, Optical Kerning. Uncheck the Ligatures option.**

Since this is not an OpenType font, you will not use ligatures. Kerning metrics are not built into ATC fonts, so Optical kerning yields the best results.

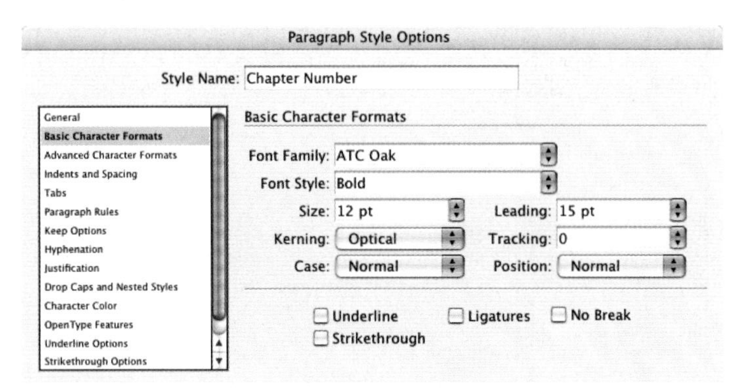

FIGURE 6.14

4 **Choose Indents and Spacing from the list on the left. Set the Alignment to Left (the default). All Indent fields, as well as Space Before and Space After fields, should be set to 0 (zero).**

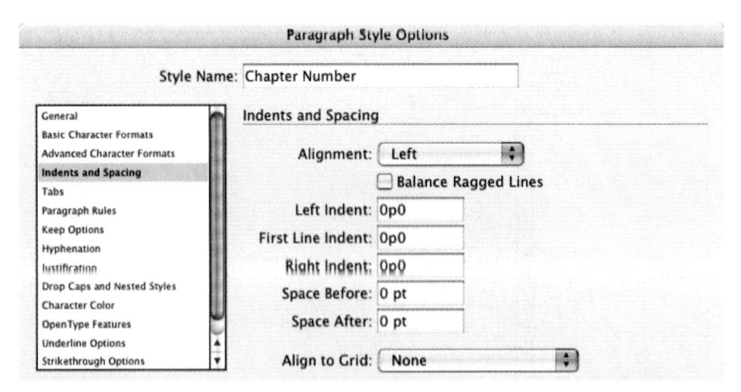

FIGURE 6.15

5 **Choose Paragraph Rules from the list. Turn on the Rule Above option. Assign it a Weight of 2 pt, a Color of PANTONE 286 C, and an Offset of 12 pt.**

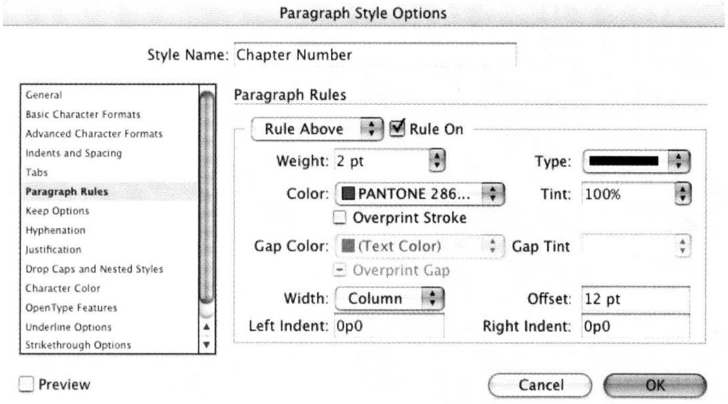

FIGURE 6.16

6 **Choose Keep Options from the list. Set the Start Paragraph field to On Next Odd Page.**

As a rule of thumb, chapters begin on right-hand pages, which are odd-numbered.

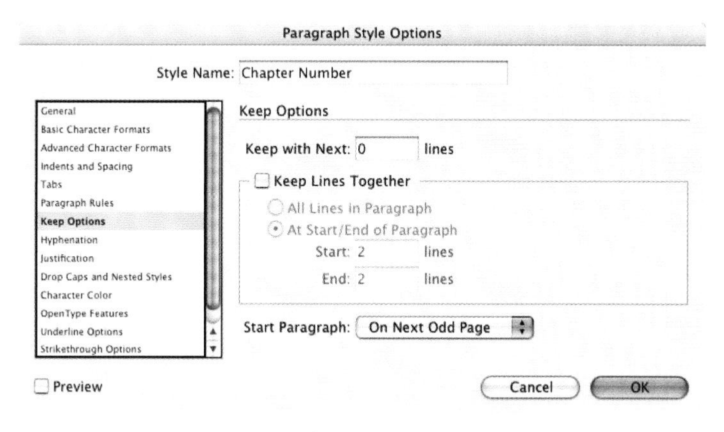

FIGURE 6.17

7 **Choose Hyphenation from the list. Uncheck Hyphenate.**

8 **Set the Character Color to Black. Click OK.**

9 **Save your changes. Leave the file open for the next exercise.**

Create the Chapter Name Style

1 In the open document, create another new paragraph style, based on [No Paragraph Style]. Name this style "Chapter Name".

2 Choose Basic Character Formats from the list. Assign Adobe Garamond Pro Bold Italic, 18/30, with Metrics Kerning.

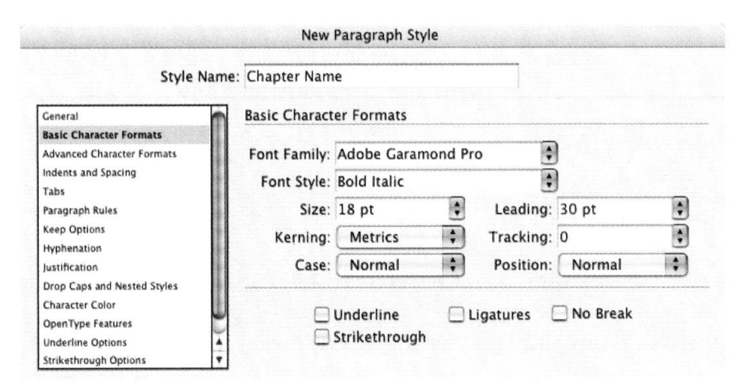

FIGURE 6.18

3 In the Indents and Spacing pane, set Alignment to Left and Space After to 30 pt. Indents and Space Before should be set to 0 (zero).

4 From the Paragraph Rules pane, be certain Rule Above is unchecked. Choose Rule Below from the drop-down menu, and click the Rule On box. Assign it a Weight of 2 pt, Color of PMS 286, and Offset of 6 pt.

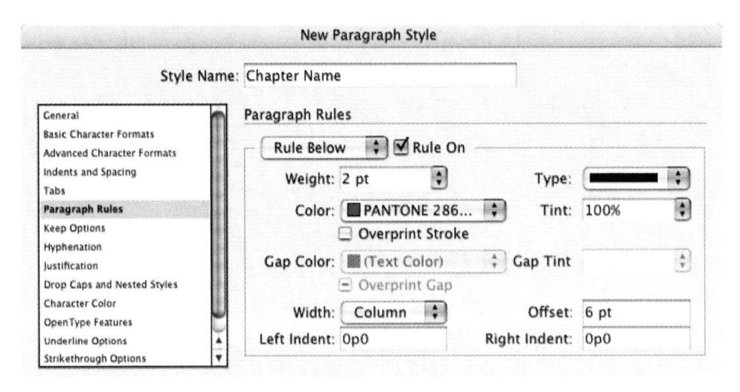

FIGURE 6.19

5 In the Keep Options pane, check the Keep All Lines in the Paragraph Together box. Choose Anywhere from the Start Paragraph menu.

6 In the Hyphenation pane, uncheck the Hyphenate box.

7 In the Character Color pane, accept Black as the default. Click OK.

8 Save your changes. Leave the document open for the next exercise.

To Extend Your Knowledge...

HYPHENATION ZONES

The hyphenation zone should be considered carefully, taking into consideration the overall line length and type size. A zone of 0.5 inch (the default) may be appropriate for 12-point type on a 3.5-inch line, but entirely inappropriate for 9-point type on a 1.5-inch line.

LESSON 3 Creating Styles Based on One Another

One of the easiest ways to create a new style is to base it upon a pre-existing style. When you do this, InDesign picks up all the attributes of the style upon which the new style is based, so you must be careful to turn off or adjust any attributes that you don't want in the new style. When shared attributes are changed in the "parent" style, they are also changed in the "child" style.

Basing one style on another maintains a relationship between styles that have similar character style, leading, or indents. For example, you may create a document with four main related styles — Body Text, Body Text Paragraph 1, Bulleted List style, and Numbered List style. These may all share the same font, size, and leading, but may have different indents, tabs, and spaces above and below.

When you create one style upon another, the base style becomes the default style for future styles. You can inadvertently insert unwanted style elements into a new style if the default is not cleared. It is usually best to Option/Alt-Shift-click [No Paragraph Style] before you create a new style after you create a style based on another.

Create Styles Based on One Another

1. **Continue in the open document. Click the Body Text style to highlight it. Choose Duplicate Style from the Paragraph Styles Options menu. Name the style "Body Text 1". Set the Shortcut to Command/Control-0 (zero).**

   Note that the style is automatically based on Body Text. If the text were being typed in the InDesign program, you would have set the Next Style option to Body Text. Since the text is pre-keyed, setting that attribute would have no effect.

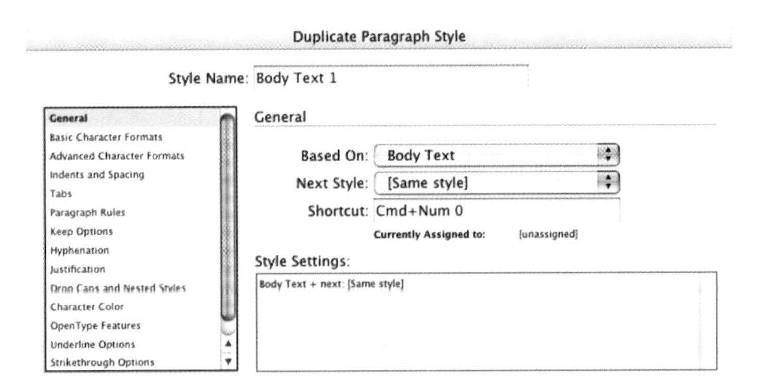

FIGURE 6.20

2 **In the Indents and Spacing pane, set the First Line Indent to 0p0.**

3 **In the Drop Caps and Nested Styles pane, set the Drop Caps Lines to 2, and accept the Characters default of 1. Click OK.**

Duplicate Paragraph Style

Style Name: Body Text 1

General
Basic Character Formats
Advanced Character Formats
Indents and Spacing
Tabs
Paragraph Rules
Keep Options
Hyphenation
Justification
Drop Caps and Nested Styles
Character Color
OpenType Features
Underline Options
Strikethrough Options

Drop Caps and Nested Styles

Drop Caps

Lines	Characters	Character Style
2	1	[No character style]

Nested Styles

Click New Nested Style button to create a nested style.

New Nested Style Delete

Preview Cancel OK

FIGURE 6.21

That's all it takes to set up a new style based on another, when there are minimal changes. Next, set up another style based on Body Text 1.

4 **Click Body Text 1 and choose Duplicate Style.**

5 **Name the style "Poem".**

6 **In the Indents and Spacing, pane, set the Alignment to Left, Left Indent to 3p0, and Space Before to 6 pt.**

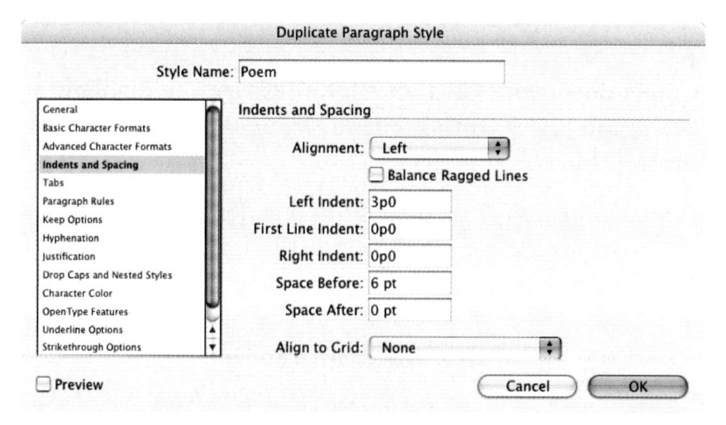

FIGURE 6.22

7 **In the Keep Options pane, click the All Lines in Paragraph button.**

8 **In the Drop Caps and Nested Styles pane, set the number of Lines to 0 (zero). Click OK.**

9 **Duplicate the Poem style. Name the copy "Poem Last".**

10 **In the Indents and Spacing pane, add a 6-pt Space After to the current definition. Click OK.**

Your Paragraph Styles palette should resemble Figure 6.23.

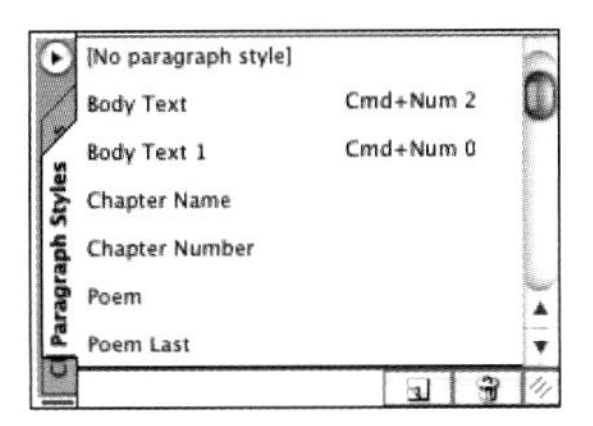

FIGURE 6.23

11 **Save your changes. Leave the document open for the next exercise.**

To Extend Your Knowledge...

HYPHENATING CAPITALIZED WORDS

Generally speaking, it is not proper to hyphenate capitalized words. If a document has very short lines and includes many long proper nouns, however, allowing them to hyphenate is often a good idea — the page looks better.

LESSON 4 Editing Existing Styles

You may discover that you made a mistake when you created a style, or (more likely) someone changed the design parameters. Editing an existing style is easy — but you must be aware of the structure of the document's styles before making wholesale changes. Before you edit anything, you need to ensure that the style you want to change has no dependent styles (unless you intend to similarly alter them, as well). When you're confident that you won't hopelessly ruin the document, you can choose the style to alter, and make the necessary changes.

If you change only the font parameter, you're (usually) on safe ground. If you change colors or spacing, however, be aware that you could create significant problems in the document. Another way to wreak havoc in your documents is to have too many levels of styles based on one another. You might find it beneficial to create a flow chart, such as the one shown in Figure 6.24, that includes all of your styles and their origins.

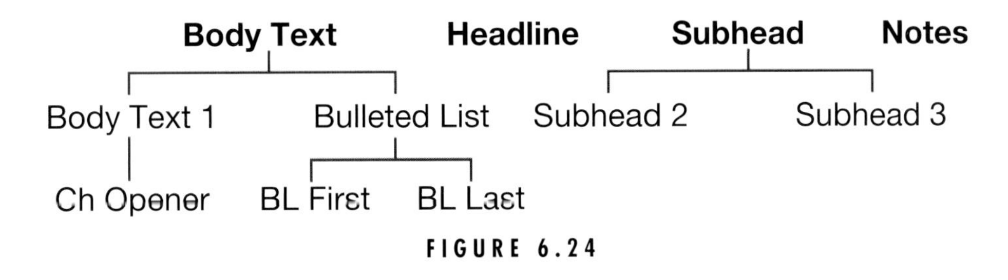

FIGURE 6.24

In Figure 6.24, you see that two styles are directly dependent on the Body Text style, and two others on the Subhead style. The Chapter Opener descends from the Body Text 1 style, and the first and last entries of a bulleted list descend from the Bulleted List style. In this example, a change in the Body Text style affects the Body Text style and all five styles dependent upon it.

Edit Styles

1. **In the open document, click the Poem style and choose Style Options.**

   You could simply double-click the style name to open it.

2. **In the Basic Character Formats pane, change the Font to 14-pt Caflish Script Pro. Click OK.**

   Caflish Script sets to a much smaller size than Adobe Garamond. You need to increase its point size to achieve balance.

3. **Open the Poem Last style, and choose Basic Character Formats.**

   Notice that it already changed to Caflish Script Pro because you based this style on the Poem style. This is an example of the parent-child relationship in styles derived from other styles.

4. **Click OK to close the style.**

5. **Save your changes. Leave the document open for the next exercise.**

LESSON 5 Applying Styles

There is a difference between the way you apply a character style versus how you apply a paragraph style. To apply a character style, you must select (highlight) all the characters that will receive the style. If you miss a letter, the style is not applied to it. After selecting the text, you need to click the name of the character style you want to apply.

To apply a paragraph style, you simply click anywhere in the paragraph and choose the desired style. You may apply the style to multiple consecutive paragraphs. It doesn't matter if character styles or paragraph styles are first applied; character styles always override paragraph styles.

You can tell if text that was assigned a style has been modified when the style displays a plus (+) sign next to it in the Character palette. For example, if you apply a character style that specifies Adobe Garamond, and then change the text to Adobe Caslon in the Character palette (not the Character Styles palette), you made a ***local override***, and the style name displays a plus sign.

Apply Styles

1 **In the open document, choose Type>Paragraph Styles (if the palette is not already open).**

The styles palettes are used to apply styles to a paragraph, a range of paragraphs, or a range of characters.

2 **Click the Type tool in the frame and choose Select All from the Edit menu (or press Command/Control-A) to select all the text in the document.**

3 **Assign the Body Text style by clicking it in the Paragraph Styles palette, or press Command/Control-2 (on the numeric keypad).**

This gets you started by applying the most common style all at once.

4 **Click the first paragraph, Chapter II, and then click the Chapter Number paragraph style name to apply it to the first paragraph.**

5 **Place the Type tool cursor in the next line and assign it the Chapter Name style.**

6 **Assign the Body Text 1 style to the next paragraph by placing the cursor in the paragraph and pressing Command/Control-0.**

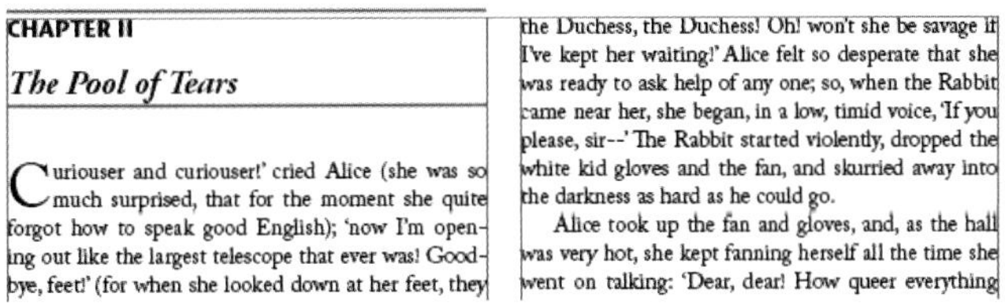

CHAPTER II

The Pool of Tears

Curiouser and curiouser!' cried Alice (she was so much surprised, that for the moment she quite forgot how to speak good English); 'now I'm opening out like the largest telescope that ever was! Good-bye, feet!' (for when she looked down at her feet, they the Duchess, the Duchess! Oh! won't she be savage if I've kept her waiting!' Alice felt so desperate that she was ready to ask help of any one; so, when the Rabbit came near her, she began, in a low, timid voice, 'If you please, sir--' The Rabbit started violently, dropped the white kid gloves and the fan, and skurried away into the darkness as hard as he could go.

Alice took up the fan and gloves, and, as the hall was very hot, she kept fanning herself all the time she went on talking: 'Dear, dear! How queer everything

FIGURE 6.25

7 **In the lower-right section on the page, eight lines do not wrap normally. Place the Type tool cursor in the first group of four lines and assign the Poem style.**

The text begins with "'How doth the little crocodile."

8 **Apply the Poem Last style to the next group of four lines.**

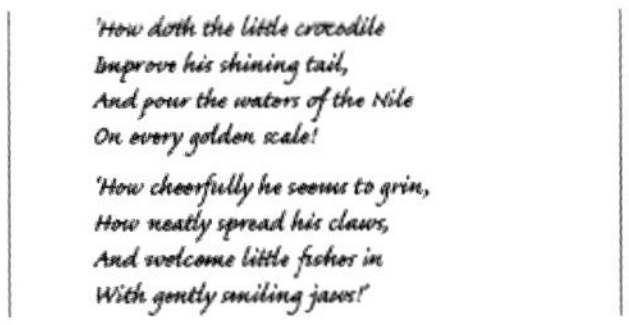

'How doth the little crocodile
Improve his shining tail,
And pour the waters of the Nile
On every golden scale!

'How cheerfully he seems to grin,
How neatly spread his claws,
And welcome little fishes in
With gently smiling jaws!'

FIGURE 6.26

9 **Click the Character Styles tab in the styles palette container.**

10 **In the first paragraph of text, highlight the words "Curiouser and curiouser!'"**

11 **Press Command/Control-1 (on the numeric keypad). Click anywhere in the document to view your work.**

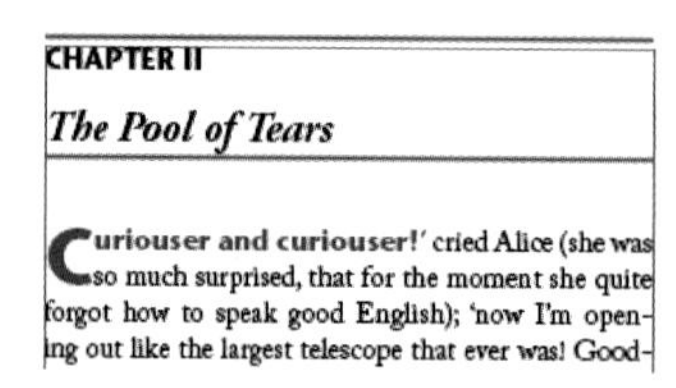

FIGURE 6.27

12 **Use the Selection tool to click the left text frame.**

You probably noticed that the rule above Chapter II is above the text frame. You could adjust this with the offset in Paragraph Rules, but that option affects the distance of the rule from the baseline, not from a frame edge.

13 **Choose Object>Text Frame Options (or press Command/Control-B). Set the Top Inset Spacing to 5 pt. Click OK.**

The rule moves inside the text frame. The page looks much better.

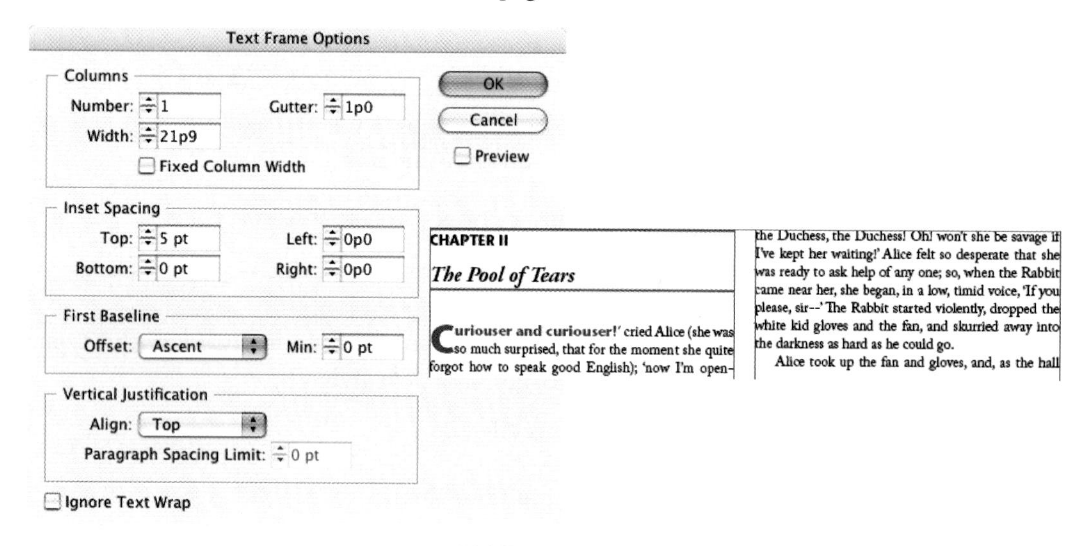

FIGURE 6.28

14 **Save your changes. Leave the document open for the next exercise.**

Apply and Remove Overrides

1. **In the open document, go to line 7 of the first paragraph. Use the Type tool to highlight the words "Oh, my poor little feet." Style them with Adobe Caslon Pro Italic by selecting the style from the Character Styles palette.**

   This produces a local override. When your cursor is within the text you styled, you see a "+" sign following the style name in the Paragraph Styles palette.

2. **Place the cursor within the first three words of the paragraph.**

   You do not see a "+" sign, because this run-in head is a character style, and is not regarded as an override.

3. **Place the cursor anywhere in the paragraph. Option/Alt-click the Body Text 1 style name.**

   This removes the local override, but does not remove the character style.

4. **Highlight the run-in phrase (the text assigned the Run-in Blue character style).**

5. **Switch to the Character Styles palette and Option/Alt-click [No Character Style].**

   The words revert to the standard paragraph style.

6. **With the words still highlighted, click the Run-in Blue character style again.**

   The phrase changes back to the character style.

7. **Save your changes. Close the document.**

To Extend Your Knowledge...

REMOVING STYLES AND OVERRIDES

To remove local character or paragraph style overrides and revert back to the style specifications, you can select the text or paragraph, press Option/Alt, and then click the name of the desired style in the appropriate palette. This preserves any character styles you applied, while it removes overrides.

To remove both character styles and formatting overrides from a paragraph, place the cursor in the paragraph, hold down the Option/Alt-Shift keys, and click the style name in the Paragraph Styles palette.

To remove the style from text, you can press the Option/Alt key and click [No Character Style] or [No Paragraph Style] in the appropriate palette.

SUMMARY

In this project, you learned how to create and apply character and paragraph styles, how to edit styles, and how to base one style upon another. You learned how styles can interact with one another, and with other elements of InDesign, such as the underlying baseline grid and the Text Frame options.

KEY TERMS

Adobe Single-Line Composer
Character style
Editorial
Hyphenation ladder
Hyphenation zone
Keep options
Lining characters
Local override
Orphan
Paragraph style
Parent-child style relationship
Style sheet
Widow

CHECKING CONCEPTS AND TERMS

MULTIPLE CHOICE

Circle the letter of the correct answer for each of the following questions.

1. What are the primary advantages of using styles?
   a. Creativity and flexibility.
   b. Ability to manipulate text and graphics.
   c. Speed and consistency.
   d. All of the above.

2. What do style sheets determine?
   a. Relative importance of paragraph elements.
   b. The look of individual tables.
   c. The definition of specific colors.
   d. The appearance of a document.

3. How are style sheets built?
   a. Acquired from existing text.
   b. Defined by entering specifications into palettes.
   c. Imported from other documents.
   d. All of the above.

4. When would you use the Next Style feature?
   a. When composing a book.
   b. When importing text from a word processor.
   c. When creating a list.
   d. When composing text directly in InDesign.

5. How are character styles applied?
   a. By highlighting the text and clicking the style name.
   b. By placing the cursor in the word and clicking the style name.
   c. Through the Character menu.
   d. By pressing the F11 key.

6. When would you not want to create styles?
   a. For a series of ads with similar elements.
   b. For a directory.
   c. For a book.
   d. For a poster displaying different typefaces.

7. What happens if elements of a character style are left blank?
   a. The elements are picked up from the underlying paragraph.
   b. The elements cannot be applied.
   c. The character style is invalid.
   d. Similar elements of the standard character style are used.

8. When is it acceptable to hyphenate a capitalized word?
   a. It is always acceptable.
   b. When you have a short line length to work with.
   c. When it is not a person's name.
   d. Anywhere but headlines.

9. When would you use the Single-Line Composer?
   a. When you want to automate composition.
   b. When you want the best overall fit.
   c. When you want absolute control over the document.
   d. When you're under a deadline.

10. How can you override a paragraph style?
   a. By applying another paragraph style.
   b. By applying a character style.
   c. By manually entering attributes.
   d. All of the above.

DISCUSSION QUESTIONS

1. There is no questioning that setting up styles is a time-consuming process. Under what circumstances would you (or would you not) choose to incorporate styles in your documents? Consider document types, and whether you would create the text in InDesign.

2. Thinking of the hyphenation and justification parameters, including the two composition options available in InDesign, what design issues would you address to compose the best-looking documents possible?

SKILL DRILL

Skill Drills reinforce project skills. Each skill reinforced is the same, or nearly the same, as a skill presented in the lessons. Detailed instructions are provided in a step-by-step format. You should complete these exercises in order.

1. Build a Seminar Promotion

Every year, the InDesign Experts Association holds an annual conference in conjunction with another organization. This year, the conference is in Chicago, in association with PrintImage. The conference features a number of seminars. In these Skill Drills, you build and apply the style sheets for this event.

1. Open idea2005.indd from the Project_06 folder. Save it under the same name to your WIP_06 folder.

   Much of text is already in place, and some has already been styled manually. You will style the bulk of the text using character and paragraph styles.
2. From the Paragraph Styles palette, create your first style. Choose New Paragraph Style, and name the style "Promo". Base it on No Paragraph Style. Do not assign a keyboard shortcut.
3. From Basic Character Formats, assign ATC Oak Bold, 12/20.
4. From Indents and Spacing, assign a Left Alignment with 10-pt Space After.
5. From Hyphenation, turn off Hyphenation.
6. From Character Color, assign Paper.
7. Click OK to save this paragraph style.
8. Highlight the text in the leftmost frame on Page 1. Click this style to apply it to the text.
9. Save your changes. Leave the document open for the next exercise.

2. Introduce the Seminar

1. In the open document, with no text selected, change to the Character Styles palette to create a new character style. Name it "Sky Red".
2. In the Character Color pane, apply the Red Sky color. Click OK to save this character style.
3. Change to the Paragraph Styles palette. Option/Alt click [No Paragraph Style] to reset it to its default. Create a new paragraph style based on [No Paragraph Style]. Name it "Intro".
4. From Basic Character Formats, assign Adobe Garamond Pro Regular, 12/15.
5. From Indents and Spacing, assign a Left Alignment, with a First Line Indent of 0.25 in. Click OK.
6. Click the Intro style, and then choose Duplicate Style from the Paragraph Styles Options menu. Name the new style "Intro 1".
7. From Indents and Spacing, assign a First Line Indent of 0 in.

8. From Drop Caps and Nested Styles, assign Drop Caps of 3 Lines and 1 Character, with a Character Style of Sky Red. Click OK.
9. Click the first paragraph in the frame on the right, and click the Intro 1 style to apply it.
10. Select the rest of the paragraphs in the frame, and apply the Intro style to them.
11. Save your changes. Leave the document open for the next exercise.

FIGURE 6.29

If you have problems...

You may discover that creating a style based on [No Paragraph Style] introduces elements from a previous paragraph style. Always Option/Alt-click [No Paragraph Style] to reset its "memory" to the default before you begin a new paragraph based on this style.

When creating new styles, it is safest to switch to the Selection tool, so you do not accidentally pick up attributes from the paragraph the cursor rests in, or assign an unwanted style to that paragraph.

3. Prepare Session Styles

1. In the open document, create a new paragraph style based on [No Paragraph Style]. Name it "Date".
2. From Basic Character Formats, assign ATC Oak Bold, 10/10.
3. From Keep Options, choose Start Paragraph in Next Frame.
4. From Character Color, choose Paper. Click OK.

5. Click the Date style and choose Duplicate Style from the Paragraph Styles Options menu. Name the new style "Session".
6. From Basic Character Formats, change the Size to 9 pt.
7. From Character Color, choose Bright Yellow. Click OK.
8. Duplicate this style and name the new style "Presentation".
9. From Indents and Spacing, set a 4-pt Space Before and 2-pt Space After. Set a Right-Justified tab at 3.4167 in.
10. From Keep Options, choose Start Paragraph Anywhere.
11. Change the Character Color to Black. Click OK.
12. Create one more new paragraph style, based on [No Paragraph Style]. Name it "Features". Assign Character Format of ATC Oak Normal, 9/10. Assign an 8-pt Left Indent, and a –8-pt First Line Indent. Assign a 2-pt Space After. Click OK.
13. Create a new character style named "Speaker". Assign a Keyboard Shortcut of Command/Control-0 (on the numeric keypad). Assign a Character Format of ATC Oak Italic. Click OK.
14. Save your changes. Leave the document open for the next exercise.

4. Finish the Sessions Page

1. Go to Page 2 of the open document. You see several frames. Click the Selection tool in the top black text frame. Click the out port, and then click in the upper-left frame (Blue to Tan) to link these text frames.
2. Link all the frames together: Blue to Tan links to Red to Tan, which links to the middle black frame. The black frame links to Brown to Ivory, which links to Green to Blue.
3. Click in the top black frame and choose File>Place. The Show Import Options and Replace Selected Item boxes should be checked. Click the file idea2005.doc, and then click Open. Only the Use Typographer's Quotes box should be checked.

   The text flows into all the frames, properly styled, because the style names had been applied in Microsoft Word. The page still needs some additional work.
4. Hold down the Shift key, and use the Selection tool to click the two black frames to select them both. Choose Object>Text Frame Options.
5. Assign a 4-pt Top Inset Spacing. Set Vertical Justification to Align Center. Click OK.
6. Select the other four frames and press Command/Control-B to access the Text Frame Options dialog box.
7. Assign Inset Spacing as follows: 6-pt Top, 6-pt Left, and 6-pt Right. Click OK.
8. In the Green to Blue box, there is a long presentation line, "Publishing for Multimedia and the World Wide Web." Insert a soft return between the words "Multimedia" and "and."

9. The speaker's name is on the right of every bold black line. Highlight each of the names and apply the Speaker character style.
10. Save your changes. Leave the document open for the Challenge exercises.

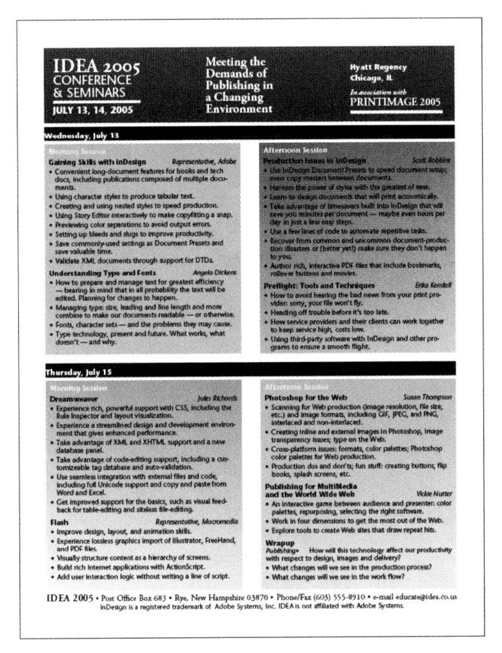

IDEA 2005
CONFERENCE
& SEMINARS
JULY 13, 14, 2005

Meeting the Demands of Publishing in a Changing Environment

Hyatt Regency
Chicago, IL
In association with
PRINTIMAGE 2005

Wednesday, July 13

Morning Session

Gaining Skills with InDesign *Representative, Adobe*
- Convenient long-document features for books and tech docs, including publications composed of multiple documents.
- Using character styles to produce tabular text.
- Creating and using nested styles to speed production.
- Using Story Editor interactively to make copyfitting a snap.
- Previewing color separations to avoid output errors.
- Setting up bleeds and slugs to improve productivity.
- Save commonly-used settings as Document Presets and save valuable time.
- Validate XML documents through support for DTDs.

Understanding Type and Fonts *Angela Dickens*
- How to prepare and manage text for greatest efficiency — bearing in mind that in all probability the text will be edited. Planning for changes to happen.
- Managing type: size, leading and line length and more combine to make our documents readable — or otherwise.
- Fonts, character sets — and the problems they may cause.
- Type technology, present and future. What works, what doesn't — and why.

Afternoon Session

Production Issues in InDesign *Scott Robbins*
- Use InDesign Document Presets to speed document setup; even copy masters between documents.
- Harness the power of styles with the greatest of ease.
- Learn to design documents that will print economically.
- Take advantage of timesavers built into InDesign that will save you minutes per document — maybe even hours per day in just a few easy steps.
- Use a few lines of code to automate repetitive tasks.
- Recover from common and uncommon document-production disasters or (better yet!) make sure they don't happen to you.
- Author rich, interactive PDF files that include bookmarks, rollover buttons and movies.

Preflight: Tools and Techniques *Erika Kendall*
- How to avoid hearing the bad news from your print provider: sorry, your file won't fly.
- Heading off trouble before it's too late.
- How service providers and their clients can work together to keep service high, costs low.
- Using third-party software with InDesign and other programs to ensure a smooth flight.

Thursday, July 15

Morning Session

Dreamweaver *Jules Richards*
- Experience rich, powerful support with CSS, including the Rule Inspector and layout visualization.
- Experience a streamlined design and development environment that gives enhanced performance.
- Take advantage of XML and XHTML support and a new database panel.
- Take advantage of code-editing support, including a customizeable tag database and auto-validation.
- Use seamless integration with external files and code, including full Unicode support and copy and paste from Word and Excel.
- Get improved support for the basics, such as visual feedback for table-editing and siteless file-editing.

Flash *Representative, Macromedia*
- Improve design, layout, and animation skills.
- Experience lossless graphics import of Illustrator, FreeHand, and PDF files.
- Visually structure content as a hierarchy of screens.
- Build rich Internet applications with ActionScript.
- Add user interaction logic without writing a line of script.

Afternoon Session

Photoshop for the Web *Susan Thompson*
- Scanning for Web production (image resolution, file size, etc.) and image formats, including GIF, JPEG, and PNG, interlaced and non-interlaced.
- Creating inline and external images in Photoshop, image transparency issues; type on the Web.
- Cross-platform issues: formats, color palettes; Photoshop color palettes for Web production.
- Production dos and don'ts; fun stuff: creating buttons, flip books, splash screens, etc.

Publishing for MultiMedia and the World Wide Web *Vickie Nutter*
- An interactive game between audience and presenter: color palettes, repurposing, selecting the right software.
- Work in four dimensions to get the most out of the Web.
- Explore tools to create Web sites that draw repeat hits.

Wrapup
Publishing• How will this technology affect our productivity with respect to design, images and delivery?
- What changes will we see in the production process?
- What changes will we see in the work flow?

IDEA 2005 • Post Office Box 683 • Rye, New Hampshire 03870 • Phone/Fax (603) 555-8910 • e-mail educate@idea.co.us
InDesign is a registered trademark of Adobe Systems, Inc. IDEA is not affiliated with Adobe Systems.

FIGURE 6.30

CHALLENGE

Challenge exercises expand on, or are somewhat related to, skills presented in the lessons. Each exercise provides a brief introduction, followed by instructions presented in a numbered-step format that are not as detailed as those in the Skill Drill exercises. You should complete these exercises in order.

1. Create Styles for Page 3

The first two pages of this promotional piece tease the audience and provide information. The last two pages ask for money and include the actual schedule. There is also a mailing panel. Part of the construction is done, but there is still plenty left to do on these pages.

1. With idea2005.indd open, go to Page 3.

   You see a number of text frames, some with text already inserted, and some without. Before you flow the text, you need to build some styles.

2. Create a new paragraph style based on [No Paragraph Style] named "Body Text". Define it as Adobe Garamond Pro, 11/13, with a 1p First Line Indent and no Space Before or Space After. Accept the default Character Color of Black.

3. Create a second style named "Body Text 1", based on Body Text. Remove the first line indent from this style.
4. Create a style named "Head 1" based on no style. Define it as Adobe Garamond Pro Semibold, 18/18, with 6-pt Space After.
5. Create a style named "Head 2" based on no style. Define it as ATC Oak Bold, 10/10, with 1-pt Space After. Assign a Color of Maroon.
6. Create a style named "Details" based on no style. Define it as ATC Oak Normal, 8/9, with 3-pt Space After.
7. Create a style named "Registration", based on Details. Change to a 10-pt Leading. Position a Right Justified tab at 4.75 inches, with the Underline [_] specified as the Leader Character.
8. Create a style named "Callout" based on no style. Define it as ATC Oak Bold, 12/14. Assign a Center Alignment. Check the Turn on Balance Ragged Lines box in the Indents and Spacing pane. Turn off Hyphenation. Assign a Color of Maroon.
9. Save your changes. Leave the document open for the next Challenge.

2. Add and Style Text

1. In the open document, link the top text frame with the frame to the left and immediately below it.
2. Place idea_1.doc into these linked frames. The Show Import Options and Replace Selected Item boxes should be checked. Only the Use Typographer's Quotes box should be checked in the Show Import Options dialog box.

   Note that the Import Options are retained from the last time you placed text.
3. Select all the text and assign the Body Text style.
4. Select the first-line of text and override the style with Adobe Garamond Pro Semibold, 36/33. Remove the first line indent.

   This is the only instance of this type specification, so you did not make a style for it.
5. Select the first paragraph and assign it the Body Text 1 style.
6. Position the cursor in front of the word "We" at the beginning of the third paragraph. Press the Enter key on the numeric keypad to force a line break.

   You can access this command from Type>Insert Break Character>Column Break, as well.
7. With your cursor in the text frame below the pull-quote in the oval frame, place idea_2.doc. Only the Replace Selected Item box needs to be checked.
8. Select all the text in this frame and style it as Body Text.
9. Place your cursor in the first paragraph and style it as Head 1.
10. Style the second paragraph as Body Text 1.

11. Place idea_3.doc in the remaining uncolored frame. Apply Head 1 to the first paragraph, Body Text 1 to the second paragraph, and Body Text to the third paragraph.
12. Save your changes. Leave the document open.

3. Add and Style Detail Text

1. In the open document, place idea_4.doc in the remaining unfilled text frame, with a gradient of Brown to Ivory. Select all the text and style it as Details.
2. Press Command/Control B to access the Text Frame Options menu. Assign Top, Left, and Right Inset Spacing of 6 pt (0.0833 in).
3. Style the first two lines with the Head 2 style. Apply the same style to the Cancellation, Travel, Speaker Notes, and Who Should Attend headlines.
4. Highlight the first line of text (The Important Stuff), and then change the Size to 12 pt, the Space After to 3 pt, and the Color to Black.
5. Select the third line of text (the words Non-Member, Member, and Additional Member), and change the Size to 7 pt, and the Space After to 0 (zero).
6. Select the third and fourth lines of text, and set Centered tabs at 0.75 in, 1.3 in, and 1.875 in.
7. Select all the text in the box in the lower right (Registration Form) and apply the Registration style.
8. Select the text in the first line, Registration Form, and style it as 12-pt Adobe Garamond Pro Bold.
9. In the line third from the bottom, place the cursor immediately before the word "Idea." Insert an Indent to Here command (choose Type>Insert Special Character>Indent to Here, or press Command/Control-\).
10. Center the last line of text.
11. Save your changes. Leave the document open.

4. Add Final Touches to the Page

1. In the open document, select the elliptical text frame containing the pull-quote, and access the Text Frame Options menu.
2. Change the First Baseline Minimum to 0.4 inches.
3. Select all the text and apply the Callout style.
4. Select the last line of type and change the style to Adobe Garamond Pro Semibold Italic.
5. Select the frame and rotate it 10°. Position it appropriately in the open space.
6. At the end of the first article, create a new paragraph. Press Option/Alt and click [No Paragraph Style].

7. Change the Font to Adobe Caslon Pro Regular, and choose Glyphs from the Type menu. Show Ornaments, and pick an ornament that you feel is appropriate as an article-ender. Double-click the ornament to insert it.
8. Size the ornament appropriately, apply necessary leading, center it, and color it Maroon.
9. Copy and paste the ornament in the article in the lower left of the page.
10. Save your changes. Leave the document open.

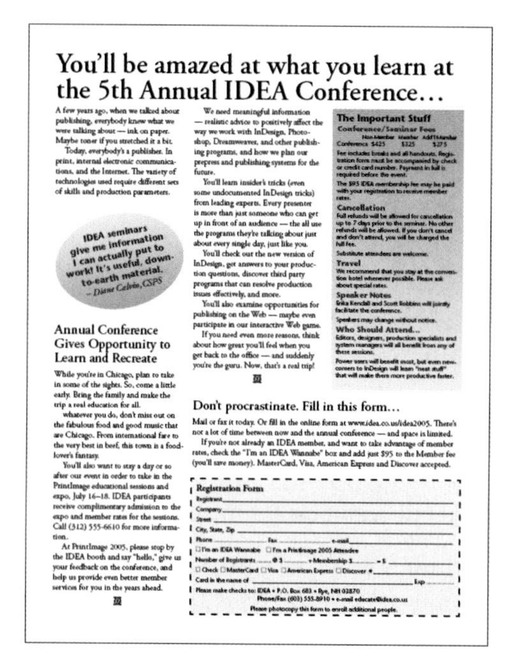

You'll be amazed at what you learn at the 5th Annual IDEA Conference…

A few years ago, when we talked about publishing, everybody knew what we were talking about — ink on paper. Maybe toner if you stretched it a bit.

Today, everybody's a publisher. In print, internal electronic communications, and the Internet. The variety of technologies used require different sets of skills and production parameters.

IDEA seminars give me information I can actually put to work! It's useful, down-to-earth material.
– Diane Calvin, CSPS

Annual Conference Gives Opportunity to Learn and Recreate

While you're in Chicago, plan to take in some of the sights. So, come a little early. Bring the family and make the trip a real education for all.

whatever you do, don't miss out on the fabulous food and good music that are Chicago. From international fare to the very best in beef, this town is a food-lover's fantasy.

You'll also want to stay a day or so after our event in order to take in the PrintImage educational sessions and expo, July 16–18. IDEA participants receive complimentary admission to the expo and member rates for the sessions. Call (312) 555-6610 for more information.

At PrintImage 2005, please stop by the IDEA booth and say "hello," give us your feedback on the conference, and help us provide even better member services for you in the years ahead.

We need meaningful information — realistic advice to positively affect the way we work with InDesign, Photoshop, Dreamweaver, and other publishing programs, and how we plan our prepress and publishing systems for the future.

You'll learn insider's tricks (even some undocumented InDesign tricks) from leading experts. Every presenter is more than just someone who can get up in front of an audience — the all use the programs they're talking about just about every single day, just like you.

You'll check out the new version of InDesign, get answers to your production questions, discover third party programs that can resolve production issues effectively, and more.

You'll also examine opportunities for publishing on the Web — maybe even participate in our interactive Web game.

If you need even more reasons, think about how great you'll feel when you get back to the office — and suddenly you're the guru. Now, that's a real trip!

The Important Stuff

Conference/Seminar Fees

	Non-Member	Member	Add'l Member
Conference	$425	$325	$275

Fee includes breaks and all handouts. Registration form must be accompanied by check or credit card number. Payment in full is required before the event.

The $95 IDEA membership fee may be paid with your registration to receive member rates.

Cancellation

Full refunds will be allowed for cancellation up to 7 days prior to the seminar. No other refunds will be allowed. If you don't cancel and don't attend, you will be charged the full fee.

Substitute attendees are welcome.

Travel

We recommend that you stay at the convention hotel whenever possible. Please ask about special rates.

Speaker Notes

Erika Kendall and Scott Robbins will jointly facilitate the conference.

Speakers may change without notice.

Who Should Attend…

Editors, designers, production specialists and system managers will all benefit from any of these sessions.

Power users will benefit most, but even newcomers to InDesign will learn "neat stuff" that will make them more productive faster.

Don't procrastinate. Fill in this form…

Mail or fax it today. Or fill in the online form at www.idea.co.us/idea2005. There's not a lot of time between now and the annual conference — and space is limited.

If you're not already an IDEA member, and want to take advantage of member rates, check the "I'm an IDEA Wannabe" box and add just $95 to the Member fee (you'll save money). MasterCard, Visa, American Express and Discover accepted.

Registration Form

Registrant ______

Company ______

Street ______

City, State, Zip ______

Phone ______ Fax ______ e-mail ______

☐ I'm an IDEA Wannabe ☐ I'm a PrintImage 2005 Attendee

Number of Registrants ____ @ $ ____ + Membership $ ____ = $ ______

☐ Check ☐ MasterCard ☐ Visa ☐ American Express ☐ Discover # ______

Card in the name of ______ Exp ______

Please make checks to: IDEA • P.O. Box 683 • Rye, NH 03870

Phone/Fax (603) 555-8910 • e-mail educate@idea.co.us

Please photocopy this form to enroll additional people.

FIGURE 6.31

5. Finish the Brochure

1. In the open document, go to Page 4.

   Most of the work has been done on this page.

2. Highlight the lines that begin with the word "Wednesday" and the session times. Assign the Body Text 1 style.
3. Select all the text in this frame and assign tabs as follows: 0.375 in, Align On Character tab, using the en dash as the Align-On Character; 1.25 in and 3.6667 in, Left-Aligning tabs.
4. In the box near the bottom of the page, style the first line as ATC Oak Normal, 10/12.
5. Use the Type tool to highlight the last line. Click the first line with the Eyedropper tool.

   The text in the last line assumes the style of the text in the first line.

6. Switch to the Type tool. Style the text on the left of the first line (July 13, 14…) as Bold, and on the left of the last line (Plan NOW…) as Bold Italic.

7. Select the second line. Assign ATC Oak Bold, 12/17, with Small Caps. Center the text and add a 3-pt Space After.
8. In the Lunch on Your Own line, add a 2-pt Space Above and 2-pt Space Below, and make the words (but not the time) Italic.
9. Add a 3-pt Space Before the last line.
10. Make the dates (Wednesday, July 13 and Thursday, July 14) Bold and add a 2-pt Space After. Add color however you prefer.
11. Select the Bulk Rate indicia. With the proxy set to the center reference point, rotate it 180°.
12. Select the frame containing the return address information and repeat the action.
13. Preview the document with Display Performance set for High Quality.
14. Save your changes. Close the document.

FIGURE 6.32

PORTFOLIO BUILDER

Redesign Magazine Pages

You were hired to redesign the inside pages of *Sharing Spaces*, a travel magazine for Condo Swap International. The organization wants a simple, elegant design that conveys the idea of an unostentatious, quality lifestyle, centering on the benefits of vacation travel and the condominium lifestyle.

The comps need to show three different kinds of pages:

- Feature stories: A feature begins on a right-facing page, and continues on at least two more pages. Each includes a title and author, at least two levels of headings within the text, body copy, and (optional) bulleted lists. Each feature highlights a country or region.
- Monthly columns. Each issue of the magazine includes several columns, which may be as small as two-thirds of a page, or as large as a full page. Monthly column pages fit into one of four categories: Members' Voice, Restaurant Reviews, From the Publisher's Desk, and A Time for Play. Each column includes the column name, the author, a main heading, one internal head, and body copy.
- Things To Do. Each issue includes four pages of things to do in the featured region. The pages include a headline, body text, and bulleted text.
- There may be ads on these pages.

You should keep in mind the following physical specifications:

- The trim size of the magazine is 8.25 × 10.5 inches.
- The live area should have a 0.75-inch inside margin and a 0.5-inch margin on the other three sides. Remember, however, to include a running head and/or running foot within that margin area.
- Incorporate a 0.125-inch bleed allowance.

The comps should show the text formatting for each editorial element that may appear on the page. Use placeholder text and define the style sheets you need to format the comps.

PROJECT 7

LEVEL 1

Using Text Utilities

OBJECTIVES

In this project, you learn how to

- Use the Find/Change feature
- Search based on formats
- Use meta characters
- Spell-check your documents
- Customize the dictionary
- Use the Story Editor

WHY WOULD I DO THIS?

Working with large amounts of text can be cumbersome when clients make changes, or when you must proofread text to ensure accurate spelling. Reading the text word-for-word to hunt for mistakes takes considerable time and effort. Instead, you can use InDesign's text utilities to replace a large percentage of these manual ***search-and-replace*** methods.

InDesign offers several text utilities that make it easy to find and replace words or phrases, as well as to check spelling. You can edit the User dictionary to include words that are not found in most dictionaries, such as proper nouns or trademarks. You can also use the special dictionaries that ship with InDesign, which you can choose through Preferences.

You can use only one dictionary at a time. There are four English dictionaries: English UK, English US, English USA Legal, and English USA Medical. Other supported languages include Catalan, Danish, Dutch, Finnish, French, French Canadian, German Reformed, German Swiss, German Traditional, Italian, Norwegian Bokmal, Norwegian Nyorsk, Portuguese, Portuguese Brazilian, Spanish Castilian, and Swedish.

Find/Change

With the ***Find/Change*** feature, you can search for specified text or special characters and decide if you want to apply a change. This dialog box behaves differently than most you've seen; it's a ***non-modal*** dialog box, which means you can leave it open while you continue to work in the document. You can perform searches and edit text without closing the Find/Change dialog box; it doesn't disappear until you click the Done button.

You have the option of searching just the story (linked text frames) you are working on, all text frames in the document, or selected text; you can also search from the cursor position to the end of the story, which can be an excellent timesaver when working with long documents. Interestingly, you are not limited to searching and replacing words — but you are limited to text styles. For example, you could change all instances of the phrase "inn door" in a style called Body to "indoor" and the color Green.

Remember that InDesign can't read your mind; it can only search for specified items. Always check whether the ***Whole Word*** or ***Case Sensitive*** check boxes are activated. If you want to find the word "cat," and search for those characters, you will find "Catherine" and "concatenate" unless you use the Whole Word option.

Meta Characters

Not all searches look for words, as we already discussed. Special characters that are accessed using combinations of keystrokes are called ***meta characters***, and you can search for those. You can look for attributes of a text block, such as the End of Paragraph marker (^p). When you select from a variety of special text characters and attributes in the Find What and Change To pop-up menus, you can easily include these characters in search or replacement terms.

The ***wildcard characters*** are "^?" (any character), "^9" (any digit), and "^$" (any letter). These wildcards are useful in situations where, for example, you want to find all occurrences of four-letter words ending in "ng". If you define your search term as "^$^$ng" and limit the search to Whole Word, InDesign finds all words such as sing, rang, and long. You can't use wildcards within replacement terms; they are only useful for finding words, or for changing the formatting of found words. If you type a wildcard into the Change To field, InDesign treats those symbols as text and performs a literal replacement.

Spell-Checking and Dictionaries

We all make mistakes, and a last-minute spell-check of text that is going to press can save a lot of embarrassment. The InDesign ***Check Spelling*** dialog box has features that can give you significant control over finding and changing words, as well as the ability to add your own words to the dictionary.

Most dictionaries contain basic words in the chosen language, but many words are specific to a particular industry, profession, or discipline, including slang or jargon. If the spell-checker continuously flags words the writer uses frequently, it may be best to add those words to the dictionary by clicking the Add button in the Check Spelling dialog box.

In addition to the US and UK English dictionaries, InDesign includes specialized dictionaries, such as English USA Legal and English USA Medical. It also includes sixteen other languages, common to areas of InDesign distribution. You can interactively assign a language to a specific group of words, so the words are not flagged as misspelled when a spell-check is performed.

Story Editor

InDesign's ***Story Editor*** is designed to function as a word processor. It is an efficient way to edit longer stories without being distracted by what is happening in the layout. You simply select a typeface, size, and theme, and make the necessary edits (see Figure 7.4).

Any changes you make in Story Editor are reflected interactively in the layout. You apply styles through the standard Character Styles and Paragraph Styles palettes, and you can change fonts and font characteristics interactively; however, you see the changes in the story, not in Story Editor, which is designed for fast editing. You can also use the Find/Change utility within Story Editor.

As you work through this project, you will discover that the text utilities can make working with text much more productive — particularly in longer documents. As you develop your work patterns, you will find how the text utilities best fit with your working style.

VISUAL SUMMARY

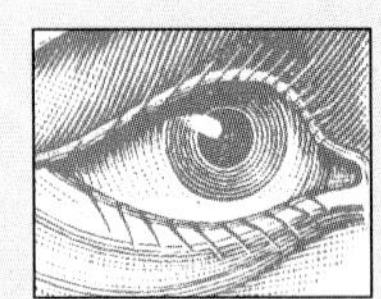

The more you can automate the composition process, the more time you'll have to spend on the enjoyable aspects of document design and production, and the less time you'll need to spend on completing tedious tasks. You would probably prefer to relegate spell checking, style tagging, and inputting editors' changes to someone who spends all her time doing word processing. In the real world, however, that doesn't happen — and it's probably best that you don't send the file you labored over for hours, tweaking every detail, to someone else who might possibly damage it, or worse.

Using the Find/Change tool is a fast way to input an editor's last-minute changes or some final tweaks to the design. (The text should have been edited before you received it; but many times, that isn't the case.) You might also choose to use it as a way to enter "substitute" characters, and then replace them with the correct characters later. For example, you could enter "x" as a multiplication symbol, and then replace it with the actual "mult" symbol, "×."

In addition to replacing words and symbols, you can change formatting — from sweeping changes to very specific ones. As you proceed through this project, you will learn to put this function to very good use, and discover ways to save significant time.

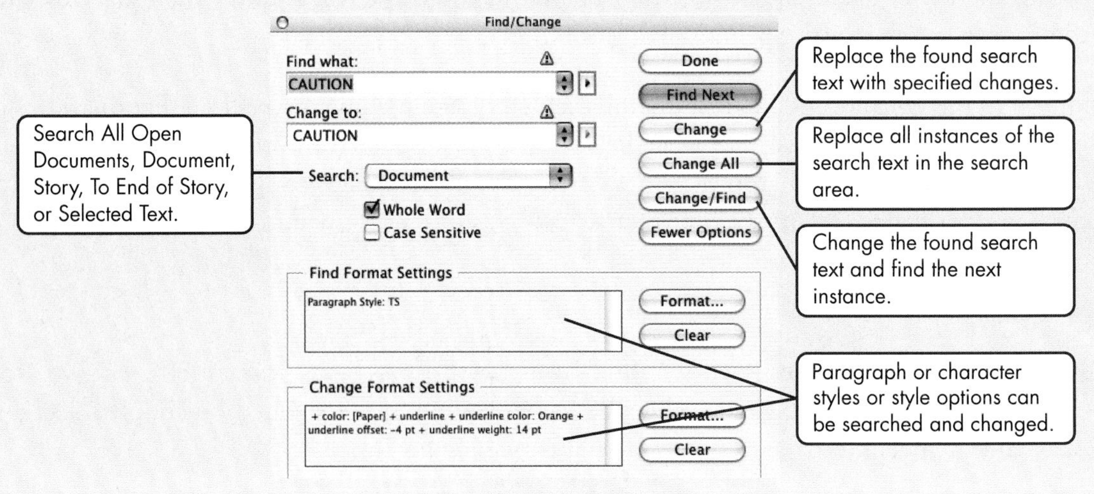

FIGURE 7.1

The document should be spell-checked in a word-processing program before it is handed off to you for composition, and then the text should be manually proofread by someone on your team — which many times, will be you. When you are working on shorter documents, such as advertisements and brochures, you will enter type directly into the InDesign document. Seldom will you be required to key booklets or books directly into InDesign.

Even though your document will likely be proofread before it goes to press, sending it through the spell-checker can appreciably lessen your task of correcting errors. Remember: when your client asks you to make changes to a document, the time you spend is billable; if you fail to discover errors that you input, you cannot bill the client for the time it takes to input the changes.

You have several options when spell-checking, ranging from accepting the dictionary's recommended change, to entering your own word, or adding the word you typed to InDesign's ***User dictionary*** so it is recognized in the future. You can also choose to ignore the "error," or instruct InDesign to ignore the spelling in every instance of this spell-check, without adding the word to the dictionary.

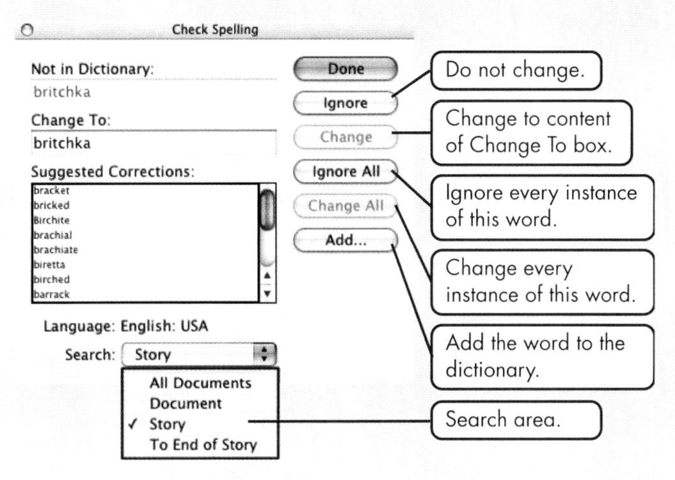

FIGURE 7.2

The spell-checker is an excellent feature, but nothing is better at proofreading than a pair of eyes. Remember, the spell-checker is designed to identify misspelled words. It does not see words in context. You may accidentally type "of" instead of "or," which is a very common error because the keys are one above the other on the keyboard; both are words, and the spell-checker won't catch it as an error. Or, you could make an embarrassing blooper, such as the [Name Deleted] Department of Public Health made on a 300-page report about STDs; their name appeared in the running head of every page, and they left out the "l" in "Public."

InDesign has a standard dictionary that you cannot edit. The standard dictionary interacts transparently with document-specific dictionaries, and with an editable User dictionary, to which you can add words and specify hyphenation. The User dictionary is available to all documents, but the ***document-specific dictionary*** can be used only within the document. The dictionary includes both spelling and hyphenation options.

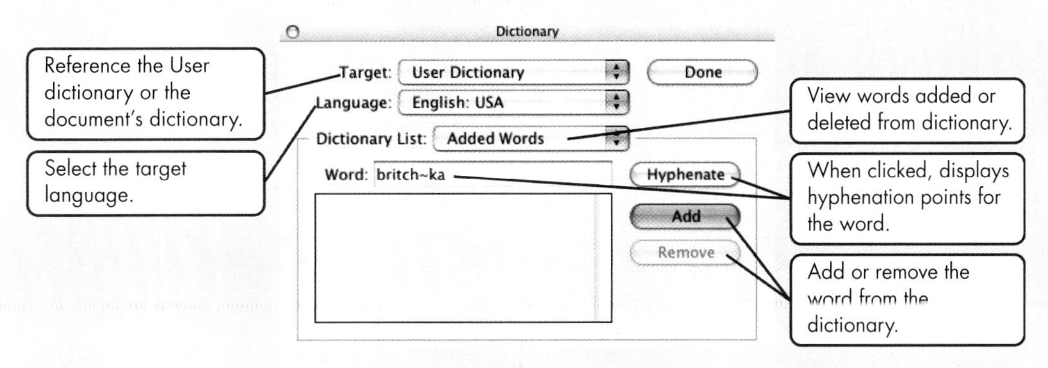

FIGURE 7.3

The Story Editor allows you to edit long passages of text without getting bogged down with screen repaints, or zooming in because you're working on smaller type, or panning your screen because you can't see the entire document. You set the preferences for this no-nonsense option in the Story Editor pane of the Preferences menu (see Figure 7.4). Using Story Editor, you can make any changes to the document that you can make when working in the document window. The changes are interactively reflected in the document, in case you need to reference the document for copyfitting purposes.

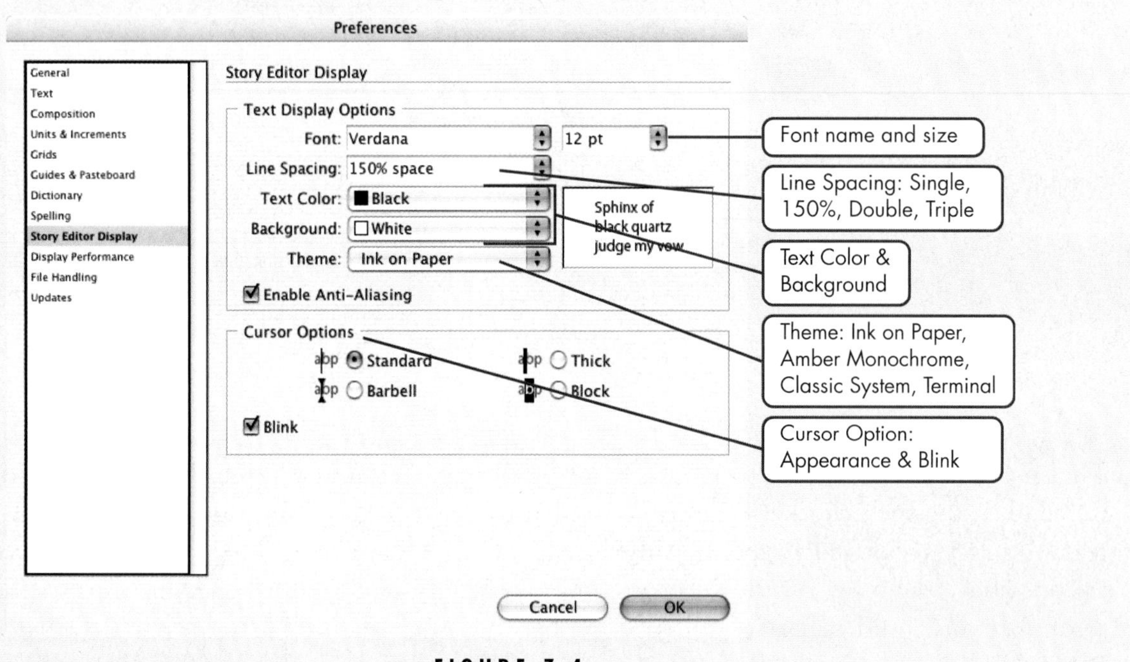

FIGURE 7.4

LESSON 1 Using Find/Change for Text

More often than not, when you use the Find/Change function, you find and change text — both standard characters and special characters that are accessed using combinations of keystrokes (meta characters). This may be because you are handling changes in the document, or because you are using Find/Change to repair imported text that was prepared badly.

InDesign provides a drop-down menu that allows you to select the meta characters that you want to replace. After a while, you will become familiar with a number of the often-used characters and will enter those characters manually — it's much faster than using the drop-down menu, which can become tedious.

Find and Replace Text

1 **Open the document dead_souls_ch1.indd from the Project_07 folder.**

This is the first chapter of *Dead Souls*, by the 19th-century Russian novelist Nokolai Gogol. You're going to take a few liberties with this masterpiece of dry wit. If you receive any missing font warnings, ignore them (although you shouldn't get any if you already installed Adobe Garamond Pro).

2 **Choose Type>Show Hidden Characters. Look at the first page. Zoom in on the beginning of the second paragraph that begins with "During the traveler's inspection."**

There is an indent, and then there are two angled brackets, which indicate that the person who originally typed the text used tabs to set the indent, rather than setting the indent as part of the style. Then the text was flowed into the document, which includes the indent as part of the style, as it should be.

3 **Click the Type tool in the first paragraph of the text frame on Page 1. Choose Edit>Find/Change, or press Command/Control-F.**

You want to remove the tabs, but how do you type a tab into the Find What field? You can copy and paste from the document, or you can click the triangle to the right of the Find What field, and choose the character from the pop-up menu.

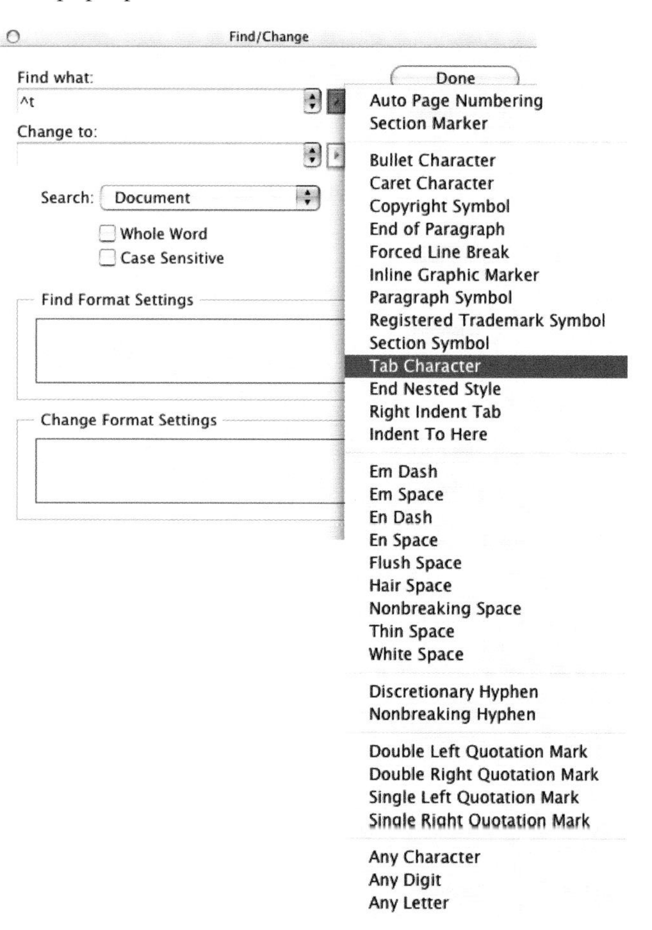

FIGURE 7.5

4 **Choose Tab Character from the Find What menu. Leave the Change To field blank.**

InDesign inserts the character for a tab, which is "^t" (Shift-6, then type "t") into the Find What field. This finds the tab character and replaces it with nothing — an effective way to remove unwanted elements.

5 **Click the Find Next button.**

The first occurrence of a tab in the text is highlighted. If you receive the error shown message in Figure 7.6, you probably have the Whole Word option selected. The tabs adjoin the first word in the paragraph, so this option must be deselected.

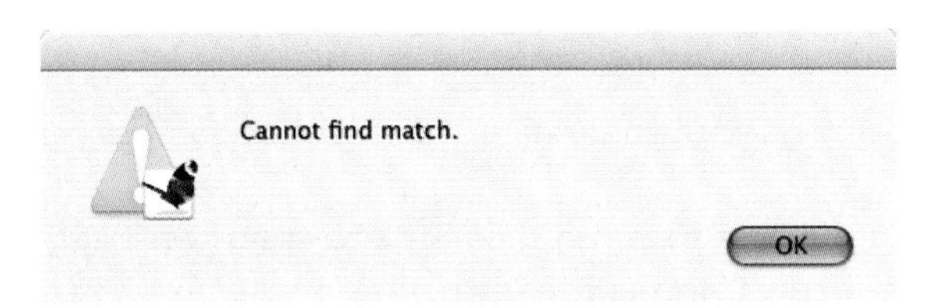
Cannot find match.
OK

FIGURE 7.6

6 **Click Change/Find.**

This removes the tab and goes to the next occurrence.

7 **Click Change All. When you see the Search Complete dialog box, click OK.**

The rest of the tabbed indents are removed and you receive the message shown in Figure 7.7.

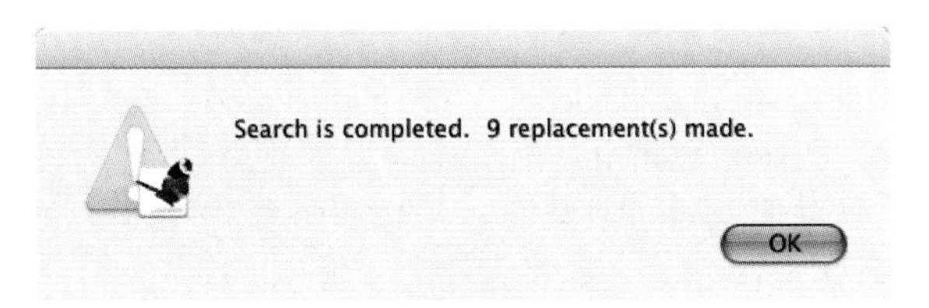
Search is completed. 9 replacement(s) made.
OK

FIGURE 7.7

You also need to replace the British spelling, "rouble," with the U.S. spelling, "ruble."

8 **Type "rouble" into the Find What field, and "ruble" into the Change To field. Make sure that Whole Word is not checked. Click Find Next to highlight the first occurrence of the search term, and then click Change/Find. Click OK to close the Search Complete dialog box.**

You see the Search Complete dialog box because there was only one instance of the word in the document. You did not check Whole Word because you wanted to be sure to change instances where "rouble" was not the entire word. As it turns out, it was contained in the word "roubles." You cannot blindly click Find Next; although it was not the case here, "rouble" could also have been contained in the word "trouble."

The editor wants to change all occurrences of the protagonist's surname, Chichikov, to the more nearly accurate translation, Tchichikov.

9 **Enter the name you want to change (Chichikov) in the Find What field, enter the desired change (Tchichikov) in the Change To field, and then click Change All.**

Twenty-one replacements are made.

You can have many stories (unlinked text frames) in a document. InDesign gives you the option of searching all open documents, all stories in the document, just the story in which the text cursor is placed, or the remaining text in the story from the placement of the text cursor.

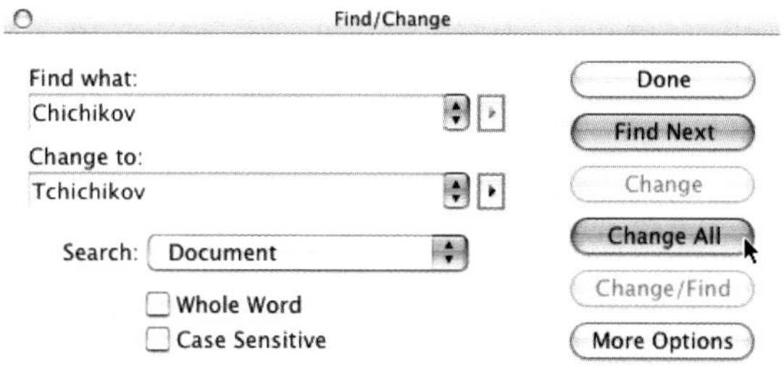

FIGURE 7.8

10 **Dismiss the completion dialog box, and then click Done.**

11 **Save the document to your WIP_07 folder using the same name. Close the file.**

LESSON 2 Searching on Formatting

Sometimes, the problems with files have less to do with the text than they do with the formatting. People who are trained as traditional "typists" often insert a tab (or worse, five spaces) at the beginning of a paragraph to create an indent; they also double-space after periods and colons, and insert multiple paragraph returns. While this was necessary on monospace typewriters, these conventions haven't been in use for years — sadly, old-school typing techniques are still taught in some places.

As you know, you can use InDesign to automatically create paragraph indents, and add space above or below a paragraph. With the variable-spaced characters we use, it is not necessary to double-space after sentences. To prepare documents for formatting in InDesign, you must remove the unnecessary characters from the text.

Change Text Styles

1 **Open formatted_text.indd from the Project_07 folder. Press Command-Option-I (Macintosh) or Control-Alt-I (Windows) to turn on Hidden Characters.**

This document contains several recipes that must fit on a single page. Notice the unnecessary empty paragraphs (two hard returns) that should be replaced with Space Before or Space After formatting.

2 **Click the Type tool in the story immediately before the word "Recipes."**

This makes the Story option available in the Find/Change dialog box.

To Extend Your Knowledge...

META CHARACTERS

You will often use some of the meta characters when searching; others will be used much less frequently. Below is the list of keyboard shortcuts, so you don't have to select from the menu every time.

References to InDesign Features:		**Dashes and Spaces:**	
Auto page numbering	^#	Em dash	^_
Section mark	^x	Em space	^m
Non-Standard Characters:		En dash	^=
Bullet character	^8	En space	^>
Caret character	^^	Flush space	^f
Copyright symbol	^2	Hair space	^|
End of paragraph	^p	Non-breaking space	^s
Forced line break	^n	Thin space	^<
Inline graphic marker	^g	White space	^w
Paragraph symbol	^7	**Hyphens:**	
Registered trademark symbol	^r	Discretionary hyphen	^-
Section symbol	^6	Non-breaking hyphen	^~
Tab character	^t	**Quotation Marks:**	
End nested style	^\	Double left quotation mark	^{
Right indent tab	^y	Double right quotation mark	^}
Indent to here	^i	Single left quotation mark	^[
Wildcard Characters:		Single right quotation mark	^]
Any character	^?		
Any digit	^9		
Any letter	^$		

3 **Choose Edit>Find/Change. Remove any terms remaining in the Find/Change dialog box from the previous exercise. Type "^p^p" into the Find What field.**

You're going to remove every instance of two sequential paragraph markers. You can also access the Find/Change dialog box by pressing the Command/Control-F keys, and then choose End of Paragraph from the drop-down list of meta characters in the Find What menu.

4 **Click the cursor in the Change To field, and type "^p". Make sure the Search option is set to Story. Click Change All, and then dismiss the completion notice.**

Fifteen double returns are replaced with single returns.

Find/Change
Find what:
^p^p
Change to:
^p
Search: Story
Whole Word
Case Sensitive
Done
Find Next
Change
Change All
Change/Find
More Options

FIGURE 7.9

5 **Click Change All again, and then dismiss the completion notice. Click Change All a third time, and then click OK when the completion notice tells you that no more changes were made.**

Sometimes there will be three, four, or even more returns in a row. Keep clicking Change All until the completion notice tells you no more changes were made.

6 **Select the first five lines of the ingredients for Orange-Glazed Bananas Foster, making certain your selection includes the ¶ markers.**

You want to change these ***hard returns*** (marked with end-of-paragraph markers) to ***soft returns***, also known as forced line breaks. Soft returns advance you to a new line without creating a new paragraph. You only want to select the first four lines because the fifth line is the end of a paragraph.

7 **In Find/Change, set Find What as "^p", and Change To as "^n" (the symbol for a forced line break. Set the Search field to Selection. Click Change All, and then click OK at the completion notice.**

Note that text selected prior to a search remains selected after the search is finished, but the search field (Selection) reverts to Story.

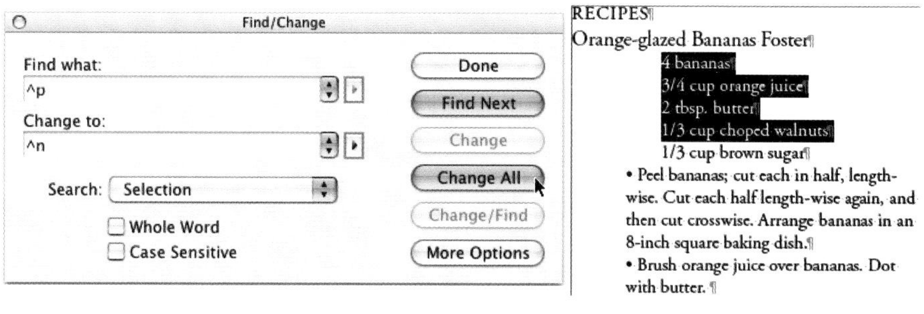

FIGURE 7.10

8 **Repeat Steps 5 and 6 for the ingredients in Key Lime Pie, Chocolate-Orange Pudding, Florida Orange Bread, and Orange Sunshine Cookies. Do not include the last ingredient in your search and replace, because this truly is the end of the paragraph. You must reset the search field to Selection each time a search is conducted.**

Check the Search pop-up menu every time, because it reverts to Story instead of retaining Selection. If you forget to change it to Selection, press Command/Control-Z to undo the last change.

9 **In the Pages palette, delete the second page.**

10 **Save the file to your WIP_07 folder. Leave the file open for the next exercise.**

All the text now fits on one page.

To Extend Your Knowledge...

TIPS AND CAUTIONS ABOUT SEARCHING

In addition to placing two hard returns at the end of a paragraph, another bad typing habit began in the days when monospaced characters (such as Courier) were regularly used. These fonts made it difficult to see the end of a sentence if only a single space was used. Typists were trained to enter two spaces at the end of every sentence; today, this practice is considered typographically incorrect. Treat two spaces the same as you do two paragraph breaks — remove of them before you begin serious page composition.

LESSON 3 Finding and Changing Using Formats

Some changes require a different approach from simply searching and replacing characters — whether the characters are visible or not. Searching on formats gives you the option to change text that shares common values. Virtually any character or paragraph style option can be searched, and any character or paragraph style can be the target of the search.

When replacing text that has been searched by format, it is not to replace a similar value. For example, you could search on all text that is blue, and replace it with text in a specific font, keeping or discarding the character color. You could also replace it with a character style. The advantage is that if the art director decides to change the colored text from blue to green, you would simply make that modification to the character style, and all text styled in that manner would automatically change.

There is a caution accompanying searching on formats: You should immediately clear a format Find/Change when the operation is complete. If this is not done, you may carry unwanted elements into the next Find/Change operation.

Modify Formats

1 **Position the Type tool at the beginning of the open formatted_text.indd.**

2 **Choose Edit>Find/Change. Click the More Options button.**

The recipe titles are set in 14-pt type. They are the only elements using that type size. You need to tag all these titles with the Recipe Title style.

3 **Delete any leftover terms in the Find What and Change To fields, and then click the Format button in the Find Format Settings section. Choose Basic Character Formats. Set the Size to 14 pt. Click OK.**

4 **Click the Format button in the Change Format Settings section. Choose Recipe Title from the Paragraph Style menu (the Style Options pane appears by default). Click OK.**

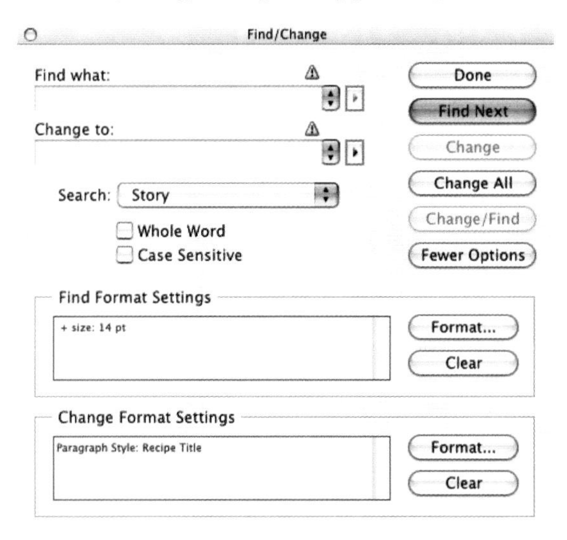

FIGURE 7.11

5 **Click Change All. Click OK in the search completion notice. Click the Clear buttons for both Find Format Settings and Change Format Settings.**

You should always clear the Find Format Settings and Change Format Settings sections at the conclusion of a search.

6 **Click the Format button in the Find Format Settings section. Choose Indents and Spacing. Type "5p0" in the Left Indent field. Click OK.**

You're going to apply the Ingredients style to the ingredients. They are currently set with a 5p0 indent, which is searchable.

7 **Click the Format button in the Change Format section. In the Change Format Settings field, choose Ingredients from the Paragraph Style menu. Click OK.**

8 **In the Find/Change box, click Change All. Dismiss the completion notice, and clear the Find and Change Format Settings sections.**

9 **Click the Format button in the Find Format Settings section. Choose Basic Character Formats, and choose 12 pt in the Size field. Click OK.**

The body text is the only text still set in 12 pt, so this is an acceptable search parameter.

10 **In the Change Format Settings section, choose Body Text from the Paragraph Style menu. Click OK. Click Change All. Dismiss the completion notice. Clear the Find and Change Format Settings sections.**

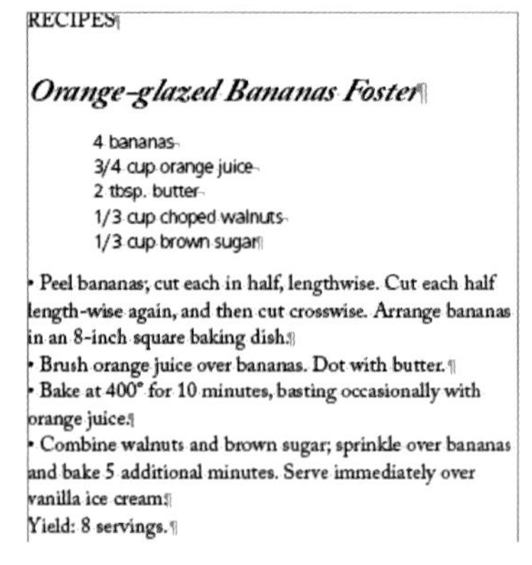

RECIPES

Orange-glazed Bananas Foster

4 bananas
3/4 cup orange juice
2 tbsp. butter
1/3 cup choped walnuts
1/3 cup brown sugar

• Peel bananas; cut each in half, lengthwise. Cut each half length-wise again, and then cut crosswise. Arrange bananas in an 8-inch square baking dish.
• Brush orange juice over bananas. Dot with butter.
• Bake at 400° for 10 minutes, basting occasionally with orange juice.
• Combine walnuts and brown sugar; sprinkle over bananas and bake 5 additional minutes. Serve immediately over vanilla ice cream.
Yield: 8 servings.

FIGURE 7.12

11 **Save your changes. Leave the file open for the next exercise.**

Fine-Tune the Document

1 **In the open document, highlight the first word, "Recipes," and change it to 24-pt Adobe Caslon Pro Bold.**

2 **In the Find What field, choose the bullet character (^8) from the drop-down menu. In the Change To field, choose the bullet character, thin space, and Indent to Here characters (^8^<^i), then click Find Next. Click Change All. Dismiss the completion notice. Click Done.**

Bullets should hang, not run into the sentence following. This Find/Change replaces a bullet followed by a space with a bullet followed by a thin space and an Indent to Here character. This forces the lines following a bullet to align properly.

RECIPES

Orange-glazed Bananas Foster

4 bananas
3/4 cup orange juice
2 tbsp. butter
1/3 cup choped walnuts
1/3 cup brown sugar

• Peel bananas; cut each in half, lengthwise. Cut each half length-wise again, and then cut crosswise. Arrange bananas in an 8-inch square baking dish.
• Brush orange juice over bananas. Dot with butter.
• Bake at 400° for 10 minutes, basting occasionally with orange juice.
• Combine walnuts and brown sugar; sprinkle over bananas and bake 5 additional minutes. Serve immediately over vanilla ice cream.
Yield: 8 servings.

FIGURE 7.13

3 Use the Selection tool to select the pie in the upper left of the pasteboard. Cut the pie.

4 Click the Type tool at the end of the Key Lime Pie recipe title. Press Return/Enter. Change the Leading of the paragraph to 75 pt.

5 With the Type tool still active, choose Edit>Paste to paste the picture of the pie into the text frame.

6 Use the Paragraph Styles palette to apply an appropriate indent.

7 Turn off Show Hidden Characters. Press the "W" key to view the page.

8 Save your changes. Leave the document open for the next lesson.

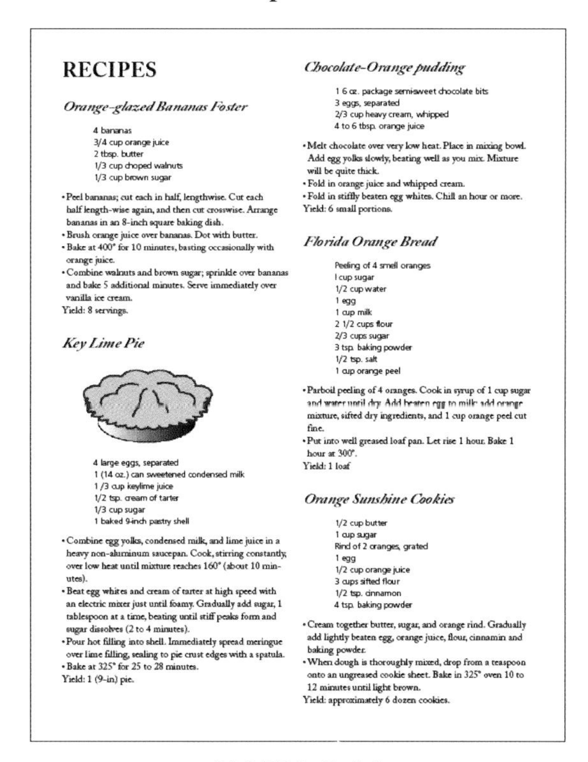

RECIPES

Orange-glazed Bananas Foster

4 bananas
3/4 cup orange juice
2 tbsp. butter
1/3 cup choped walnuts
1/3 cup brown sugar

- Peel bananas; cut each in half, lengthwise. Cut each half length-wise again, and then cut crosswise. Arrange bananas in an 8-inch square baking dish.
- Brush orange juice over bananas. Dot with butter.
- Bake at 400° for 10 minutes, basting occasionally with orange juice.
- Combine walnuts and brown sugar; sprinkle over bananas and bake 5 additional minutes. Serve immediately over vanilla ice cream.

Yield: 8 servings.

Key Lime Pie

4 large eggs, separated
1 (14 oz.) can sweetened condensed milk
1 /3 cup keylime juice
1/2 tsp. cream of tarter
1/3 cup sugar
1 baked 9-inch pastry shell

- Combine egg yolks, condensed milk, and lime juice in a heavy non-aluminum saucepan. Cook, stirring constantly, over low heat until mixture reaches 160° (about 10 minutes).
- Beat egg whites and cream of tarter at high speed with an electric mixer just until foamy. Gradually add sugar, 1 tablespoon at a time, beating until stiff peaks form and sugar dissolves (2 to 4 minutes).
- Pour hot filling into shell. Immediately spread meringue over lime filling, sealing to pie crust edges with a spatula.
- Bake at 325° for 25 to 28 minutes.

Yield: 1 (9-in) pie.

Chocolate-Orange pudding

1 6 oz. package semi-sweet chocolate bits
3 eggs, separated
2/3 cup heavy cream, whipped
4 to 6 tbsp. orange juice

- Melt chocolate over very low heat. Place in mixing bowl. Add egg yolks slowly, beating well as you mix. Mixture will be quite thick.
- Fold in orange juice and whipped cream.
- Fold in stiffly beaten egg whites. Chill an hour or more.

Yield: 6 small portions.

Florida Orange Bread

Peeling of 4 smell oranges
l cup sugar
1/2 cup water
1 egg
1 cup milk
2 1/2 cups flour
2/3 cups sugar
3 tsp. baking powder
1/2 tsp. salt
1 cup orange peel

- Parboil peeling of 4 oranges. Cook in syrup of 1 cup sugar and water until dry. Add beaten egg to milk; add orange mixture, sifted dry ingredients, and 1 cup orange peel cut fine.
- Put into well greased loaf pan. Let rise 1 hour. Bake 1 hour at 300°.

Yield: 1 loaf

Orange Sunshine Cookies

1/2 cup butter
1 cup sugar
Rind of 2 oranges, grated
1 egg
1/2 cup orange juice
3 cups sifted flour
1/2 tsp. cinnamon
4 tsp. baking powder

- Cream together butter, sugar, and orange rind. Gradually add lightly beaten egg, orange juice, flour, cinnamin and baking powder.
- When dough is thoroughly mixed, drop from a teaspoon onto an ungreased cookie sheet. Bake in 325° oven 10 to 12 minutes until light brown.

Yield: approximately 6 dozen cookies.

FIGURE 7.14

To Extend Your Knowledge...

TIPS ABOUT CHANGING FORMAT SETTINGS

When you use format settings to find and make changes to text, you should click the Clear button before proceeding to other tasks. The format settings are retained and applied to the next search unless they are cleared. If you forget that you were using them, and conduct a new search, the resulting problems in your document may take hours to resolve.

LESSON 4 Using the Spell-Checker

Whether your document is large or small, it is always worthwhile to take the few moments necessary to check your spelling. Even if you receive your text from a word processor, you should check it — never assume the person who passed the document to you performed his job completely.

As you complete the next exercise, you will discover the importance of thinking while you perform a spell-check. Sometimes you know a word will be repeated, and that the spelling will be correct in every instance. At other times, you may want to check the word each and every time it appears — just to be sure.

One trap that is easy to fall into, especially when the spell-checker finds a number of sequential "problems" that you ignore, is to lose focus on the task. When this happens, you may ignore an actual spelling error. This is often the case if you spell-check technical documents, where jargon is used.

Check the Spelling

1 **In the open formatted_text.indd document, deselect all text and/or text frames. Choose Edit>Check Spelling.**

2 **Click the Start button.**

If the button says Ignore, click it. Either button starts the Check Spelling search.

3 **The first word questioned is "tbsp," the abbreviation for tablespoon. Click Ignore All.**

This abbreviation is common in recipes, so there are probably more references in the document. The spell-checker will not question the word again.

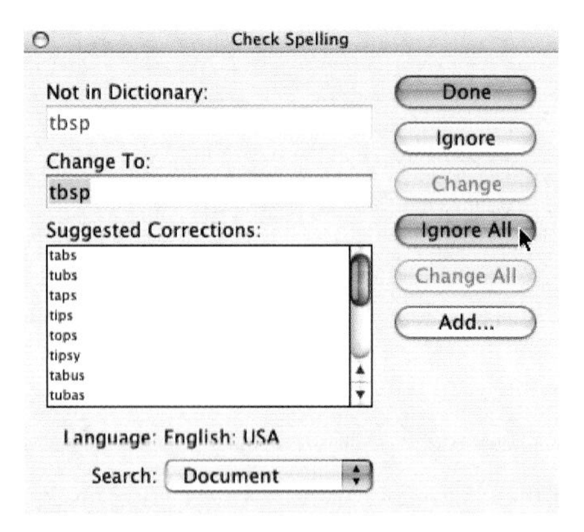

FIGURE 7.15

4 **The next word questioned is "butter." Click Ignore.**

At the top of the dialog box, you see the words "Capitalization Error." The checker sees that the abbreviated word prior to "butter" ends with a period and interprets this as the end of a sentence. It recommends that "butter," as the start of a new sentence, should begin with a capital letter.

5 **The next word, "choped," is a misspelled word. The suggested replacement, "chopped," appears in the dictionary list. Click this word, and then click Change.**

Check Spelling
Not in Dictionary:
choped
Change To:
chopped
Suggested Corrections:
hoped
chopped
cooped
coped
copped
copied
chapped
chipped
Done
Ignore
Change
Ignore All
Change All
Add...
Language: English: USA
Search: Document

FIGURE 7.16

6 **The checker finds "8-inch." Click Ignore.**

7 **The next word questioned is "keylime." The replacement in the dictionary list separates this into two words, "key lime." Choose the replacement and click Change.**

8 **Next, the word "tsp" is questioned. Similar to "tbsp," this abbreviation for teaspoon is often used in recipes.**

9 **Continue through the spell-check session, changing or ignoring as appropriate:**

cream	Ignore
9-inch	Ignore
9-in	Change to 9-inch
orange	Ignore
l	Change to 1
baking, salt, cinnamon, baking	Ignore
cinnaminn	Change to cinnamon

10 **The word "ungreased" is the last you encounter. The word is correct, but is not in the dictionary. Click Add in the dialog box. It changes to the Dictionary dialog box. Click Hyphenate. Click Add, and then click Done.**

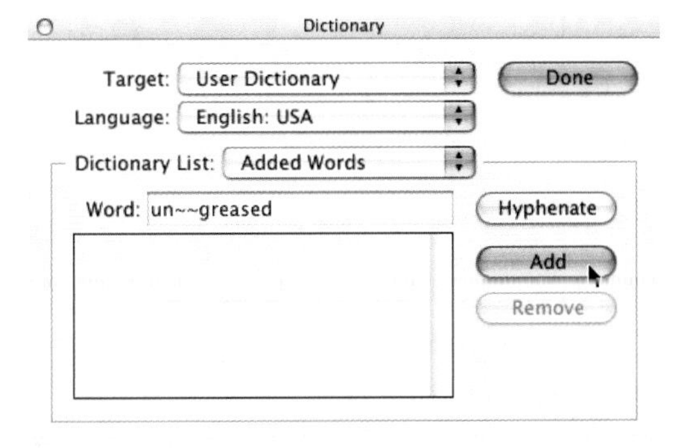

FIGURE 7.17

11 **You return to the Check Spelling dialog box. Click Ignore. The Check Spelling session is finished. Click Done to close the dialog box.**

12 **Read the document and make any necessary changes the spell-checker missed.**

The third ingredient in the Key Lime Pie recipe is "1 /3," which should be changed to "1/3." In both the fourth ingredient and the second bulleted item of the Key Lime Pie recipe, the word "tarter" appears. Although that is a word, you should use cream of "tartar," instead. Florida Orange Bread's first item is listed as "smell oranges." You'd probably prefer to use "small" oranges.

13 **Save your changes. Close the document.**

LESSON 5 Setting Story Editor Preferences

When setting the preferences for the Story Editor display, you should set the display so it is easy on your eyes because you're likely going to be looking at the screen for a long time. While we chose black on white in the following exercise, you may find that a light green or yellow is a better setting for you. Setting the line spacing is important, too, because line spacing aids readability. Since you are going to be editing, a little extra space than you might normally use works well. You should experiment with the features to discover which preferences are best for your eyes.

Story Editor preferences are located in InDesign's Preferences menu. Perhaps more than any other preference, this one will likely remain constant from document to document, because the settings do not directly affect the document's appearance — Story Editor preferences simply make it easier for you to work more efficiently.

Set Your Story Editor Preferences

1 **From your Preferences menu, choose Story Editor Display.**

2 **Choose a Font that displays well on screen, and includes Italics and Bold.**

We prefer fonts such as Verdana, which were designed for Internet use and display well on the monitor.

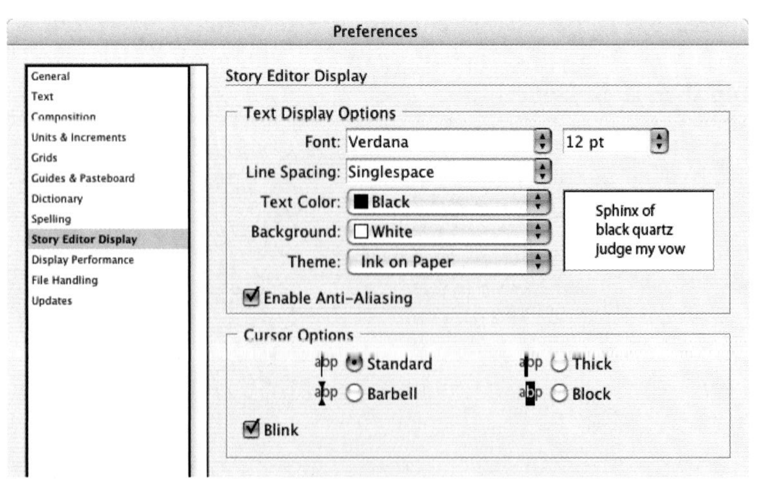

FIGURE 7.18

3 **Choose a Size.**

The 12-point default size is good; if you have difficulty seeing, you can choose a larger size. The whole point of the Story Editor is to enable you to edit quickly and easily.

4 **Choose your Line Spacing.**

The extra readability that 150% line spacing provides works well, but you may prefer tighter spacing.

5 **Leave the Text Color as Black, and Background as White.**

Look at the small preview box on the right side of the dialog box to see how the colors appear. If you prefer, experiment with other colors to see if a different color combination is more soothing for your eyes.

6 **View the four Themes in the display. Choose one that is comfortable for you.**

7 **Leave the Enable Anti-Aliasing box checked.**

The type looks better with this feature turned on.

8 **Choose a cursor option that will help you see your position in the document most readily.**

Most find that either the Standard or Barbell option is best.

9 **Leave the Blink box selected. This helps you find the cursor more readily.**

10 **Click OK to save the preferences for the next exercise.**

LESSON 6 Using Story Editor

The Story Editor could be used to actually write documents; but, as its name implies, it is really designed for editing. When you use the Story Editor, you concentrate on the edits, not on line wraps in the document. You also have the advantage of being able to work in one continuous text stream, instead of going from page to page, as you would if you were editing a longer document. The pages do not have to repaint along with graphics, so edits can be performed much more quickly in Story Editor than in layout.

When in Story Editor, you have access to all the text-editing functions that are available in the layout. Even though you see bold and italic when they are applied to text, you do not see font changes; all type appears in the font you select as your display style. As an added benefit, paragraph styles are visible next to each paragraph, as they are in word-processing programs.

In most cases, when you are working with Story Editor, you will be in an editing stage after your client has seen the document, and realized that certain phraseology could be better. You will not have an art director looking over your shoulder when you work with this tool; but as soon as you are finished, you should return to the document (with a previous proof in front of you) and make sure that your editing did not create design problems.

Use Story Editor

1 **Open alice_5.indd from your Project_07 folder. Click the text cursor in the frame, in front of the word "Chapter."**

2 **Choose Edit>Edit in Story Editor.**

The keyboard shortcut is Command/Control-Y.

3 **Adjust the editing window so the line length of the text is comfortable for you, and ideally, so you can see the underlying document.**

You can see the paragraph styles in the left part of Story Editor's split window, and the text in the right window.

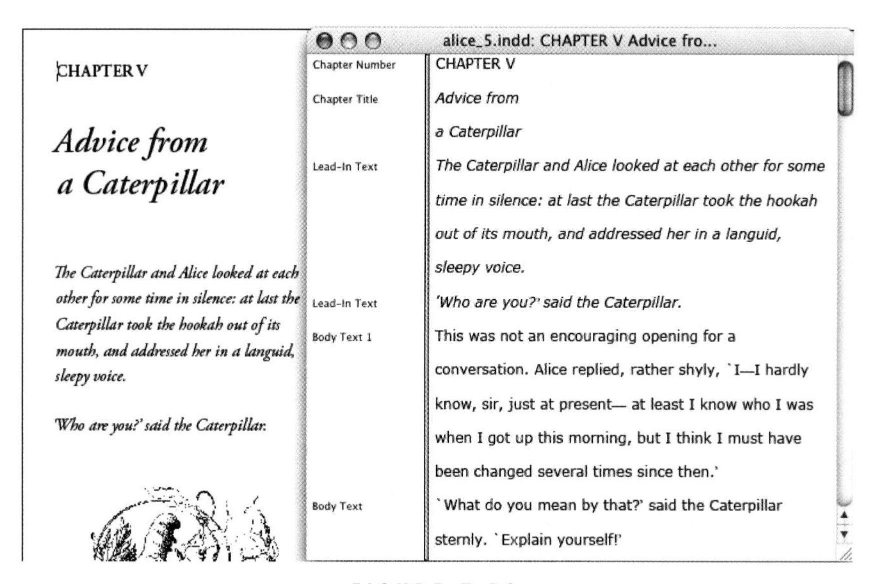

FIGURE 7.19

4 **Choose Edit>Find/Change, and perform three replacements for misspelled words, using Change All:**

Find What	Change To
Caterpiller	Caterpillar
pooka	hookah
aires	airs

5 **In Find What, enter "`" (the first key on the left end of the top row of your keyboard). Enter Single Left Quotation Mark (^[ ) in the Change To box, and choose Change All. Click Done when the Find/Change is complete.**

Some very strange characters are used for an open quote.

6 **With the first column of the document visible, and while still in Story Editor, choose Type>Insert Break Character>Forced Line Break (Shift-Return/Enter) to place a soft return immediately before the word "at," following the word "silence" in the second line of lead-in text.**

You can see the change made interactively, but it doesn't affect your ability to continue editing. This non-intrusive method of viewing your edits is called ***passive preview***.

7 **Save the file to your WIP_07 folder under the same name. Close the document.**

SUMMARY

In this project, you used InDesign's powerful text utilities to automate the editing process. You learned to find and change text elements based on a variety of criteria. You became acquainted with the various dictionaries, and learned to add words when necessary. You discovered the power of InDesign's spell-checker. You also became aware of some of the general deficiencies of spell-checking programs, which are very effective at checking spelling, but cannot check context or grammar. In addition, you learned to set up and use the Story Editor to edit your documents quickly, without interference from the layout, or having to change views because of differences in type sizes.

KEY TERMS

Case Sensitive option
Check Spelling utility
Document-specific dictionary
Find/Change
Hard return
Meta character
Non-modal
Passive preview
Search and replace
Soft return
Story Editor
User dictionary
Whole Word option
Wildcard characters

CHECKING CONCEPTS AND TERMS

MULTIPLE CHOICE

Circle the letter of the correct answer for each of the following questions.

1. What is a primary value for using the Find/Change utility?

a. It corrects the original word-processed document.

b. It is fast and accurate.

c. It automatically hyphenates.

d. It can access multiple dictionaries.

2. What is the User dictionary?

a. The dictionary that ships with InDesign.

b. The dictionary that is attached to an individual document.

c. A dictionary you can edit.

d. Part of online help.

3. The Find/Change dialog box is non-modal. What does that mean?
   a. It does not have to be re-launched for every Find/Change.
   b. It is always accessible.
   c. You must open it for every Find/Change.
   d. You can search for specific text.

4. What does the Whole Word option do?
   a. It treats the characters you are searching for as one word, even if there are several words in the phrase.
   b. It limits the search to words containing the characters you are searching for.
   c. It ignores words that contain the characters you are searching for, unless those characters comprise the entire word, not a part of a word.
   d. It accepts words that sound like the characters you typed into the search field.

5. When do you need to click the Clear button after a search?
   a. When you are searching for specific words.
   b. When you are searching for and replacing specific words.
   c. When you used the Case Sensitive option.
   d. When you search or replace format settings.

6. What are meta characters?
   a. Characters that are larger than others.
   b. Characters that represent invisible characters, such as the ¶ or › symbols.
   c. Pi characters.
   d. Character combinations used in place of invisible characters, such as ^p or ^t.

7. When does the Check Spelling utility allow access to the dictionary?
   a. Whenever the Add button is clicked in the spell-checker.
   b. Whenever you highlight a word.
   c. When you choose Ignore.
   d. Never.

8. What is the value of Story Editor?
   a. It is a WYSIWYG word processor.
   b. It shows you the text, in the face and size specified, but without graphics.
   c. It shows you the text in a single stream.
   d. It is a read-only file, so you can quickly see what needs to be changed.

9. When should you trust InDesign's spell-checker with the final "look" at the document?
   a. When time is short.
   b. When you received your text from a word processor.
   c. When the client is going to proofread before press.
   d. Never.

10. What types of elements can you search for in Find/Change?
   a. Text and graphics.
   b. Words and meta characters.
   c. Colors.
   d. Anything in the document.

DISCUSSION QUESTIONS

1. When would you choose to use the Story Editor, and when would you choose not to use it? Keep in mind the types of documents, their complexity, and their length.
2. Why must care be exercised when performing Find/Change functions, using features such as search and replace?
3. What sorts of documents would you not want to spell-check, and why?

SKILL DRILL

Skill Drills reinforce project skills. Each skill reinforced is the same, or nearly the same, as a skill presented in the lessons. Detailed instructions are provided in a step-by-step format. You should complete these exercises in order.

1. Use Find/Change for Text

You received a chapter of a book that just came back from the editors, who made several changes on the hard-copy document. Your task is to use the Find/Change utility to make these changes in the electronic file.

1. Open type_mechanics.indd from the Project_07 folder.
2. Press Command/Control-F to access the Find/Change utility.
3. Click the Text tool in the document and set the Search for Story.
4. In the Find What field, enter "skewing".
5. In the Change To field, enter "skewing (fake italics)". Click Find Next.
6. Click Change.

   You only want to change the first instance to define it. You could have simply searched for the word and changed it manually; the amount of time spent would have been roughly equal.
7. Save the file. Leave it open for the next exercise.

2. Use Find/Change for Formats

1. In the open document, click the More Options button.
2. In the Find What field, enter "CAUTION".
3. In the Change To field, enter "^>CAUTION^>".

   This inserts an en space on either side of the word.
4. In the Find Format field, choose the paragraph style "TS."
5. In the Change Format field, choose Paper as the Character Color. In the Underline options, set Underline to On, Weight to 15 pt, Offset to –4 pt, Type to Solid, and Color to Orange. Click OK.
6. Click Change All.
7. Click OK to dismiss the completion notice.
8. Clear the Format settings. Click Done to close the Find/Change dialog box.
9. Save the file. Leave it open for the next exercise.

3. Spell-Check the Document

1. In the open document, press Command/Control-I to access the Check Spelling utility.
2. Click the text cursor in the document and set the Search for Story.
3. In the Check Spelling dialog box, click Start.
4. The first word questioned is "letterforms." Click Ignore All.
5. The next word questioned is "bitmapped." Click the Add button, and change the target to "type_mechanics.indd" to add it to the document dictionary. Click Add, and then click Done.
6. The next word challenged is "TrueType." Click the Add button and add it to the User dictionary. Do not include hyphenation.
7. Treat the following words as indicated:

Installable	Ignore
Editable	Ignore
bitmap (all varieties of the word)	Add to document dictionary
metrics	Add to User dictionary
superset	Add to document dictionary
TruType	Change to TrueType
Microsoft	Add to User dictionary; select Hyphenate and place a tilde (~) in front of the word so it will not hyphenate
rasterize (all varieties of the word)	Add to document dictionary
multiplatform	Change to multi-platform
oldstyle	Ignore All
Macromedia	Ignore

8. Stop spell-checking after Macromedia. From there on, the document uses technical jargon. Click Done.
9. Save and close the document.

CHALLENGE

Challenge exercises expand on, or are somewhat related to, skills presented in the lessons. Each exercise provides a brief introduction, followed by instructions presented in a numbered-step format that are not as detailed as those in the Skill Drill exercises. You should complete these exercises in order.

1. Correct Formatting for a Book

You flowed the text for a new version of Sir Walter Scott's classic, *Ivanhoe*. Since the text is in public domain, it is somewhat suspect. Your task is to find and resolve the problems with the layout of the text, as well as apply some changes that you want to make to enhance the document.

1. Open ivanhoe.indd from the Project_07 folder. Go to the third page, which is numbered as Page 1.
2. Show Hidden Characters.

   You see that each line ends with a hard return, there are double-spaces after each sentence, each paragraph begins with two spaces, and there are two spaces between paragraphs.

   The Body Text style was already applied to the chapter. You must perform the corrections in a logical order, or you will be unable to use the power of Find/Change to make the necessary changes.
3. Click the text cursor at the beginning of the document. Open Find/Change. Set the Search to Story. In the Find What box, enter "^p[space][space]". In the Change To box, enter "^p".

   This removes the two spaces at the beginning of each paragraph.
4. Click Find Next, and then click Change. Once you are sure the change works correctly, click Change All. Repeat to ensure you make all the changes.
5. In the Find What box, enter "^p^p". In the Change To box, enter "| (Shift-\)".

   The purpose of this step is simply to enter a character that does not appear in the story. You'll see the logic as you progress.
6. Click Change All. Repeat to ensure you make all the changes.
7. In the Find What box, enter "^p". In the Change To box, enter "[space]". Click Change All.
8. Change the "|" character back to a paragraph end.

   Now the document is starting to resemble a book.
9. Convert all double-spaces to single-spaces.

10. Apply the Chapter style to the "CHAPTER I" paragraph. Apply the Body Text 1 style to the first paragraph of text (following Chapter I).
11. Save your changes and leave the document open.

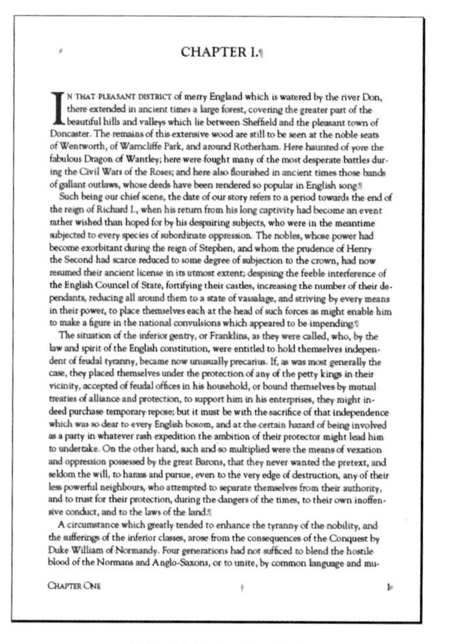

CHAPTER I.¶

IN THAT PLEASANT DISTRICT of merry England which is watered by the river Don, there extended in ancient times a large forest, covering the greater part of the beautiful hills and valleys which lie between Sheffield and the pleasant town of Doncaster. The remains of this extensive wood are still to be seen at the noble seats of Wentworth, of Warncliffe Park, and around Rotherham. Here haunted of yore the fabulous Dragon of Wantley; here were fought many of the most desperate battles during the Civil Wars of the Roses; and here also flourished in ancient times those bands of gallant outlaws, whose deeds have been rendered so popular in English song.¶

Such being our chief scene, the date of our story refers to a period towards the end of the reign of Richard I., when his return from his long captivity had become an event rather wished than hoped for by his despairing subjects, who were in the meantime subjected to every species of subordinate oppression. The nobles, whose power had become exorbitant during the reign of Stephen, and whom the prudence of Henry the Second had scarce reduced to some degree of subjection to the crown, had now resumed their ancient license in its utmost extent; despising the feeble interference of the English Councel of State, fortifying their castles, increasing the number of their dependants, reducing all around them to a state of vassalage, and striving by every means in their power, to place themselves each at the head of such forces as might enable him to make a figure in the national convulsions which appeared to be impending.¶

The situation of the inferior gentry, or Franklins, as they were called, who, by the law and spirit of the English constitution, were entitled to hold themselves independent of feudal tyranny, became now unusually precarius. If, as was most generally the case, they placed themselves under the protection of any of the petty kings in their vicinity, accepted of feudal offices in his household, or bound themselves by mutual treaties of alliance and protection, to support him in his enterprises, they might indeed purchase temporary repose; but it must be with the sacrifice of that independence which was so dear to every English bosom, and at the certain hazard of being involved as a party in whatever rash expedition the ambition of their protector might lead him to undertake. On the other hand, such and so multiplied were the means of vexation and oppression possessed by the great Barons, that they never wanted the pretext, and seldom the will, to harass and pursue, even to the very edge of destruction, any of their less powerful neighbours, who attempted to separate themselves from their authority, and to trust for their protection, during the dangers of the times, to their own inoffensive conduct, and to the laws of the land.¶

A circumstance which greatly tended to enhance the tyranny of the nobility, and the sufferings of the inferior classes, arose from the consequences of the Conquest by Duke William of Normandy. Four generations had not sufficed to blend the hostile blood of the Normans and Anglo-Saxons, or to unite, by common language and mu-

CHAPTER ONE 1

FIGURE 7.20

2. Make Changes in Text and Format

There are some additional changes to make. One major change affects text characters, and another change should be made through format settings.

1. In the open document, find and change all instances of "``" with double left quotation marks (open quotes, "). Choose the double left quotation mark from the pull-down menu.

   The characters you are replacing are two instances of the first character in the top row of your keyboard.

2. Change "English constitution" to "Great Charter".
3. Clear all the text in the Find What and Change To boxes.
4. Set Find Format Settings>Basic Character Formats for Adobe Caslon Pro Regular.
5. Set Change Format Settings to the Break paragraph style.
6. Conduct the Find/Change, and then clear the Format Settings section.
7. Click Done to close the Find/Change dialog.
8. Save your changes and leave the document open.

3. Conduct a Spell-Check

You're converting this document into an American version, and you can be sure there are a number of "Britishisms" in the text. Do not confuse British spellings (which should change) with flavorful dialog (which should not change). There are also some misspelled words. To make your task less onerous, a number of proper nouns were added to the document dictionary. Take your time with this exercise.

1. In the open document, press Command/Control-I to access the Check Spelling utility.
2. Set the spell-checker to Story, and check only the story beginning with "Chapter I" on Page 3. Click Start.
3. The utility questions "Doncaster." Click Ignore All.
4. Correct the spelling of any word that is actually misspelled. The program questions "Councel," "precarius," "richley," "copsewood," "silvan," "unhewn," "hawkks," "fidgety," "St" (should be St.), "lurcher," and "foreclaws."

   If you need to use a dictionary, do so.
5. When you get into the dialog section, you are presented with "o'," "thous't," "mayst," "thee," "unfriendship," "burte" (should be brute), "speakest," "hath," "thou," "brings't," "thinkest," "wouldst," "wilt," and "notwithstanding," "canst." Change the words that are misspelled and either ignore or add to the Ivanhoe.indd dictionary those that are correct.
6. Change "tendance" to "tending." For the expression "him.---" replace the three hyphens with a space. Change the expression "purport:---" to "purport:" In other instances, change three hyphens (---) to an em dash (—).
7. Be sure to translate British spellings, such as "neighbour" and "colour" into their U.S. spellings. You may wish to use the Change All button for this sort of word.
8. Add as many words to the document dictionary as you wish.
9. When you finish the spell-check, save your changes and close the document.

PORTFOLIO BUILDER

Check Your Projects

When you present your portfolio to a potential client or employer, you have already cleared the first hurdle — review of your resumé. You should view the portfolio as an extension of the resumé, and more. Your portfolio shows prospective clients and employers what you have made of your education and experience, and what you have accomplished; you want to present your portfolio in the best possible light.

Review the projects you created in previous Portfolio Builder assignments. For each project, complete the following steps:

- Check and correct the spelling in each document.
- Check for and replace missing fonts, or fonts that have been menu-styled rather than selected from the list of fonts.
- Check and correct widows and orphans, as well as bad hyphenation, kerning, and tracking.

LEVEL 1

PROJECT 8

Printing and Packaging

OBJECTIVES

In this project, you learn how to

- Set up the proper driver and print settings
- Proof a color document for printing on a color or black-and-white printer
- Tile and scale oversized documents
- Become familiar with printer's marks
- Set the Print dialog box options
- Package documents for service providers

WHY WOULD I DO THIS?

Chances are, you successfully printed a document in Project 1. In this project, you learn how to set up to print a variety of documents. As you build a document, you typically need to print and review numerous drafts. After you finalize the content and layout, you either print the document or prepare it for a service provider for imaging to film or printing plates. Even documents designed for the Web need to be printed so they can be proofed, reviewed, or referenced.

If your document is larger than the paper size your printer can accommodate, or if you want to proof specifications for commercial printing (such as bleed, trim, and color), you can adjust some of the print settings to produce the output you need. When you're ready to hand off the file to a service provider, you can use InDesign's Package feature to simplify the process and ensure the service provider receives all the necessary components to image your InDesign file successfully.

In addition, you can print thumbnails of the pages of your document, so you have a visual preview of the entire document in just a few pages. You can also print your master pages and show objects that normally do not print, which can be useful references when you create a template. You can actually sit down with the template and measure it, to make sure it is accurate.

Setting Up to Print

Before printing to a desktop printer connected to your computer, you need to do some document and system preparation. InDesign creates PostScript files suitable for high-end commercial printing, so you must have a PostScript printer driver installed on your computer. Although some non-PostScript printers can output InDesign pages, these types of printers aren't suitable for high-quality reproduction; some printing features and document elements, such as EPS files, do not print well — if at all.

If you don't have a suitable printer, you can create portable PostScript files, and then move them to another computer that is connected to a suitable printer. As an alternative, you can export one or more pages of an InDesign document to Acrobat PDF files and print those elsewhere. These advanced functions are discussed in *Essentials for Design: InDesign Level 2.*

Adobe provides its own PostScript drivers on the InDesign installation CD. Most operating systems include their own PostScript drivers; but to obtain the greatest functionality from InDesign, we recommend that you install and use the Adobe PostScript driver appropriate for your computer's operating system.

In addition to the printer driver, InDesign requires that the appropriate ***PostScript Printer Description (PPD)*** file is available. The "appropriate" PPD file is the one that matches the printer you're using. Macintosh users choose the PPD in the Print Center when setting up a new printer. Windows users can add a printer through the Add Printer wizard, or by running the Adobe PS PostScript driver installation utility. On the Macintosh, PPDs are generally located at Library>Printers>PPD>Contents>Resources>en.lproj. Under Windows XP, PPDs are generally located at C:\Win2kMS.

Once the PostScript driver and the PPD file are correctly installed, you're ready to prepare the specific document. See your operating system's documentation for printer driver installation instructions.

The print functions are standardized across both Macintosh and Windows platforms. The example shown in Figure 8.1 was created on the Macintosh; but aside from cosmetic appearances, there is almost no difference between the Print dialog box on the Macintosh and on Windows.

VISUAL SUMMARY

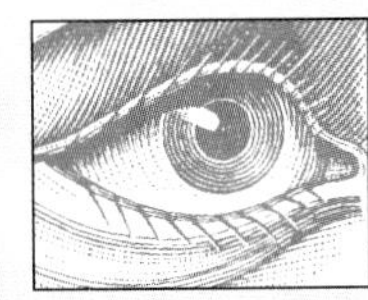

Printing documents from InDesign is a relatively straightforward procedure. You do, however, have several options that come into play when printing large images, spreads (two adjoining pages), or when printing to film. In addition, you can manage your printing preferences.

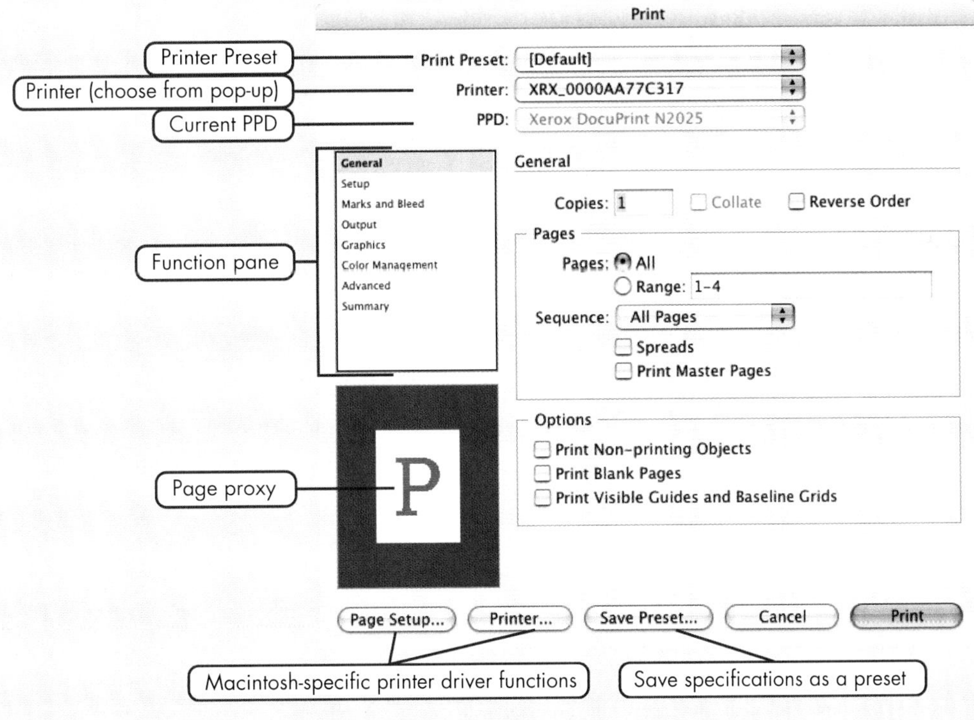

FIGURE 8.1

- The ***Printer Preset menu*** lists available printer styles; you can click the Save Preset button at the bottom of the dialog box to save your choice. Printer presets are useful when there is a specific output format that you use frequently, or if you use different formats with different output devices, such as a color printer and a black-and-white printer.

- The ***Printer menu*** shows all currently available printers installed on your computer. If you prefer to create a PostScript file instead of actually printing the job, you can choose PostScript File from this menu.

- The ***PPD menu*** is only active if you choose PostScript File from the Printer pop-up menu. If you select an actual printer, the PPD pop-up is grayed-out and unavailable. You need to select a new PPD (Macintosh) or re-install the printer (Windows) to change the PPD.
- The ***function pane*** is a list of all available output options. A different pane of options appears in the dialog box, depending on the function you choose from this list.
- The ***page proxy*** shows a miniature representation of a page of the current document. It reflects the orientation and sizing of the page relative to the selected paper size and orientation of the output device.
- The ***OS-specific buttons*** (Macintosh: Page Setup and Printer; Windows: Setup) should not be used to set printer parameters. The settings you make in the InDesign Print dialog box generally override the settings in the dialog boxes accessed by these buttons.
- If you have a printer that prints tabloid (or A3) paper, you can print letter- or legal-size documents that have bleeds, and trim back the pages to the edges of their finished size, retaining the true bleed. At some point, however, you might need to send an oversized document to a printer that cannot handle larger paper sizes. There are two options to help you, depending on what quality you need to proof: you can use tiling or scaling.

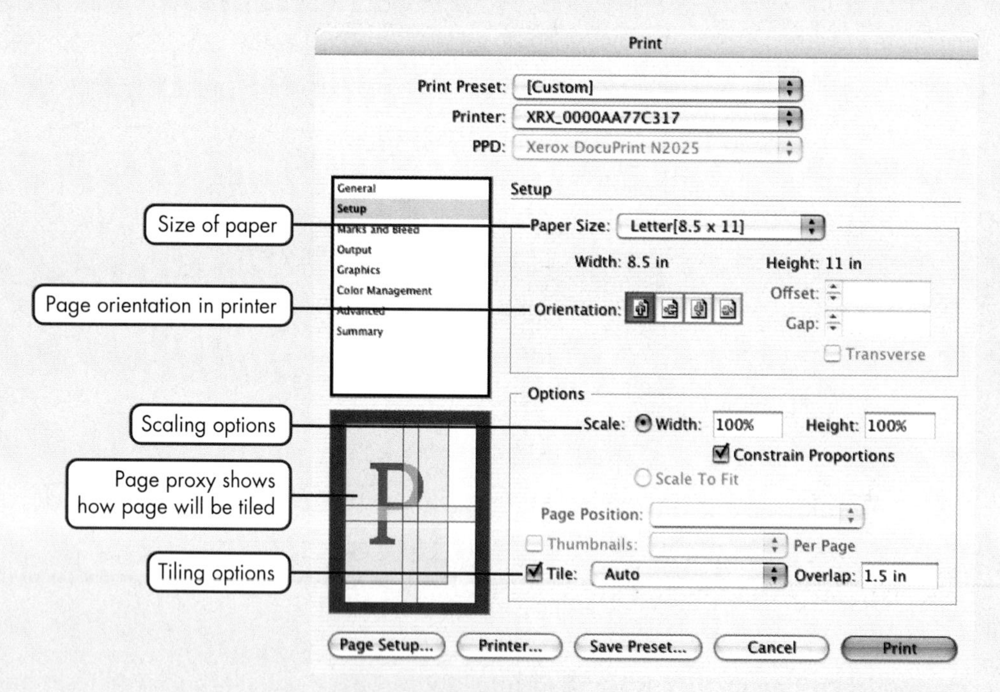

FIGURE 8.2

Tiling crops blocks of the oversized document page and prints the sections onto several sheets of paper. Once printed, you have a full-size proof that you can cut out of the different sheets, assemble, and tape together.

When proofing at exact size is not a critical factor, you can use scaling. The ***Scaling*** option of the Print dialog box reduces the size of the document, allowing more of the image to print on the sheet. Elements in the document are proportionally sized, but are not true to the finished size. This is sufficient for a general overview of the page, but you should always print your final proofs at 100%.

Printer's marks are one of the keys to successful proofing. These include trim, bleed, and registration marks, as well as file and color information. You can also include a slug, which is information about the job that is more detailed than the document can automatically provide. All this information is printed outside the page margins. InDesign can automatically print five kinds of printer's marks to ensure that the commercial printer has the proper instructions to successfully reproduce your document.

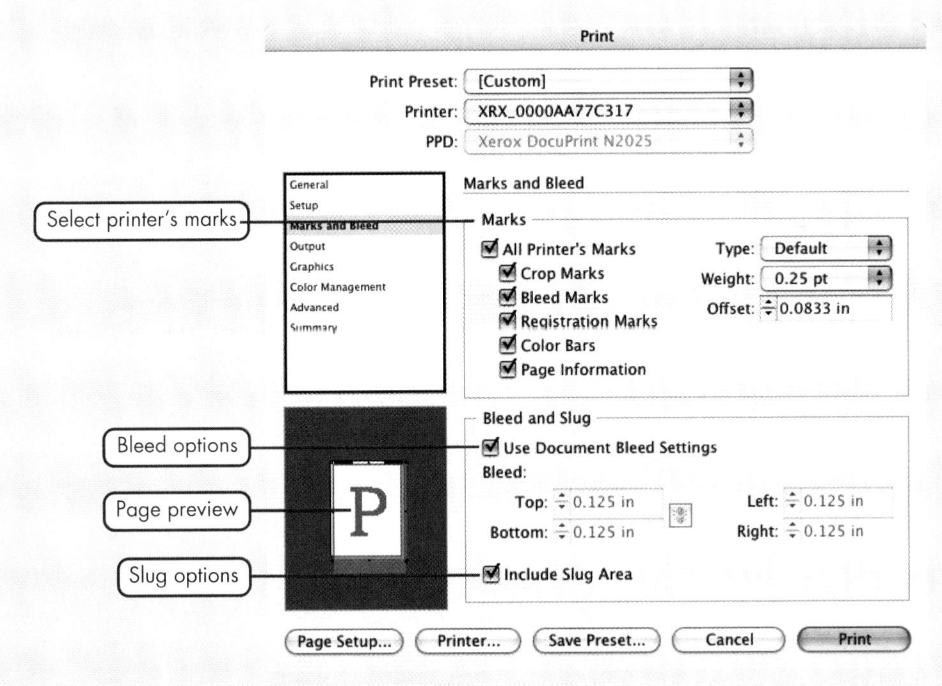

FIGURE 8.3

Bleed and slug areas are defined in Preferences, as we discussed earlier in this book. If ink is to print to the edge of the page, the image must actually extend (bleed) beyond the page boundaries. Your printer will tell you how much bleed he prefers, but it should be at least 0.125 inch. A slug is information about the job that appears on the printed sheet, but is trimmed off the final document.

You will often export a document to PDF, whether you are going to send it to a client as a proof, display it on the Web, or use it as the format to send the file to the service provider. PDF is a rich document format that is discussed in more depth in *Essentials for Design: InDesign Level 2*; however, Adobe includes a number of presets that are, for the most part, quite adequate for your needs. You explore and use the presets to export PDF documents in this project.

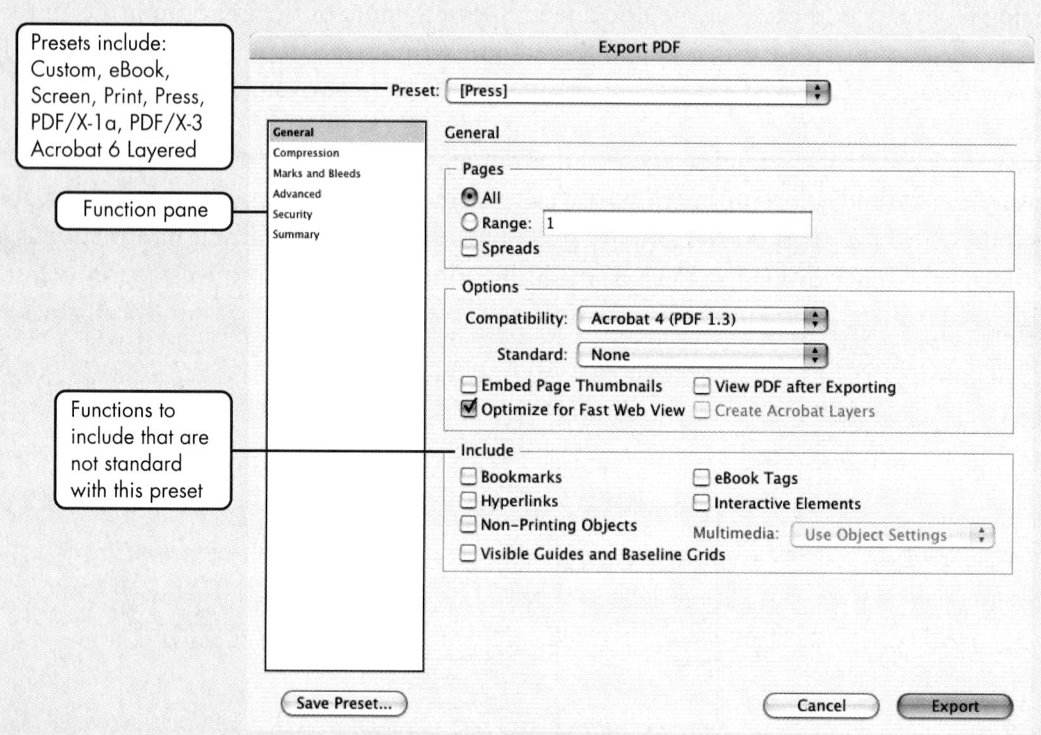

FIGURE 8.4

When everyone has approved the proof of your document, you will probably send the files to another company for final output. This can involve creating high-resolution film or plates for a press run, or using your document files to print the job digitally on a high-speed printer or a digital color press. Service providers use their own equipment, computers, and networks to produce this output — they do not have access to the files that you used to create the job, unless you supply them. In addition to the InDesign file itself, service providers need all external files used to create the document, including the fonts used in the page-layout document and in imported EPS files, the EPS files themselves, and all other imported graphic files not embedded in the document. Ensuring that all necessary components are given to the service provider is called ***packaging*** the document.

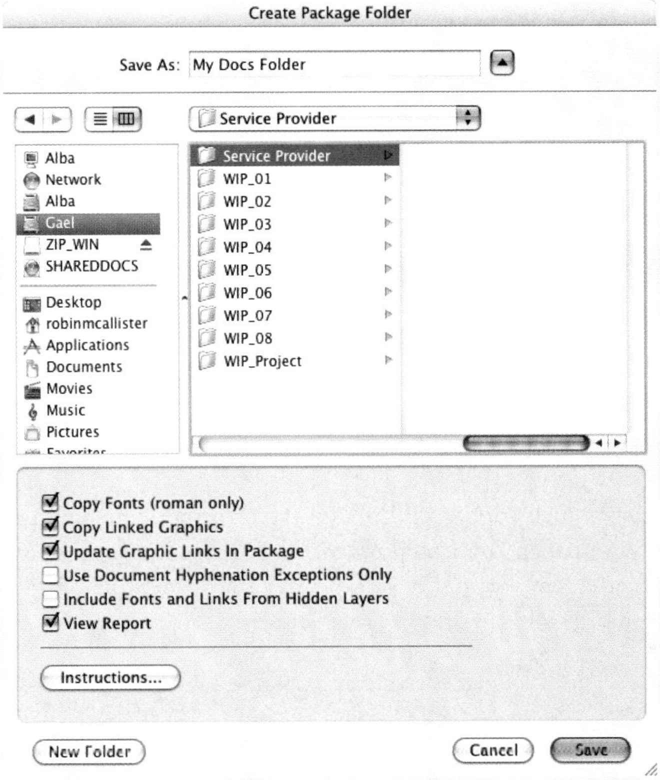

FIGURE 8.5

From printing to your desktop printer, to sending proofs around the office or around the world, to packaging your documents for a service provider, you will often use InDesign's printing options. In this project, you learn the basics of printing, proofing, and packaging.

LESSON 1 Setting Up to Print

Everyone's printing situation is different, and each job has its own specifications — from one-color ink to four-color process, or printing with additional inks and varnishes. The following real-life printing situation gives you a feeling for the entire printing process.

Faire Isles Trading Company sends a flyer featuring monthly specials to its customer list. Sometimes, the special product is an overstock item; at other times, Faire Isles obtains some special pricing that they pass along to their customers. This process-color (CMYK) brochure will be printed front and back, trimmed to letter size. Most of the press run will be folded for insertion into envelopes; the balance will be held in the store as flat sheets to hand out to customers. You will send a composite of the file to your desktop printer to proof copy, placement, and the general design of the piece.

While you can ***soft proof*** the document on your computer monitor, you usually get a better feel for the piece when you handle an actual sheet of paper. In addition, while the spell-checker allows you to read and proof text on the screen, you often do a better job of catching errors when you proofread from paper. Printing a proof is a critical step in the process of producing documents.

Prepare a File for Printing (All Operating Systems)

1. **Open special_flyer.indd from the Project_08 folder.**

2. **Open the Links palette (Window>Links, or Command/Control-Shift-D). Scroll through the palette to view the links.**

   You should not see any symbols indicating broken or modified links. If you see these symbols, you need to re-link before you print.

3. **Choose File>Print (or press Command/Control-P) to show the General pane of the Print dialog box.**

   Here, you can specify which pages to print, and the printing sequence. You can also choose to print spreads on one sheet of paper. You would probably scale the output to fit a spread on the sheet, unless the spread is half-letter size, or you have a printer that can print on tabloid-size sheets of paper. InDesign defaults to printing all pages in the document.

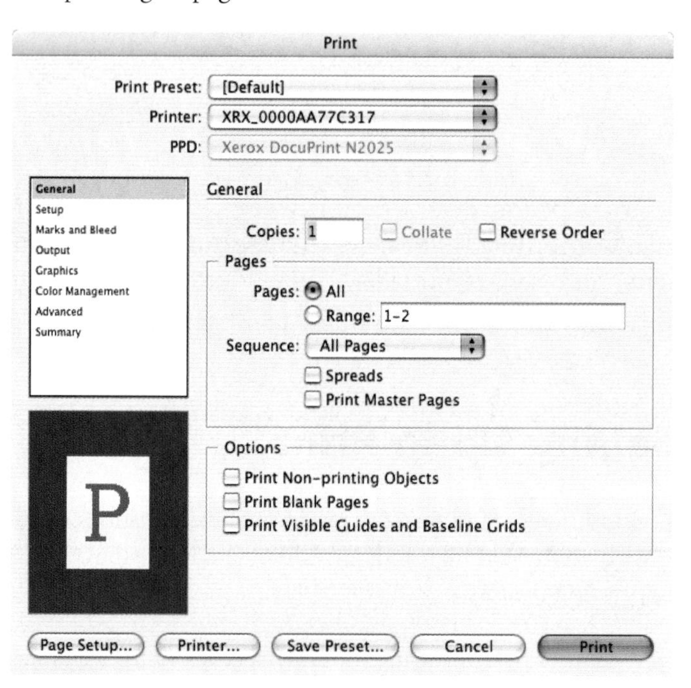

FIGURE 8.6

4. **Click Setup in the function pane (the list on the left) to apply the document's size and orientation to the print job. Change the Paper Size to Letter Extra, Tabloid, A3, or 11 × 17, if your printer supports these sizes. If your printer doesn't support these larger paper sizes, leave the**

paper size set to Letter and click the Scale to Fit button. Choose Centered (the default) in the Page Position menu.

The Page Position option is not available if you clicked Scale to Fit.

Although the document is letter-size, it requires a bleed and printer's marks, so you need to choose a paper size that provides enough room to print these marks.

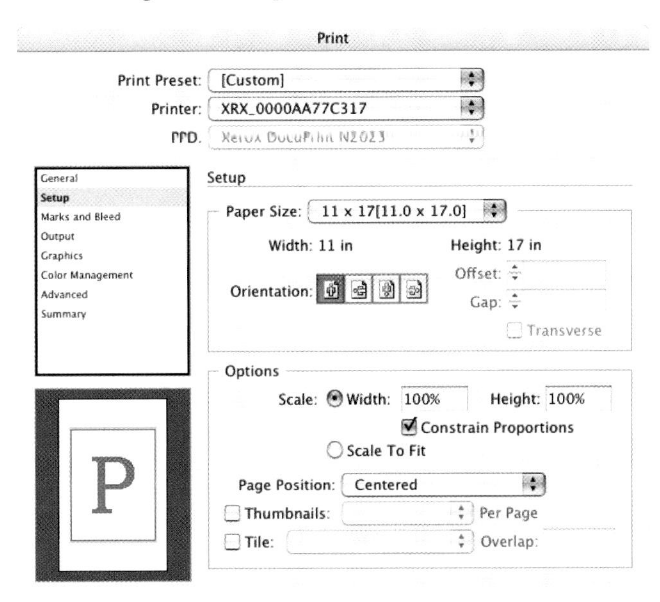

FIGURE 8.7

5 **Click Marks and Bleeds in the function pane. Click the All Printer's Marks check box. If it is not already selected, check the Use Document Bleed Settings box.**

If you chose a custom paper size and used the Auto width and height function, the size changes to accommodate the marks and bleed settings.

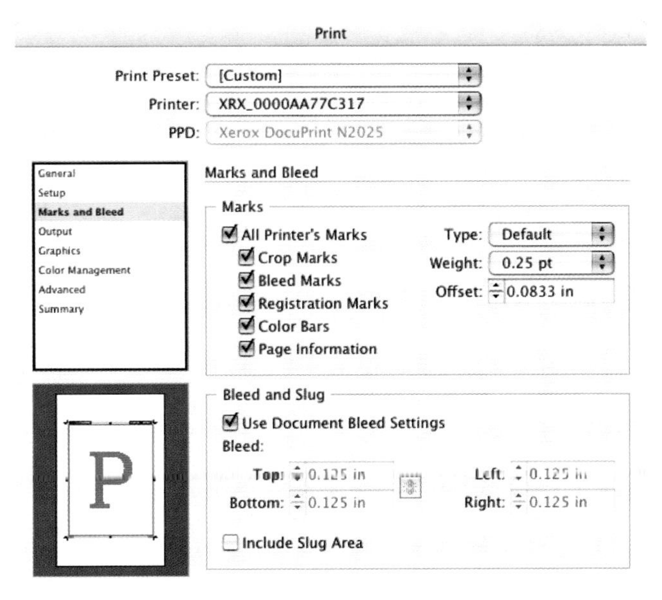

FIGURE 8.8

6 **Click Output in the function pane. Choose the appropriate color from the Color menu.**

If you have a black-and-white printer, choose Composite Gray. If you have a non-PostScript inkjet printer, choose Composite RGB. If you have a PostScript color printer, choose Composite CMYK. You can click the Text as Black check box to print all text in the document as black, which is helpful when printing proofs of colored text to a black-and-white printer.

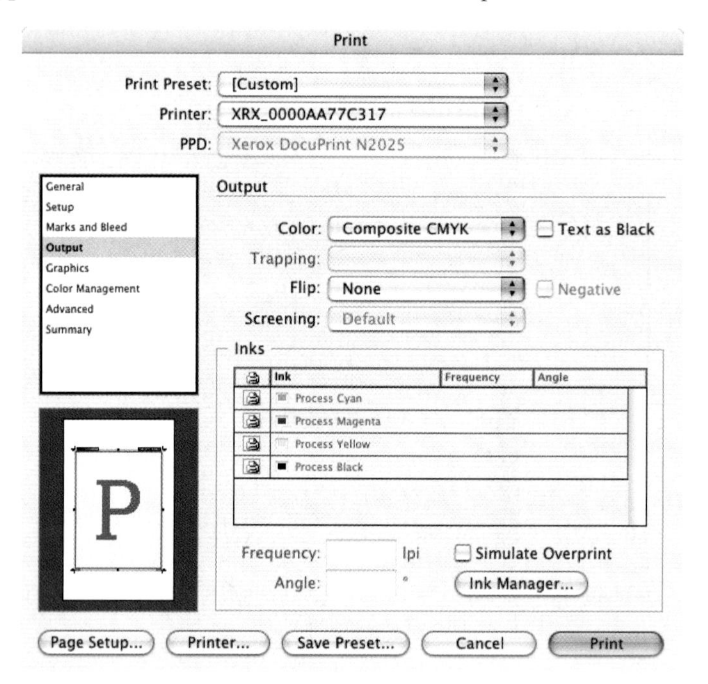

FIGURE 8.9

7 **Click Graphics in the function pane. You shouldn't need to change any of these settings.**

The data should be sent as Optimized Subsampling. If the file were being sent to a high-resolution imagesetter, all data would be sent. Optimized Subsampling sends just enough data to achieve the best image your printer can produce.

To Extend Your Knowledge...

PRINTER REQUIREMENTS FOR PROOFS

Usually, the printer asks you to provide an actual-size proof with no printer's marks; but sometimes he may ask for a color-separated version, especially if you are using spot inks. This eliminates the possibility of costly errors.

You should never apply scaling when printing the final version of your document. Make sure scaling is turned off before you make the final prints, and before you save the file and send it to your service provider.

Accept the default to download the complete font set. You would choose to subset fonts if you had used only one or two characters from a font set, such as an ornament. In addition, you should download PPD fonts; otherwise, even though they reside in your printer, the metrics may not exactly match those in the printer.

Depending on your printer and how it's connected to your computer or network, the value in the PostScript menu is either Level 2 or Level 3. This value is derived from the PPD. The Data Format is either Binary or ASCII. If your printer supports binary data, then Binary is the default; otherwise, ASCII is the default. You can't change this setting, because it, too, is derived from the PPD.

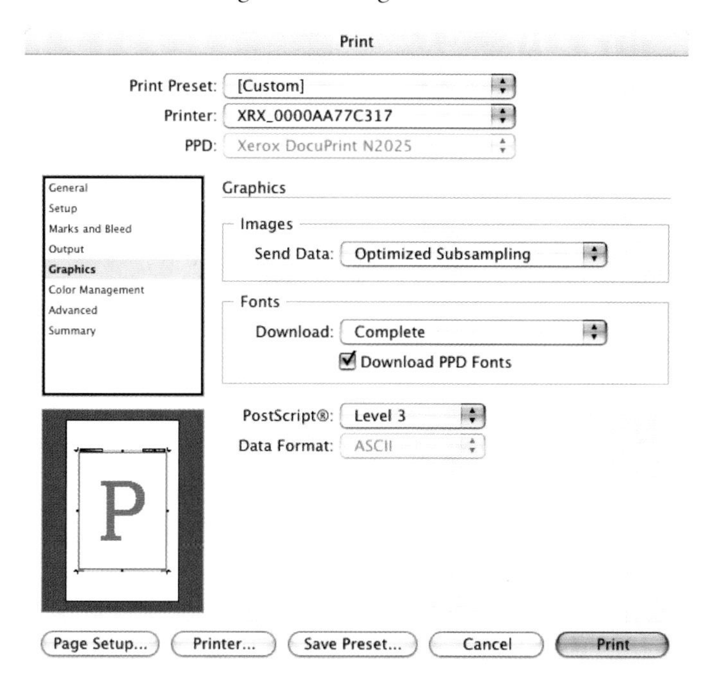

FIGURE 8.10

8 **Click Summary in the function pane. Review the Summary pane, and then click the Print button.**

The Summary pane provides a summary of all the print parameters you selected. InDesign provides information about the print process while the file downloads. In a few minutes, two pages should come out of your printer. Color Management and Advanced functions are discussed in detail in *Essentials for Design: InDesign Level 2.*

9 **Examine the output.**

Note the printer's marks, which include the trim (cutting) marks, the bleed area marks, and some document information. There are also color bars, which are used for quality control when the job is on press, as well as registration marks, which are used on press to ensure that all separations are in proper alignment.

10 **Save the document to your WIP_08 folder under the same name. Close the file.**

LESSON 2 Printing Oversized Documents

Even when documents exceed the size of your printer, you still need to provide a to-size proof for the printer; this is the best way to remove the chance of errors. When a printer reviews your proof, he will often place it right next to a proof made from the film negative he will use to make the printing plate. If the two proofs do not match exactly, he will undoubtedly call you to discuss the situation. So remember: even if you are producing a 9 × 12-inch brochure on your letter-size printer, you should not scale the document to fit; spend the extra time producing a to-size proof.

You can print an oversized document in a scaled-down version to check spatial relationships and/or to proofread it. When you produce the final proof for the printer, you will have two or more sheets of paper that you taped together to create a to-size proof.

Tile and Print an Oversized Document

1 **Open kindergarten.indd from the Project_08 folder.**

2 **Choose File>Print.**

In the General pane of the Print dialog box, the page proxy (lower-left corner) shows you that the document is too large to print on the default paper size of your current printer.

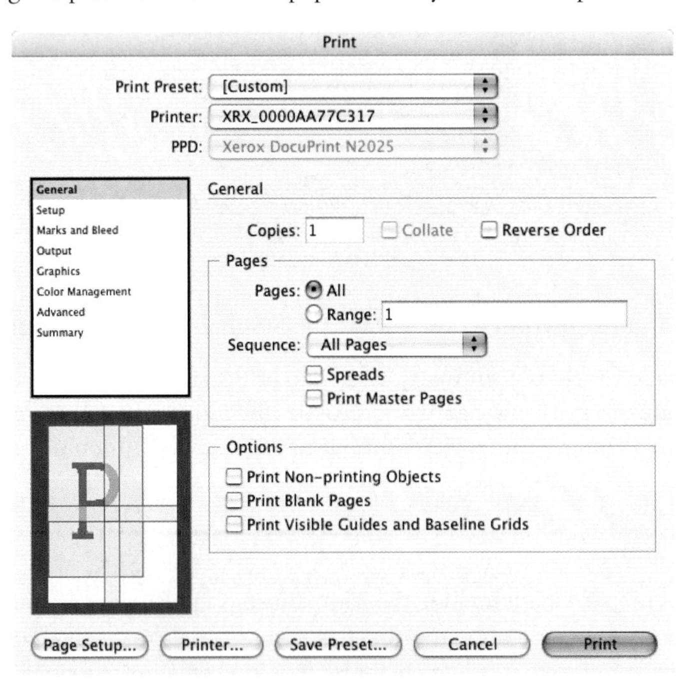

FIGURE 8.11

3 **Click Setup in the function pane. In the Setup pane, choose Letter from the Paper Size menu, if it is not already selected. In the Options section, click the Tile button. Leave the Tile menu set to Auto. Use the default Overlap of 1.5 in.**

The overlap determines how much of the image intersects on adjoining sheets as the page is divided into tiles. If the document contained a lot of space with large gaps between type or images, the overlap would be greater to match the pieces more accurately. Note how the page proxy shows the tiles and overlap.

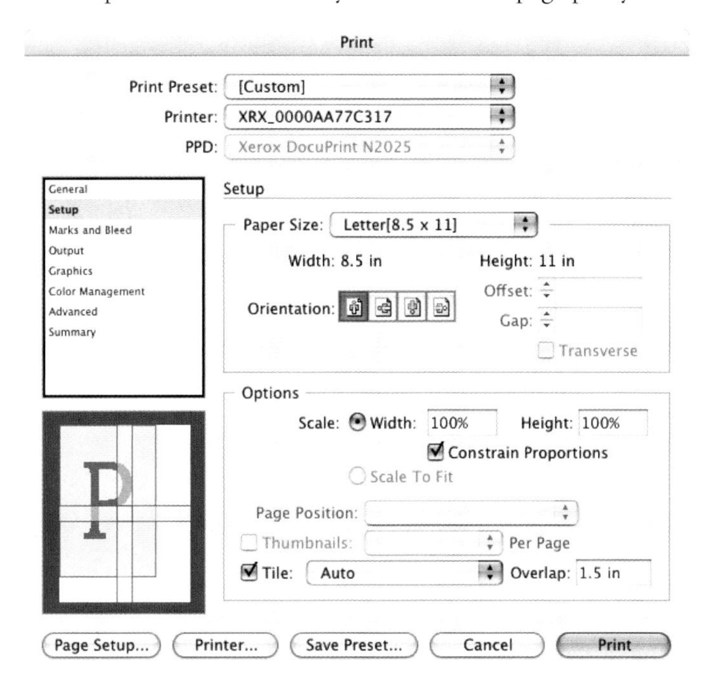

FIGURE 8.12

4 **Choose Graphics from the function pane. In the Graphics pane, be sure Optimized Subsampling is selected in the Send Data menu.**

This option speeds printing and can avoid a printer error. If you get a printer error when using Optimized Subsampling, choose Proxy from the Send Data menu to send a low-resolution version of the image.

5 **Click Print.**

When the pages come out of the printer, use a pair of scissors to cut out the image pieces, and tape them together like a jigsaw puzzle to accurately reproduce the full image of the page.

6 **Close the document without saving.**

To Extend Your Knowledge...

AUTO AND MANUAL TILING

The Auto tiling option centers the page image among the tiled sheets, automatically adjusts the sheet overlap, and prints as many sheets as necessary to accommodate the document's actual size. The Manual tiling option allows you to print a portion of a large page. You simply drag the zero-point crosshair from the rulers to the upper-left corner of the area you want to print. In the Scale and Fit options of the Print dialog box, you choose Manual and designate the overlap distance.

LESSON 3 Proofing with PDFs

PDF (Portable Document Format) is the de facto standard for proofing documents on-screen, as well as for electronically transmitting documents to clients for proofing. All the images and fonts are embedded in a PDF file in a highly compressed format, so PDF is ideal for submitting documents to clients at remote locations. The client needs only to view the single file, which is seen correctly on screen or prints properly on a desktop printer, even if the client does not possess the fonts used to create the document.

Export PDFs for Proofing

1 Open sock_hop.indd from the Project_08 folder.

This document could be used as an ad, or it could be distributed as a flyer, either printed or photocopied. Before you do anything to the file, however, you need to get your client's approval on the proof.

2 Choose File>Export. Choose your WIP_08 folder. Click Save.

The Export PDF dialog box appears.

3 Choose the Screen preset and click the View PDF after Exporting button.

The preset changes to Custom. InDesign includes seven standard export presets. You can also create your own, if you have specific needs. For the most part, however, the presets are fine. If you click the View PDF after Exporting button, Acrobat Reader is launched and the file is opened when the export is completed.

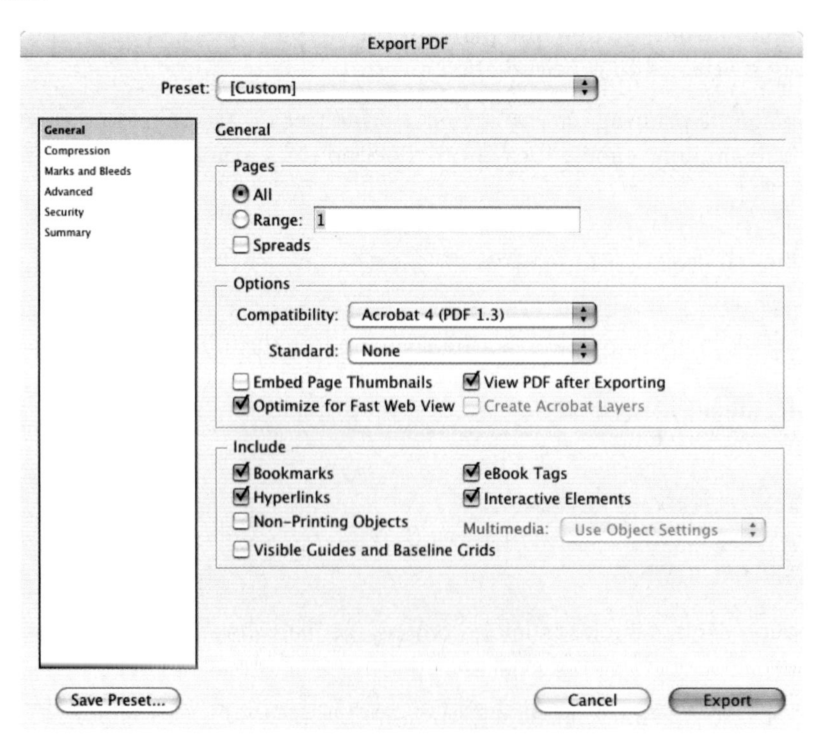

FIGURE 8.13

4 **Click Compression in the function pane.**

The Compression menu shows downsampling values for images. ***Downsampling*** reduces the number of pixels per inch, and is performed when the images have substantially more resolution than necessary. Color and grayscale images are downsampled to 72 pixels per inch (the number of pixels per inch normally used on Web pages), and monochrome (bitmap) images are downsampled to 300 pixels per inch. This removes excess data and is adequate for proofing documents.

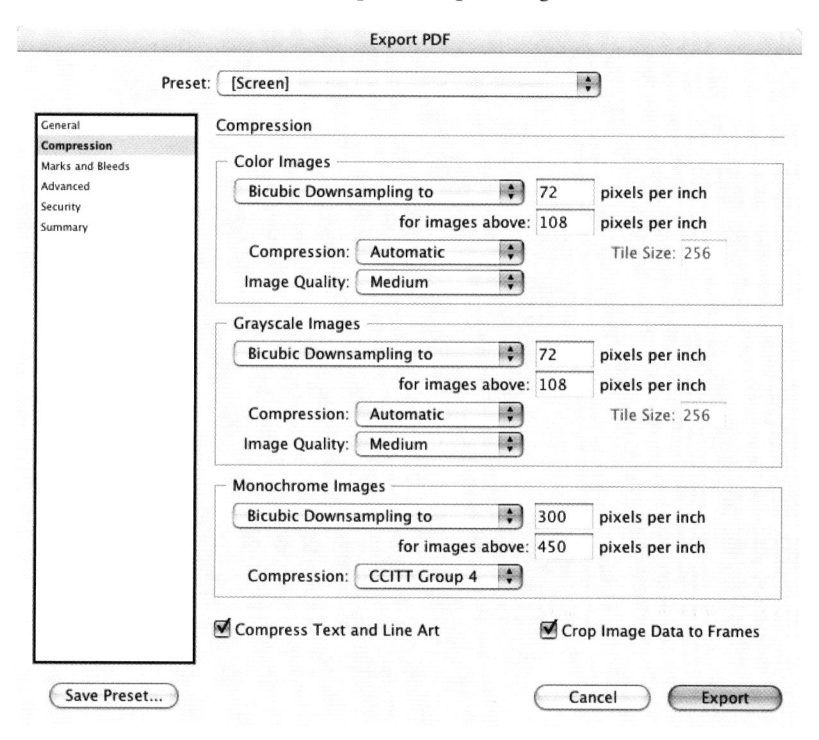

FIGURE 8.14

5 **Click Marks and Bleeds in the function pane. Ensure that they are turned off.**

You're proofing this document on screen, so these features are not necessary.

6 **Click Summary in the function pane.**

In the Summary pane, you can check all the specifications before exporting the file. You could also save the preset if you were to use this specification again.

7 **Click Export.**

The page you are exporting has transparency, so you receive the following warning.

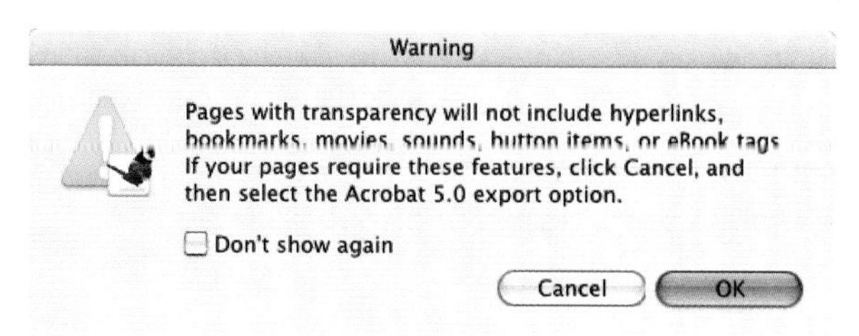

FIGURE 8.15

8 **Click OK to dismiss the warning.**

A second warning appears.

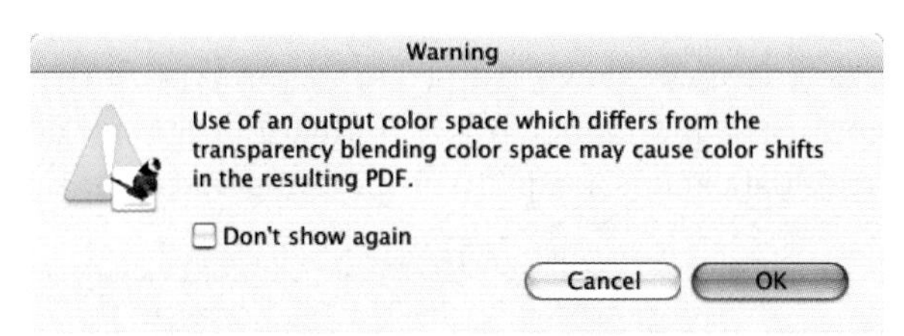

FIGURE 8.16

9 **Click OK to dismiss the warning.**

The file exports to your WIP_08 folder. Adobe Acrobat Reader launches and displays your PDF.

10 **Leave the file open for the next exercise.**

To Extend Your Knowledge...

PRINTER'S MARKS

Printer's marks provide information about your document; but more important, they help the printer control the quality of the final output. The accuracy of colors can be measured, and the all-important alignment of printing plates can be determined from these marks. Printer's marks include:

Crop Marks. These short lines outside the image area indicate where to trim or cut the sheet to its final size.

Bleed Marks. These short perpendicular lines indicate the edge of the image area, including ink that prints beyond the final trim size.

Registration Marks. These marks are small concentric circles intersected by a crosshair. These fine lines (the default is 0.25 pt, or 1/288 inch) are used to precisely align color separations, ensuring that elements printed in different inks fit and appear as designed. These marks can also be used to overlay different versions on the same base design, such as different names printed in identical positions alongside the art and address of a preprinted business card.

Color Bars. This row of small squares reproduces different tints and tint combinations of ink colors. The value and consistency of these color patches is measured during a press run with an instrument called a densitometer to establish and maintain consistent print reproduction.

Page Information. This information is printed outside the image area at the bottom of the page. InDesign automatically prints the file name, the date and time the page was printed, and the page number of the image. If you are printing separations, InDesign also prints the name of the ink intended for each separation (for example, Cyan, Magenta, or PANTONE 231).

LESSON 4 Preparing PDF for a Print Workflow

PDF is the current standard for submitting ads for many publications. It is used as the primary imaging workflow in some manufacturing plants, as well. In this lesson, you learn the basics of exporting files to PDF in preparation for printing on a press.

When used in a printing workflow, PDF is essentially a pre-processed PostScript file. All the necessary components are included in the file, which prints more quickly than a file printed from the originating publishing program. We provide an in-depth discussion about creating PDF files in *Essentials for Design: InDesign Level 2.*

Export PDFs for Press

1 **In the open file, choose File>Export. Choose your WIP_08 folder. Click Save.**

2 **Choose the Press preset.**

The Press pane opens with the standard settings.

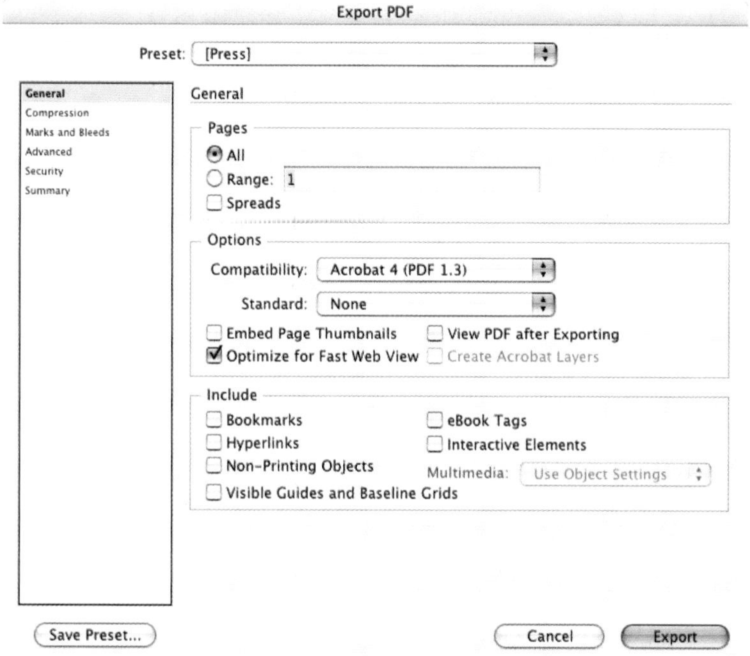

FIGURE 8.17

3 **Click Compression in the function pane.**

Note that the pixels per inch are substantially higher than when exporting for proofing.

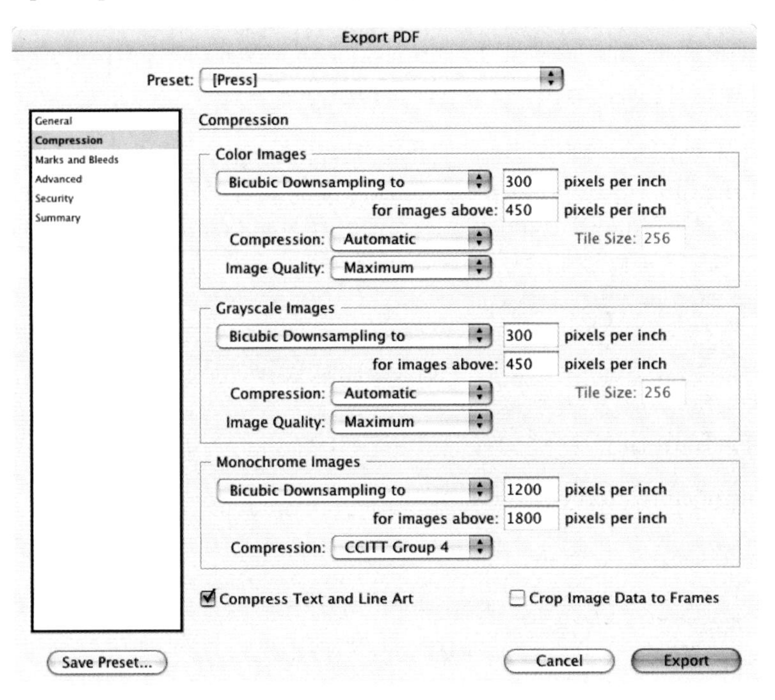

FIGURE 8.18

4 **Click Marks and Bleeds in the function pane.**

You're going to print this as a flyer, so turn on the All Printer's Marks and Bleed options. Note that the preset changes to Custom.

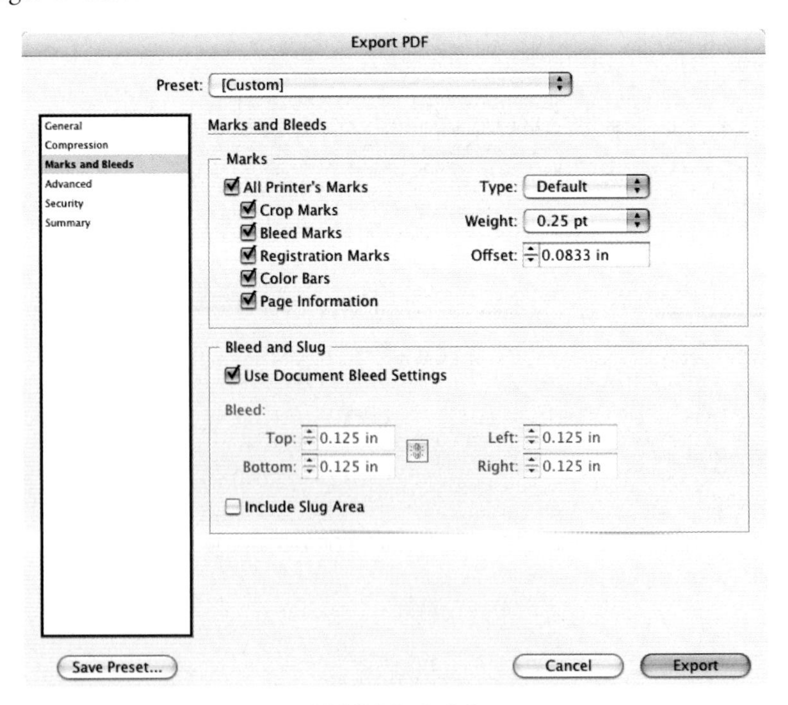

FIGURE 8.19

5 **Click Summary in the function pane.**

In the Summary pane, you can check all the specifications before exporting the file.

6 **Click Export.**

The file exports to your WIP_08 folder.

7 **Close the file.**

LESSON 5 Preflight a Document

Before you send your document to the printer or another graphic arts service provider (***GASP***) to be printed, you must preflight the document to ensure it is ready for printing in every respect — all elements must be there, and the elements must be in the proper format.

Preflighting is simply going through an electronic checklist to ensure that there are no surprises when the service provider prints your file. The last thing you want to hear is that your document would have been printed on last night's third shift, except for the bad image on page three. You were unavailable at that time of night, so the pressman pulled the job. Now, you have to wait two days until there is room in the printer's schedule to accommodate your job. A scenario such as this could be disastrous to both you and your client.

Preflight a Document

1 **Open special_flyer.indd from the Project_08 folder.**

This document includes a number of images and several fonts. You would not want to manually keep track of them, so you can let InDesign do the job for you.

2 **Check both pages to ensure that no fonts are missing.**

Missing fonts would appear highlighted in pink. You can also use the Type>Find Font command to ensure that no fonts are missing.

3 **Check the Links palette to ensure that all linked graphics are in place and have not been modified.**

The Links palette is available from Window>Links, or by pressing Command/Control-Shift-D.

4 **Choose File>Preflight.**

InDesign checks all the images and ensures that all the fonts are in place. You receive the following warning, telling you there are no problems with the document except that there is one RGB image, which will print improperly.

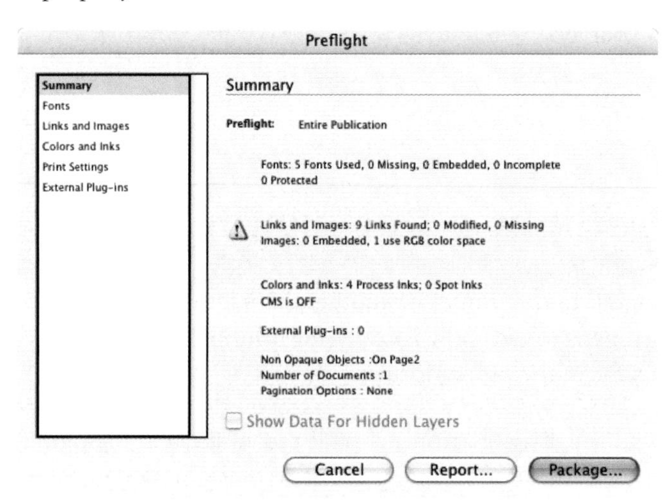

FIGURE 8.20

5 **Click Links and Images in the function pane.**

Fairy.tif is the problem image. It is highlighted, and you see its format is RGB. You need to exchange this image for a CMYK image.

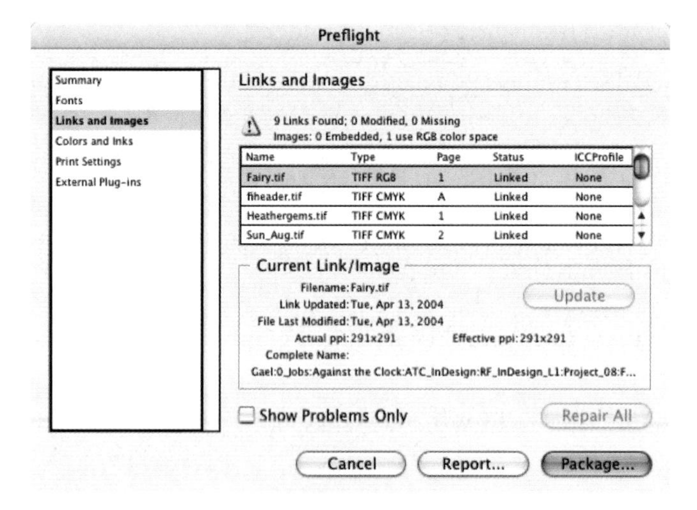

FIGURE 8.21

6 **Click Cancel.**

7 **On Page 1 of the InDesign document, and use the Direct Selection tool to click the Fairy.tif image. Place Fairy_CMYK.tif. Be sure the Replace Selected Item button is checked.**

This replaces the RGB fairy with the CMYK version of the image.

8 **Save the document. Re-run your preflight.**

The document passes preflight.

9 **Click Cancel. Leave the document open for the next lesson.**

LESSON 6 Package a Document

After your document passes preflight and you are confident that it is ready to go to the GASP to be imaged to film (or printed directly to press), you need to gather together all the elements in the file — including linked images and fonts. While your service provider probably has the fonts you use, you should include your fonts just in case the service provider has a different version; if that is the case, the font metrics may vary.

Anytime you send an InDesign document outside your network for printing or editing, it should be packaged to ensure that all the elements are included. If a document is not packaged using InDesign's packaging option, you may forget to include an element when you send it to the printer. This can be especially true when you reproduce a new version of a document that includes a few changes to the original. While you may remember each and every graphic in a document you created yesterday, you may be less confident when you make an address change to a brochure you created six months ago.

In the previous exercise, you probably noticed that you could have simply clicked the Package button when you were done preflighting. Instead, you're going to complete the entire packaging process.

Package a Document

1 **In the open special_flyer.indd, check both pages to ensure that no fonts are missing.**

2 **Check the Links palette to ensure that all linked graphics are in place and have not been modified.**

3 **Choose File>Package. If you made any modifications to the file, you receive a message that says, "Publication must be saved before continuing. Save it now." If you receive this message, save the file to your WIP_08 folder.**

This function runs the preflight process that you ran in the previous lesson. If there's anything amiss, such as a lost image link, or an image in the RGB color space, the file is not ready to package and a warning appears. Always check to see what is wrong with the file when you receive a warning.

The Printing Instructions dialog box appears.

4 **Fill in your name, contact information, and the following instructions:**

Qty:	5,000, 4/4, 80 lb., Matte Coated Text
Bleed:	0.125 in
Trim:	8.5 × 11, Letter-fold 4,000, 1,000 flat

The text does not automatically wrap.

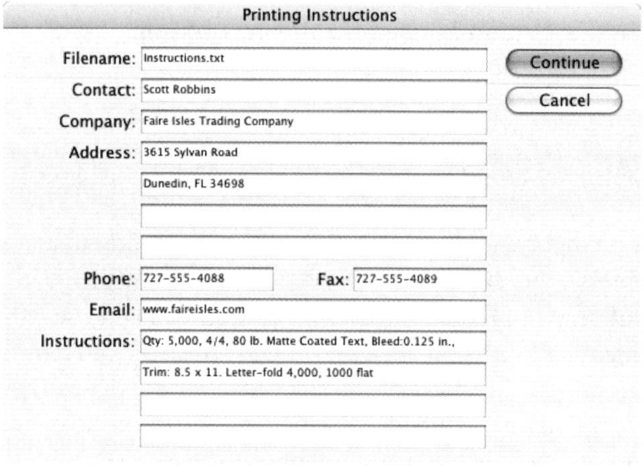

Printing Instructions

Filename: Instructions.txt
Contact: Scott Robbins
Company: Faire Isles Trading Company
Address: 3615 Sylvan Road
Dunedin, FL 34698
Phone: 727-555-4088 Fax: 727-555-4089
Email: www.faireisles.com
Instructions: Qty: 5,000, 4/4, 80 lb. Matte Coated Text, Bleed:0.125 in.,
Trim: 8.5 x 11. Letter-fold 4,000, 1000 flat
Continue
Cancel

FIGURE 8.22

5 **Click Continue.**

The Create Package Folder dialog box asks you where to copy the folder that contains the package components. You can store the packaged document anywhere, including on removable media.

6 **Make a new folder within your WIP_08 folder. Name it "To GASP". Open the new folder.**

The folder containing the packaged files is placed inside this new folder. By default, it has the same name as the document, but you can rename it.

7 **Check View Report, and then click the Save/Package button.**

The first three boxes are checked by default. The third box, Update Graphic Links in Package, is particularly important. If it is not checked, InDesign looks for the graphics in their original locations, which do not exist on the service provider's computer.

FIGURE 8.23

8 **Read the Font Alert message. Click OK.**

Font vendors' licensing agreements vary widely with regard to copying fonts for imaging at other locations. Some vendors prohibit it, and some allow a one-time use.

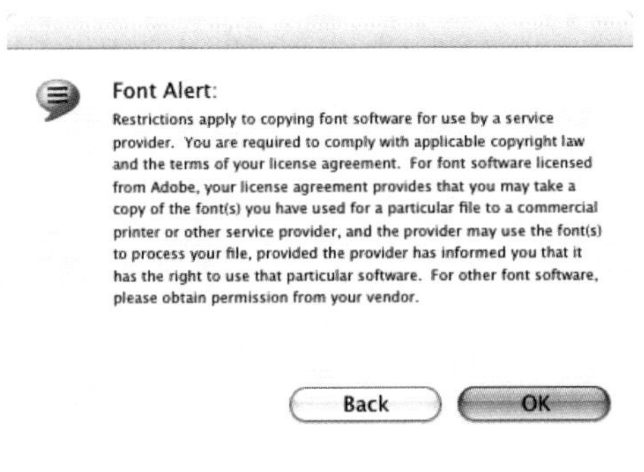

FIGURE 8.24

A progress bar displays while the files are copied and packaged with the document and instructions. The instructions file opens in your system's default text editor. The report contains the information you entered in the Printing Instructions dialog box, as well as a list of all fonts and colors used in the document and in imported files, link information, the print settings last used for the document, the status of InDesign's color management system, the presence of any applied transparency, and the files packaged in the folder.

9 **Review the report and print a copy. Quit the text editor. Go to the location where you saved the package and look at the content of the folder you made.**

The folder should contain two documents (the InDesign special_flyer.indd file, and the instructions.txt file) and two folders (Fonts and Links). The required printer and screen fonts used in the document are inside the Fonts folder. Entire font families are not copied; only the actual fonts used in the job are packaged. The Links folder includes several TIFF files. The To GASP folder is ready to deliver to a service provider that supports printing InDesign documents.

10 **Return to InDesign. Close the file without saving.**

To Extend Your Knowledge...

READ YOUR WARNINGS

If you receive a warning, do not simply click the Continue button. Click View Info and find out what issues are present. You may, for example, receive a warning that images are in the RGB color space; but if you are printing to a color copier that uses more than the standard CMYK inks, that may be preferable. Always check with your service provider to determine which color space is preferred.

SUMMARY

In this final project of the book, you learned to print files to a desktop printer, export to PDF, preflight a finished document, and collect all the elements of your document prior to submitting a job to a service provider. You set up and printed a document with printer's marks, and learned how/why those marks are used. You also tiled and printed an oversized document, and you packaged a job for delivery to an external service provider.

CAREERS IN DESIGN

DISTRIBUTING DOCUMENTS

As you discovered while reading this book, it takes both creative vision and technical expertise to design and create documents, ranging from business cards to multi-chapter publications — but the best document ever created is completely ineffective if it simply remains in the designer's computer.

In the past, when you were ready to present a comp to a client, you needed to enlist the services of a printer or other service provider who could prepare a proof photographically — and expensively. If the client ordered changes, another proof had to be prepared. This review process could take days to complete, especially if the client's office was a long distance from the designer or agency. Once the proof was approved, all parts of the document had to be delivered to the service provider for scanning, color separation, and combining into negatives prior to printing.

Today's process — while exacting — is much quicker and simpler. A PDF file is made in minutes (sometimes seconds), and can be transmitted just as quickly to a number of locations anywhere in the world. Approvals (and changes) can be made almost instantaneously, instead of wasting valuable time in transit. Hard-copy proofs can be made on an ink jet or laser printer and delivered to the printer along with the electronic file. The electronic file contains all the images in place, making image assembly (combining elements in the negatives) unnecessary — a process that used to take days can now be accomplished in hours.

Even though the process has changed and been streamlined, it remains essentially the same: the client still signs off on the job, and the designer still must deliver all elements to the service provider, which is why the packaging procedure is so important — it ensures that all elements are included when the document is delivered to the printer.

In addition to documents that are prepared for printing, the PDF file format is used to share documents throughout an organization. For example, a number of companies distribute their newsletters electronically. PDF files can also be posted on Web sites, making information available to virtually anyone.

KEY TERMS

Bleed marks
Color bars
Crop marks
Downsampling
Font metrics
GASP
Optimized Subsampling
Packaging
Page proxy
PPD
Preflight
Printer driver
Printer's marks
Registration marks
Scaling
Service provider
Soft proof
Tiling
Trim marks

CHECKING CONCEPTS AND TERMS

MULTIPLE CHOICE

Circle the letter of the correct answer for each of the following questions.

1. Why should you print to a PostScript printer?
  a. To get accurate color.
  b. To get high-quality reproduction.
  c. To achieve rich blacks.
  d. To print TIFF files.

2. What does a PPD do?
  a. It handles the download of the file to the printer.
  b. It ensures that all parts of a document are included.
  c. It gives InDesign information about the printer.
  d. It converts files for non-PostScript printers.

3. What is a printing spread?
  a. A range of consecutive pages.
  b. Right-hand pages.
  c. Non-consecutive pages.
  d. Pages printed with printer's marks.

4. When should you use a printer preset?
  a. When you frequently use a specific output format.
  b. When outputting to a PostScript printer.
  c. When outputting to a non-PostScript printer.
  d. When creating a PostScript file as output.

5. When should you tile a document?
  a. Whenever you need to see crop marks.
  b. When the whole document fits on one page of the paper in your printer.
  c. When you need to see a general overview of the page.
  d. When the document is too large to fit on one page of your printer's paper.

6. Which of the following is not a function of printer's marks?
  a. Date and time the page is printed.
  b. The job number.
  c. Color bars and bleed marks.
  d. Registration and crop marks.

7. When should you export a document to PDF?
  a. When it will be printed from InDesign.
  b. When you need to provide a color proof.
  c. When you are sending it to a remote client.
  d. When you need an HTML document.

8. Which of the PDF Print presets are you most likely to alter?
  a. Standards
  b. Compression
  c. Marks and Bleeds
  d. Security

9. When packaging a file for a service provider, ____________.
  a. all the files are included in the InDesign file
  b. you need to include all linked files
  c. you need to include only fonts included in EPS files
  d. you need to include all embedded files

10. When should you package a file for the service provider?
  a. Anytime you send it outside your network.
  b. When there are missing fonts.
  c. When there are missing or modified linked images.
  d. When it doesn't need to be preflighted.

DISCUSSION QUESTIONS

1. PDF is a ubiquitous file format that has many uses. Discuss the ways you can use this format in a production setting. Be creative in your uses of PDF.

2. Whether you package your document for a service provider, or you print it across your network, you have the same concerns: availability of files and fonts. Discuss how you can control the use of fonts and graphics within the network, as well as when you send files off the network.

SKILL DRILL

Skill Drills reinforce project skills. Each skill reinforced is the same, or nearly the same, as a skill presented in the lessons. Detailed instructions are provided in a step-by-step format. You must complete the Skill Drills in order.

1. Banks for Congress — Proof to Your Printer

This political flyer is typical of many jobs, from the perspective of what is required once the job is composed. The flyer is a 2-sided 8.5 × 11-inch document that bleeds on all four sides.

In this series of exercises, you print the job to your laser printer for a final proofing run-through. Then, you send it to the client to proof, and finally, send it to the service provider.

1. Open banks.indd from the Project_08 folder. Visually check both pages to ensure that no fonts are missing.
2. Check the Links palettes to ensure that all linked files are present and have not been modified.
3. Choose File>Print to open the Print dialog box.

   You're going to print to your laser printer so you can check positioning and proofread the document.
4. In the General pane, be sure the correct printer is selected, and that all pages are to be printed.
5. In the Setup pane, choose Letter as the Paper Size. The Scale should be set to 100%. The Orientation should be set to Portrait. The Tile button should not be checked.
6. In the Marks and Bleeds pane, nothing should be selected.

   If you select any bleeds, the printer will choose the edge of the bleed as the edge of the page, and your image will be improperly centered.
7. In the Output pane, select the appropriate color mode for your printer.
8. In the Graphics pane, be sure data is sent with Optimized Subsampling. Choose to download the complete font and download the PPDs.
9. Click Print.
10. Review the printed document.
11. Save the file and leave it open for the next exercise.

2. Banks for Congress — Proof to Client

As is so often the case with this type of job, the process must be completed in a hurry. Your client, who is several miles away, needs to proof the job so you can send it to the printer. The best solution is to send a viewable PDF file that the client can print on his desktop printer.

1. In the open document, choose File>Export.
2. With the Adobe PDF format active, choose your WIP_08 folder as the destination. Click Save.
3. In the General pane, choose the Print preset, ensure that all pages are selected, and choose View PDF After Exporting. Deselect all other options.
4. In the Compression pane, accept the defaults.
5. Marks and Bleeds should be deselected. Your client does not need them.
6. Click Export.
7. View the PDF document, and then close it. Leave the banks.indd file open for the next exercise.

3. Banks for Congress — Proof to Service Provider

Even though this is a letter-size document, it must be printed to an oversized printer to show bleed and trim marks. Assume that the maximum paper size available is letter-size. You need to provide a proof to the service provider at full size, including all printer's marks.

1. In the open document, press Command/Control-P to open the Print dialog box.
2. In the General pane, be sure the correct printer is selected. Choose All Pages.
3. In the Setup pane, set the Paper Size to Letter, the Orientation to Landscape, the Scale to 100%, and click Tile.

   Setting the orientation to landscape allows you to print two pages instead of four.
4. In the Marks and Bleed frame, select All Printer's Marks and Use Document Bleed Settings. Accept the default Weight and Offset.
5. In the Output frame, select the appropriate color mode for your printer.
6. Optimized Subsampling should be selected in the Graphics pane.
7. Click Print.
8. When the pages emerge from the printer, tape them together, and then review them.
9. Leave the document open for the next exercise.

4. Banks for Congress — Package for Service Provider

You're finally ready to send this document to the service provider for printing. Since you must deliver the proof along with the electronic file, you would normally save the document to a Zip disk or other removable medium. For the sake of this exercise, however, you save it into your WIP_08 folder.

1. In the open document, choose File>Package.
2. You may receive a message stating that the publication must be saved before continuing. If so, click Save.
3. The Printing Instructions pane appears; it contains the information from the previous document you packaged. In the Instructions section, make the following changes:

Job:	Banks for Congress 4-color Process
Qty:	60,000, 70 lb. Dull Coated Text
Bleed:	0.125 in.
Trim:	8.5 × 11, Letterfold 45,000, 15,000 flat

4. Click Continue.
5. Choose the To GASP folder you created earlier in the Create Package Folder dialog box. The same boxes you previously selected as options in this pane should be selected. Click Save/Package.
6. At the Font Alert, click OK.
7. InDesign packages your document, and your instructions appear in a text window.
8. Save and close the document. Close the text editor.

CHALLENGE

Challenge exercises expand on, or are somewhat related to, skills presented in the lessons. Each exercise provides a brief introduction, followed by instructions presented in a numbered-step format that are not as detailed as those in the Skill Drill exercises. You should complete these exercises in order.

1. Banks for Congress — Proof to Your Printer

Just as you're ready to call the messenger to send the Banks for Congress job to your service provider, you get a frantic call from the client's fiscal agent. They can't afford to print full-color flyers. You have to convert to a two-color job. Of course, the job has lost none of its urgency, so you have to burn some midnight oil to get it done on time. You call the printer and tell him the job will be on his doorstep before the midnight shift starts. After some frantic work, you're ready to begin the process of preparing for press — again.

1. Open banks_2color.indd from your Project_08 folder. Visually check the file.
2. Check the Links palette to ensure that all linked files are present and have not been modified.
3. Open the Print dialog box.
4. Be sure the correct printer is selected, and that all pages are to be printed.
5. Choose Letter as the Paper Size and set the Scale to 100%.
6. You aren't going to print any printer's marks or bleeds on this proof. You're just checking it to make sure you didn't damage the file in any way when you made your changes.
7. Select the appropriate color mode for your printer.
8. Be sure data is sent with Optimized Subsampling.
9. Print the document, and then review it.
10. Save the file and leave it open for the next exercise.

2. Banks for Congress — Proof to Client (Round 2)

Banks still wants to see a proof — and you want him to see the file, so he can assume sign-off responsibility. You need to create another PDF.

1. In the open document, choose File>Export. Choose the Adobe PDF format.
2. Save the document to your WIP_08 folder.
3. Choose the Print preset, ensure that all pages are selected, and choose only View PDF After Exporting.

   If the Optimize for Fast Web View, Bookmarks, or Hyperlinks buttons are checked, you receive a warning. Click OK to dismiss the warning.
4. In the Compression pane, accept the defaults.

5. Your client does not need to see the printer's marks and bleeds.
6. Export the file.
7. View the PDF document. Leave the file open for the next exercise.

3. Banks for Congress — Proof to Service Provider (Round 2)

Even though you already created a proof for the service provider, it's a good idea to provide a proof from the current file, in case images shifted even a little bit.

1. In the open document, access the Print menu.
2. Be sure the correct printer is selected, and then choose All Pages.
3. Set the Paper Size to Letter, the Orientation to Landscape, the Scale to 100%, and click Tile.
4. In the Marks and Bleed frame, choose All Printer's Marks and Use Document Bleed Settings.
5. Select the appropriate color mode for your printer.
6. Optimized Subsampling should be selected in the Graphics pane.
7. Click Print.
8. When the pages emerge from the printer, assemble them, and then review the to-size proof.
9. Leave the document open for the next exercise.

4. Banks for Congress — Separations Proof to Service Provider

This is a spot color job, so the service provider wants you to submit a secondary proof that shows the color breaks. This proof does not have to be to size.

1. In the open document, access the Print menu.
2. Be sure the correct printer is selected, and then choose All Pages.
3. Set the Paper Size to Letter, the Orientation to Portrait, uncheck Tile, and check Scale to Fit.
4. In the Marks and Bleed frame, choose All Printer's Marks and Use Document Bleed Settings.
5. In the Output frame, choose Separations from the Color drop-down menu.
6. Optimized Subsampling should be selected in the Graphics pane.
7. Click Print.

   Oops — and this is a big oops — you printed 10 pages instead of 4. The process color gradient is so close to the PANTONE 287 blue that you can't tell the difference. You need to modify the document — and you're very thankful the service provider required the separations proof.
8. Leave the file open for the next exercise.

5. Banks for Congress — Fix the Document

1. Continue in the open document.
2. With nothing selected, click PANTONE 287C, and choose New Tint Swatch from the Swatches palette.
3. Type "20%" in the Tint % box. Click OK.
4. Double-click on BG Gradient, and assign PMS 287 to the first stop.
5. Assign the 20% tint of PMS 287 to the right stop. Click OK.
6. Delete the two process color swatches from the palette.
7. Save the document. Print another separated proof.

   You should send another PDF file to your client, too. Chances are, though, that you'd rather keep this embarrassing error to yourself.
8. Leave the file open for the final exercise.

6. Banks for Congress — Package for Service Provider (Round 2)

You're finally ready to send this document to the service provider for printing.

1. In the open document, choose File>Package.
2. In the Printing Instructions pane, make the following changes:

Job:	Banks for Congress 2-color: Black and PMS 287
Qty:	60,000, 70 lb. Dull Coated Text
Bleed:	0.125 in.
Trim:	8.5 × 11, Letterfold 45,000, 15,000 flat

3. Click Continue.
4. Create a folder named "GASP_2 Color" so you don't inadvertently send the service provider the wrong file. The same boxes you previously selected as options in this pane should be selected. Click Save.
5. Dismiss the Font Alert warning.

   InDesign packages your document, and your instructions appear in a text window.
6. Save and close the document. Close the text editor.

PORTFOLIO BUILDER

Prepare Your Portfolio

A portfolio is only valuable when it is presented. Today, you can present your portfolio in person, as hard copy, or electronically. Review the Portfolio Builders, Skill Drills, and Challenges in your WIP folders, and prepare the best projects for inclusion in your portfolio. You should prepare PDF files for electronic presentation and print the files to a color printer for presentation in person.

- Check each document on screen to ensure that all graphics are linked and all fonts are available.
- Print a black-and-white proof so you can check for any composition errors, such as bad line breaks or poor kerning.
- Create a PDF file of each document, so you can send your portfolio for electronic review.
- Print your documents to a color printer, and arrange them for presentation.

INTEGRATING PROJECT

This Integrating Project is designed to reflect a real-world design job, drawing on the skills you learned throughout this book. The files you need to complete this project are located in the RF_InDesign_L1>IP folder.

Design a Travel Brochure

A travel agency may feature many vacation packages. More important than those packages is convincing customers to use the agency, rather than booking vacations for themselves, especially when booking online is so easy. In this project, you create a six-panel brochure (a standard marketing piece) that includes images and text, presented in a highly effective manner.

All object coordinates included in this project assume that the upper-left proxy-reference point is selected in the Control palette; be sure to check frequently, because the proxy-reference point may default to the center.

Whether your next vacation is designed to take you around the world in eighty days (more or less), or you're constrained to a long weekend closer to home, we're the people who can make your vacation fun, exciting, romantic, or relaxing – in other words, the kind of vacation you're looking to have. Located in "vacation central" – Florida's sunny Gulf coast, we're familiar with what people want from their vacations, and, with two decades behind us, we have the experience to help you maximize your vacation.

We'll work with your desires (and your budget) to help you get the most from a guided vacation, a cruise, an "on your own" experience, or a combination of any of these.

Meet Our Travel Specialists

Judy, believe it or not, is our resident ski bum. Last winter she was the guide for six (count 'em) trips to the American Rockies and Sierras. This summer where else would she be but taking ski tours "down under" to the Chilean Andes and to New Zealand. Seems like all she knows how to do is take fun to the max!

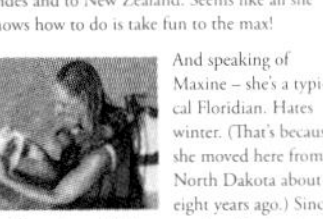

And speaking of Maxine – she's a typical Floridian. Hates winter. (That's because she moved here from North Dakota about eight years ago.) Since she's been here she's been comfortable showing up at work in shorts and a polo shirt – except when she's having fun with our customers diving off the Keys, or sailing the Caribbean. Maxine is a registered dive instructor and holds her pilot's license for sailing craft. She also knows when the big fish are running for those of you who really enjoy big game fishing.

What can we tell you about Laurie, except that she's a Celtophile. Her specialty is trips to Ireland, Scotland, England, Wales, Australia and New Zealand. Whether it's helping folks get the most from their trip to "the Homeland" or accompanying them on cycling and hiking trips through the beautiful mountains, trying to spy Nessie, exploring the towns, or watching the changing of the guard at Buckingham Palace, she's right at home in the British Isles and Down Under.

John is our computer geek. He keeps track of all the best airfares and cruise line fares, so we can pass them along to you. Like everybody else, he has a "life." In addition to living online, he's our resident expert on Florida theme parks – and has extended that expertise to cover other parks, like Colonial Williamsburg. Since we're so close, he's been known to take a mid-week theme park break, just to see what's new and exciting that he can share with you.

Glen is the person we all rely on to keep us together. He's the manager of the mailing list, keeper of the schedule – and all 'round expert on night life, concerts, and theatre. If you're planning an evening On the Town (New York, Chicago, San Francisco, Rome, or wherever) Glen will help you find the kind of fun you seek.

How Can We Serve You?

By now, you have a pretty good idea of what we can do for you. We specialize in vacation travel (but, of course, we'll be happy to book your travel for whatever reason).

- Guided Tours
- The British Isles
- Trips "Down Under"
- Dive Trips and Tours
- Sailing Trips
- Cruises
- Theatre and On the Town

Call us and see for yourself just how muc[h] you can have!

SPECIAL EVENTS AROUND THE WORLD

Caribbean Sail and Dive. April 23 – 29.
ATWV's Maxine Taylor leads you in this 7-day, 6-night sail and dive in the pristine waters of the West Indies. You'll sail the 51-foot sloop *Ligature*, with a home port of Nassau, Bahamas. This combination sail and dive will provide a variety of experiences for all participants. We dive in the clear waters of the West Indies, and come face-to-face with a variety of flora and fauna. A Gala in Nassau ends your week of frolic on and in the water. This tour fills up fast!
Beginning and intermediate sailors. Dive certification required. Call for details.

Caribbean Sail. April 30 – May 6.
Sail the waters of the West Indies for 7 days and 6 nights in the 51-foot sloop *Dipthong* along with ATWV's Maxine Taylor. You'll learn some of the finer points of sailing, including the all-important lesson of how to function as a crew, instead of a group of individuals. But sailing isn't all we do on this trip. There's also ample opportunity to slip into the warm, crystalline waters of the Caribbean for a dip, or to snorkel off the many reefs. And, of course, you won't want to miss the gala End-of-Sail party in Nassau.
Beginning and intermediate sailors. No prerequisite. Call for details.

Down Under Ski & Boogie. May 20 – 28.
You'll fly from Los Angeles to Auckland, NZ – then take a short flight to Christchurch on South Island where you'll begin the skiing adventure of a lifetime! ATWV's Judy Jackson knows the ski trails of these rugged mountains – and she'll help you navigate them from top to bottom, or schuss straight down the hill – unless, of course, you can convince her that you really want to get airborn on a boogie board. There's plenty of time [illegible] especially on that last night, before you (almost) literally go back in time, when you return to the States. (You lose a day when you cross the Date Line.)
Intermediate and Advanced Skiers. Call for details and info about our special side-trip to Fiji.

Event	Price	Depart	Flight
Sail & Dive	$1395	Miami	$189
Sail	$1195	Miami	$189
Ski & Boogie	$1725	Los Angeles	Included

Bulk Rate
U.S. Postage
PAID
Permit #112
Tampa, FL

AROUND THE WORLD VACATIONS
Suite 100
Dockside Quay
Tampa
Florida
35232

Set Up the Brochure Format

1 Create a new document. Set the Number of Pages to 2, and uncheck the Facing Pages and Master Text Frame boxes. Set the Page Size to Letter and the Orientation to Landscape. Set all Margins to 0.25 in. Set the number of Columns to 1, and allow a 0.125-in Bleed all around.

2 Access InDesign Preferences. In the Units and Increments pane, set the Ruler Units to Inches, and the Display Performance default View to Typical (if you did not previously set this as your default).

3 Set up your guides to delineate your fold marks and panel margins. On the first page, place vertical guides at 3.625 in and 7.3125 in.

This is the inside page, where you place the bulk of your text. Creating three equal columns will not work, because automatic folding machines require that the inward-folding panel be slightly narrower than the two outer panels.

4 Double-click Page 2 in the Pages palette. Place vertical guides at 3.6875 in and 7.375 in.

This is the outside sheet, including the front cover and the back cover, which is the mailing panel.

5 Remain on Page 2. Drag the guides for your live copy area to 0.25 in on either side of the fold marks. Position the guides at 3.4375 in, 3.9375 in, 7.125 in, and 7.625 in.

6 Drag the cursor horizontally to select all the guides. Choose Object>Lock Position, so you don't accidentally move them.

7 Go to Page 1. Drag guides to 3.375 in, 3.875 in, 7.0625 in, and 7.5625 in. Lock these guides as you did for the guides on Page 2.

8 Save your file as "atwv_brochure.indd" to your WIP_IP folder. Leave the file open for the next exercise.

Establish the Color Scheme

Use process colors in this brochure, and print it 4/4 (four process colors on both sides). Specify a Color Type of Process and a Color Mode of CMYK for all the colors.

1. In the open file, delete all colors in the Swatches palette except [None], [Paper], [Black], and [Registration].
2. From the Swatches palette, choose New Color Swatch.
3. Uncheck the Name with Color Value box. Type the name "Dark Green" in the Swatch Name field. Set the CMYK specifications to C:100, M:0, Y:75, K:50.
4. Create a new color named "Dark Blue", defined as C:100, M:75, Y:0, K:25.
5. Create another color named "Light Blue", defined as C:85, M:5, Y:0, K:0.
6. Save your changes. Leave the document open for the next exercise.

Set Up Styles

1. In the open file, choose New Paragraph Style from the Paragraph Styles palette menu. Name it "Body Text".
2. In the Basic Character Formats pane, set the Font to Adobe Garamond Pro, Regular, 12/15.
3. In the Indents and Spacing pane, set the First Line Indent to 1p0.

   You can enter measurements in any measurement unit. InDesign converts them to their equivalent in the unit you selected in Preferences; in the case of this document, inches.
4. Do not hyphenate capitalized words.
5. Click OK to save the style.
6. You need another style without a first-line indent. Make sure the Body Text style is selected in the Paragraph Styles palette. Choose Duplicate Style from the palette menu. Name the style "Body Text 1". From the Indents and Spacing pane, set the First Line Indent to 0. Click OK to save the new style.
7. Now you need a headline style. Option/Alt-Click [No Paragraph Style] to clear it, then choose New Paragraph Style from the palette menu. Name it "Head 1".

   Remember, new paragraph styles pick up attributes from the last style created; if you create a style based on another, that information is retained in the [No Paragraph Style] memory. You must Option/Alt click [No Paragraph Style] to clear its memory.

8 Set the Head 1 style as follows:

Basic Character Formats:	ATC Oak, Bold, 12/15.
Indents and Spacing:	Left with No Indents, 10-pt Space Before.
Keep Options:	Keep with Next 1 Line, Keep Lines Together: All Lines in Paragraph.
Hyphenation:	Off
Character Color:	Dark Green with Stroke of None.

9 Make a duplicate of the Body Text 1 style and name it "List Bullet", the primary style for a bulleted list. Set the Left Indent to 3p0 and the First Line Indent to –0p9. Click OK.

10 Duplicate the List Bullet style and name it "List Bullet 1". Set the Space Before to 7.5 pt.

This style is for the first item in a bulleted list.

11 Duplicate the List Bullet style and name it "List Bullet Last". Set the Space After to 7.5 pt.

This style is for the last item in a bulleted list.

12 Make a duplicate of Body Text 1 called "Bio". Set the Space After to 7.5 pt.

13 Save your changes. Leave the document open for the next exercise.

Place Text and Apply Styles

All position coordinates in this project are measured from the upper-left corner of the object, unless otherwise specified. Be sure the proxy-reference point is set to the upper-left corner.

1 On the first page of the open document, create three rectangular text frames filling the three "columns" on the page, as follows:

X: 0.25 in	Y: 0.25 in	W: 3.125 in	H: 8 in
X: 3.875 in	Y: 0.25 in	W: 3.1875 in	H: 8 in
X: 7.5625 in	Y: 0.25 in	W: 3.1875 in	H: 8 in

2 Link all three text frames by clicking the Selection tool in the out port, and then in the following text frame.

3 Click in the leftmost text frame with the Type tool.

4 Place the file atwv_text.rtf. Do not check the Show Import Options box. Check the Replace Selected Items box.

5 Place the Type tool cursor in the first paragraph and choose the Body Text 1 style.

6. Select the second paragraph and define its style as Body Text.

7. Select the third paragraph (Meet Our Travel Specialists) and apply the Head 1 style.

8. Select the next paragraphs (stop when you get to the heading "How Can We Serve You") and apply the Bio style.

9. Style the "How Can We Serve You" paragraph as Head 1.

10. Style the next paragraph as Body Text 1.

11. The next 7 lines comprise a bulleted list. Apply the List Bullet 1 style to the first item, the List Bullet Last style to the last item, and the List Bullet style to the rest of the bulleted items.

12. Select the last paragraph and define it as Body Text 1.

13. Select the first paragraph and apply a Drop Cap with a Depth of 4 Lines and specify the Number of Characters as 1.

14. Place the cursor between the "W" and the "h" of the first word, and press Shift-Return/Enter to force a line break.

15. Assign a Color of Dark Blue to the drop cap.

16. Save your changes. Leave the file open for the next exercise.

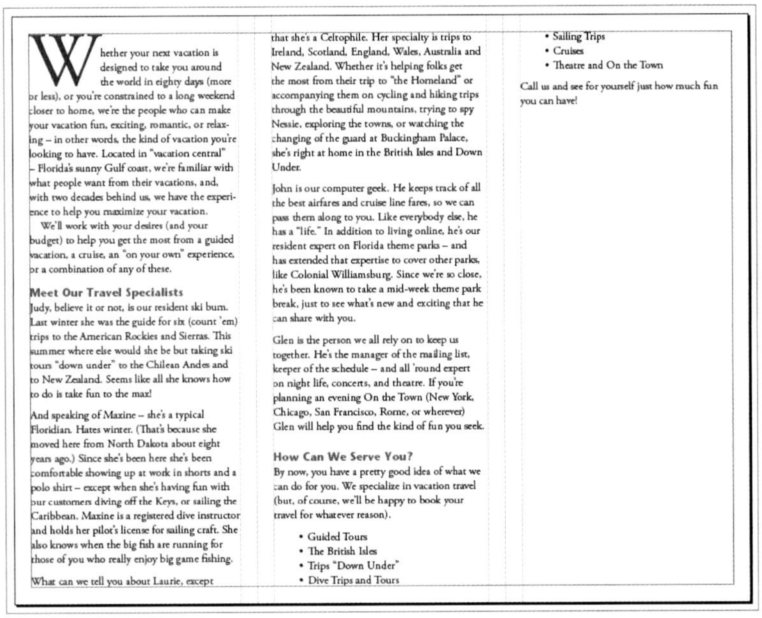

Whether your next vacation is designed to take you around the world in eighty days (more or less), or you're constrained to a long weekend closer to home, we're the people who can make your vacation fun, exciting, romantic, or relaxing – in other words, the kind of vacation you're looking to have. Located in "vacation central" – Florida's sunny Gulf coast, we're familiar with what people want from their vacations, and, with two decades behind us, we have the experience to help you maximize your vacation.

We'll work with your desires (and your budget) to help you get the most from a guided vacation, a cruise, an "on your own" experience, or a combination of any of these.

Meet Our Travel Specialists

Judy, believe it or not, is our resident ski bum. Last winter she was the guide for six (count 'em) trips to the American Rockies and Sierras. This summer where else would she be but taking ski tours "down under" to the Chilean Andes and to New Zealand. Seems like all she knows how to do is take fun to the max!

And speaking of Maxine – she's a typical Floridian. Hates winter. (That's because she moved here from North Dakota about eight years ago.) Since she's been here she's been comfortable showing up at work in shorts and a polo shirt – except when she's having fun with our customers diving off the Keys, or sailing the Caribbean. Maxine is a registered dive instructor and holds her pilot's license for sailing craft. She also knows when the big fish are running for those of you who really enjoy big game fishing.

What can we tell you about Laurie, except that she's a Celtophile. Her specialty is trips to Ireland, Scotland, England, Wales, Australia and New Zealand. Whether it's helping folks get the most from their trip to "the Homeland" or accompanying them on cycling and hiking trips through the beautiful mountains, trying to spy Nessie, exploring the towns, or watching the changing of the guard at Buckingham Palace, she's right at home in the British Isles and Down Under.

John is our computer geek. He keeps track of all the best airfares and cruise line fares, so we can pass them along to you. Like everybody else, he has a "life." In addition to living online, he's our resident expert on Florida theme parks – and has extended that expertise to cover other parks, like Colonial Williamsburg. Since we're so close, he's been known to take a mid-week theme park break, just to see what's new and exciting that he can share with you.

Glen is the person we all rely on to keep us together. He's the manager of the mailing list, keeper of the schedule – and all 'round expert on night life, concerts, and theatre. If you're planning an evening On the Town (New York, Chicago, San Francisco, Rome, or wherever) Glen will help you find the kind of fun you seek.

How Can We Serve You?

By now, you have a pretty good idea of what we can do for you. We specialize in vacation travel (but, of course, we'll be happy to book your travel for whatever reason).

- Guided Tours
- The British Isles
- Trips "Down Under"
- Dive Trips and Tours
- Sailing Trips
- Cruises
- Theatre and On the Town

Call us and see for yourself just how much fun you can have!

Place Images in Frames

In large part, this brochure is about the people at the agency; they are the prime reason you would choose to book your vacation with the agency instead of online. A paragraph about each person at the travel agency is included under the headline, "Meet Our Travel Specialists." You need to place faces beside the names, so clients can identify the people who are booking their travel arrangements.

1. In the open document, use the Rectangle Frame tool to create the first picture frame with the following specifications: X: 0.25 in, Y: 4.375 in, W: 1 in, H: 1.5 in.

2. Choose Window>Type & Tables>Text Wrap. Click the second button, Wrap Around Bounding Box. Leave the Top and Left Offsets at 0 (zero), and set the Bottom and Right Offsets to 0.125 in.

   You use these offsets for all pictures in the biography section.

3. Switch to the Selection tool. Choose File>Place and place judy.tif.

4. Choose Object>Fitting>Fit Frame to Content.

5. Click Judy's image frame, copy it, and choose Edit>Paste in Place to put a duplicate exactly on top of the original.

6. Hold down the Shift key while you drag the copy of Judy down to the paragraph about Max. Visually align the top of the frame with the top of the paragraph about Max.

7. Place max.tif into the frame, replacing Judy's picture.

8. Choose Object>Fitting>Fit Frame to Content.

   The bottom offset is too large; it creates an unattractive white area under Max's picture.

9. Change the Bottom Offset in the Text Wrap dialog box to 0 (zero).

   This causes the last line to align with the left margin. Note how Adobe Paragraph Composer considers these things when composing text, and how the entire paragraph is recomposed.

   There is still too much white space under the image.

10. Press Command/Control-Shift and enlarge the frame and its content by dragging the lower-right handle until the bottom of the image aligns with the baseline of the seventh line of type in this paragraph.

    This is an adjustment of just a few points.

11. Click Judy's picture. Hold down the Option/Alt key while you drag the picture to the second column, next to Laurie's bio paragraph. Place laurie.tif into the frame and fit the frame to the content.

    You have a similar problem with Laurie as you did with Max — too much white space under her image. Reducing the bottom text wrap offset to zero still doesn't completely resolve the problem.

    Holding the Option/Alt key while you drag an object to copy it is called a ***drag copy***.

12 Reduce Laurie's image to resolve the space issue.

13 Drag-copy Judy's frame into position for John's picture. Place john1.tif into the copy of Judy's frame, and adjust the fit, offset, and size appropriately.

Pay attention to what's happening with the type. You don't want to end up with a single short word on the last line of the paragraph.

14 Switch to the Type tool. At the beginning of Glen's bio, Control/right-click, and choose Insert Break Character>Frame Break from the menu.

The type following the break character moves to the next frame. There was not enough room for Glen's picture. This leaves some white space under John's bio, but you can fill that space. You will discover that no matter how well you plan, you end up doing some designing "on the fly."

15 Drag-copy Judy's picture frame into position next to Glen's bio. Place glen.tif into the frame. Resize, fit, and position the offsets to achieve a good-looking text wrap.

16 Place your_vacation.tif at the bottom of the third column. No text wrap offsets are necessary. You want this image to span the column, so hold down the Command/Control-Shift keys and drag until the image fills the width of the column and abuts the bottom margin.

If you look carefully, you see that the descender of the "y" is cut off.

17 With the image selected, choose Object>Arrange>Send to Back.

18 Save your changes. Leave the document open for the next exercise.

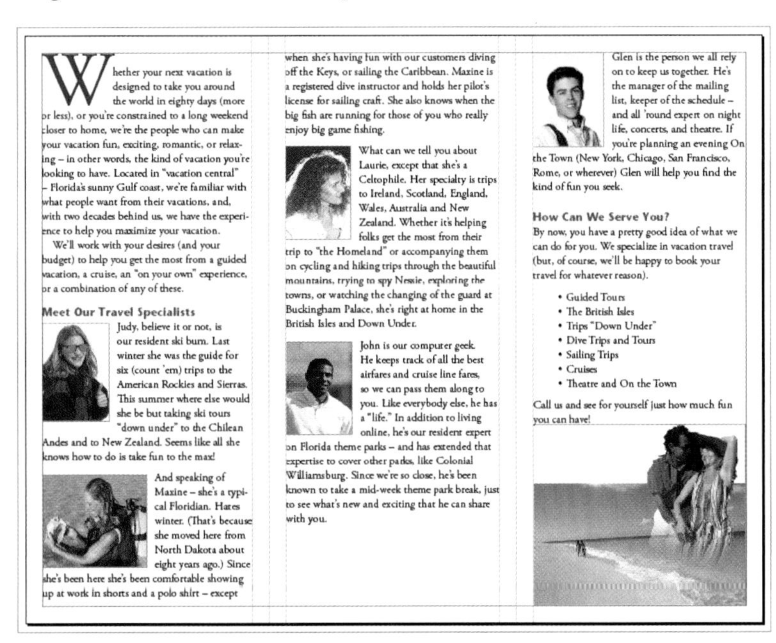

Whether your next vacation is designed to take you around the world in eighty days (more or less), or you're constrained to a long weekend closer to home, we're the people who can make your vacation fun, exciting, romantic, or relaxing – in other words, the kind of vacation you're looking to have. Located in "vacation central" – Florida's sunny Gulf coast, we're familiar with what people want from their vacations, and, with two decades behind us, we have the experience to help you maximize your vacation.

We'll work with your desires (and your budget) to help you get the most from a guided vacation, a cruise, an "on your own" experience, or a combination of any of these.

Meet Our Travel Specialists

Judy, believe it or not, is our resident ski bum. Last winter she was the guide for six (count 'em) trips to the American Rockies and Sierras. This summer where else would she be but taking ski tours "down under" to the Chilean Andes and to New Zealand. Seems like all she knows how to do is take fun to the max!

And speaking of Maxine – she's a typical Floridian. Hates winter. (That's because she moved here from North Dakota about eight years ago.) Since she's been here she's been comfortable showing up at work in shorts and a polo shirt – except when she's having fun with our customers diving off the Keys, or sailing the Caribbean. Maxine is a registered dive instructor and holds her pilot's license for sailing craft. She also knows when the big fish are running for those of you who really enjoy big game fishing.

What can we tell you about Laurie, except that she's a Celtophile. Her specialty is trips to Ireland, Scotland, England, Wales, Australia and New Zealand. Whether it's helping folks get the most from their trip to "the Homeland" or accompanying them on cycling and hiking trips through the beautiful mountains, trying to spy Nessie, exploring the towns, or watching the changing of the guard at Buckingham Palace, she's right at home in the British Isles and Down Under.

John is our computer geek. He keeps track of all the best airfares and cruise line fares, so we can pass them along to you. Like everybody else, he has a "life." In addition to living online, he's our resident expert on Florida theme parks – and has extended that expertise to cover other parks, like Colonial Williamsburg. Since we're so close, he's been known to take a mid-week theme park break, just to see what's new and exciting that he can share with you.

Glen is the person we all rely on to keep us together. He's the manager of the mailing list, keeper of the schedule – and all 'round expert on night life, concerts, and theatre. If you're planning an evening On the Town (New York, Chicago, San Francisco, Rome, or wherever) Glen will help you find the kind of fun you seek.

How Can We Serve You?

By now, you have a pretty good idea of what we can do for you. We specialize in vacation travel (but, of course, we'll be happy to book your travel for whatever reason).

- Guided Tours
- The British Isles
- Trips "Down Under"
- Dive Trips and Tours
- Sailing Trips
- Cruises
- Theatre and On the Town

Call us and see for yourself just how much fun you can have!

Fill In the Blanks

The hole at the bottom of the center panel needs to be filled and (of course) the art director is standing over your shoulder, trying to see what last-minute changes she can make — now that the page is composed.

1. In the open document, draw a text frame as follows: X: 3.875 in, Y: 7.375 in, W: 3.1875 in, H: 0.875 in.

2. Type the following, using a forced line break to separate the two lines:

   For your next vacation, call
   813/555-ATWV

3. Center the text. Access the Text Frame Options and apply a vertical justification to Align Center.

4. Set both lines in Caflisch Script Pro, Regular, 18/18.

   You want the telephone number to occupy roughly the same width as the first line, which means enlarging the point size, tracking the type, or both.

5. Enlarge the point size by selecting the text in the second line, and then pressing Command/Control-Shift-> (Greater Than key) until the type is the same width as the first line.

6. Adjust the Leading appropriately.

7. Select all the text. Set its Fill to Paper.

8. Switch to the Selection tool. Set the frame's Fill to Dark Blue.

   Remember the art director? She noticed that the picture of John is the wrong John.

9. Choose the Direct Selection tool, click the picture of (wrong) John, and then choose john2.tif. In the Place dialog box, make sure Replace Selected Item is checked.

   This action replaces the selected image with the new one (every time), and maintains scaling and other transformations applied to the original image — *only* if you start by selecting the original object with the Direct Selection tool.

10 Save your changes. Leave the document open for the next exercise.

The figure below shows how our document looks at this point in development. You made some decisions about picture sizing, so your brochure may differ from ours. Make any modifications necessary to ensure that all text appears properly.

Set the Style for a Special Offer

Even though the primary thrust of this brochure is to acquaint customers with the agency's staff, it would be silly to miss the opportunity to make sales. The special-offer panel provides an opportunity to make some money, while it helps clients have fun. This special-events panel requires some new styles, and you make it stand out with color.

1 In the open file, double-click the Page 2 icon in the Pages palette to go to the second spread.

2 Use the Rectangle tool to draw a rectangle with the following specifications: X: –0.125 in, Y: –0.125 in, W: 3.8055 in, H: 8.75 in.

This begins the rectangle at the bleed edges and extends it to the fold.

3 In the Swatches palette, click the Light Blue swatch. Then, choose New Color Swatch from the Options menu. Assign 43% Cyan, 3% Magenta, 0% Yellow, and 0% Black. Name the swatch "Very Light Blue". Click OK.

You could have simply created a tint at 50%, but doing so using process color is not advisable, because the results are unpredictable.

4. Fill the rectangle with the new color. Be sure the Stroke is set to None.

5. Choose Object>Lock Position, so you don't accidentally move this object.

6. Draw a text frame with the following specifications: X: 0.25 in, Y: 0.25 in, W: 3.1875 in, H: 8 in. Assign it a 1-pt Black Stroke.

7. From the Text Frame Options dialog box, set a 6-pt Inset Spacing for all sides (0.0833 in).

8. Option/Alt-click [No Paragraph Style] to reset it. Create a new paragraph style named "Body Text Special" with these specifications: ATC Oak Normal, 9/11, 3-pt Space After, Left Justified, and do not hyphenate capitalized words.

9. Create another new paragraph style named "Body Text Special 2" based on Body Text Special. Set its specification to ATC Oak Italic, 8/9, Align Left, with 5-pt Space After.

10. Create another new paragraph style named "Body Text Special Head" based on Body Text Special. Set its specification to ATC Oak Normal, 10/11, 3-pt Space Before, and 2-pt Space After, with a Color of Dark Blue.

11. Create "Head 2" based on the Head 1 style. Set its specification to ATC Oak Bold, 14/14, All Caps, with 10-pt Space After, keeping the 10-pt Space Before setting. Set the Alignment to Center, and set the Color to Dark Green.

12. Create a character style named "Body Text Special Head" and assign it the keyboard shortcut Command/Control-0 (on the numeric keypad). Assign ATC Oak Bold as the Font.

13. Save your changes. Leave the document open.

Flow and Style Special Text

1. Switch to the Type tool. Place atwv_events.rtf into the text frame of the open file.

2. Select the first paragraph, Special Events, and assign the Head 2 style.

3. Select the second paragraph and assign the Body Text Special Head style.

4. Highlight the words "Caribbean Sail and Dive." Press Command/Control-0 to apply the Body Text Special Head character style.

5. Assign the Body Text Special style to the next paragraph.

6. Assign the Body Text Special 2 style to the next paragraph.

7 Format the next two events the same way. The event name uses the Body Text Special Head style, the description uses the Body Text Special style, and the prerequisite uses the Body Text Special 2 style. Style the event names with the character style.

Two words, Ligature and Diphthong, are highlighted because there is no italic for ATC Oak Normal.

8 Select the highlighted words (the names of boats) and style them as ATC Oak Italic.

9 Assign the Body Text Special style to the chart (4 lines) at the end of the story.

10 Deselect the frame. Save your changes. Leave the document open for the next steps.

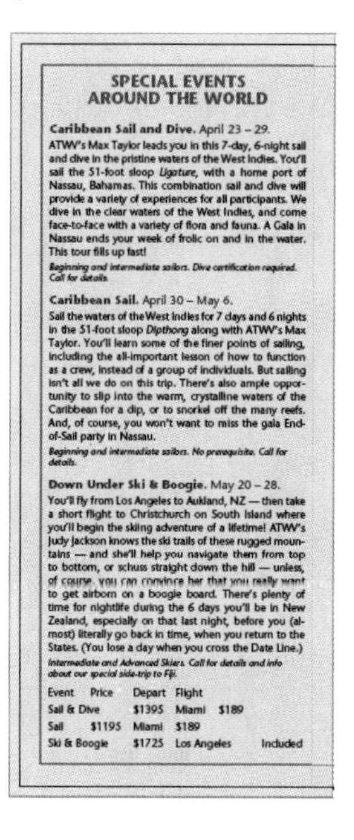

SPECIAL EVENTS
AROUND THE WORLD

Caribbean Sail and Dive. April 23 – 29.

ATWV's Max Taylor leads you in this 7-day, 6-night sail and dive in the pristine waters of the West Indies. You'll sail the 51-foot sloop *Ligature*, with a home port of Nassau, Bahamas. This combination sail and dive will provide a variety of experiences for all participants. We dive in the clear waters of the West Indies, and come face-to-face with a variety of flora and fauna. A Gala in Nassau ends your week of frolic on and in the water. This tour fills up fast!

Beginning and intermediate sailors. Dive certification required. Call for details.

Caribbean Sail. April 30 – May 6.

Sail the waters of the West Indies for 7 days and 6 nights in the 51-foot sloop *Dipthong* along with ATWV's Max Taylor. You'll learn some of the finer points of sailing, including the all-important lesson of how to function as a crew, instead of a group of individuals. But sailing isn't all we do on this trip. There's also ample opportunity to slip into the warm, crystalline waters of the Caribbean for a dip, or to snorkel off the many reefs. And, of course, you won't want to miss the gala End-of-Sail party in Nassau.

Beginning and intermediate sailors. No prerequisite. Call for details.

Down Under Ski & Boogie. May 20 – 28.

You'll fly from Los Angeles to Aukland, NZ — then take a short flight to Christchurch on South Island where you'll begin the skiing adventure of a lifetime! ATWV's Judy Jackson knows the ski trails of these rugged mountains — and she'll help you navigate them from top to bottom, or schuss straight down the hill — unless, of course, you can convince her that you really want to get airborn on a boogie board. There's plenty of time for nightlife during the 6 days you'll be in New Zealand, especially on that last night, before you (almost) literally go back in time, when you return to the States. (You lose a day when you cross the Date Line.)

Intermediate and Advanced Skiers. Call for details and info about our special side-trip to Fiji.

Event Price Depart Flight
Sail & Dive $1395 Miami $189
Sail $1195 Miami $189
Ski & Boogie $1725 Los Angeles Included

Set Up the Chart

You want the chart at the bottom of the page to stand out — after all, that's where the money is going to be made. You do so by applying rules to the text and reversing the type out of the underlying rules.

1 In the open document, select all the text in the four lines at the bottom of the page.

2 Activate the Tab ruler by choosing Window>Type & Tables>Tabs, or pressing Command/Control-Shift-T.

3 Click the magnet icon to position it above the text frame.

There must be enough room above the frame for the Tab ruler to physically fit, or this will not work.

4 Insert Centered tabs at 1.2 in, 1.92 in, and 2.7 in.

5 From the Paragraph Styles palette, set a Left Indent of 4 pt.

6 Select the top line and style the type as ATC Oak Bold.

7 With the first line still selected, choose Paragraph Rules from the Paragraph Styles palette's Options menu. Turn on the Rule Above and assign it a 1-pt Weight, Color of Dark Blue, Width of Column, and 10-pt Offset (0.1389 in). Click OK.

8 Assign a 2-pt Space Before.

9 Select the last line in the chart. Access the Paragraph Rules menu. Turn on the Rule Above and assign a 56-pt Weight, Color of Light Blue, Width of Column, and –4-pt Offset (–0.0556 in).

10 Turn on Rule Below. Assign a 1-pt Weight, Color of Dark Blue, Width of Column, and 4-pt Offset. Click OK.

11 Select all the text in the last four lines. Assign a Color of Paper.

12 Save your changes. Leave the document open.

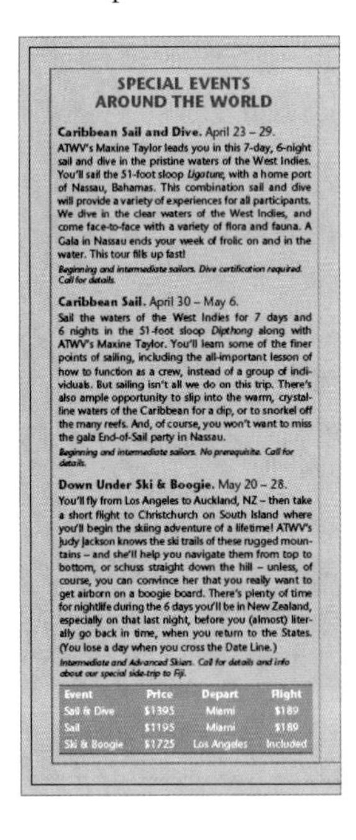

SPECIAL EVENTS
AROUND THE WORLD

Caribbean Sail and Dive. April 23 – 29.
ATWV's Maxine Taylor leads you in this 7-day, 6-night sail and dive in the pristine waters of the West Indies. You'll sail the 51-foot sloop *Ligature*, with a home port of Nassau, Bahamas. This combination sail and dive will provide a variety of experiences for all participants. We dive in the clear waters of the West Indies, and come face-to-face with a variety of flora and fauna. A Gala in Nassau ends your week of frolic on and in the water. This tour fills up fast!

Beginning and intermediate sailors. Dive certification required. Call for details.

Caribbean Sail. April 30 – May 6.
Sail the waters of the West Indies for 7 days and 6 nights in the 51-foot sloop *Dipthong* along with ATWV's Maxine Taylor. You'll learn some of the finer points of sailing, including the all-important lesson of how to function as a crew, instead of a group of individuals. But sailing isn't all we do on this trip. There's also ample opportunity to slip into the warm, crystalline waters of the Caribbean for a dip, or to snorkel off the many reefs. And, of course, you won't want to miss the gala End-of-Sail party in Nassau.

Beginning and intermediate sailors. No prerequisite. Call for details.

Down Under Ski & Boogie. May 20 – 28.
You'll fly from Los Angeles to Auckland, NZ – then take a short flight to Christchurch on South Island where you'll begin the skiing adventure of a lifetime! ATWV's Judy Jackson knows the ski trails of these rugged mountains – and she'll help you navigate them from top to bottom, or schuss straight down the hill – unless, of course, you can convince her that you really want to get airborn on a boogie board. There's plenty of time for nightlife during the 6 days you'll be in New Zealand, especially on that last night, before you (almost) literally go back in time, when you return to the States. (You lose a day when you cross the Date Line.)

Intermediate and Advanced Skiers. Call for details and info about our special side-trip to Fiji.

Event	Price	Depart	Flight
Sail & Dive	$1395	Miami	$189
Sail	$1195	Miami	$189
Ski & Boogie	$1725	Los Angeles	Included

Add the Return Address Frame

This brochure is designed as a self-mailer. The middle panel in the spread is designated as the mailing panel. It needs to include the return address and the first-class permit stamp.

1. In the open document, use the Rectangle Frame tool to draw a frame as follows: X: 3.9375 in, Y: 5.0625 in, W: 1.5 in, H: 3.1875 in.

2. Position a vertical guide at X: 4.6875 in, and a horizontal guide at Y: 5.85 in.

3. Choose the Add Anchor Point tool (it is one of the optional Pen tools). Click at the intersection of the top of the frame and the guide.

4. Switch to the Direct Selection tool. Drag each of the top two corner points of the rectangle to the horizontal guide at Y: 5.85 in.

5. Switch to the Convert Direction Point tool (another of the optional Pen tools). Click the point you added. While you hold down the Shift key to constrain the angle, drag left to the guide at X: 3.9375.

6. Delete the two guides you just added.

   You don't need them anymore.

7. In the Swatches palette, click the New Gradient Swatch icon. Set the Stop Colors by Swatches. Assign Very Light Blue to the left stop, and assign Dark Green to the right stop. Click in the center to position a third stop, and assign the Light Blue color. You do not need to assign this gradient a name. Click OK.

8. Click on the frame and apply the new gradient as the Fill.

9. In the Gradient palette, assign an Angle of –90 degrees.

10. Save your changes. Leave the document open.

Add the Return Address and Mail Indicia

1. In the open document, click the Type tool in the frame and type:

   Around the World Vacations
   Suite 100
   Dockside Quay
   Tampa
   Florida
   35232

2. Access the Text Frame Options menu. Set a First Baseline Minimum of 0.5 in.

3. Apply the Head 2 style to the company name.

4. Style the remaining two paragraphs as ATC Oak Normal, 14/14, with 0.5-in Space Before, Centered. Deselect the paragraphs.

5. Assign the address type a Fill of Paper.

6. In the Control panel, Rotate the text block 90 degrees, and position it at X: 3.9375 in, Y: 8.25 in.

   After it is rotated, the reference point changes to the lower left.

7. Create another 1-inch-square frame. Assign it a 1-pt Black Stroke and a Fill of None.

8. Click in the frame and type the following lines, ending each line with Shift-Return/Enter:

   Bulk Rate
   U.S. Postage
   PAID
   Permit #112
   Tampa, FL

9. Style the type as ATC Oak Normal, 10/12, Centered, with a Color of Black.

10. From the Text Frame Options dialog box, set the vertical justification to Center.

11. Rotate the frame 90 degrees. With the proxy-reference set to upper left, position it at X: 3.9375 in, Y: 0.25 in.

12. Save your changes. Leave the document open.

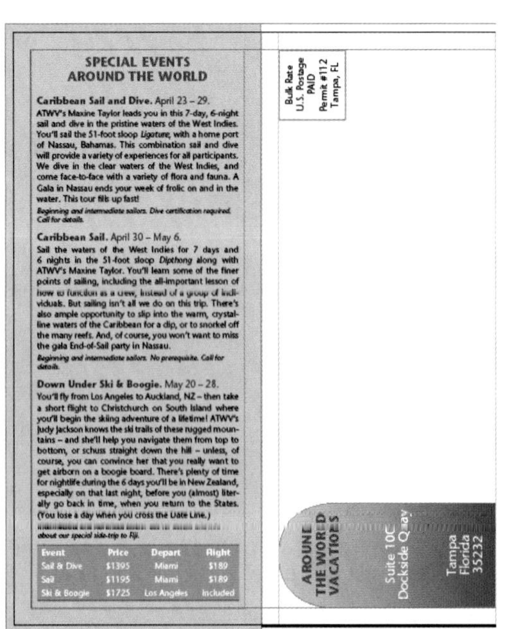

Build the Cover

The cover initially grabs a customer's attention. In this exercise, you build a cover that hints at a number of vacations that clients can take when they book with Around the World Vacations.

1. In the open document, use the Rectangle Frame tool to create a frame with the following specifications: X: 7.375 in, Y: –0.125 in, W: 3.75 in, H: 8.75 in.

2. Place atwv_cov_photo.tif into this frame.

3. Click the image with the Direct Selection tool. When the icon changes to a hand, move the image around until you are satisfied with the position of the elements. Then, release the mouse button.

   A client would normally tell you what part of the image to use; but here, you get to make the decision. A ghosted preview of the entire image helps you decide what part of the image to show.

4. On the pasteboard, draw two rectangular frames, 1.25 in square. Apply a 1-pt Black Rule to each.

5. Place picnic.tif in one frame, and place hottub.tif in the other.

6. Select the frame with picnic.tif.

7. Switch to the Rotate tool, and then move the rotation point to the center of the frame.

8. Double-click the Rotate tool. Set the Angle to 45 degrees, and be sure the Rotate Contents button is not checked. Click OK.

9. Use the Direct Selection tool to position the image to taste within the frame. If you wish, you can resize the image by holding down the Shift key and dragging the corners. Be sure the image fills the frame.

10. Select the frame that contains hottub.tif. Repeat Steps 7–9.

11. With the proxy-reference point at the top, position the picnic.tif image at X: 8.5 in, Y: 4.75 in, and position the hottub.tif image at X: 9.8775 in, Y: 4.75 in. Choose Object>Arrange>Bring to Front to position the picnic image in front, if necessary.

12. Save your changes. Leave the document open.

Finish the Cover

1. In the open document, use the Type tool to drag a new text frame with the following specifications: X: 7.625 in, Y: 6.625 in, W: 3.125 in, H: 1.625 in.

2. Type "Where in the world would you like to go?" into the frame.

3. Select the text and format it as Caflisch Script Pro, 48/36, Centered.

4 Assign a Color of Paper and a 0.5-pt Stroke of Paper.

Although you "never" stroke type, you can make an exception here. Caflisch is a bit weak for the cover; the large point size allows you to stroke the characters to make them acceptably bold.

5 Check the document for bad hyphenation and kerning in headlines that you think should be repaired. Fix any such problems.

6 You're almost done. Save your changes. Leave the document open.

Your document should resemble the figure below.

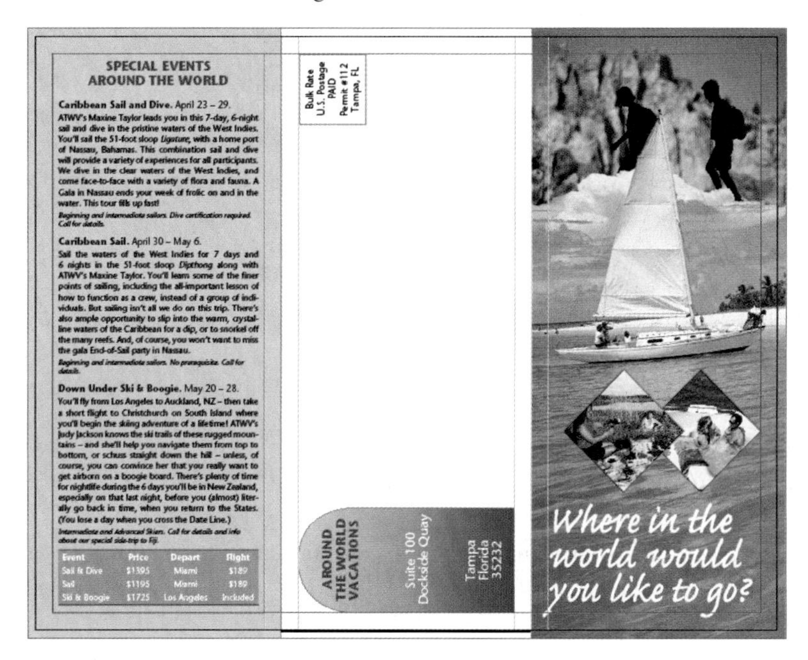

Check Spelling

1 In the open document, go to the first spread, and click the text cursor at the beginning of the text. Choose Edit>Edit in Story Editor.

2 Choose Edit>Check Spelling>Search Document. Click the Start button in the Check Spelling dialog box. The first errors flagged relate to the drop cap you created earlier because you forced a line break between the "W" and the rest of the word. Ignore these possible capitalization errors.

3 The first misspelled word is "Americian," but an appropriate replacement doesn't show up in the Suggested Corrections list. Edit the word in the Change To field by removing the last "i" in the word. Click the Change button.

4 The next misspelled word is "Chilian," and the correct replacement appears in the Suggested Corrections list. Click "Chilean," and then click Change.

5 The next word, "Zeland," is clearly wrong. Click "Zealand" in the Suggested Corrections list, and then click Change All to make sure there aren't any other occurrences. The next word, "max" is flagged as a possible capitalization error, but it's okay the way it is. Click Ignore.

6 The next word, "Celtophile," isn't necessarily misspelled, but it's not in the default InDesign dictionary, either. Assume the word is correct as submitted by the client, and click Ignore.

7 Next, "Nessie" is flagged because it's not in the dictionary. Click the Add button to add this word to the document dictionary.

Since you don't want this proper noun to hyphenate, just click the Add button, then click Done.

8 The next two words, "Buckingham" and "geek" aren't found in the dictionary. Add them.

9 Change the next word, "cruiseline," to "cruise line".

10 The next word, "Williamsburg," is okay; but the one after it, "Fransisco," is incorrect. Choose the correct spelling from the list of suggestions, and then click Change.

11 The spell-checker switches to the next story, and flags ATWV. Click Ignore All. The only remaining misspelled word in the document is "Aukland," which should be spelled "Auckland." Add the correct spelling to the dictionary.

The spell-checker questions a few more words. After the last one, you should see a message stating that the spell-check is complete.

12 Save your changes. Leave the document open.

Use Find/Save and Perform a Final Check

Clients sometime hide their instructions in the darndest places. A couple of "by-the-way" changes are inserted on a sticky note (comment) on the last page of instructions. Luckily, you can use Find/Change to resolve these problems.

1 With the cursor at the beginning of Page 1 of the open document (just as you did when spell-checking), choose the Story Editor.

Using Story Editor is a much faster way of editing than working through the actual document.

2 Choose Edit>Find/Change (or press Command/Control-F). Click the pop-up menu next to the Find What field. Choose Em Dash from the list of special characters, and then press the Tab key to move to the Replace With/Change To field. Click the pop-up menu next to this field and choose En Dash.

As an alternative, you could enter the meta-character for each: for an em dash, type "^_", and for an en dash, type "^=".

3 Be sure Search Document is selected, and then click the Change All button to perform the replacement.

A completion dialog box tells you how many replacements were made.

It is not typographically correct to use an en dash instead of an em dash, but the "right thing" to do is to follow the client's wishes. There's no sense arguing with your client; you run the risk of losing the account.

4 Replace Max's name with her full name, Maxine, using the method described above. Search the entire document with a case-sensitive, whole-word search.

You could do this manually, but using Find/Change ensures that you won't miss an occurrence.

5 Click Done, and then close the Story Editor.

6 Now that you made changes that might affect the flow of the document, check it again to ensure there are no bad line breaks or hyphenation — or worse.

7 Go to Page 1.

"Worse" happened. Due to the change from em dashes to en dashes, you lost an entire line of type in the first column, throwing off the first four pictures.

8 Use the Selection tool to click the first four photos (Judy, Max, Laurie, and John).

9 In the "Y" position in the Control palette, click the cursor after "in" and enter "–15 pt", since the leading is 15 pt.

All the photos move to their proper position.

10 Go to Page 2 and check it thoroughly. Nothing should have been affected.

11 Save your changes. Leave the document open for proofing and printing.

Print a Proof to Your Printer

No job is finished until the paperwork is done. When it comes to printing, "paperwork" means proofing for your own — and your client's — peace of mind.

1 With atwv_brochure.indd open, choose Window>Links and ensure that all linked files are present and have not been modified.

2 Open the Print dialog box.

3 Be sure the correct printer is selected, and that all pages are to be printed.

4 Choose Letter as the Paper Size and set the Scale to 100%.

5. In the Marks and Bleeds pane, nothing should be selected.

   If you select any bleeds, the printer will choose the edge of the bleed as the edge of the page, and your image will be improperly centered.

6. In the Output pane, select the appropriate color mode for your printer.
7. In the Graphics pane, be sure data is sent with Optimized Subsampling.
8. Click Print.
9. Review the printed document. Save the file. Leave it open.

Send a Proof to Your Client

Around the World Vacations wants to see a proof, and sending the client a proof is a company policy. You want the client to have the ultimate responsibility, not you.

1. In the open document, choose File>Export, and then choose the Adobe PDF format.
2. Save the document.
3. Choose the Print preset, ensure that all pages are selected, and choose View PDF After Exporting.
4. In the Compression pane, accept the defaults.
5. Your client does not need to see the printer's marks and bleeds.
6. Export the file.
7. View the PDF document. Leave the file open.

Prepare a Proof for the Service Provider

Unlike your client, your service provider needs a proof that shows printer's marks and bleeds. Graphic artists have been known to prepare documents that do not have appropriate bleed allowance, and the printer wants to know what he is up against before he begins — not after completing all the prepress work and setting up his schedule.

1. In the open document, access the Print menu.
2. Be sure the correct printer is selected, and then choose All Pages.
3. Set the Paper Size to Letter, the Orientation to Landscape, and the Scale to 100%. Click Tile.
4. In the Marks and Bleed frame, choose All Printer's Marks and Use Document Bleed Settings.

5. Select the appropriate color mode for your printer.

6. Optimized Subsampling should be selected in the Graphics frame.

7. Click Print.

8. When the pages emerge from the printer, assemble and review the to-size proof.

9. Leave the document open.

Package the Job for the Service Provider

You're ready to send this document to the service provider for printing.

1. In the open document, choose File>Package.

2. You may receive a message stating that the publication must be saved before continuing. If so, click Save.

3. The Printing Instructions pane appears, containing the information from the last document you packaged. In the Instructions section, make the following changes:

   Job: Around the World Vacations
   4-Color Process
   Qty: 10,000
   70 lb. Dull Coated Text
   Bleed: 0.125 in
   Trim: 8.5 × 11 in
   Letterfold

4. Click Continue.

5. Create a "GASP" folder within the WIP_IP folder. The same boxes you previously selected as options in this pane should still be selected. Click Save/Package.

6. Dismiss the Font Alert.

7. InDesign packages your document, and your instructions appear in a text window.

8. Save and close the document. Close the text editor.

Creating what appears to be a simple brochure can be demanding. Style sheets made this job much easier than it might have been. Using the techniques you learned in this project will help you produce better-than-average publications.

TASK GUIDE

Viewing Documents and Document Workspaces

NAVIGATING DOCUMENTS AND PAGES

Task	Macintosh	Windows
Open new default document	Command-Option-N	Control-Alt-N
Switch to next document window	Command-~ [tilde]	Control-~ [tilde]
Switch to previous document window	Command-Shift-~ [tilde]	Control-Shift-~ [tilde]
Scroll up one screen	Page Up	Page Up
Scroll down one screen	Page Down	Page Down
Go back to last-viewed page	Command-Page Up	Control-Page Up
Go forward to last-viewed page	Command-Page Down	Control-Page Down
Go to previous spread	Option-Page Up	Alt-Page Up
Go to next spread	Option-Page Down	Alt-Page Down
Select page number in page box	Command-J	Control-J
Go to master page (Pages palette closed)	Command-J, type prefix of master, Return	Control-J, type prefix of master, Enter

CONTROLLING THE DOCUMENT WINDOW

Task	Macintosh	Windows
Toggle between Normal View and Preview Mode	W	W
Zoom to 50%	Command-5	Control-5
Zoom to 200%	Command-2	Control-2
Zoom to 400%	Command-4	Control-4
Access zoom percent field	Command-Option-5	Control-Alt-5
Switch between current and previous zoom levels	Command-Option-2	Control-Alt-2
Redraw screen	Shift-F5	Shift-F5
Optimize screen redraw	Command-. [period]	Control-. [period]
Fit selection in window	Command-Option- + [plus sign]	Control-Alt- + [plus sign]
Select magnification box in document window	Command-Option-5 (main keyboard)	Control-Alt-5 (main keyboard)

MANAGING GUIDES

Task	Macintosh	Windows
Cycle through units of measurement	Command-Option-Shift-U	Control-Alt-Shift-U
Snap guide to ruler increments	Shift-drag guide	Shift-drag guide
Switch between page and spread guides (creation only)	Command-drag guide	Control-drag guide
Create vertical and horizontal ruler guides for the spread	Command drag from zero point	Control drag from zero point
Select all guides	Command-Option-G	Control-Alt-G
Lock or unlock zero point (contextual menu option)	Control-click zero point	Right-click zero point
Use current magnification for view threshold of new guide	Option-drag guide	Alt-drag guide

Selecting Tools

Task	Macintosh	Windows
Selection tool	V	V
Direct Selection tool	A	A
Toggle between Selection and Direct Selection tool	Command-Control-Tab	Control-Tab
Temporarily select Selection or Direct Selection tool (last used)	Command	Control
Temporarily select Group Selection tool (Direct Selection tool active)	Option	Alt
Temporarily select Group Selection tool (Pen, Add Anchor Point, or Delete Anchor Point tool active)	Command-Option	Control-Alt
Pen tool	P	P
Add Anchor Point tool	=	=
Delete Anchor Point tool	- [hyphen]	- [hyphen]
Convert Direction Point tool	Shift-C	Shift-C
Type tool	T	T
Type on a Path tool	Shift-T	Shift-T
Pencil tool	N	N
Line tool	\	\
Rectangle Frame tool	F	F
Rectangle tool	M	M
Ellipse tool	L	L
Rotate tool	R	R
Scale tool	S	S
Shear tool	O	O
Free Transform tool	E	E
Eyedropper tool	I	I
Measure tool	K	K
Gradient tool	G	G
Button tool	B	B
Scissors tool	C	C
Hand tool	H	H
Temporarily select Hand tool (Layout mode)	Spacebar	Spacebar
Temporarily select Hand tool (Text mode)	Option	Alt
Temporarily select Hand tool (Layout or Text mode)	Option-Spacebar	Alt-Spacebar
Zoom tool	Z	Z
Temporarily select Zoom In tool	Command-Spacebar	Control-Spacebar
Temporarily select Zoom Out tool	Command-Option-spacebar	Control-Alt-spacebar

Task	Macintosh	Windows

Using Palettes

Task	Macintosh	Windows
Delete without confirmation	Option-click Trash icon	Alt-click Trash icon
Create item and set options	Option-click New icon	Alt-click New icon
Apply value and keep focus on option	Shift-Enter	Shift-Enter
Activate last-used option in last-used palette	Command-Option-~ [tilde]	Control-Alt-~ [tilde]
Select range of items*	Shift-click	Shift-click
Select nonadjacent items*	Command-click	Control-click
Apply value and select next value	Tab	Tab
Move focus to selected object, text, or window	Esc	Esc

** Styles, Layer, Links, Swatches, or Library objects*

DISPLAYING PALETTES

Task	Macintosh	Windows
Show/Hide Align palette	Shift-F7	Shift-F7
Show/Hide Character palette	Command-T	Control-T
Show/Hide Character Styles palette	Shift-F11	Shift-F11
Show/Hide Color palette	F6	F6
Show/Hide Control palette	Command-Option-6	Control-Alt-6
Show/Hide Index palette	Shift-F8	Shift-F8
Show/Hide Info palette	F8	F8
Show/Hide Layers palette	F7	F7
Show/Hide Links palette	Command-Shift-D	Control-Shift-D
Show/Hide Pages palette	F12	F12
Show/Hide Paragraph palette	Command-Option-T	Control-Alt-T
Show/Hide Paragraph Styles palette	F11	F11
Show/Hide Separations palette	Shift-F6	Shift-F6
Show/Hide Stroke palette	F10	F10
Show/Hide Swatches palette	F5	F5
Show/Hide Table palette	Shift-F9	Shift-F9
Show/Hide Tabs palette	Command-Shift-T	Control-Shift-T
Show/Hide Text Wrap palette	Command-Option-W	Control-Alt-W
Show/Hide Transform palette	F9	F9
Show/Hide Transparency palette	Shift-F10	Shift-F10
Show/Hide all palettes	Tab	Tab
Show/Hide all palettes except Toolbox and Control palette	Shift-Tab	Shift-Tab
Stash a palette group	Option-drag a palette tab to edge of window	Alt-drag a palette tab to edge of screen
Open or close all stashed palettes	Command-Option-Tab	Control-Alt-Tab

Using Palettes (Cont'd)

Task	Macintosh	Windows
CHARACTER AND PARAGRAPH STYLES PALETTE		
Make character style definition match selected text	Command-Option-Shift-C	Control-Alt-Shift-C
Make paragraph style definition match selected text	Command-Option-Shift-R	Contaol-Alt-Shift-R
Change options without applying style	Command-Option-Shift-double-click style	Control-Alt-Shift-double-click style
Remove style and local formatting	Option-click paragraph style name	Alt-click paragraph style name
Clear overrides from paragraph style	Option-Shift-click paragraph style name	Alt-Shift-click paragraph style name
COLOR PALETTE		
Move color sliders in tandem	Shift-drag slider	Shift-drag slider
Select a color for the nonactive fill or stroke	Option-click color bar	Alt-click color bar
Switch between color modes (CMYK, RGB, LAB)	Shift-click color bar	Shift-click color bar
CONTROL PALETTE		
Enable/Disable controls	Spacebar	Spacebar
Toggle Character/Paragraph text attributes mode	Command-Option-7	Control-Alt-7
Change reference point when proxy has focus	Any numeric-keypad key or keyboard numbers	Any numeric-keypad key or keyboard numbers
Open Character Style Options dialog box	Option-click Character Style icon	Alt-click Character Style icon
Open Drop Caps & Nested Styles dialog box	Option-click Drop Cap Number of Lines or Drop Cap One or More Characters icon	Alt-click Drop Cap Number of Lines or Drop Cap One or More Characters icon
Open Justification dialog box	Option-click Leading icon	Alt-click Leading icon
Open Move dialog box	Option-click X or Y icon	Alt-click X or Y icon
Open New Character Style Options dialog box	Double-click Character Style icon	Double-click Character Style icon
Open Paragraph Style Options dialog box	Option-click Paragraph Style icon	Alt-click Paragraph Style icon
Open Rotate dialog box	Option-click Angle icon	Alt-click Angle icon
Open Scale dialog box	Option-click X or Y Scale icon	Alt-click X or Y Scale icon
Open Shear dialog box	Option-click Shear icon	Alt-click Shear icon
Open Strikethrough Options dialog box	Option-click Strikethrough icon	Alt-click Strikethrough icon
Open Text Frame Options dialog box	Option-click Number of Columns icon	Alt-click Number of Columns icon
Open Underline Options dialog box	Option-click Underline icon	Alt-click Underline icon
Open Grids pane of the Preferences dialog box	Option-click Align to Baseline Grid or Do Not Align to Baseline Grid icon	Alt-click Align to Baseline Grid or Do Not Align to Baseline Grid icon
Open Text pane of the Preferences dialog box	Option-click Superscript, Subscript, or Small Caps icon	Alt-click Superscript, Subscript, or Small Caps icon
Open Units & Increments pane of Preferences dialog box	Option-click Kerning icon	Alt-click Kerning icon

Task	Macintosh	Windows

Using Palettes (Cont'd)

LAYERS PALETTE

Task	Macintosh	Windows
Select all objects on layer	Option-click layer	Alt-click layer
Copy selection to new layer	Option-drag small square to new layer	Alt-drag small square to new layer

LINKS PALETTE

Task	Macintosh	Windows
Go to linked item	Option-double-click link file name	Alt-double-click link file name
Select all file names	Command-double-click link file name	Control-double-click link file name

PAGES PALETTE

Task	Macintosh	Windows
Apply master to selected page	Option-click master	Alt-click master
Create master page	Command-click Create New Page icon	Control-click Create New Page icon
Open Insert Pages dialog box	Option-click New Page icon	Alt-click New Page icon
Override all master page items for current spread	Command-Option-Shift-L	Control-Alt-Shift-L
Add new page after last page	Command-Shift-P	Control-Shift-P

SEPARATIONS PREVIEW PALETTE

Task	Macintosh	Windows
Turn on Overprint preview	Command-Option-Shift-Y	Control-Alt-Shift-Y
Show all plates	Command-Option-Shift-~ [tilde]	Control-Alt-Shift-~ [tilde]
Show Cyan plate	Command-Option-Shift-1	Control-Alt-Shift-1
Show Magenta plate	Command-Option-Shift-2	Control-Alt-Shift-2
Show Yellow plate	Command-Option-Shift-3	Control-Alt-Shift-3
Show Black plate	Command-Option-Shift-4	Control-Alt-Shift-4
Show 1st Spot plate	Command-Option-Shift-5	Control-Alt-Shift-5
Show 2nd Spot plate	Command-Option-Shift-6	Control-Alt-Shift-6
Show 3rd Spot plate	Command-Option-Shift-7	Control-Alt-Shift-7
Show 4th Spot plate	Command-Option-Shift-8	Control-Alt-Shift-8
Show 5th Spot plate	Command-Option-Shift-9	Control-Alt-Shift-9

SWATCHES PALETTE

Task	Macintosh	Windows
Create new swatch based on current swatch	Option-click New Swatch icon	Alt-click New Swatch icon
Create spot color swatch based on current swatch	Command-Option-click New Swatch icon	Control-Alt-click New Swatch icon
Change options without applying swatch	Command-Option-Shift-double-click swatch	Control-Alt-Shift-double-click swatch

TABS PALETTE

Task	Macintosh	Windows
Switch between alignment options	Option-click tab	Alt-click tab

TRANSFORM PALETTE

Task	Macintosh	Windows
Apply value and copy object	Option-Return	Alt-Enter
Apply width, height, or scale value proportionally	Command-Return	Control-Enter

Selecting and Moving Objects

Task	Macintosh	Windows
Add to or subtract from a selection of multiple objects (Selection, Direct Selection, or Group Selection tool active)	Shift-click	Shift-click
Select master page item from document page (Selection or Direct Selection tool active)	Command-Shift-click	Control-Shift-click
Select next object behind (Selection tool active)	Command-click	Control-click
Select next object in front (Selection tool active)	Command-Option-click	Control-Alt-click
Move selection*	Arrow keys	Arrow keys
Move selection by 10×*	Shift-Arrow keys	Shift-Arrow keys
Duplicate selection (Selection, Direct Selection, or Group Selection tool active)	Option-drag	Alt-drag
Duplicate and offset selection*	Option-Arrow keys	Alt-Arrow keys
Duplicate and offset selection by 10×*	Option-Shift-Arrow keys	Alt-Shift-Arrow keys

**Amount is set in Units & Increments pane of the Preferences dialog box*

Transforming Objects

Task	Macintosh	Windows
Duplicate and transform selection*	Transformation tool-Option-drag	Transformation tool-Alt-drag
Open Transform tool dialog box**	Double-click Scale, Rotate, or Shear tool in Toolbox	Double-click Scale, Rotate, or Shear tool in Toolbox
Decrease size by 1%	Command-<	Control-<
Decrease size by 5%	Command-Option-<	Control-Alt-<
Resize frame and content	Selection tool-Command-drag	Selection tool-Control-drag
Resize frame and content proportionately	Selection tool-Shift	Selection tool-Shift

**After you select a transformation tool, hold down the mouse button, then hold down Option/Alt and drag.*

***Transformation applies to selected object*

Editing Paths and Frames

Task	Macintosh	Windows
Temporarily switch between Direct Seletion and Convert Direction Point tool	Command-Option	Control-Alt
Temporarily switch between Pen and Convert Direction Point tool	Option	Alt
Temporarily switch between Add Anchor Point and Delete Anchor Point tool	Option	Alt
Temporarily switch between Add Anchor Point and Scissors tool	Option	Alt
Keep Pen tool selected when pointer is over path/anchor point	Shift	Shift
Move anchor point and handles while drawing with Pen tool	Spacebar	Spacebar

Working with Color

Task	Macintosh	Windows
Toggle Fill and Stroke	X	X
Swap Fill and Stroke	Shift-X	Shift-X
Apply color	, [comma]	, [comma]
Apply gradient	. [period]	. [period]
Apply No color	/	/

Working with Type

NAVIGATING AND SELECTING TEXT

Task	Macintosh	Windows
Move right one character*	Right Arrow	Right Arrow
Move left one character*	Left Arrow	Left Arrow
Move up one line*	Up Arrow	Up Arrow
Move down one line*	Down Arrow	Down Arrow
Move right one word	Command-Right Arrow	Control-Right Arrow
Move left one word	Command-Left Arrow	Control-Left Arrow
Move to start of line*	Home	Home
Move to end of line*	End	End
Move to beginning of current or to previous paragraph*	Command-Up Arrow	Control-Up Arrow
Move to beginning of next paragraph*	Command-Down Arrow	Control-Down Arrow
Move to start of story*	Command-Home	Control-Home
Move to end of story*	Command-End	Control-End
Select one word	Double-click word	Double-click word
Select one paragraph	Triple- or quadruple-click paragraph**	Triple- or quadruple-click paragraph**
Select current line	Command-Shift-\	Control-Shift-\
Select all in story	Command-A	Control-A
Select characters from insertion point	Shift-click	Shift-click
Select first frame	Command-Option-Shift-Page Up	Control-Alt-Shift-Page Up
Select last frame	Command-Option-Shift-Page Down	Control-Alt-Shift-Page Down
Select previous frame	Command-Option-Page Up	Control-Alt-Page Up
Select next frame	Command-Option-Page Down	Control-Alt-Page Down
Update missing font list	Command-Option-Shift-/	Control-Alt-Shift-/

**Add the Shift key to select intervening text*

***Depends on settings in the Text pane of the Preferences dialog box*

Task	Macintosh	Windows

Working with Type (Cont'd)

PLACING TEXT

Task	Macintosh	Windows
Automatically flow story	Shift-click loaded text icon	Shift-click loaded text icon
Semi-automatically flow story	Option-click loaded text icon	Alt-click loaded text icon
Recompose all stories	Command-Option-/	Control-Alt-/
Align to grid (on/off)	Command-Option-Shift-G	Control-Alt-Shift-G

APPLYING CHARACTER FORMATTING

Task	Macintosh	Windows
Bold	Command-Shift-B	Control-Shift-B
Italic	Command-Shift-I	Control-Shift-I
Normal	Command-Shift-Y	Control-Shift-Y
Underline	Command-Shift-U	Control-Shift-U
Strikethrough	Command-Shift-/	Control-Shift-/
All caps (on/off)	Command-Shift-K	Control-Shift-K
Small caps (on/off)	Command-Shift-H	Control-Shift-H
Superscript	Command-Shift- + [plus sign]	Control-Shift- + [plus sign]
Subscript	Command-Option-Shift- + [plus sign]	Control-Alt-Shift- + [plus sign]
Reset horizontal scale to 100%	Command-Shift-X	Control-Shift-X
Reset vertical scale to 100%	Command-Option-Shift-X	Control-Alt-Shift-X
Increase point size*	Command-Shift->	Control-Shift->
Decrease point size*	Command-Shift-<	Control-Shift-<
Increase point size by 5×*	Command-Shift- Option->	Control-Alt-Shift->
Decrease point size by 5×*	Command-Shift- Option-<	Control-Alt-Shift-<
Increase kerning and tracking (horizontal text)	Option-Right Arrow	Alt-Right Arrow
Decrease kerning and tracking (horizontal text)	Option-Left Arrow	Alt-Left Arrow
Increase kerning and tracking (vertical text)	Option-Up Arrow	Alt-Up Arrow
Decrease kerning and tracking (vertical text)	Option-Down Arrow	Alt-Down Arrow
Increase kerning and tracking by 5× (horizontal text)	Command-Option-Right Arrow	Control-Alt-Right Arrow
Decrease kerning and tracking by 5× (horizontal text)	Command-Option-Left Arrow	Control-Alt-Left Arrow
Increase kerning and tracking by 5× (vertical text)	Command-Option-Up Arrow	Control-Alt-Up Arrow
Decrease kerning and tracking by 5× (vertical text)	Command-Option-Down Arrow	Control-Alt-Down Arrow
Increase kerning between words*	Command-Option-\	Control-Alt-\
Decrease kerning between words*	Command-Option-Delete	Control-Alt-Backspace
Clear manual kerning and reset tracking to 0	Command-Option-Q	Control-Alt-Q
Select or deselect preferences setting for typographer's marks	Command-Option-Shift-" [quote]	Control-Alt-Shift-" [quote]

Task	Macintosh	Windows

Working with Type (Cont'd)

APPLYING PARAGRAPH FORMATTING

Task	Macintosh	Windows
Open Justification dialog box	Command-Option-Shift-J	Control-Alt-Shift-J
Open Paragraph Rules dialog box	Command-Option-J	Control-Alt-J
Open Keep Options dialog box	Command-Option-K	Control-Alt-K
Align left	Command-Shift-L	Control-Shift-L
Align right	Command-Shift-R	Control-Shift-R
Align center	Command-Shift-C	Control-Shift-C
Justify all lines (but last line)	Command-Shift-J	Control-Shift-J
Justify all lines (including last line)	Command-Shift-F	Control-Shift-F
Increase leading (horizontal text)*	Option-Up Arrow	Alt-Up Arrow
Decrease leading (horizontal text)*	Option-Down Arrow	Alt-Down Arrow
Increase leading (vertical text)*	Option-Right Arrow	Alt-Right Arrow
Decrease leading (vertical text)*	Option-Left Arrow	Alt-Left Arrow
Increase leading by 5× (horizontal text)*	Command-Option-Up Arrow	Control-Alt-Up Arrow
Decrease leading by 5× (horizontal text)*	Command-Option-Down Arrow	Control-Alt-Down Arrow
Increase leading by 5× (vertical text)*	Command-Option-Right Arrow	Control-Alt-Right Arrow
Decrease leading by 5× (vertical text)*	Command-Option-Left Arrow	Control-Alt-Left Arrow
Auto leading	Command-Option-Shift-A	Control-Alt-Shift-A
Auto-hyphenate (on/off)	Command-Option-Shift-H	Control-Alt-Shift-H
Increase baseline shift (horizontal text)**	Option-Shift-Up Arrow	Alt-Shift-Up Arrow
Decrease baseline shift (horizontal text)**	Option-Shift-Down Arrow	Alt-Shift-Down Arrow
Increase baseline shift (vertical text)**	Option-Shift-Right Arrow	Alt-Shift-Right Arrow
Decrease baseline shift (vertical text)**	Option-Shift-Left Arrow	Alt-Shift-Left Arrow
Increase baseline shift by 5× (horizontal text)**	Command-Option-Shift-Up Arrow	Control-Alt-Shift-Up Arrow
Decrease baseline shift by 5× (horizontal text)**	Command-Option-Shift-Down Arrow	Control-Alt-Shift-Down Arrow
Increase baseline shift by 5× (vertical text)**	Command-Option-Shift-Right Arrow	Control-Alt-Shift-Right Arrow
Decrease baseline shift by 5× (vertical text)**	Command-Option-Shift-Left Arrow	Control-Alt-Shift-Left Arrow

**Press Shift to increase or decrease kerning between words by five times.*

***Amount is set in Units & Increments pane of the Preferences dialog box*

Working with Type (Cont'd)

USING SPECIAL CHARACTERS

Task	Macintosh	Windows
Column Break	Enter	Numeric Enter
Forced Line Break	Shift-Return	Shift-Enter
Frame Break	Shift-Enter	Shift-Numeric Enter
Page Break	Command-Enter	Control-Numeric Enter
Indent to Here	Command-\	Control-\
Right Indent Tab	Shift-Tab	Shift-Tab
Auto Page Number	Command-Option-Shift-N	Control-Alt-Shift-N
Previous Page Number	Command-Option-Shift-[	Control-Alt-Shift-[
Next Page Number	Command-Option-Shift-]	Control-Alt-Shift-]
Current Page Number	Command-Option-N	Control-Alt-N
Bullet Character (•)	Option-8	Alt-8
Copyright Symbol (©)	Option-G	Alt-G
Ellipsis (...)	Option-;	Alt-;
Paragraph Symbol (¶)	Option-7	Alt-7
Registered Trademark Symbol (®)	Option-R	Alt-R
Section Symbol (§)	Option-6	Alt-6
Single Left Quotation Mark (‘)	Option-]	Alt-]
Single Right Quotation Mark (’)	Option-Shift-]	Alt-Shift-]
Double Left Quotation Mark (“)	Option-[	Alt-[
Double Right Quotation Mark (”)	Option-Shift-[	Alt-Shift-[
Discretionary Hyphen	Command-Shift- - [hyphen]	Control-Shift- - [hyphen]
Nonbreaking Hyphen	Command-Option- - [hyphen]	Control-Alt- - [hyphen]
Em Dash	Option-Shift- - [hyphen]	Alt-Shift- - [hyphen]
En Dash	Option- - [hyphen]	Alt- - [hyphen]
Em Space	Command-Shift-M	Control-Shift-M
En Space	Command-Shift-N	Control-Shift-N
Hair Space	Command-Option-Shift-I	Control-Alt-Shift-I
Nonbreaking Space	Command-Option-X	Control-Alt-X
Thin Space	Command-Option-Shift-M	Control-Alt-Shift-M

Task	Macintosh	Windows

Finding and Changing Text

Task	Macintosh	Windows
Insert selected text into Find What box	Command-F1	Control-F1
Insert selected text into Find What box and finds next	Shift-F1	Shift-F1
Find next occurrence of Find What text	Shift-F2 or Command-Option-F	Shift-F2 or Control-Alt-F
Insert selected text into Change To box	Command-F2	Control-F2
Replace selection with Change To text	Command-F3	Control-F3

Working with Tables

Task	Macintosh	Windows
Insert or delete rows or columns while dragging	Begin dragging row or column border, then hold down Option as you drag	Begin dragging row or column border, then hold down Alt as you drag
Resize rows or columns without changing table size	Shift-drag interior row/column border	Shift-drag interior row/column border
Resize rows or columns proportionally	Shift-drag right or bottom table border	Shift-drag right or bottom table border
Move to next cell	Tab	Tab
Move to previous cell	Shift-Tab	Shift-Tab
Move to first cell in column	Option-Page Up	Alt-Page Up
Move to last cell in column	Option-Page Down	Alt-Page Down
Move to first cell in row	Option-Home	Alt-Home
Move to last cell in row	Option-End	Alt-End
Move to first row in frame	Page Up	Page Up
Move to last row in frame	Page Down	Page Down
Move up, down, left, or right one cell	Arrow keys	Arrow keys
Select cell above the current cell	Shift-Up Arrow	Shift-Up Arrow
Select cell below the current cell	Shift-Down Arrow	Shift-Down Arrow
Select cell to the right of the current cell	Shift-Right Arrow	Shift-Right Arrow
Select cell to the left of the current cell	Shift-Left Arrow	Shift-Left Arrow
Start row on next column	Enter (numeric keypad)	Enter (numeric keypad)
Start row on next frame	Shift-Enter (numeric keypad)	Shift-Enter (numeric keypad)
Toggle between text selection and cell selection	Esc	Esc

Indexing

Task	Macintosh	Windows
Create index entry without dialog box	Command-Option-U	Control-Alt-U
Open Index entry dialog box	Command-U	Control-U
Create proper name index entry (last name, first name)	Command-Shift-F8	Control-Shift-F8

Navigating XML

Task	Macintosh	Windows
Expand/Collapse element	Right Arrow/Left Arrow key	Right Arrow/Left Arrow key
Expand/Collapse element and child elements	Option-Right Arrow/Left Arrow key	Alt-Right Arrow/Left Arrow key
Extend XML selection up/down	Shift-Up Arrow/Down Arrow key	Shift-Up Arrow/Down Arrow key
Move XML selection up/down	Up Arrow/Down Arrow key	Up Arrow/Down Arrow key
Scroll structure pane up/down one screen	Page Up/Page Down key	Page Up/Page Down key
Select first/last XML node	Home/End key	Home/End key
Extend selection to first/last XML node	Shift-Home/End key	Shift-Home/End key
Go to previous/next validation error	Command-Left Arrow/Right Arrow key	Control-Left Arrow/Right Arrow key

GLOSSARY

A/As Author's Alterations. Changes made to the copy by the author after typesetting, and thus chargeable to the author.

Acrobat A program developed by Adobe Systems, Inc. that allows the conversion of any document from any Macintosh or Windows application to PDF format. It is widely used for distributing documents online.

Acrobat Reader A stand-alone program or Web browser plug-in from Adobe that allows you to view a PDF file. Acrobat Reader is free and can be downloaded from the Adobe Web site.

additive color The process of mixing red, green, and blue light to achieve a wide range of colors, as on a color television screen.

Adobe Paragraph Composer The text composition engine present in Adobe InDesign. Loosely based on Donald Knuth's TeX composition algorithms, this is the only desktop product that can perform text composition on multiple lines of text at one time.

align panel A panel that provides a number of options for aligning objects, relative to each other or to the document.

alignment Positioning content to the left, right, center, top, or bottom.

anchor points The individual points that define the shape of a vector-based graphic element. Anchor points are connected by line segments.

anti-aliasing A graphics software feature that eliminates or softens the jaggedness of low-resolution curved edges.

ascender Part of a lowercase letter that exceeds the height of the letter "x". The letters b, d, f, h, k, l, and t have ascenders.

ASCII American Standard Code for Information Interchange. Worldwide, standard ASCII text does not include formatting, and therefore can be exchanged and read by most computer systems.

aspect ratio The width-to-height proportions of an image.

ATM Adobe Type Manager. A utility that causes fonts to appear smooth on screen at any point size. It's also used to manage font libraries.

attribute Information included in the start tag of an element.

automatic text box A text box that appears on the default master page; it snaps to the defined margin guides.

auxiliary dictionary A supplementary file that is used to store unusual, technical, or other words that do not appear in the built-in dictionary.

backslant A name for characters that slant the opposite direction from italic characters.

banding A visible stair-stepping of shades in a gradient.

baseline The implied reference line on which the bases of capital letters sit.

baseline shift A formatting option that moves selected characters above or below the baseline of normal text.

Bézier curves Vector curves that are defined mathematically. These curves can be scaled without the "jaggies" inherent in enlarging bitmapped fonts or graphics.

binding In general, the various methods used to secure signatures or leaves in a book. Examples include saddle-stitching (the use of staples in a folded spine), and perfect-bound (multiple sets of folded pages sewn or glued into a flat spine).

binding edge The edge of a page that is inserted into the publication's binding.

bitmap image An image constructed from individual dots or pixels set to a grid-like mosaic. The file must contain information about the color and position of each pixel, so the disk space needed for bitmap images can be very large.

bitmapped Forming an image with a grid of pixels whose curved edges have discrete steps because of the approximation of the curve due to a finite number pixels.

bitmapping The stairstepped appearance of graphics, caused by enlarging raster images.

black The absence of color. An ink that absorbs all wavelengths of light.

bleed Page data that extends beyond the trim marks on a page.

bleed allowance The extra portion of an element that extends beyond the page trim edge.

bleed size An element of page geometry; the trim size plus the bleed allowance.

BMP A Windows bitmap image format that features low-quality and large file sizes.

body copy The text portion of the copy on a page, as distinguished from headlines.

boldface A heavier, blacker version of a typeface.

border A continual line that extends around an element.

bounding box An area that defines the outer border of an object.

bullet A marker preceding text, usually a solid dot, used to add emphasis; generally indicates the text is part of a list.

by-line A short phrase or paragraph that names and gives credit to the author of a piece.

calibration bars A strip of color blocks or tonal values on film, proofs, and press sheets, used to check the accuracy of color registration, quality, density, and ink coverage during a print run.

callout A descriptive label referenced to a visual element, such as several words connected to the element by an arrow.

cap line The theoretical line to which the tops of capital letters are aligned.

caps Abbreviation for capital letters.

caps and small caps A style of typesetting in which capital letters are used in the normal way, while the type that would normally be in lowercase is changed to capital letters of a smaller point size. A true small-caps typeface does not contain any lowercase letters.

caption The lines of text that identify a picture or illustration, usually placed beneath it or otherwise in close proximity.

center marks Press marks that appear on the center of all sides of a press sheet to aid in positioning the print area on the paper.

character count The number of characters (letters, figures, signs, or spaces) in a selected block of copy.

character style sheet A style sheet that defines only character formatting attributes, including font, type size, text color, and type style.

clip art Collections of predrawn and digitized graphics.

clipboard The portion of computer memory that holds data that has been cut or copied. The next item cut or copied replaces the data already in the clipboard.

clipping path A path that determines which parts of an image show on the page. Anything inside the path shows and prints; anything outside the path won't. The clipping path essentially knocks out the unwanted part of the image.

CMYK Cyan, Magenta, Yellow, Black. The subtractive primaries, or process colors, used in four-color printing.

coated Printing papers that have a surface coating (of clay or other material) to provide a smoother, more even finish with greater opacity.

collate To gather together separate sections or leaves of a publication in the correct order for binding.

color chart A printed chart of various combinations of CMYK colors used as an aid for the selection of colors during the design phase of a project.

color composition The ink components that are combined to make up a specific color.

color key An overlay color proof of acetate sheets, one for each of the four primary printing inks. The method was developed by 3M Corporation and remains a copyrighted term.

color mode A system for describing color, such as RGB, HLS, CIELAB, or CMYK.

color picker A function within a graphics application that assists in selecting or setting a color.

color proof A printed or simulated printed image of the color separations intended to produce a close representation of the final reproduction for approval and as a guide to the press operator.

color separation The process of transforming color artwork into components corresponding to the colors of ink being used, whether process or spot, or a combination of the two.

color space A three-dimensional coordinate system in which any color can be represented as a point.

column 1. A vertical area for type, used to constrain line length to enhance design and readability. 2. A series of cells arranged vertically.

column guides The guides that denote the location of gutters between columns.

commercial printing Typically, printing on high-capacity, high-resolution presses; processes include offset lithography, flexography, gravure, and screen printing. Offset printing is the most widely used commercial printing process.

comp Comprehensive artwork used to present the general color and layout of a page.

composite proof A version of an illustration or page in which the process colors appear together to represent full color. When produced on a monochrome output device, colors are represented as shades of gray.

contextual menu A menu containing options that are only relative to the object for which the menu is activated.

control handle Nonprinting lines that define the shape or segments that connect two anchor points.

coordinates Numbers signifying a place in a Cartesian plane, represented by (x,y).

copy 1. Written matter intended to be reproduced in printed form. 2. The text of a news story, advertisement, television commercial, etc., as distinguished from related visual material.

copyfitting Making sure you don't write more text than you have room to accommodate.

copyright Ownership of a work. Permits the owner of material to prevent its use without express permission or acknowledgement of the originator. Copyright may be sold, transferred, or given up contractually.

corner radius The distance between the anchor points that define the corners of beveled-, rounded-, or concave-corner boxes.

crop marks Printed lines used as guides for final trimming of the pages within a press sheet. Also called "trim marks."

cropping The elimination of parts of a photograph or other original that are not required to be printed.

curly quotes See *smart quotes.*

cursor A small symbol that can be moved around a video screen. Used to indicate the position where data will be entered or an action taken.

dash A short horizontal rule of varying lengths used to indicate a pause or clause in a sentence. See *en dash, em dash.*

dateline In a news release, the identification of the city where the company issuing the release is located, as well as the date on which the release was written.

decorative font Display type that is typically an artistic representation of some theme, which is commonly indicated in the font name (e.g., Eyechart or Papyrus).

default A specification for a mode of computer operation that occurs if no other is selected. The default font size might be 12 point, or a default color for an object might be white with a black border.

device-independent color Reproduction in which the output color is absolute, and is not determined by the output device characteristics.

DICColor A special-color library commonly used in Japan.

dictionary A collection of words used to determine appropriate spelling and hyphenation.

dingbat 1. A font character that displays a picture instead of a letter, number, or punctuation mark. There are entire font families of pictographic dingbats. 2. A printer's typographical ornament.

discretionary hyphen A hyphen coded for display and printing only when formatting of the text puts the hyphenated word at the end of a line. Also called a "soft hyphen."

display performance In InDesign, this option allows you to choose Optimized Display, Typical Display, or High-Quality Display. Optimized Display grays out images, so the pages repaint faster; High-Quality Display enhances the display quality of images, and the page repaints slower.

document The general term for a computer file containing text and/or graphics.

double-page spread A design that spans the two pages visible to the reader at any open spot in a magazine, periodical, or book.

draw-type pictures Pictures created from a series of instructions that tell the computer to draw lines, curves, rectangles, and other objects. Also called "object-oriented images" or "vector graphics." See *bitmap image.*

drop cap Text formatting in which the first one or more characters in a paragraph is enlarged to occupy more than one line in the paragraph.

drop-down menu A selection list.

duplicate Make a copy.

editable text A text element that the user can modify by entering or deleting keystrokes.

editorial priority The order of importance for text in a document.

effective resolution The final resolution of an image, calculated by dividing the image resolution (pixels per inch) by the magnification percentage.

element The smallest unit of a graphic, or a component of a page layout or design. Any object, text block, or graphic might be referred to as a design element.

em A printers measurement; the height, in points, of the font size.

em dash A dash (—) that indicates the separation of elements of a sentence or clause.

em space A space that is of equal width in points to the point size. An em space in 10 point type is 10 points wide.

embedded font A font that is made part of a document.

embedding Including a complete copy of a text file or image within a document, with or without a link.

en dash A dash (–), half the width of an em dash, that often replaces the word "to" or "through," such as 9–5 or Monday–Friday.

en space A space that is equal to half the width of an em space.

EPS Encapsulated PostScript. File format used to transfer PostScript data within compatible applications. EPS files can contain text, vector artwork, and images.

expanded type A typeface in which the width of the letters is wider than that of the standard letters of the font. Expanded type can be a designed font, or the effect may be approximated using a horizontal scaling feature. Also called extended type.

expert set A font that includes "cut" small caps, meaning that they were specially designed from the start to be used as small caps, and they maintain the same weight as the regular cap.

export To save a file generated in one application into a format that is readable in another.

extended characters Characters that cannot be accessed directly from the keyboard; for the most part, characters with an ASCII value higher than 128.

facing pages A type of layout in which the pages of a design appear opposite each other, as in the pages of a book. See *non-facing pages*.

fair use Using copyrighted work without obtaining permission from the copyright holder for purposes such as critique, education, or research.

fill To add a tone or color to the area inside a closed object in a graphic illustration program.

fill character The character that appears between the text at each tab location.

Focoltone A special-color library used in the United States.

folder The digital equivalent of a paper file folder, used to organize files in the Macintosh and Windows operating systems. Double-clicking the icon opens it to reveal the files stored inside.

folding dummy A template used for determining page arrangement on a form to meet folding and binding requirements.

font A font is the complete collection of all the characters (numbers, uppercase and lowercase letters, and in some cases, small caps and symbols) of a given typeface in a specific style; for example, Helvetica Bold.

font embedding The technique of saving font data as a part of a PDF file, which eliminates problems caused by missing font files.

font family In Web design, a grouping of (supposedly) similar fonts, which will be used to display text in the Web page.

font license The legal right to use a font you purchased; most licenses limit fonts to use on a single computer.

font metrics The physical characteristics of a font, as defined in the font data file.

font subsetting Embedding only the used characters of a font into the final file. The advantage of font subsetting is that it decreases the overall size of a file. The disadvantage is that it limits the ability to makes corrections at the printing service.

font substitution A process in which your computer uses a font other than the one you used in your design to display or print your publication. Usually occurs when a used font is missing on the computer used to output the design.

force justify A type alignment command that causes the space between letters and words in a line of type to expand to fit within a line.

four-color process Process color printer. See *process colors.*

FPO For position only. A term applied to low-quality images or simple shapes used to indicate placement and scaling of an art element on mechanicals or camera-ready artwork.

frame The physical characteristics of a box edge.

full measure A line set to the entire line length.

GASP Graphic arts service provider. A firm that provides a range of services somewhere on the continuum from design to fulfillment.

glyph Any character of a font.

gradient A gradual transition from one color to another. The shape of the gradient and the proportion of the two colors can be varied. Also known as blends, gradations, graduated fills, and vignettes.

grayed out Any option (menu selection, button, etc.) that is not available.

grayscale 1. An image composed in grays ranging from black to white, usually using 256 different tones. 2. A tint ramp used to measure and control the accuracy of screen percentages. 3. An accessory used to define neutral density in a photographic image.

Greeking 1. A software technique where areas of gray are used to simulate lines of text below a certain point size. 2. Nonsense text used to define a layout before copy is available.

grid A division of a page by horizontal and vertical guides into areas where text or graphics may be placed accurately.

gutter Extra space between pages in a layout. Sometimes used interchangeably with "alley" to describe the space between columns on a page. Gutters can appear either between the top and bottom of two adjacent pages or between two sides of adjacent pages.

gutter width The space between columns on a layout page.

H & J Hyphenation and Justification. Parameters used by a page-layout program to determine how a line of text should be hyphenated, or how its inter-word and inter-character space should be adjusted.

hairline rule The thinnest rule that can be printed on a given device. A hairline rule on a 1200-dpi imagesetter is 1/1200 of an inch; on a 300-dpi laser printer, the same rule would print at 1/300 of an inch.

halftone An image generated for use in printing in which a range of continuous tones is simulated by an array of dots that create the illusion of continuous tone when seen at a distance.

halftone tint An area covered with a uniform halftone dot size to produce an even tone or color. Also called flat tint or screen tint.

hanging indent Text in which the first line of a paragraph is placed farther left than the rest of the paragraph.

horizontal scale A technique used for creating artificially condensed type.

hyphenation exception A user-defined change to the way a specific word will be hyphenated in a layout.

hyphenation zone The space at the end of a line of text in which the hyphenation function will examine the word to determine whether it should be hyphenated and wrapped to the next line.

imagesetter A raster-based device used to output a digital file at high resolution (usually 1000–3000 dpi) onto photographic paper or film, from which printing plates are made, or directly to printing plates (called a "platesetter").

imposition The arrangement of pages on a printed sheet, which, when the sheet is finally printed, folded, and trimmed, will place the pages in their correct order.

impression cylinder In commercial printing, a cylinder that provides back pressure, thus allowing the image to be transferred from the blanket to the substrate.

initial caps Text in which the first letter of each word (except articles) is capitalized.

inline graphic A graphic that is inserted within a body of text, and may be formatted using normal text commands for justification and leading; inline graphics move with the body of text in which they are placed.

input An element, such as a text box, that receives information from the user.

insertion point A flashing bar that indicates the location at which text will be placed.

intellectual property Any product of human intelligence that is unique, novel, unobvious, and valuable (such as a literary work, idea, or invention).

international paper sizes The International Standards Organization (ISO) system of paper sizes based on a series of three sizes — A, B, and C. Each size has the same proportion of length to width as the others.

invisible characters See *non-printing characters.*

jaggies Visible steps in the curved edge of a graphic or text character that result from enlarging a bitmapped image.

job package The collected group of all elements that must be sent to a service provide or printer, including a desktop proof, the project file, any images or graphics placed in the layout, and all fonts used in the design.

job specifications Detailed information about a particular job; required to complete the design and print the final product. Includes page geometry, number of ink colors, type of paper being used, finishing requirements, delivery instructions, and other relevant information.

JPEG A compression algorithm that reduces the file size of bitmapped images, named for the Joint Photographic Experts Group, which created the standard. JPEG is "lossy" compression; image quality is reduced in direct proportion to the amount of compression.

justified alignment Straight left and right alignment of text — not ragged. Every line of text is the same width, creating even left and right margins.

keyboard equivalents User-defined shortcuts to style sheets.

L*a*b* The lightness, red-green attribute, and yellow-blue attribute in the CIE L*a*b* color space, a three-dimensional color mapping system.

laser printer A printing system using a laser beam to produce an image on a photosensitive drum. The image is transferred to paper by a conventional xerographic printing process. Current laser printers used for desktop publishing have a resolution of 600 dpi.

lasso tool A selection tool in graphics applications.

layer A function of graphics applications in which elements may be isolated from each other, so a group of elements can be hidden from view, reordered, or otherwise manipulated as a unit, without affecting other elements in the composition.

layout The arrangement of text and graphics on a page, usually produced in the preliminary design stage.

layout space Another term for layout.

leading Space added between lines of type. Named after the strips of lead that used to be inserted between lines of metal type. In specifying type, lines of 12-pt type separated by a 14-pt space is abbreviated "12/14," or "twelve over fourteen."

left alignment Text having a straight left edge and a ragged or uneven right edge.

letter spacing The insertion or addition of white space between the letters of words.

ligature Letters that are joined together as a single unit of type such as œ and fi.

line art A drawing or piece of black-and-white artwork with no screens. Line art can be represented by a graphic file having only 1-bit resolution.

line coordinates The location and length of a line; defined according to the position and type of anchor points that comprise the line.

line segment The part of a line between two anchor points.

line style The physical appearance of a line; can be plain (solid), dotted, dashed, thin-and-thick, etc.

lithography A mechanical printing process based on the principle of the natural aversion of water to grease. In modern offset lithography, the image on a photosensitive plate is first transferred to the blanket of a rotating drum, and then to the paper.

live area One of the elements of page geometry; the area of a page that can be safely printed without the possibility of being lost in the binding or cut off when the job is trimmed.

lpi Lines per inch. The number of lines per inch used when converting a photograph to a halftone. Typical values range from 85 for newspaper work to 150 or higher for high-quality reproduction on smooth or coated paper. Also called "line screen."

margin guides Guides that denote the live area of a layout page.

margins The non-printing areas of a page, or the line at which text starts or stops.

master font The primary font in a font family, from which variations are derived.

master pages Page-layout templates containing elements common to all pages to which the master is applied.

mechanical A pasted-up page of camera-ready art that is photographed to produce a plate for the press.

menu A list of choices of functions or items, such as fonts.

menu bar The strip across the top of your screen that contains the names of the menus available to you.

menu styling Artificial type styling, typically applied by choosing shortcuts from a menu or palette, or by using a keyboard shortcut.

misregister The unwanted result of incorrectly aligned process inks and spot colors on a finished printed piece. Misregistration can be caused by many factors, including paper stretch and improper plate alignment. Trapping can compensate for misregistration.

monospace A font in which all characters occupy the same amount of horizontal width regardless of the character. See also *proportional spacing.*

named colors A set of colors specifically designated for reference by name, rather than by RGB or hexadecimal values.

nesting Placing graphic files within other graphic files. This practice often results in errors in printing.

non-breaking space A typographic command that connects two words with a space, but prevents the words from being broken apart if the space occurs within the hyphenation zone.

non-facing pages A type of layout in which the pages of a design do not appear opposite each other. See *facing pages.*

non-printing characters Formatting characters (such as paragraph returns and tabs) that do not appear in the final printed piece.

nudge To move a graphic or text element in small, preset increments, usually with the Arrow keys.

object A reference to a collection of properties and methods.

object-oriented art Vector-based artwork composed of separate elements or shapes described mathematically, rather than by specifying the color and position of every point. This is in contrast to bitmap images, which are composed of individual pixels.

oblique A slanted character; often used when referring to italic versions of sans-serif typefaces.

offset The distance at which rules are placed above or below paragraphs of text; can be defined as a specific measurement or as a percentage of paragraph spacing.

offset lithography A printing method whereby the image is transferred from a plate onto a rubber-covered cylinder, from which the printing takes place. See *lithography.*

OpenType A font format developed by Adobe and Microsoft that can be used on both the Windows and Macintosh platforms, can contain over 65,000 distinct glyphs, and offers advanced typographic features.

optical margin alignment In InDesign, with the Optical Margin Alignment option selected, certain characters are placed to the left or right of the escapement of a text frame, "hanging" into the margin.

ordered list A list of numbered items.

orphan A single or partial word, or a partial line of a paragraph appearing at the bottom of a page. See *widow.*

output device Any hardware equipment, such as a monitor, laser printer, or imagesetter, that depicts text or graphics created on a computer.

outset The distance at which text flows around the edge of a picture or box.

page geometry The physical attributes of a layout page. See *trim size, live area, bleed size.*

palette 1. As derived from the term in the traditional art world, a collection of selectable colors. 2. Another name for a dialog box or menu of choices.

PANTONE Matching System PMS. A system for specifying colors by number for both coated and uncoated paper; used by print services and in color desktop publishing to assure uniform color matching.

paragraph style sheet A style sheet that defines the appearance of the paragraph, combining the character style to be used in the paragraph with the line spacing, indents, tabs, rules, and other paragraph attributes.

parent style sheet The style sheet on which other styles are based; changing the definition of the parent affects any style sheet that is based on the parent.

pasteboard In a page-layout program, the desktop area outside the printing-page area.

PDF Portable Document Format. Developed by Adobe Systems, Inc. (read by Acrobat Reader), this format has become a de facto standard for document transfer across platforms.

PDF workflow A workflow in which PDF files are used to transmit designs to a service provider for output.

pi fonts A collection of special characters, such as timetable symbols and mathematical signs. Examples are Zapf Dingbats and Symbol. See *dingbat.*

pica A traditional typographic measurement of 12 points, or approximately 1/6 of an inch. Most applications specify a pica as exactly 1/6 of an inch.

placeholder text In InDesign, a utility for placing nonsense text into a text box. Used to experiment with formatting and layout before the actual job text is ready.

pop-up menu A menu of choices accessed by clicking and dragging the current choice.

portrait Printing from left to right across the narrow side of the page.

PostScript 1. A page-description language, developed by Adobe Systems, Inc., that describes type and/or images and their positional relationships on the page. 2. A computer-programming language.

preferences A set of modifiable defaults for an application.

preflight check A final check of a page layout that verifies all fonts and linked graphics are available, that colors are properly defined, and that any necessary traps have been applied.

prepress All work done between writing and printing, such as typesetting, scanning, layout, and imposition.

preproduction Preparation of all production details.

printer driver The device that communicates between the software program and the printer. When using an application, the printer driver tells the application what the printer can do, and also tells the printer how to print the publication.

printer fonts The image outlines for type in PostScript that are sent to the printer.

printer's marks See *trim marks, registration marks.*

printer's spread The two pages that abut on press in a multi-page document.

process colors The four inks (cyan, magenta, yellow, and black) used in four-color process printing. A printing method in which a full range of colors is reproduced by combining four semi-transparent inks. See *color separation, CMYK.*

proof A representation of the printed job that is made from plates (press proof), film, or electronic data (prepress proofs). It is generally used for customer inspection and approval before mass production begins.

proportional spacing A method of spacing whereby each character is spaced to accommodate the varying widths of letters or figures, thus increasing readability. For example, a proportionally spaced "m" is wider than an "i."

pt. Abbreviation for point.

pull quote An excerpt from the body of a story used to emphasize an idea, draw readers' attention, or generate interest.

pull-down menu A menu that displays additional options.

range kerning Another term for tracking.

raster A bitmapped representation of graphic data.

raster graphics A class of graphics created and organized in a rectangular array of bitmaps. Often created by paint software or scanners.

raster image A type of picture created and organized in a rectangular array of bitmaps. Often created by paint software, scanners, or digital cameras.

reader's spread The two (or more) pages a reader views when the document is open.

registration Aligning plates on a multicolor printing press so the images superimpose properly to produce the required composite output.

registration color A default color selection that can be applied to design elements so they will print on every separation from a PostScript printer. "Registration" is often used to print identification text that will appear outside the page area on a set of separations.

registration marks Figures (often crossed lines and a circle) placed outside the trim page boundaries on all color separation overlays to provide a common element for proper alignment.

resolution The density of graphic information expressed in dots per inch (dpi) or pixels per inch (ppi).

resolution dependent A characteristic of raster images, in which the file's resolution is determined when the file is created, scanned, or photographed.

resolution independent A characteristic of vector graphics, in which the file adopts its resolution at the time of output based on the capabilities of the device being used.

RGB 1. The colors of projected light from a computer monitor that, when combined, simulate a subset of the visual spectrum. 2. The color mode of most digital artwork. See also *CMYK, additive color.*

right alignment Text having a straight right edge and a ragged or uneven left edge.

robust kerning A feature of professionally designed fonts, in which kerning values for specific letter pairs are built into the font metrics.

ruler Similar to a physical ruler, a feature of graphics software used for precise measurement and alignment of objects. Rulers appear in the top and left edges of the document window. See *grid.*

ruler guides Horizontal and vertical guides that can be placed anywhere on the page by dragging from the rulers at the edge of the document window.

rules 1. Straight lines. 2. Lines that are placed above or below paragraphs of text.

runaround A technique used to flow text around the outside of another shape; text can be wrapped around the edges of a box, or contoured to the shape of a placed image. Also called text wrap.

running head Text at the top of the page that provides information about the publication. Chapter names and book titles are often included in the running head. Also called a "header."

sans serif Fonts that do not have serifs. See *serif.*

scaling The means within a program to reduce or enlarge the amount of space an image occupies by multiplying the data by a factor. Scaling can be proportional, or in one dimension only.

script font Typefaces that appear to have been created with a pen or a brush, whether the letters are connected or unconnected.

select Place the cursor on an object and click the mouse button to make the object active.

select option A potential choice listed in a select list.

selection The currently active object,s in a window. Often made by clicking with the mouse or by dragging a marquee around the desired object/s.

serif A line or curve projecting from the end of a letterform. Typefaces designed with such projections are called serif faces.

serif font Font characterized by a stroke at the top or base of letters, or the ear or spur on some letters.

service bureau An organization that provides services, such as scanning and prepress checks, that prepare your publication to be printed on a commercial printing press. Service bureaus do not, however, print your publication.

service mark A legal designation that identifies and protects the ownership of a specific term or phrase.

service provider Any organization, including a commercial printer, that processes design files for output.

shade A color mixed with black: a 10% shade is one part of the original color and nine parts black. See *tint.*

shortcut 1. A quick method for accessing a menu item or command, usually through a series of keystrokes. 2. The icon that can be created in Windows to open an application without having to penetrate layers of various folders.

silhouette To remove part of the background of a photograph or illustration, leaving only the desired portion.

small caps A type style in which lowercase letters are replaced by uppercase letters set in a smaller point size.

smart quotes The curly quotation marks used by typographers, as opposed to the straight marks on the typewriter. Use of smart quotes is usually a setup option in a word-processing or page-layout application.

snap-to An optional feature in graphics applications that drives objects to line up with guides, margins, or other objects if they are within a preset pixel range. This eliminates the need for very precise manual placement of an object with the mouse.

soft return A return command that ends a line but does not apply a paragraph mark that would end the continuity of the style for that paragraph.

special color Colors that are reproduced using premixed inks, often used to print colors that are outside the CMYK gamut.

spine The binding edge at the back of a book that contains title information and joins the front and back covers.

spot color Any pre-mixed ink that is not one of the four process-color inks.

spot-color printing The printing method in which special ink colors are used independently or in conjunction with process colors to create a specific color that is outside the gamut of process-color printing.

spread 1. Two abutting pages. 2. A trapping process that slightly enlarges a lighter foreground object to prevent white paper gaps caused by misregistration.

stacking order 1. The order of elements on a PostScript page, where the topmost item can obscure underlying items. 2. The order in which elements are placed on a page; the first is at the bottom and the last is at the top. 3. The order of layers, from top to bottom.

stripping The act of manually assembling individual film negatives into flats for printing. Also referred to as "film assembly.

stroke The width and color attributes of a line.

style A defined set of formatting instructions for font and paragraph attributes, tabs, and other properties of text.

style sheet A defined set of formatting instructions for font and paragraph attributes, tabs, and other properties of text.

subhead A second-level heading used to organize body text by topic.

subscript Small-size characters set below the normal letters or figures, usually to convey technical information.

superior Small characters set above the normal letters or figures; set as a percentage of the defined type size and aligned to the top edge of ascenders in that type size/font combination.

superscript Small characters set above the normal letters or figures, such as numbers referring to footnotes; similar to superior characters, but raised in percentages from the baseline instead of aligned to the ascender height.

SVG Scalable Vector Graphics. A language for the creation of graphics using only tags.

tabloid 11 × 17 inch paper.

tags The various formats in a style sheet that indicate paragraph settings, margins and columns, page layouts, hyphenation and justification, widow and orphan control, and other parameters. An indication of the start and end of an element.

template A document file containing layout, styles, and repeating elements (such as logos) by which a series of documents can maintain the same look and feel. A model publication you can use as the basis for creating a new publication.

text The characters and words that form the main body of a publication.

text attribute A characteristic applied directly to a letter or letters in text, such as bold, italic, or underline.

text box A box into which users can type.

text converters/filters Tools that convert word-processing and spreadsheet documents created in other programs into files that can be imported into another program.

text editor An application used to create or make changes to text files.

text effects Means by which the appearance of text can be modified, such as bolding, underlining, and italicizing.

text inset The distance from the edge of the box to the position of the placed text.

text string Any sequence of alphanumeric characters that are not code commands.

text-overflow icon An icon at the end of a text box that indicates more text exists at the end of the story, but does not fit into the box (or chain of boxes).

thin space A fixed space, equal to half an en space or the width of a period in most fonts.

TIFF Tagged Image File Format. A common format used for scanned or computer-generated bitmapped images.

tint 1. A halftone area that contains dots of uniform size; that is, no modeling or texture. 2. A percentage of a color; a 10% tint is one part of the original color and nine parts substrate color. See *shade.*

toggle A command that switches between either of two states at each application. Switching between Hide and Show is a toggle.

tool tip Small text explaining the item to which the mouse is pointing.

tracking Adjusting the spacing of letters in a line of text to achieve proper justification or general appearance.

trademark A legal designation that identifies and protects the ownership of a specific device (such as a name, symbol, or mark).

transformation A change in the shape, color, position, velocity, or opacity of an object.

trapping The process of creating an overlap between abutting inks to compensate for imprecise registration in the printing process. Extending the lighter colors of one object into the darker colors of an adjoining object.

trim marks Printer's marks that denote the edge of the layout before it is printed and cut to final size.

trim size Area of the finished page after the job is printed, folded, bound, and cut.

TrueType An outline font format used in both Macintosh and Windows systems that can be used both on the screen and on a printer.

Trumatch A special-color library used in the United States.

Type 1 fonts PostScript fonts based on Bézier curves encrypted for compactness.

type family A set of typefaces created from the same basic design, but in different variations, such as bold, light, italic, book, and heavy.

type size Typeface as measured (in points) from the bottom of descenders to the body clearance line, which is slightly higher than the top of ascenders.

typeface A unique and distinctive design of a font alphabet; the combined group of all the letters, figures, and punctuation of a specific font.

typesetting The arrangement of individual characters of text into words, sentences, and paragraphs.

typo An abbreviation for typographical error. A keystroke error in the typeset copy.

typographer's quotes See *smart quotes.*

typography The art and process of placing, arranging, and formatting type in a design.

uppercase The capital letters of a typeface as opposed to the lowercase, or small, letters. When type was hand composited, the capital letters resided in the upper part of the type case.

vector graphics Graphics defined using coordinate points and mathematically drawn lines and curves, which may be freely scaled and rotated without image degradation in the final output.

vertical justification The ability to automatically adjust the interline spacing (leading) to make columns and pages end at the same point on a page.

weight 1. The thickness of the strokes of a typeface. The weight of a typeface is usually denoted in the name of the font; for example, light, book, or ultra (thin, medium, and thick strokes, respectively). 2. The thickness of a line or rule.

white space Areas on the page that contain no images or type. Proper use of white space is critical to a well-balanced design.

widow A short line ending a paragraph that appears at the top of the page. See *orphan.*

word break The division of a word at the end of a line in accordance with hyphenation principles.

word space The space inserted between words in a desktop publishing application. The optimal value is built into the typeface, and may usually be modified within an application.

wrap Type set on the page so it wraps around the shape of another element.

x-height The height of the lowercase letter "x" in a given typeface, which represents the basic size of the bodies of all of the lowercase letters (excluding ascenders and descenders).

zero point The mathematical origin of the coordinates of the two-dimensional page. The zero point may be moved to any location on the page, and the ruler dimensions change accordingly.

zooming The process of electronically enlarging or reducing an image on a monitor to facilitate detailed design or editing and navigation.

INDEX

A

B

C

D

E

F

G

H

I

J

K

L

M

N

O

P

Q

R